STEVE EMANUEL'S
BOOTCAMP FOR THE MBE

EMANUEL'S ESSENTIALS
Q&A BY TOPIC
VOLUME II

EMANUEL BAR REVIEW ADVISORS

Steven L. Emanuel
Founder and Editor-in-Chief
Emanuel Bar Review

Joel Wm. Friedman
Jack M. Gordon Professor of Procedural Law and Jurisdiction and
   Director of Tulane ITESM Ph.D. Program
Tulane University Law School

James J. Rigos
Owner and Editor-in-Chief
Rigos Professional Education Programs

STEVE EMANUEL'S
Bootcamp for the MBE

EMANUEL'S ESSENTIALS

VOLUME II:
EVIDENCE
REAL PROPERTY
CONSTITUTIONAL LAW

STEVEN L. EMANUEL

Founder & Editor-in-Chief,
Emanuel Bar Review
Member, NY, CT, MD and VA bars

www.emanuelbarprep.com

Emanuel Bar Review is a division of Aspen Publishers, a Wolters Kluwer company.

© 2010 Aspen Publishers. All Rights Reserved.
http://lawschool.aspenpublishers.com

Certain publicly disclosed questions and answers from past MBE examinations have been included herein with the permission of the NCBE, the copyright owner. These questions and answers are the only actual MBE questions and answers included in Aspen Publisher's materials. Permission to use the NCBE's questions does not constitute an endorsement by NCBE or otherwise signify that NCBE has reviewed or approved any aspect of these materials or the company or individuals who distribute these materials.

Some questions that have been included herein come from the following NCBE publications:
"Multistate Bar Examination Questions 1992," Copyright © 1992, National Conference of Bar Examiners. All Rights Reserved.
"Sample MBE," Copyright © 1995 by the National Conference of Bar Examiners. All Rights Reserved.
"Sample MBE II," Copyright © 1997 by the National Conference of Bar Examiners. All Rights Reserved.
"Sample MBE III," Copyright © 2002 by the National Conference of Bar Examiners. All Rights Reserved.
"MBE-OPE 1," Copyright © 2006 by the National Conference of Bar Examiners. All Rights Reserved.
"MBE-OPE 2," Copyright © 2009 by the National Conference of Bar Examiners. All Rights Reserved.

No part of this publication may be reproduced or transmitted in any form or by any means, electronic or mechanical, including photocopy, recording, or any information storage and retrieval system, without permission in writing from the publisher. Requests for permission to make copies of any part of this publication should be mailed to:

> Aspen Publishers
> Attn: Permissions Department
> 76 Ninth Avenue, 7th Floor
> New York, NY 10011-5201

For information about Emanuel Bar Review (including Emanuel Multistate Review), contact:

> email: info@emanuelbarprep.com
> phone: 1-888-MBE-PREP
> fax: 781-207-5815
> website: www.emanuelbarprep.com

Printed in the United States of America.

3 4 5 6 7 8 9 0

ISBN 978-0-7355-9743-3

SUMMARY OF CONTENTS

Preface xxiii
   Evidence 1
   Real Property 113
   Constitutional Law 219

TABLE OF CONTENTS

Preface xxiii

EVIDENCE

Chapter 1

BASIC CONCEPTS

II. CONDITIONS FOR ADMITTING EVIDENCE 3
    A. Relevant 3
    B. Offering testimonial evidence 8
    C. Making and responding to objections 9
    D. Sequestration of witnesses 10

Chapter 2

CIRCUMSTANTIAL PROOF: SPECIAL PROBLEMS

II. CHARACTER EVIDENCE 11
    B. Character is essential element of case 11
    C. Other-crimes (and "bad acts") evidence in criminal cases 12
    E. Character of victim 18
    H. Must be pertinent 19

III. METHODS OF PROVING CHARACTER: REPUTATION, OPINION AND PROOF OF SPECIFIC ACTS 19
    A. FRE 19

V. HABIT AND CUSTOM 22
    A. Generally allowable 22
    B. Business practices 22

VII. SUBSEQUENT REMEDIAL MEASURES 24
    B. Other purposes 24

VIII. LIABILITY INSURANCE 26
    A. General rule 26

IX. SETTLEMENTS AND PLEA BARGAINS 27

A.	Settlements	27
C.	Offer to pay medical expenses	30

Chapter 3

EXAMINATION AND IMPEACHMENT OF WITNESSES

V.	PRESENT RECOLLECTION REFRESHED AND OTHER TECHNIQUES	31
	A. Present recollection refreshed	31
VII.	IMPEACHMENT — GENERALLY	32
	B. Impeaching one's own witness	32
VIII.	IMPEACHMENT BY PRIOR CRIMINAL CONVICTION	33
	A. Federal Rule	33
IX.	IMPEACHMENT BY PRIOR BAD ACTS	34
	A. Federal Rule	34
XI.	IMPEACHMENT BY PRIOR INCONSISTENT STATEMENT	39
	A. General rule	39
	B. Special rules from FRE 613	40
XIV.	IMPEACHMENT BY CONTRADICTION; THE "COLLATERAL ISSUE" RULE	42
	B. Collateral issue rule	42

Chapter 4

HEARSAY

I.	DEFINITION	44
	B. Definition	44
	D. Illustrations of hearsay on MBE	45
II.	SPECIAL ISSUES	48
	B. "Truth of matter asserted"	48
	D. Multiple hearsay	50

Chapter 5

HEARSAY EXCEPTIONS AND EXCLUSIONS

I.	ADMISSIONS	53
	B. Personal admissions	53

  C. Adoptive 57

III. SPONTANEOUS, EXCITED, OR CONTEMPORANEOUS UTTERANCES (INCLUDING STATEMENTS ABOUT PHYSICAL OR MENTAL CONDITION) 59
  B. Statements made for purposes of medical diagnosis or treatment 59
  C. Declaration of present mental, emotional, or physical condition 60
  D. Excited utterance 64
  E. Present sense impression 66

IV. PAST RECOLLECTION RECORDED 68
  A. Exception under the FRE 68

V. RECORDS OF REGULARLY CONDUCTED ACTIVITY (a/k/a "BUSINESS RECORDS") 72
  B. Various requirements 72
  C. Person supplying info 74
  H. Absence of entry 74

VI. PUBLIC RECORDS AND REPORTS 75
  A. Public records and reports 75
  D. Absence of public record 77

VII. LEARNED WRITINGS AND COMMERCIAL PUBLICATIONS 78
  A. Learned writings 78

X. DYING DECLARATIONS 80
  B. Requirements in detail 80

XI. DECLARATIONS AGAINST INTEREST 83
  A. Generally 83
  B. Meaning of "against interest" 85

XIII. PRIOR STATEMENTS OF AVAILABLE WITNESS 85
  A. Prior inconsistent statements 85

Chapter 6

CONFRONTATION AND COMPULSORY PROCESS

[Omitted]

Chapter 7
PRIVILEGES

II. THE ATTORNEY-CLIENT PRIVILEGE	87
A. Generally	87
B. Professional relationship	88
III. PHYSICIAN-PATIENT PRIVILEGE	88
A. No federal privilege	88
IV. THE PRIVILEGE AGAINST SELF-INCRIMINATION	89
G. Negative inference allowed in civil cases	89

Chapter 8
REAL AND DEMONSTRATIVE EVIDENCE, INCLUDING WRITINGS

II. AUTHENTICATION	90
C. Authentication of writings and recordings	90
D. Self-authentication	94
III. THE "BEST EVIDENCE RULE" FOR RECORDED COMMUNICATIONS	95
B. Communications covered	95
C. Proving the contents	96
E. Duplicates	98
IV. SUMMARIES OF VOLUMINOUS WRITINGS	99
A. Summaries generally	99

Chapter 9
OPINIONS, EXPERTS, AND SCIENTIFIC EVIDENCE

I. FIRST-HAND KNOWLEDGE AND LAY OPINIONS	100
A. First-hand knowledge required	100
C. Opinion on "ultimate issue"	101
II. EXPERT WITNESSES	102
B. Illustration	102
C. Basis for expert's opinion	103

Chapter 10

BURDENS OF PROOF, PRESUMPTIONS, AND OTHER PROCEDURAL ISSUES

II. PRESUMPTIONS 105
    B. Effect of presumptions in federal civil cases 105

III. JUDGE-JURY ALLOCATION 107
    B. Issues of fact 107

Chapter 11

JUDICIAL NOTICE

II. ADJUDICATIVE FACTS 109
    A. General rule 109
    B. Must take if requested, and may take without a request 110
    C. Instructions, and jury's right to disregard 111

REAL PROPERTY

Chapter 1
ADVERSE POSSESSION

IV. "HOSTILE" POSSESSION 115
    B. Boundary disputes 115

V. CONTINUITY OF POSSESSION 117
    A. Continuity of possession 117

Chapter 2
FREEHOLD ESTATES

II. THE FEE SIMPLE 118
    A. Fee simple absolute 118
    B. Fee simple defeasible 119

IV. THE LIFE ESTATE 121
    B. Duties and powers of life tenant 121

Chapter 3
FUTURE INTERESTS

II. POSSIBILITY OF REVERTER; RIGHT OF RE-ENTRY 124
    A. Possibility of reverter and right of re-entry 124

IV. REMAINDERS 126
    C. Contingent remainders 126

V. EXECUTORY INTERESTS 129
    A. Executory interests 129

VI. THE RULE AGAINST PERPETUITIES 130
    B. Applicability of Rule to various estates 130
    D. Special situations 134

Chapter 4
CONCURRENT OWNERSHIP

II. JOINT TENANCY 135
    C. Severance 135

III. TENANCY IN COMMON 137
A. Tenancy in common 137

IV. RELATIONS BETWEEN CO-TENANTS 138
B. Payments made by one tenant 138
C. Partition 139

Chapter 5

LANDLORD AND TENANT

III. TORT LIABILITY OF LANDLORD AND TENANT 140
B. Landlord's liability 140

IV. TENANT'S DUTIES 142
B. Fixtures 142

VI. TRANSFER AND SALE BY LESSOR; ASSIGNMENT AND SUBLETTING BY LESSEE 143
A. Generally allowed 143
B. Running of benefit and burden 145
E. Agreement by the parties about transfer 146

Chapter 6

EASEMENTS AND SERVITUDES

II. CREATION OF EASEMENTS 147
E. Easement by prescription 147

III. SCOPE OF EASEMENTS 148
B. Development of dominant estate 148

IV. REPAIR AND MAINTENANCE OF EASEMENTS 149
B. Dominant owner has right to maintain 149

V. TRANSFER AND SUBDIVISION OF EASEMENTS 152
B. Transfer of benefit 152

VI. TERMINATION OF EASEMENTS 152
A. Abandonment 152

VII. LICENSES 154
A. Definition 154

IX. EQUITABLE SERVITUDES / RESTRICTIVE COVENANTS 156

C. Plaintiff's parcel must be intended to be benefitted 156
C. Running of benefit and burden 157
D. Developer's building plan 162

X. MODIFICATION AND TERMINATION OF COVENANTS AND SERVITUDES 164
A. Modification and termination generally 164

Chapter 7

LAND SALE CONTRACTS, MORTGAGES, DEEDS AND WILLS

I. LAND SALE CONTRACTS 167
A. Statute of Frauds 167
C. Marketable title 168
D. Remedies for failure to perform 173
E. Equitable conversion 177

II. MORTGAGES AND INSTALLMENT CONTRACTS 179
A. Nature of mortgage 179

III. DEEDS 188
B. Formalities 188
C. Delivery of deed 190
E. Covenants for title in warranty deed 194
F. Estoppel by deed 196
G. Undisclosed condition in house 198

IV. CONVEYANCING BY WILL: ADEMPTION, EXONERATION AND LAPSE 198
C. Exoneration 198

Chapter 8

RECORDING ACTS

IV. WHAT INSTRUMENTS MUST BE RECORDED 199
A. What instruments must be recorded 199

V. WHO IS PROTECTED BY THE RECORDING ACT 200
B. Who is a bona fide purchaser (BFP) 200
C. The "gave value" requirement 203
E. Recording first in a race or race-notice state 207

VI. PURCHASER MUST TAKE "WITHOUT NOTICE" 208

    A. Notice to subsequent claimants 208
    C. Purchaser from one without notice 211

Chapter 9
RIGHTS INCIDENT TO LAND

I. NUISANCE 213
    C. Private nuisance 213

II. LATERAL AND SUBJACENT SUPPORT 215
    B. Lateral support 215

III. WATER RIGHTS 216
    A. Drainage of surface waters 216

IV. AIR RIGHTS 217
    B. Other air-rights issues 217

CONSTITUTIONAL LAW

Chapter 1

THE SUPREME COURT'S AUTHORITY AND THE FEDERAL JUDICIAL POWER

I. THE SUPREME COURT'S AUTHORITY AND THE FEDERAL JUDICIAL POWER 221
   B. Supreme Court review of state court decision 221
   C. Federal judicial power 223

II. CONGRESS'S CONTROL OF FEDERAL JUDICIAL POWER 225
   B. Congress's power to decide 225

Chapter 2

FEDERALISM AND FEDERAL POWER GENERALLY

I. THE CONCEPT OF FEDERALISM 227
   B. Federal government has limited powers 227

Chapter 3

POWERS OF THE FEDERAL GOVERNMENT; THE SEPARATION OF POWERS

I. POWERS OF THE THREE FEDERAL BRANCHES 228
   A. Powers of the three branches 228

II. THE FEDERAL COMMERCE POWER 231
   B. Summary of modern view 231
   C. The Tenth Amendment as a limit on Congress's power 234

III. THE TAXING AND SPENDING POWERS 237
   A. Taxing power 237
   B. Spending power 240

IV. THE SEPARATION OF POWERS 242
   A. Separation of powers generally 242

Chapter 4

TWO LIMITS ON STATE POWER: THE DORMANT COMMERCE CLAUSE AND CONGRESSIONAL ACTION

I. THE DORMANT COMMERCE CLAUSE 246
   A. Dormant Commerce Clause generally 246
   B. State taxation of interstate commerce 250

II. CONGRESSIONAL PRE-EMPTION AND CONSENT; THE SUPREMACY CLAUSE 252
   B. The Supremacy Clause and federal pre-emption 252
   C. Consent by Congress 257

Chapter 5

INTERGOVERNMENTAL IMMUNITIES; INTERSTATE RELATIONS

I. TAX AND REGULATORY IMMUNITIES 260
   A. Several types of immunities 260

II. THE INTERSTATE PRIVILEGES AND IMMUNITIES CLAUSE 263
   A. Interstate Privileges and Immunities 263

III. THE FULL FAITH AND CREDIT CLAUSE 265
   A. How tested on MBE 265

Chapter 6

THE DUE PROCESS CLAUSE

III. SUBSTANTIVE DUE PROCESS — ECONOMIC AND SOCIAL WELFARE REGULATION 267
   C. Economic and social-welfare regulation 267

IV. SUBSTANTIVE DUE PROCESS — REGULATIONS AFFECTING FUNDAMENTAL RIGHTS 268
   C. Abortion 268

V. PROCEDURAL DUE PROCESS 270
   A. Introduction 270
   D. Process required 272

Chapter 7
EQUAL PROTECTION

I. EQUAL PROTECTION GENERALLY	275
A. Text of clause	275
II. ECONOMIC AND SOCIAL LAWS — THE "MERE RATIONALITY" TEST	276
A. Non-suspect, non-fundamental rights (economic and social legislation)	276
III. SUSPECT CLASSIFICATIONS, ESPECIALLY RACE	280
A. Suspect classifications	280
V. MIDDLE-LEVEL REVIEW (GENDER, ILLEGITIMACY AND ALIENAGE)	281
B. Gender	281
VI. FUNDAMENTAL RIGHTS	283
B. Voting rights	283
C. Ballot access	284
F. Necessities	285

Chapter 8
MISCELLANEOUS CLAUSES

I. FOURTEENTH AMENDMENT PRIVILEGES AND IMMUNITIES	287
A. Privileges and Immunities Clause (P&I) Generally	287
II. THE "TAKING" CLAUSE	287
A. The "Taking" Clause Generally	287
IV. *EX POST FACTO* LAWS	290
A. Constitutional prohibition	290
V. BILLS OF ATTAINDER	291
B. Definition of "punishment"	291

Chapter 9
THE "STATE ACTION" REQUIREMENT; CONGRESS'S ENFORCEMENT OF THE CIVIL WAR AMENDMENTS

I. STATE ACTION	292

C. "State involvement" doctrine 292

II. CONGRESSIONAL ENFORCEMENT OF CIVIL RIGHTS 293
    B. Congress's power to enforce 293
    C. Congress's power to reach private conduct 294

Chapter 10

FREEDOM OF EXPRESSION

I. GENERAL THEMES 296
    C. Analysis of content-based government action 296
    E. Overbreadth 296

III. TIME, PLACE AND MANNER REGULATIONS 298
    A. Time, place and manner generally 298
    G. Regulation of "hate speech" 299

V. DEFAMATION AND INVASION OF PRIVACY 300
    B. Other state-law tort claims 300

VI. OBSCENITY 301
    C. Significance 301
    G. Regulating secondary effects of adult speech 302

VII. COMMERCIAL SPEECH 303
    A. Commercial speech generally 303
    C. Lawyers 304

IX. FREEDOM OF ASSOCIATION, AND DENIAL OF
    PUBLIC BENEFITS OR JOBS 305
    C. Denial of public benefit or job 305

X. SPECIAL PROBLEMS OF THE MEDIA 309
    A. The media (and its special problems) 309

Chapter 11

FREEDOM OF RELIGION

II. THE ESTABLISHMENT CLAUSE 311
    B. Three-part test 311
    F. Ceremonies and displays 312

III. THE FREE EXERCISE CLAUSE 314
    E. Generally-applicable laws 314

Chapter 12
JUSTICIABILITY

III. STANDING 316
    D. Cases not based on taxpayer or citizen status 316
    E. Third-party standing 319

IV. MOOTNESS 319
    B. Exceptions 319

V. RIPENESS 321
    A. Ripeness problem generally 321
    C. Reasonable probability of harm required 322

VI. THE ELEVENTH AMENDMENT AND SUITS AGAINST THE STATES 324
    A. The Eleventh Amendment generally 324

VII. POLITICAL QUESTIONS 326
    B. "Commitment to other branches" strand 326

PREFACE

Dear Bootcamp enrollee:

Thank you for enrolling in Steve Emanuel's Bootcamp for the MBE.

The present volume gives you a large number of MBE-format questions and answers on Evidence, Real Property and Constitutional Law, organized by sub-topic. (The first volume covers the remaining three MBE subjects: Contracts, Criminal Law and Procedure, and Torts.) Headings in this Q&A material for each subject are the same as in the subject-matter outline on the subject included in your Bootcamp materials, and are presented in the same order as in that outline. Therefore, to locate questions on any topic, check the topic in the subject-matter outline, then look under the same heading in this book. (A few chapters in the subject-matter outline don't have any corresponding questions in this book, in which case the Table of Contents for this book states "Omitted" for that chapter.) Some questions are reprinted multiple times; when that occurs, one version of the question usually includes a discussion of all four choices, whereas the other version(s) typically discuss just one particular wrong choice. Occasionally, in the interests of clarity we have chosen to use a heading here that was not present in the subject-matter outline; when that happens, we indicate this by putting the header in italics.

Questions from the 200-Question Simulated MBE are not reprinted or referred to in this book. (A book containing the questions and answers to the Simulated MBE is separately included in your materials.) Questions from the Self-Assessment Test that is also part of your materials are reprinted here in full, as are many questions that were not part of either the Self-Assessment Test or the Simulated MBE.

The entire Emanuel Bar Review team joins me in saying that we're glad you chose Steve Emanuel's Bootcamp for the MBE. GOOD LUCK on your upcoming bar exam!

Steve Emanuel

Larchmont, NY

April, 2010

EVIDENCE

EVIDENCE Q&A BY TOPIC

Headings in this Q&A material are the same as in the *Steve Emanuel's Bootcamp for the MBE: Evidence* subject-matter outline, and are presented in the same order as in that outline. Therefore, to locate questions on any topic, check the topic in the subject-matter outline, then look under the same heading in this book. Some questions are reprinted multiple times; when that occurs, one version of the question usually includes a discussion of all four choices, whereas the other version(s) typically discuss just one particular wrong choice. Occasionally, in the interests of clarity we have chosen to use a heading here that was not present in the subject-matter outline; when that happens, we indicate this by putting the header in italics.

Questions from the Self-Assessment Test that is part of your materials are reprinted here in full, as are many questions that were not part of the Self-Assessment Test. Questions from the 200-Question Simulated MBE are not reprinted or referred to here (a book with the questions and answers to the Simulated MBE is also part of your materials).

All answers assume that the Federal Rules of Evidence ("FRE") are in force as to all issues. "ACN" refers to "Advisory Committee Notes" to a particular Federal Rule of Evidence. "M&K" refers to Mueller & Kirkpatrick, Evidence hornbook (Aspen, 3d Ed., 2003). "McC" refers to McCormick on Evidence (West, 4th Ed., 1992). "Lilly" refers to Lilly, An Introduction to the Law of Evidence (West, 2d Ed., 1987).

CHAPTER 1
BASIC CONCEPTS

II. CONDITIONS FOR ADMITTING EVIDENCE

A. Relevant:

1. Definition:

Question: In a prosecution for aggravated battery, a police officer testified that when he arrested the defendant, he took a knife from the defendant and delivered it to the medical examiner. The medical examiner testified that the knife blade was consistent with the victim's wound but admitted on cross-examination that any number of other knives could also have caused the wound.

Should the judge grant a motion to strike the medical examiner's testimony?

(A) No, because the probative worth of this evidence is for the jury to assess.

(B) Yes, because in light of the medical examiner's admission, his testimony has insufficient probative value.

(C) Yes, because the medical examiner could not state the probability that the wound was caused by the defendant's knife.

(D) Yes, because the probative value is substantially outweighed by the danger of unfair prejudice.

[QA074]

Answer: Choice **(A)** is correct. This evidence has some probative value, because it links the knife in defendant's possession to the type of knife that could have caused the victim's wound. The evidence is not very strong, because other knives could also have caused the wound. But how much weight to give to the evidence is a decision for the jury. FRE 401 requires only that evidence have "any tendency to make the existence of any fact that is of consequence to the determination of the action more probable or less probable than it would be without the evidence." Thus to be relevant, evidence need only have *some* probative value in establishing a fact. The Advisory Committee's Note to Rule 401 quotes the famous statement "A brick is not a wall," making the point that evidence is admissible even if it is only a single brick that is a part of a large wall of evidence establishing a party's case.

(B) is wrong because evidence meets the relevancy requirement of FRE 401 if it has "any tendency to make the existence of any fact that is of consequence to the determination of the action more probable or less probable than it would be without the evidence." The medical examiner's testimony meets this minimal standard of probativity. And it is probative of a material fact — whether this knife was the crime weapon.

(C) is wrong because no statement of probability is required for admissibility. The medical examiner's testimony does not have to establish that defendant's knife caused the wound by any particular standard of proof, such as beyond a reasonable doubt, by clear and convincing evidence, or by a preponderance of the evidence — it's up to the jury to assess the value of the evidence in determining guilt. The testimony only needs to have some unspecified-but-minimal probative value to be admissible. That's shown by FRE 401, under which evidence is deemed to have probative value, and to be admissible (assuming it doesn't violate some other specific prohibition), if it has "any tendency to make the existence of any fact that is of consequence to the determination of the action more probable or less probable than it would be without the evidence."

(D) is wrong because it mischaracterizes the evidence here. It's true that FRE 403 requires a weighing of probative value against unfair prejudice, as this choice suggests. That rule establishes what might be described as a presumption of admissibility: evidence meeting Rule 401's definition of relevance is admissible unless its probative value is "*substantially* outweighed" by the danger of unfair prejudice. Here, the medical examiner's testimony does not appear to pose *any* significant degree of unfair prejudice, let alone enough to "substantially outweigh" the probative value of that testimony.

Question: In a civil action for breach of an oral contract, the defendant admits that there had been discussions, but denies that he ever entered into an agreement with the plaintiff.

Which of the following standards of admissibility should be applied by the court to evidence proffered as relevant to prove whether a contract was formed?

(A) Whether a reasonable juror would find the evidence determinative of whether the contract was or was not formed.

(B) Whether the evidence has any tendency to make the fact of contract formation more or less probable than without the evidence.

(C) Whether the evidence is sufficient to prove, absent contrary evidence, that the contract was or was not formed.

(D) Whether the evidence makes it more likely than not that a contract was or was not formed.

[Q7078]

Answer: Choice **(B)** is correct. This is the standard of relevance applied by the judge in determining admissibility under FRE 401. Under that rule, evidence is relevant if it has "any tendency to make the existence of any fact that is of consequence to the determination of the action more probable or less probable than it would be without the evidence."

(A) is wrong because the test for admissibility is whether the judge believes that the evidence is probative, not whether a reasonable jury could believe it to be so. This is established by FRE 104(a).

(C) is wrong because the judge determines admissibility and the jury determines sufficiency. It would be impossible for a party to build a case if every piece of evidence had to be sufficient to prove the point in dispute.

(D) is wrong because the preponderance standard is applied by the jury to all of the evidence admitted. It is not applied by the court to determine whether a particular piece of evidence can be considered by the jury on the ultimate question. Thus, this answer confuses the standard of proof used by the jury with the standard of admissibility used by the judge.

Question: PullCo sued Davidson, its former vice president, for return of $230,000 that had been embezzled during the previous two years. Called by PullCo as an adverse witness, Davidson testified that his annual salary had been $75,000, and he denied the embezzlement. PullCo calls banker Witt to show that, during the two-year period, Davidson had deposited $250,000 in his bank account.

Witt's testimony is

(A) admissible as circumstantial evidence of Davidson's guilt.

(B) admissible to impeach Davidson.

(C) inadmissible, because its prejudicial effect substantially outweighs its probative value.

(D) inadmissible, because the deposits could have come from legitimate sources.

[Q3024]

Answer: Choice **(A)** is correct. Circumstantial evidence is evidence which, even if it is believed, does not resolve the matter at issue unless additional reasoning is used to reach the proposition to which the evidence is directed. Circumstantial evidence will be admitted only if it has probative value, that is, only if it affects the probability of the existence of a fact consequential to the action. Evidence that Davidson deposited nearly twice his salary over a two-year period is circumstantial evidence of Davidson's embezzlement, because this evidence makes it more likely than it would otherwise be that Davidson had a major non-salary source of income. There is no evidentiary rule that would bar the admission of this very-relevant evidence.

(B) is wrong because the use of Witt's testimony for impeachment purposes would violate FRE 608(b). FRE 608(b) says that "Specific instances of the conduct of a witness, for the purpose of *attacking or supporting the witness's credibility,* other than conviction of crime as provided in rule 609, *may not be proved by extrinsic evidence.*" The evidence here consists of "specific instances" of Davidson's conduct. If the evidence is being offered to "impeach" Davidson as Choice (B) specifies, it is being offered to "attack the witness's credibility," and falls within 608(b), given that there has been no criminal conviction. Therefore, the specific instances of conduct can't be proved by "extrinsic evidence" (which is what separate testimony from Witt would be). Instead, impeachment could only happen by bringing out the instances while Davidson was on the stand (e.g., "Isn't it true that according to bank records you deposited almost twice the amount of your salary?").

(C) is wrong because the evidence is highly probative of embezzlement, and there is no "unfair" prejudice. FRE 403 says that "Although relevant, evidence may be excluded if its probative value is substantially outweighed by the danger of unfair prejudice...." However, this provision wouldn't apply here because: (1) the probative value is quite large (surely a person who deposits almost twice his salary into a bank account is significantly more likely to be an embezzler than one who does not); and (2) there is minimal "unfairness" in showing that a person has made bank deposits, certainly not enough unfairness to "substantially outweigh" the major probative value of the evidence.

(D) is wrong because a piece of evidence, to be admissible (assuming no special rule of exclusion applies) must merely make some issue of disputed fact more likely to be true than it would be in the absence of the evidence. The evidence doesn't have to conclusively "prove" the ultimate proposition to which it's addressed, or even render that proposition "more likely than not" true. As the idea is sometimes put, "a brick is not a wall." Here, the fact that a person has made bank deposits of almost twice his salary in a two-year period makes it more likely that he's an embezzler than if he had only deposited the amount of his salary or less. So this evidence satisfies the "makes some disputed fact more likely or less likely" standard, even though there may well be a legitimate explanation for the deposits. As the court might say, the possibility of an innocent explanation here merely "goes to weight, not admissibility."

Question: A defendant's house was destroyed by fire and she was charged with arson. To prove that the defendant had a motive to burn down her house, the government offered evidence that the defendant had fully insured the house and its contents.

Should the court admit this evidence?

(A) No, because the probative value of the evidence of insurance upon the issue of whether the defendant intentionally burned her house down is substantially outweighed by the dangers of unfair prejudice and confusion of the jury.

(B) No, because evidence of insurance is not admissible upon the issue of whether the insured acted wrongfully.

(C) Yes, because evidence of insurance on the house has a tendency to show that the defendant had a motive to burn down the house.

(D) Yes, because any conduct of a party to the case is admissible when offered against the party.

[QA018]

Answer: Choice **(C)** is correct. This is a relevance problem. The main issue is whether the evidence meets the general relevance standard of FRE 401. Under that rule, evidence need only have "any tendency to make the existence of a fact that is of consequence to the determination of the action more probable or less probable than it would be without the evidence." Thus, evidence that has only the slightest probative value can be admitted under this rule. While evidence that the property is insured is not conclusive that the defendant committed arson (many people fully insure their houses), it is relevant to the issue of whether the defendant would have had a financial incentive or motive to commit the arson — the defendant might be able to generate cash more quickly by burning down the house and collecting insurance proceeds than by attempting to sell the house. This evidence meets the minimal probativity standard of FRE 401. (There is a special rule concerning the admissibility of evidence of insurance, but that rule doesn't bar the evidence here; see the discussion of Choice (B) for more about this.)

(A) is wrong because although the probative value of this evidence on the issue of whether defendant intentionally burned her house down is not particularly strong, it is somewhat probative of the issue of possible motive, so it meets the easy-to-satisfy probativity standard of FRE 401 (quoted in the discussion of Choice (C) above). FRE 403 provides that relevant evidence should be admitted unless its probative value is "substantially outweighed" by the dangers of unfair prejudice, confusion, or waste of time. Here, the evidence of insurance is probably not unfairly prejudicial at all (in the sense that it does not have an undue tendency to produce decision on an improper basis such as emotion); in any event, whatever small prejudicial tendency the evidence might have is certainly not enough to "substantially outweigh" the probative value of the evidence.

(B) is wrong because, although it is true that FRE 411 bars evidence of insurance to establish that the insured acted negligently or otherwise wrongfully, such evidence is admissible for *other purposes*, and proof of motive is such a purpose. (In this respect, Rule 411 is similar to Rule 404(b), under which evidence of past conduct cannot be admitted to prove a propensity to engage in such conduct but can be admitted for other purposes, such as to prove motive.)

(D) is wrong because there is no such broad rule that any conduct of a party may be admitted against that party.

2. **Exclusion:**

   Question: Deeb was charged with stealing furs from a van. At trial, Wallace testified she saw Deeb take the furs.

   The jurisdiction in which Deeb is being tried does not allow in evidence lie detector results. On cross-examination by Deeb's attorney, Wallace was asked, "The light was too dim to identify Deeb, wasn't it?" She responded, "I'm sure enough that it was Deeb that I passed a lie detector test administered by the police." Deeb's attorney immediately objects and moves to strike.

   The trial court should

   (A) grant the motion, because the question was leading.

   (B) grant the motion, because the probative value of the unresponsive testimony is substantially outweighed by the danger of unfair prejudice.

   (C) deny the motion, because it is proper rehabilitation of an impeached witness.

   (D) deny the motion, because Deeb's attorney "opened the door" by asking the question.
   [Q1031]

   Answer: Choice **(B)** is correct. FRE 403 provides: "Although relevant, evidence may be excluded if its probative value is substantially outweighed by the danger of unfair prejudice..." The fact pattern tells us that the jurisdiction excludes evidence of lie detector results, indicating that the jurisdiction questions the reliability of the test and considers evidence of the test results to be of low probative value. "Unfair" prejudice...means "an undue tendency to suggest decision on an improper basis..." Advisory Committee Note to FRE 403. It is reasonable to assume that some members of a jury may regard the results of a lie detector test as more scientific than they actually are, and consequently give the test too much weight. Therefore, in this jurisdiction, the danger of unfair prejudice would substantially outweigh the (low) probative value of the lie detector test.

   (A) is wrong because, although the motion would be granted, it would not be for the stated reason. Leading questions are generally permissible on cross examination. FRE 611(c).

(C) is wrong because, even apart from the FRE 403 problem discussed in Choice (B), the reasoning supporting this answer mischaracterizes the concept of "rehabilitation." Once a witness has been impeached, rehabilitation is brought out through separate testimony that is offered by counsel representing the party who is a proponent of the impeached witness's testimony. It is incorrect to characterize the witness's own response to opposing counsel's "impeaching" question as "rehabilitation" of that witness's credibility.

(D) is wrong because (1) the motion would be granted for the reason discussed in Choice (B); and (2) the reasoning supporting this answer misapplies the concept of "opening the door." A topic which is otherwise off-limits to an opposing party is considered "opened for questioning" once it has been introduced by the other party — the rationale is that if the topic has been "opened" by one party it would be unfair to prohibit the opposing party from addressing it. In this case, the question "The light was too dim to identify Deeb, wasn't it?" is not even arguably related to the topic of Wallace's passing a lie detector test, so there is no unfairness in not allowing Wallace to talk about the lie detector test.

Question: A defendant's house was destroyed by fire and she was charged with arson. To prove that the defendant had a motive to burn down her house, the government offered evidence that the defendant had fully insured the house and its contents.

Should the court admit this evidence?

(A) No, because the probative value of the evidence of insurance upon the issue of whether the defendant intentionally burned her house down is substantially outweighed by the dangers of unfair prejudice and confusion of the jury.

(B) No, because evidence of insurance is not admissible upon the issue of whether the insured acted wrongfully.

(C) Yes, because evidence of insurance on the house has a tendency to show that the defendant had a motive to burn down the house.

(D) Yes, because any conduct of a party to the case is admissible when offered against the party.

[QA018]

Answer: Choice **(A)** is **incorrect**, because although this rule correctly articulates the prejudice-probativity balancing test, it misapplies that test to these facts. First, although the probative value of this evidence on the issue of whether defendant intentionally burned her house down is not particularly strong, it is somewhat probative of the issue of possible motive, so it meets the easy-to-satisfy probativity standard of FRE 401. (401 says that evidence need only have "any tendency to make the existence of a fact that is of consequence to the determination of the action more probable or less probable than it would be without the evidence.") Next, FRE 403 provides (as this choice correctly suggests) that relevant evidence should be admitted unless its probative value is "substantially outweighed" by the dangers of unfair prejudice, confusion, or waste of time. Here, the evidence of insurance is probably not unfairly prejudicial at all (in the sense that it does not have an undue tendency to produce decision on an improper basis such as emotion); in any event, whatever small prejudicial tendency the evidence might have is certainly not enough to "substantially outweigh" the probative value of the evidence. Nor would the evidence have any particular tendency to confuse the jury.

(The correct answer is (C); for more about this, see *supra*, p. 6.)

B. Offering testimonial evidence:

4. *Testimony by trial judge:*

Question: A defendant was charged with murder. While walking down the hallway during a recess in the defendant's trial, the judge overheard the defendant say to his attorney, "So what if I did it? There's not enough proof to convict." Upon the judge's reporting the incident to counsel, the prosecutor called the judge as a witness in the trial.

Is the judge's testimony regarding the defendant's statement admissible?

(A) Yes, as the statement of a party-opponent.

(B) Yes, because the defendant's statement, although otherwise privileged, was made without reasonable efforts to preserve confidentiality.

(C) No, because the statement was a privileged attorney-client communication.

(D) No, because a judge may never testify in a trial over which he or she is presiding.

[QA015]

Answer: Choice **(D)** is correct. Although the judge is being asked to recount an out-of-court statement made by a party that is offered against that party, admissibility here does not turn on the hearsay rule. Regardless of whether the evidence is admissible under the hearsay rule, FRE 605 provides that a "judge presiding at the trial may not testify in that trial as a witness." Thus, the judge cannot offer any testimony of any kind, no matter how probative and important his testimony.

(A) is wrong because even though the statement is the admission of a party-opponent and would be otherwise admissible non-hearsay under Rule FRE 801(d)(2)(A), FRE 605 says that the presiding judge cannot be called as a witness to testify about anything.

(B) is wrong because, although it is true that reasonable efforts were not made by the defendant and his attorney to preserve confidentiality, this means only that the communication was not privileged — it does not mean the statement is necessarily admissible. The problem here is that under FRE 605, the statement cannot be proven through the testimony of the presiding judge because that rule bars the presiding judge from offering any testimony of any kind. The defendant's lack of efforts to preserve confidentiality mean that the statement probably *would* be admissible if someone other than the presiding judge had heard it and been asked to testify about it.

(C) is wrong because, although it reaches the right outcome, it uses incorrect reasoning. The statement would *not* be privileged. That's because reasonable efforts were not made by the defendant and his attorney to preserve confidentiality, since the statement was made in a hallway open to the public in a voice loud enough to be overheard.

C. **Making and responding to objections:**

3. *Hearing outside of presence of jury:*

Question: A defendant was on trial for burglary. The prosecutor called the arresting officer to testify that shortly after the arrest the defendant had orally admitted her guilt to him. Before the officer testified, the defendant objected that no *Miranda* warning had been given, and she requested a hearing outside the presence of the jury to hear evidence on that issue.

How should the court proceed?

(A) The court should grant the request, because the hearing on the admissibility of the confession must be conducted outside the presence of the jury.

(B) The court may grant or deny the request, because the court has discretion whether to conduct preliminary hearings in the presence of the jury.

(C) The court should deny the request and rule the confession inadmissible, because only signed confessions are permitted in criminal cases.

(D) The court should deny the request and rule the confession admissible, because it is the statement of a party-opponent.

[QA010]

Answer: Choice **(A)** is correct. The admissibility of the officer's testimony turns on two issues: (1) whether a *Miranda* warning had to be given to the defendant before his confession can be admitted; and (2) whether the judge's determination of the first issue must be preceded by a hearing conducted in front of or outside the hearing of the jury. With respect to the first question, *Miranda* warnings must be given before a confession made by a person under arrest can be admitted. Since the defendant contends that no *Miranda* warnings were given, she is entitled to a hearing on the issue. The rule resolving the second question is contained in the first sentence of FRE 104(c), which says that "Hearings on the admissibility of confessions shall *in all cases* be conducted outside of the hearing of the jury." (Note that this provision goes on to say that hearings on all *other* preliminary matters shall be conducted outside the presence of the jury *only* when either justice requires or when a criminal defendant is a witness and requests a hearing outside of the jury's presence.) Thus under FRE 104(c), the hearing must be conducted outside the presence of the jury.

(B) is wrong because FRE 104(c) mandates that the admissibility of confessions "shall" be conducted out of the hearing of the jury. So the trial court has no discretion in this matter.

(C) is wrong because oral confessions, like signed written confessions, are admissible in criminal cases, assuming that any required *Miranda* warnings were given.

(D) is wrong because it ignores the effect of *Miranda*. It's true that a confession of a criminal defendant is an out-of-court statement made by a party-opponent, which makes it non-hearsay under FRE 801(d)(2)(A) and thus admissible — as a matter of evidence law — to prove the truth of the matter asserted within that statement. But the rules of evidence cannot alter the *constitutional* requirement that *Miranda* warnings must be given before a confession made by a person under arrest is admissible.

D. Sequestration of witnesses:

1. FRE 615:

Question: The plaintiff has sued the defendant for personal injuries arising out of an automobile accident. Which of the following would be ERROR?

(A) The judge allows the defendant's attorney to ask the defendant questions on cross-examination that go well beyond the scope of direct examination by the plaintiff, who has called the defendant as an adverse witness.

(B) The judge refuses to allow the defendant's attorney to cross-examine the defendant by leading questions.

(C) The judge allows cross-examination about the credibility of a witness even though no question relating to credibility has been asked on direct examination.

(D) The judge, despite the defendant's request for exclusion of witnesses, allows the plaintiff's eyewitness to remain in the courtroom after testifying, even though the eyewitness is expected to be recalled for further cross-examination.

[Q3153]

Answer: Choice **(D)** is correct. FRE 615 says that "At the request of a party the court shall order witnesses excluded so that they cannot hear the testimony of other witnesses..."

Although the eyewitness has already testified, the fact that he is expected to be re-called for further cross means that he's still to be treated as a witness who has not yet testified. By using the word "shall," the rule does not give the trial judge the discretion to allow the witness to remain. (The purpose of the sequestration rule is to prevent the witness from tailoring his testimony to that of other witnesses. This purpose would be thwarted by letting the eyewitness here be in the courtroom before his re-cross.)

(A) is wrong because the court has the discretion to permit inquiry into additional matters. FRE 611(b) says that as a general rule cross "should be limited to the subject matter of the direct examination and matters affecting the credibility of the witness." But that section goes on to say, "The court may, in the exercise of discretion, permit inquiry into additional matters as if on direct examination." The court's discretion would be especially proper in this case, since the defendant is effectively the direct examiner (because the plaintiff called the defendant as an adverse, or "hostile," witness).

(B) is wrong because leading questions are not proper on these facts. Here, if the defendant's lawyer is conducting "cross examination" of the defendant, it must be because the plaintiff called the defendant as an adverse witness (which is, indeed, what Choice (A) specifies happened). In that scenario, this "cross" is to be treated by the court as if it were a direct exam, since the questioner is sympathetic to the witness. In that instance, the cross should not be allowed to make use of leading questions, any more than a standard direct exam may use leading questions. See FRE 611(c), stating the general rule that leading questions "should not be used on the direct examination of a witness except as may be necessary to develop the witness's testimony."

(C) is wrong because matters of credibility are within the scope of cross-examination. FRE 611(b), in defining the permissible scope of cross-examination, says that the cross may include, in addition to "the subject matter of the direct examination," "matters affecting the credibility of the witness." So the fact that credibility was not placed in issue in the direct does not bar it from being covered on cross.

CHAPTER 2

CIRCUMSTANTIAL PROOF: SPECIAL PROBLEMS

II. CHARACTER EVIDENCE

B. **Character is essential element of case:**

3. **Types of evidence:**

    Question: At a civil trial for slander, the plaintiff showed that the defendant had called the plaintiff a thief. In defense, the defendant called a witness to testify, "I have been the plaintiff's neighbor for many years, and people in our community generally have said that he is a thief."

    Is the testimony concerning the plaintiff's reputation in the community admissible?

    (A) No, because character is an essential element of the defense, and proof must be made by specific instances of conduct.

    (B) Yes, to prove that the plaintiff is a thief, and to reduce or refute the damages claimed.

    (C) Yes, to prove that the plaintiff is a thief, but not on the issue of damages.

(D) Yes, to reduce or refute the damages claimed, but not to prove that the plaintiff is a thief.

[Q7087]

Answer: Choice **(B)** is correct. In slander cases, where the defendant makes a statement that the plaintiff has an unsavory character, the plaintiff's character is considered "in issue" (i.e., an essential element of the claim or defense under the substantive law) in two respects: First, the plaintiff's actual character will determine whether the defendant was incorrect in his assessment, and thus liable for slander, because truth is a defense. Second, the plaintiff will allege that he is damaged by the statement, which is another way of saying that his true character has been besmirched; but if the plaintiff actually has a bad reputation anyway, then damages are limited. Thus, in slander cases like the one in this question, character evidence is relevant both to whether the plaintiff has a certain character (here, being a thief) and to the extent of damages. Under FRE 405(a) and (b), when character is "in issue" it can be proved by evidence of reputation, opinion, or specific acts.

(A) is wrong because in slander cases, where the defendant makes a statement that the plaintiff has an unsavory character, the plaintiff's character is considered "in issue," for the reasons discussed in the above analysis of Choice (B). Under FRE 405(a) and (b), when character is "in issue" it can be proved by evidence of reputation, opinion, or specific acts, so specific instances are not the only allowable method as this choice asserts.

(C) and (D) are wrong because in slander cases like the one in this question, character evidence is relevant *both* to whether the plaintiff has a certain character (here, the character of being a thief) and to the extent of damages, and such character evidence may be proved by reputation evidence under FRE 405(a), as described in the discussion of Choice (B) above.

C. **Other-crimes (and "bad acts") evidence in criminal cases:**

   2. **Proof of other relevant factor:**

      c. **Plan:**

      Question: The defendant was arrested after she used a credit card bearing the name of Timothy Nolan to pay for a purchase. The defendant was subsequently charged with fraudulent use of a credit card. At her trial, a police officer testified that when she arrested the defendant, she found her to be in possession of 5 credit cards bearing the name of Timothy Nolan and 36 other credit cards bearing a total of 36 different names. In addition, the officer stated that the defendant's wallet contained driver's licenses to match each of the various names on the credit cards.

      If the defendant's attorney moves to exclude evidence that the defendant possessed credit cards or driver's licenses other than that which she was charged with fraudulently using, which of the following would be the prosecutor's most effective argument in opposition to that motion?

      (A) The number of credit cards and driver's licenses in the defendant's possession tends to establish a criminal plan.

      (B) The number of credit cards in the defendant's possession makes it likely that she had stolen them.

      (C) the defendant should be required to explain why she possessed so many credit cards belonging to other people.

      (D) the defendant's possession of 41 credit cards bearing names other than her own is an admission by conduct.

      [Q5134]

Answer: Choice **(A)** is correct. Although FRE 404(a) says that evidence of unconvicted bad acts is generally substantively inadmissible to prove a character trait so as to show conduct in conformity with that trait on the present occasion, FRE 404(b) provides that such evidence may be admissible for "other purposes." One of the most common permissible "other purposes" for such evidence is to create an inference that the defendant is guilty of the crime charged by showing that the crime was part of a general criminal plan or scheme. Since the defendant's possession of 41 different credit cards bearing 36 different names suggests that she planned to make fraudulent use of them all, evidence of that fact may be admissible. Such circumstantial evidence must be subjected to close examination to determine whether its probative value is outweighed by its prejudicial effect, so it is not certain that a court would admit the evidence. But of all the arguments set forth, (A) is the only one which could possibly provide the prosecutor with an effective argument in opposition to the motion to exclude.

(B) is wrong because the defendant is not charged with stealing credit cards, making an inference that she did so not relevant to any fact of consequence in the prosecution. It might be logical to argue that such an inference is relevant because a person who would steal credit cards is probably disposed to make fraudulent use of them. Such an argument would fail, however, because evidence of unconvicted acts is inadmissible for the purpose of proving a mere criminal disposition.

(C) is wrong because, under the Fifth Amendment privilege against self-incrimination, a criminal defendant cannot be required to explain her conduct.

(D) is wrong because an admission by conduct occurs when a party engages in conduct which indicates her own belief that she is guilty of the crime charged (e.g., attempting to bribe an arresting officer to let the defendant go free or attempting to flee after being charged with a crime). Since possession of credit cards bearing other names does not indicate that the defendant believed herself to be guilty of fraudulently using the card bearing the name of Timothy Nolan, it is not an admission by conduct.

e. **Identity:**

Question: A defendant is on trial for attempted fraud. The state charges that the defendant switched a price tag from a cloth coat to a more expensive fur-trimmed coat and then presented the latter for purchase at the cash register. The defendant testified in her own behalf that the tag must have been switched by someone else. On cross-examination, the prosecutor asks whether the defendant was convicted on two prior occasions of misdemeanor fraud in the defrauding of a retailer by the same means of switching the price tag on a fur-trimmed coat.

Is the question about the convictions for the earlier crimes proper?

(A) It is not proper either to impeach the defendant or to prove that the defendant committed the crime.

(B) It is proper both to prove that the defendant committed the crime and to impeach the defendant.

(C) It is proper to impeach the defendant, but not to prove that the defendant committed the crime.

(D) It is proper to prove the defendant committed the crime, but not to impeach the defendant.

[Q7068]

Answer: Choice **(B)** is correct. Under FRE 404(b), prior bad acts can be admitted to prove the defendant's conduct if offered for some purpose other than to show that the defendant is a bad person. In this case, the bad acts are very similar to the acts in dispute, and tend to show a non-character purpose, namely "identity" (that the defrauder was defendant rather than someone else). Thus the bad acts can be offered as proof that the defendant committed the crime charged. Moreover, the convictions are automatically admissible to impeach the defendant's character for truthfulness; fraud convictions clearly involve dishonesty or false statement, and so the court "shall" admit the convictions under Rule 609(a)(2).

Choices (A), (C), and (D) are wrong because each is in some way inconsistent with the correct answer given in (B).

f. "Absence of mistake or accident":

Question: A defendant is on trial for the murder of his father. The defendant's defense is that he shot his father accidentally. The prosecutor calls as a witness a police officer to testify that on two occasions in the year prior to this incident, he had been called to the defendant's home because of complaints of loud arguments between the defendant and his father, and had found it necessary to stop the defendant from beating his father.

The evidence is

(A) inadmissible, because it is improper character evidence.

(B) inadmissible, because the witness lacks firsthand knowledge of who started the quarrels.

(C) admissible to show that the defendant killed his father intentionally.

(D) admissible to show that the defendant is a violent person.
[Q3064]

Answer: Choice **(C)** is correct. This answer is correct because the beatings would tend to prove that the killing was not accidental. Under FRE 404(b), "Evidence of other crimes, wrongs, or acts is not admissible to prove the character of a person in order to show action in conformity therewith." So if the prosecution were offering the prior beatings on the theory that "These beatings showed that the defendant had a violent character, making it more likely that he acted violently on this occasion," the evidence would be barred by the above-quoted portion of 404(b). However, FRE 404(b) goes on to say that such other-crimes-or-wrongs evidence "may, however, be admissible for other purposes, such as proof of motive, opportunity, intent, preparation, plan, knowledge, identity, or *absence of mistake or accident*..." Here, that's exactly what's happening: the defendant has claimed that the shooting was accidental, and the prosecution is offering the prior beatings to show "absence of mistake or accident." So the evidence is admissible.

(A) is wrong because the acts of violence here are not being offered as character evidence. It's true that if the evidence were offered as pure character evidence, to show that the defendant acted in conformity with his character (character for violence, say) on the present occasion, the evidence would be barred by FRE 404(b). But as described in the analysis of Choice (C), the evidence here is being offered to show "absence of mistake or accident," not to show "character," so it's admissible.

(B) is wrong, because the beatings show lack of accident regardless of who started the fights. The fact that the witness doesn't know first-hand who started the fights is irrelevant, if the mere existence of the fights would tend to show that the shooting on the present occasion was no mistake. For instance, even if the father started the two prior fights, the fact that the defendant responded by beating his father would make it at least somewhat less likely than it would otherwise be that the shooting now was an accident. So the evidence is relevant, and it's admissible (as described in Choice (C)) as tending to prove absence of accident.

(D) is wrong because evidence of a character for violence is not admissible under these circumstances. Under FRE 404(b), "Evidence of other crimes, wrongs, or acts is not admissible to prove the character of a person in order to show action in conformity therewith." So if the evidence of the prior beatings were really being offered to show that "the defendant has a character for violence, and is thus likely to have acted violently on the present occasion," the quoted sentence would apply to make the evidence inadmissible (not admissible, as this choice posits). However, "character for violence" is not what the prior-acts evidence is being offered for. Instead (as shown in the analysis of Choice (C)), it's being offered to show absence of accident, and that purpose is admissible under 404(b).

Question: A drug enforcement agent had been informed that a person arriving from Europe on a particular airline flight, and answering to a particular description, would be carrying cocaine in his baggage. When the agent saw a man answering that description (the defendant), the agent stopped him and searched his bag. In it, he found a small brass statue with a false bottom. Upon removing the false bottom, the agent found one ounce of cocaine. At the defendant's drug trial, he claimed that he had purchased the statue as a souvenir and was unaware that there was cocaine hidden it its base.

At trial the prosecution now offers to prove that the defendant was convicted fifteen years earlier of illegally importing cocaine by hiding it in the base of a brass statue.

If the defendant's attorney objects, the court should rule that proof of the defendant's prior conviction is

(A) admissible, as evidence of habit.

(B) admissible, because it is evidence of a distinctive method of operation.

(C) inadmissible, because evidence of previous conduct by a defendant may not be used against him.

(D) inadmissible, because the prior conviction occurred more than ten years before the trial.

[Q5136]

Answer: Choice **(B)** is correct. In general, evidence of a defendant's character or disposition is inadmissible for the purpose of proving that he acted in a particular way on a particular occasion. See FRE 404(a), first sentence. But 404(b) qualifies this rule by saying that "evidence of other crimes, wrongs, or acts ... may, however, be admissible for other purposes, such as ... absence of mistake or accident[.]" Since the defendant has claimed that he was "unaware that there was cocaine hidden in [the statue's] base," the fact that he was previously convicted of (knowingly) smuggling cocaine hidden in the base of another brass statue tends to prove absence of mistake or accident, and is thus admissible.

(A) is wrong because, although FRE 406 permits evidence of habit to be used as circumstantial evidence that on a particular occasion the defendant's conduct was consistent with his habit, such habit evidence requires a showing that the actor in question *consistently* acts in a particular way, and one prior experience is not sufficient to establish a habit.

(C) is wrong because, although evidence of a defendant's previous conduct is inadmissible if offered against him for some purposes, it may be admissible if offered against him for others. (C) is therefore overinclusive — for instance, it does not correctly reflect that the defendant's previous conduct here tends to prove absence of mistake, as discussed in (B) above.

(D) is wrong because, although FRE 609(b) indeed says that evidence of a prior conviction is not usually admissible for the purpose of impeaching a witness if the conviction occurred more than ten years prior to the trial at which it is offered, the defendant's prior conviction is not being offered to impeach his credibility.

h. Not an exclusive list:

Question: Plaintiff sued Defendant Auto Manufacturing for his wife's death, claiming that a defective steering mechanism on the family car caused it to veer off the road and hit a tree when his wife was driving. Defendant claims that the steering mechanism was damaged in the collision and offers testimony that the deceased wife was intoxicated at the time of the accident.

Testimony concerning the wife's intoxication is

(A) admissible to provide an alternate explanation of the accident's cause.

(B) admissible as proper evidence of the wife's character.

(C) inadmissible, because it is improper to prove character evidence by specific conduct.

(D) inadmissible, because it is substantially more prejudicial than probative.

[Q7074]

Answer: Choice **(A)** is correct, because Defendant is not attempting to prove a character trait, but is trying to provide an alternate explanation. An issue in the case (indeed, the core issue) is whether the accident was caused by a defective steering wheel or, instead, by some other cause not associated with Defendant. If the wife was intoxicated at the time she was driving the car, this fact would obviously make it more likely than it would otherwise be that the intoxication, not a steering-wheel defect, was the cause of the accident. Therefore, the wife's intoxication was directly relevant evidence that does not fall within any exclusion. (As to the argument that the evidence is inadmissible character evidence, see the discussion of Choice (C).)

(B) is wrong because Defendant is not trying to prove a trait of Plaintiff's deceased wife's character. If the evidence being offered by Defendant was evidence that the wife was often drunk, then the evidence would in effect be character evidence. In that event, this choice would still be wrong, because character evidence, offered to prove that the person acted in conformity therewith on a particular occasion, is generally inadmissible. FRE 404(a). But here, what's being offered is not character evidence (evidence that the wife was often or generally drunk) but rather direct evidence of behavior on the particular occasion in question (evidence that she was drunk while driving into the fatal accident). This is not character evidence at all.

(C) is wrong because, although it more or less correctly states a rule, that rule does not apply on these facts. It's true that under FRE 404(a), evidence of a person's character or a trait of character "is not admissible for the purpose of proving action in conformity therewith on a particular occasion" (with some exceptions not applicable here). It's also true that under FRE 404(b), "evidence of other ... acts is not admissible to prove the character of a person in order to show action in conformity therewith." Therefore, if Defendant were trying to show that the wife was drunk on particular occasions other than the one now in question, that evidence would indeed be excludible under 404(b)'s ban on specific-acts evidence to prove conduct in conformity with character. But that's not what's being offered here: what's offered is direct evidence that the wife was drunk on the particular occasion in issue, and that's not "character" evidence of any sort.

(D) is wrong because proof of Plaintiff's wife's intoxication would be probative of Defendant's defense. It's true that under FRE 403, relevant evidence may be excluded "if its probative value is substantially outweighed by the danger of unfair prejudice..." But given that the key issue in the case is "What caused the accident?", and given that the wife's intoxication, if it existed, would have tremendous probative value on the issue of the accident's cause, no court would conclude that there was a danger of "unfair" prejudice, or that that prejudice substantially outweighed the evidence's probative value.

3. **Other aspects of other-crimes evidence:**

   d. **Rule 403 balancing:**

   Question: Decker, charged with armed robbery of a store, denied that he was the person who had robbed the store.

   In presenting the state's case, the prosecutor seeks to introduce evidence that Decker had robbed two other stores in the past year.

   This evidence is

   (A) admissible, to prove a pertinent trait of Decker's character and Decker's action in conformity therewith.

   (B) admissible, to prove Decker's intent and identity.

   (C) inadmissible, because character must be proved by reputation or opinion and may not be proved by specific acts.

   (D) inadmissible, because its probative value is substantially outweighed by the danger of unfair prejudice.

   [Q1062]

   Answer: Choice **(D)** is correct. Although evidence of Decker's previous two robberies may arguably be relevant as to whether Decker robbed the store in the present case, its probative value is low and dwarfed by the prejudicial value of the evidence. FRE 403 says that "Although relevant, evidence may be excluded if its probative value is substantially outweighed by the danger of unfair prejudice..." "Unfair" prejudice means "an undue tendency to suggest decision on an improper basis..." ACN to FRE 403. The probative value of the evidence is pretty low, since the other acts don't bear very strongly on whether Decker is the robber in the present case (there's no indication that the m.o.'s are all that similar, for instance — see Choice (B) below). Conversely, there's a large risk that if the evidence were admitted, some members of the jury would likely regard it as more probative than it actually is, and consequently give the evidence too much weight.

   (A) is wrong because the general rule is that "evidence of a person's character or a trait of character is not admissible for the purpose of proving action in conformity therewith on a particular occasion." FRE 404(a). There are some exceptions, but none applies here. This choice asserts a rule — admissibility of character-trait evidence to prove action in conformity with the trait on the present occasion — that is the exact opposite of the real rule of 404(a).

   (B) is wrong for two reasons. First, the previous robberies are probably not sufficiently probative of Decker's identity or his intent (the latter isn't even an issue in this case). It's true that evidence of other acts may be admissible for purposes other than to show action in conformity with a person's character, and that two of these acceptable purposes are to prove identity and intent. FRE 404(b). But generally, when other acts are offered to prove identity, the prosecution's theory is that the other acts by the accused are so similar in method to the crime charged that all bear his "signature" (thus justifying the inference that if the defendant committed the prior acts, he also must have committed the present one). Here, the other robberies aren't similar enough to meet this "signature" standard.

Secondly, this evidence poses an extremely high risk of prejudice, far outweighing its limited probative value, and is thus excludible under FRE 403 (see the discussion of Choice (D) above).

(C) is wrong because (1) it at least slightly misstates the law; and (2) more importantly, it gives an explanation that is inapplicable here. While it's true that in general, character or a trait of character must be proved by reputation or opinion evidence, not specific-acts evidence (FRE 405(a)), there are some scenarios in which specific-acts evidence *is* admissible (e.g., where a character trait is an "essential element of a charge, claim or defense" — see FRE 405(b)). But the bigger problem is that what the prosecution is offering here is not, strictly speaking, character evidence — the prosecution is not offering the evidence to show that Decker has a character or tendency to commit robbery; rather, it's trying to qualify for one or more of the "other purposes than character" exceptions mentioned by 404(b), e.g., identity.

E. **Character of victim:**

3. **Rape or sexual assault:**

   a. **FRE:**

   Question: Charged with forcible rape, the defendant relied on a defense of alibi. At the trial, the alleged victim testified that the defendant was the man who accosted her on the street, dragged her into the basement of an apartment building, and forced her to submit to sexual intercourse. During the case, the defendant's attorney offered the testimony of a woman who stated that she was familiar with the victim's reputation in the community and that the victim was thought of as a prostitute. The defendant's attorney also offered into evidence a certified court record indicating that the victim had been convicted of prostitution, a misdemeanor, two months prior to the alleged rape.

   Upon proper objection by the prosecution to both the woman's testimony and the court record, which of the following should the court admit?

   (A) The woman's testimony only.

   (B) The court record only.

   (C) The woman's testimony and the court record.

   (D) Neither the woman's testimony nor the court record.

   [Q5030]

   Answer: Choice **(D)** is correct. FRE 412, the federal "rape shield" provision, applicable to civil and criminal cases "involving alleged sexual misconduct," puts tight limits on evidence of an alleged victim's past sexual behavior and sexual predisposition. Except for a few narrow exceptions, evidence is inadmissible if offered either to "prove that any alleged victim engaged in other sexual behavior" or to "prove any alleged victim's sexual predisposition." Both the testimony and the court record here are evidence of the alleged victim's "other sexual behavior" and/or "sexual predisposition." Therefore, they're inadmissible under FRE 412 unless they fall within one of that rule's narrow exceptions. In criminal cases, the main exceptions are for (1) conduct with the defendant offered to support a defense of consent (covered in FRE 412(b)(1)(B)), and (2) conduct with others offered to show that the defendant was not the source of semen or the victim's injury (covered in FRE 412(b)(1)(A)). Since the defendant is relying on an alibi defense rather than on a consent defense, the first of these exceptions doesn't apply. Since the defendant is not offering the victim's history of prostitution to show that he was not the source of semen or of the victim's injuries, the second exception doesn't apply. So both pieces of evidence are excluded by FRE 412.

(A), (B), and (C) are each inconsistent with the above analysis and thus wrong.

H. Must be pertinent:

Question: At the defendant's murder trial, the defendant calls, as his first witness, a man to testify that the defendant has a reputation in their community as a peaceable and truthful person. The prosecutor objects on the ground that the witness's testimony would constitute improper character evidence.

The court should

(A) admit the testimony as to peaceableness, but exclude the testimony as to truthfulness.

(B) admit the testimony as to truthfulness, but exclude the testimony as to peaceableness.

(C) admit the testimony as to both character traits.

(D) exclude the testimony as to both character traits.

[Q3164]

Answer: Choice **(A)** is correct. Only the testimony about peaceableness is a "pertinent trait" of the accused. FRE 404(a), after stating the general rule against character evidence to prove action in conformity therewith, gives an exception for "evidence of a pertinent trait of character offered by an accused[.]" Since peaceability and truthfulness are each "traits of character," the evidence will be admissible if and only if it concerns a "pertinent" trait. What traits are "pertinent" depends on the nature of the crime charged and any defenses raised. Here, what's charged is a crime that involves violence, but not untruthfulness. Therefore, the accused's reputation for peaceableness involves a "pertinent" trait (one who is peaceable is less likely to have committed a crime involving violence). However, the accused's reputation for truthfulness would probably be held not to be pertinent (since one who is truthful is not less likely to have committed a murder than one who is untruthful.) (Note, however, that if the defendant took the stand and the prosecution attacked his credibility, then the "reputation for truthfulness" testimony would become admissible because the defendant's truthfulness or untruthfulness would be in issue and thus a "pertinent" trait.)

To the extent that Choices (B), (C), and (D) each fail to admit the peaceableness testimony or admit the truthfulness testimony, each is wrong for the reasons described in the analysis of Choice (A).

III. METHODS OF PROVING CHARACTER: REPUTATION, OPINION AND PROOF OF SPECIFIC ACTS

A. FRE:

1. D's good-character evidence:

a. Rebuttal:

Question: The defendant was charged with the crime of assaulting the victim. He admitted striking the victim, but claimed to have acted in self-defense when he was attacked by the victim, who was drunk and belligerent after a football game.

The defendant offered testimony of defendant's employer that he had known and employed the defendant for twelve years and knew the defendant's reputation among the people with whom he lived and worked to be that of a peaceful, law-abiding, nonviolent person. The trial judge admitted this testimony.

On cross-examination of the employer, the state's attorney asked the employer if he had heard that the defendant often engaged in fights and brawls. The trial judge should rule the question

(A) admissible, because evidence of the defendant's previous fights and brawls may be used to prove his guilt.

(B) admissible, because it tests the employer's knowledge of the defendant's reputation.

(C) inadmissible, because it seeks to put into evidence separate, unrelated offenses.

(D) inadmissible, because no specific time or incidents are specified and inquired about.

[Q4026]

Answer: Choice **(B)** is correct. The evidence will be admissible to impeach the employer as a reputation witness. The problem here is that the evidence the prosecutor is seeking is character evidence. Choice (B) offers a way to overcome this problem. Under these facts, the employer is testifying as a reputation witness on the defendant's behalf; that is, he's testifying that the defendant is known as a peaceful, nonviolent person. This evidence is admissible under FRE 404(1), which allows an accused to offer evidence of his own "pertinent trait of character." Then, FRE 405(a) says that where evidence of a "trait of character of a person is admissible" (which the evidence here is, as described in the prior sentence), "On cross-examination, inquiry is allowable into relevant specific instances of conduct." So once the employer gave the testimony favorable to the defendant about the defendant's peaceable reputation, the prosecution was entitled to make "inquiry ... into relevant specific instances of conduct." The specific instances being inquired about (frequent engaging in fights and brawls) are "relevant," because if the employer didn't know about these instances, his testimony about the defendant's reputation for peaceability would be of questionable accuracy (if the employer didn't know these true facts, is he really knowledgeable about the defendant's reputation on this subject?)

(A) is wrong because it is unduly broad. Since the defendant offered favorable reputation evidence of his peaceability as he was permitted to do under 404(a)(1), the prosecution was permitted to rebut that evidence. The rebuttal evidence was in fact substantively admissible to prove that the defendant was not peaceable, and therefore probably wasn't acting in self-defense. However, this choice suggests that independent (extrinsic) evidence of the fights would have been admissible. In fact, only questioning of the defendant's character witness (the employer) was permissible, on account of FRE 405(a) — the prosecution couldn't have introduced extrinsic proof of the defendant's previous fights (e.g., by testimony from a different witness who observed them), and his choice falsely implies that such evidence could have been admitted.

(C) is wrong because it fails to identify that the evidence can be brought out on the cross of the employer, as further discussed in Choice (B).

(D) is wrong because, while impeachment of a reputation witness with specific instances is possible, the specific instances need not be identified as precisely as (D) suggests. Under FRE 404(a) a reputation witness (of which the employer is one) may be questioned about specific instances bearing on the reputation, since *not* knowing such information reflects on the witness's *competence* to testify as to the person's reputation in the community. However, the testimony here is specific enough to constitute specific acts; it clearly does not amount to opinion or reputation testimony.

ii. No extrinsic evidence of specific acts:

Question: The defendant, a young doctor, is charged with falsely claiming deductions on her federal income tax return. At trial, a witness testified for the defendant that she has a reputation in the community for complete honesty. After a sidebar conference at which the prosecutor gave the judge a record showing that the defendant's medical school had disciplined her for altering her transcript, the prosecutor proposes to ask the witness on cross-examination: "Have you ever heard that the defendant falsified her medical school transcript?"

Is the prosecutor's question proper?

(A) No, because it calls for hearsay not within any exception.

(B) No, because its minimal relevance on the issue of income tax fraud is substantially outweighed by the danger of unfair prejudice.

(C) Yes, because an affirmative answer will be probative of the defendant's bad character for honesty and, therefore, her guilt.

(D) Yes, because an affirmative answer will impeach the witness's credibility.

[Q7074]

Answer: Choice **(D)** is correct. The incident can be offered on cross-examination of the character witness, the proper purpose being to show that the witness's assessment of the defendant's character for honesty is not credible. FRE 405(a) says that if evidence of character or a character trait is admissible, proof may be made by testimony as to reputation. Furthermore, in the case of such character evidence, FRE 405(a), last sentence, says that on cross, "inquiry is allowable into relevant specific instances of conduct." Here, this last sentence applies. The intent of the question is to test the witness's knowledge of the defendant's reputation. If the witness hasn't heard about the falsification, he might not be very plugged in to the community and is thus a poor reputation witness. If the witness *has* heard of it, and still believes that the defendant has a good reputation in the community for honesty, this would mean either that the community itself is not very knowledgeable about the defendant's past (making it a poor judge of the defendant's honesty) or that the community is knowledgeable about the defendant's past but ridiculously forgiving (giving it low standards for honesty, and thus making it a poor judge of that trait).

So the alleged falsification is a specific incident of conduct the witness's knowledge of which is probative of the credibility of the witness's reputation testimony. (Note that the courts require that the cross-examiner must have a good faith belief that the event actually occurred before inquiring into the act on cross-examination. In this case, that good faith standard is met by the evidence presented at the sidebar conference that the defendant was disciplined in medical school.)

(A) is wrong because the question does not call for a statement that would be used for its truth. Therefore, it is not hearsay. Rather, the intent of the question is to test the witness's knowledge of the defendant's reputation, and is admissible for the reasons stated in the discussion of Choice (D) above.

(B) is wrong because the alleged incident is not offered to prove income tax fraud, but, rather, to test the witness's knowledge of the defendant's reputation. Therefore, it is admissible for the reasons stated in the discussion of Choice (D) above.

(C) is wrong, because the "bad character" explanation is not a correct statement of law. If an affirmative answer were offered to prove that defendant had a bad character for honesty and therefore was likely guilty, the evidence would be inadmissible. That's because FRE 404 and 405, taken together, prohibit evidence of specific acts indicative of a person's character when that character evidence is offered to prove that a person acted in accordance with the character trait on the occasion in question at trial. Thus, the prosecutor may not introduce the incident involving the medical school transcript for the inference that, because the defendant acted dishonestly on that occasion, she likely acted dishonestly with regard to her tax return.

V. HABIT AND CUSTOM

A. Generally allowable:

2. **Three factors:**

   Question: In a negligence action brought by Pauling against Davidson, Pauling alleged that Davidson failed to signal before making a left turn onto Front Street. During the presentation of Davidson's direct case, Weigand was called as a witness. Weigand testified that she was Davidson's secretary and that Davidson drove her to work every morning. She said that she was in Davidson's car on the morning of the accident, but did not see him signal because she was reading a magazine at the time. She added, however, that she had seen Davidson turn at that intersection many times, and that he always signaled before doing so.

   If Pauling's attorney objects to this testimony by Weigand, her testimony should be

   (A) excluded, unless there were no eyewitnesses to Davidson's behavior on the morning in question.

   (B) excluded, because evidence of past behavior is inadmissible for the purpose of proving reasonable care on a particular occasion.

   (C) admitted, as circumstantial evidence that Davidson signaled on the morning of the accident.

   (D) admitted, but only if it is corroborated by Davidson's testimony.

   [Q5109]

   Answer: Choice **(C)** is correct. Circumstantial evidence is proof of one fact from which another can be inferred. The fact that Davidson always signals at that intersection may permit the inference that he did so on this particular occasion, if it is logically relevant to that conclusion. FRE 406 provides that evidence of a person's habit, "whether corroborated or not and regardless of the presence of eyewitnesses," is relevant to prove that his conduct on a particular occasion was consistent with that habit. Weigand's testimony should, therefore, be admitted as circumstantial evidence of that fact.

   (A) is wrong because the FRE 406, as quoted in the discussion of (C) above, specifically dispenses with the requirement that there were no eyewitnesses.

   (B) is wrong because, while this choice correctly states a general rule (a version of the broad ban on "character" evidence to prove action in conformity therewith), FRE 406 is a more specific rule that allows "habit" evidence to show that the habit was followed on a particular occasion, as detailed in Choice (C) above.

   (D) is wrong because the language of the portion of FRE 406 quoted in (C) makes corroboration unnecessary.

B. Business practices:

1. **Practices relating to copies and mailings:**

   Question: Plaintiff Construction Co. sued Defendant Development Co. for money owed on a cost-plus contract that required notice of proposed expenditures beyond original estimates. Defendant asserted that it never received the required notice. At trial Plaintiff calls its general manager, Witness, to testify that it is Plaintiff's routine practice to send cost overrun notices as required by the contract. Witness also offers a photocopy of the cost overrun notice letter to Defendant on which Plaintiff is relying, and which he has taken from Plaintiff's regular business files.

On the issue of giving notice, the letter copy is

(A) admissible, though hearsay, under the business record exception.

(B) admissible, because of the routine practices of the company.

(C) inadmissible, because it is hearsay not within any exception.

(D) inadmissible, because it is not the best evidence of the notice.

[Q3077]

Answer: Choice **(B)** is correct. The issue is whether the copy found in Plaintiff's files is indeed a copy of a letter that was actually sent to Defendant. Therefore, FRE 406 is relevant. That rule says that "Evidence of the habit of a person or of the routine practice of an organization, whether corroborated or not and regardless of the presence of eyewitnesses, is relevant to prove that the conduct of the person or organization on a particular occasion was in conformity with the habit or routine practice." So here, the general manager's testimony that it was the organization's habit to send such a notice as required by its contracts tends to establish that the photocopy was indeed a photocopy of a letter that was sent, as contemplated by FRE 406. (Nor is the letter here hearsay [whether within an exception or not] — see Choice (A) for an explanation.)

(A) is wrong because the letter is not hearsay at all, since it's not offered to prove the truth of any matter asserted therein. It's true that the letter is an "out of court declaration." But the letter is not being offered to prove the "truth of the matter asserted." The matter asserted is that there was a cost overrun. But the purpose for offering the letter in evidence is merely to show that the contractual requirement of a notice was satisfied. (The letter would be equally relevant on the issue of notice even if the letter was incorrect in its assertion that there was a cost overrun. So it's not offered to prove the truth of the matter asserted therein.)

(C) is wrong because the letter is not hearsay at all. See the discussion of Choice (A) for why this is so.

(D) is wrong because even though the Best Evidence Rule applies, the duplicate copy is admissible. FRE 1002's version of the Best Evidence Rule (called "Requirement of Original"), says that in proving the terms of a writing, the original writing must ordinarily be produced. So on the face of this rule, since the contents of the letter are being proved, FRE 1002 seems to require use of the original. But FRE 1003 says that "A *duplicate is admissible* to the same extent as an original unless (1) a genuine question is raised as to the authenticity of the original or (2) in the circumstances it would be unfair to admit the duplicate in lieu of the original." Since Defendant has not raised a genuine question about the authenticity of the original, and since it would be not be unfair to admit the duplicate (Plaintiff obviously couldn't possess the original any more if its story of having sent it to Defendant is true), FRE 1003 allows use of the copy here.

Question: A state's code of civil procedure provides that no appeal may be prosecuted unless a notice of such appeal is mailed within twenty days after the entry of the final judgment which is being appealed. An appellee moves to dismiss an appeal on the ground that the notice of appeal was not timely served. At a hearing on the motion to dismiss, a secretary in the office of the appellant's attorney testifies that he personally enclosed the notice of appeal in a properly addressed envelope which he then sealed. He states further that he placed the envelope in a basket marked "outgoing mail" in the office conference room at 2 p.m. on the eighteenth day after the judgment appealed from was entered. He states that as a matter of office routine the "outgoing mail" basket is emptied and its contents taken to the post office every day at 4 p.m. by another employee, although he does not personally know whether it was done on that particular day.

The testimony should be

(A) excluded, since evidence of past conduct is not relevant to what was done on any particular day.

(B) excluded, unless some evidence is offered that the envelope which was deposited in the basket was actually mailed that day.

(C) admitted, only if the office employee who usually mails the contents of the "outgoing mail" basket testifies to what is customarily done.

(D) admitted, to prove that the notice of appeal was actually mailed on that day.

[Q5087]

Answer: Choice **(D)** is correct. Under FRE 406, evidence of an established business practice is admissible as circumstantial proof that it was followed on a particular day. So the proof here of the daily mailing practice is admissible to prove that the notice was mailed on the particular day in question.

(A) is wrong because when past conduct has a regularity amounting to a "routine practice of an organization," it is deemed relevant to the issue of whether the practice was followed on a particular day, and under FRE 406 is admissible on that issue.

(B) is wrong for the same reason (D) is right: evidence of an established business practice is admissible as circumstantial proof that it was followed on a particular day, without the need to prove directly that the practice was followed on the day in question.

(C) is wrong because FRE 406 says that the regular practice is admissible to prove that the practice was followed on the particular occasion in question, "whether corroborated or not and regardless of the presence of eyewitnesses." So, any office employee who knows about the practice of his own knowledge may testify to it.

VII. SUBSEQUENT REMEDIAL MEASURES

B. Other purposes:

2. Control:

Question: Pitt sued Dow for damages for injuries that Pitt incurred when a badly rotted limb fell from a curbside tree in front of Dow's home and hit Pitt. Dow claimed that the tree was on city property and thus was the responsibility of the city. At trial, Pitt offered testimony that a week after the accident, Dow had cut the tree down with a chainsaw.

The offered evidence is

(A) inadmissible, because there is a policy to encourage safety precautions.

(B) inadmissible, because it is irrelevant to the condition of the tree at the time of the accident.

(C) admissible to show the tree was on Dow's property.

(D) admissible to show the tree was in a rotted condition.

[Q4035]

Answer: Choice **(C)** is correct. The problem here is that cutting down the tree, after a limb fell on Pitt, would be considered a subsequent remedial measure. The general rule is that subsequent remedial measures are not admissible to show negligence or wrongdoing. FRE 407. However, such evidence *is* admissible for other purposes, e.g., to show ownership, control, or to prove the opponent destroyed evidence. (C) correctly identifies why the evidence of subsequent remedial measures will be admissible here: to prove ownership. That is, the evidence here will tend to prove that the tree was in fact, on Dow's property, which he denies at trial.

(A) is wrong because it misidentifies the purpose for which the evidence is offered. As this choice suggests, there is a rule (FRE 407) against proof of subsequent safety measures in order to encourage the taking of such safety measures. However, the rule is limited to situations where the evidence is offered to show negligence, defect, or the like — it doesn't extend to situations where the remedial-measures evidence is offered on some other issue such as the one here: ownership of the tree.

(B) is wrong, because it mischaracterizes the evidence as irrelevant, and it fails to recognize a purpose for which the evidence could be admitted. Here, Dow's cutting the tree down within a week of the accident would tend to suggest that it was rotted, and *that* would tend to indicate that he was negligent in failing to care for it, or cut it down earlier. Thus, Dow's cutting down the tree would be relevant to the condition of the tree at the time of the accident, but it's excludible for this purpose by FRE 407. However, as Choice (C) suggests, it is admissible for the alternative purpose of showing ownership.

(D) is wrong because it states an impermissible motive for the evidence. To the extent that the evidence is offered to prove the tree's rottenness, this purpose is directly tied to showing that the Dow's failure to cut it down earlier was negligence — the rottenness is part of the plaintiff's prima facie case of negligence. So this purpose would fall within FRE 407's ban on subsequent-remedial-measures evidence offered to show negligence or defect.

Question: A state statute provides that the owner of any motor vehicle operated on the public roads of the state is liable for damage resulting from the negligence of any person driving the vehicle with the owner's permission. A woman was injured when a vehicle operated by a priest struck her while she was walking across the street. At the scene of the accident, the priest apologized to the woman, saying, "I'm sorry. It isn't my car. I didn't know that the brakes were bad." The woman subsequently instituted an action against an accountant for her damages, asserting that the accountant owned the vehicle. She alleged that the accountant was negligent in permitting the vehicle to be driven by the priest while he (the accountant) knew that the brakes were in need of repair, and that he was also vicariously liable under the statute for the negligence of the priest. The accountant denied ownership of the vehicle. At the trial, the plaintiff offered testimony by a car mechanic that on the day after the accident the accountant hired him to completely overhaul the brakes.

Upon objection by the accountant, the evidence is

(A) admissible, to show that the accountant was the owner of the vehicle.

(B) admissible, to show that the brakes were in need of repair on the day of the accident.

(C) inadmissible, because the condition of the vehicle on any day other than that of the accident is irrelevant to show its condition at the time the accident occurred.

(D) inadmissible, under a policy which encourages safety precautions.

[Q5072]

Answer: Choice **(A)** is correct. FRE 407 seeks to encourage safety precautions by prohibiting evidence of subsequent remedial measures from being used for the purpose of showing fault or defect. Such evidence may be admissible for other purposes, however. Here, the accountant had denied ownership of the vehicle. Since it is unlikely that anyone other than the owner would arrange to have the brakes overhauled, the testimony of the mechanic is relevant to establish the accountant's ownership and should, therefore, be admitted.

(B) is wrong because of the above-stated policy of encouraging safety precautions.

(C) is wrong because the evidence is being used to establish that the accountant was the owner of the vehicle, not to establish the condition of the brakes on any particular day. (Also, the condition of the brakes on the day after the accident is relevant to show their probable condition on the day of the accident — FRE 407 keeps out this evidence if offered to show fault or defect not because it's irrelevant, but because allowing it would discourage the taking of socially-valuable remedial measures.)

(D) is wrong because the evidence is being offered to establish ownership, a purpose that is not forbidden by FRE 407's rule against the offering of remedial measures to show fault or defect.

VIII. LIABILITY INSURANCE

A. General rule:

1. **Other purposes:**

   a. **Usually wrong answer:**

   Question: A defendant's house was destroyed by fire and she was charged with arson. To prove that the defendant had a motive to burn down her house, the government offered evidence that the defendant had fully insured the house and its contents.

   Should the court admit this evidence?

   (A) No, because the probative value of the evidence of insurance upon the issue of whether the defendant intentionally burned her house down is substantially outweighed by the dangers of unfair prejudice and confusion of the jury.

   (B) No, because evidence of insurance is not admissible upon the issue of whether the insured acted wrongfully.

   (C) Yes, because evidence of insurance on the house has a tendency to show that the defendant had a motive to burn down the house.

   (D) Yes, because any conduct of a party to the case is admissible when offered against the party.

   [QA018]

   Answer: Choice **(B)** is **incorrect**, because although it is true that FRE 411 bars evidence of insurance to establish that the insured acted negligently or otherwise wrongfully, such evidence is admissible for *other purposes*, and proof of motive is such a purpose. In this respect, Rule 411 is similar to Rule 404(b), under which evidence of past conduct cannot be admitted to prove a propensity to engage in such conduct but can be admitted for other purposes, such as to prove motive. (The correct answer is (C); see p. 6 for a full discussion of all choices.)

   Question: A passenger is suing a defendant for injuries suffered in the crash of a small airplane, alleging that the defendant had owned the plane and negligently failed to have it properly maintained. The defendant has asserted in defense that he never owned the plane or had any responsibility to maintain it. At trial, the passenger calls a witness to testify that the witness had sold to the defendant a liability insurance policy on the plane.

The testimony of the witness is

(A) inadmissible, because the policy itself is required under the original document rule.

(B) inadmissible, because of the rule against proof of insurance where insurance is not itself at issue.

(C) admissible to show that the defendant had little motivation to invest money in maintenance of the airplane.

(D) admissible as some evidence of the defendant's ownership of or responsibility for the airplane.

[Q3136]

Answer: Choice **(D)** is correct. The FRE (like the common law) provide that evidence that a person carried or did not carry liability insurance is not admissible on the issue of whether that person acted negligently. (See FRE 411, first sent.) This rule bars such evidence when it is offered by a plaintiff to suggest that because the defendant was insured, the defendant was probably careless. However, the rule does not apply where the evidence is offered for some other purpose, "such as proof of agency, *ownership, or control* ..." (FRE 411, second sent.) That's what's happening here — the evidence is being used to show that because the defendant bought a liability policy on the plane, he had ownership or control of it.

(A) is wrong because the terms of the policy are not at issue, only the policy's existence. The Best Evidence Rule (B.E.R.) states that in proving the terms of a writing or a recording, where the terms are material, the original must be produced. Here, the B.E.R. would apply if the terms of the insurance policy were in question. But the terms are not in question here and are not material — Witness's testimony involves only the existence of the policy, not its terms, so the B.E.R. does not apply.

(B) is wrong because it misstates the rule. The rule against proof of liability insurance is not a general rule against "proof of insurance where insurance is not itself the issue" (as this choice asserts). Instead, the rule prohibits proof of a liability policy's existence when offered to prove negligence (and that rule applies here, as Choice (D) asserts).

(C) is wrong because such evidence is offered to suggest the defendant was probably careless. FRE 411, first sentence, says that "Evidence that a person was or was not insured against liability is not admissible upon the issue whether the person acted negligently or otherwise wrongfully." Since this choice suggests that an insured plane owner would be less likely to properly maintain the plane, it's a method of asserting the defendant's negligence, and thus flies squarely in the face of FRE 411.

IX. SETTLEMENTS AND PLEA BARGAINS

A. Settlements:

Question: Carr, a driver, ran into and injured Pedersen, a pedestrian. Pedersen has sued Carr, alleging that Carr, while drunk, struck Pedersen who was in a duly marked crosswalk. Pedersen's counsel wishes to prove that after the accident Carr went to Pedersen and offered $1,000 to settle Pedersen's claim.

The trial judge should rule this evidence

(A) admissible as an admission of a party.

(B) admissible as an admission to show Carr's liability, provided the court gives a cautionary instruction that the statement should not be considered as bearing on the issue of damages.

(C) inadmissible since it is not relevant either to the question of liability or the question of damages.

(D) inadmissible because even though it is relevant and an admission, the policy of the law is to encourage settlement negotiations.

[Q4029]

Answer: Choice **(D)** is correct. This choice correctly characterizes the statement as relevant and an admission, and correctly concludes that the evidence will be inadmissible due to public policy considerations. What's being proffered is a settlement offer by Carr. But under FRE 408, admissions in conjunction with settlement negotiations are inadmissible to prove negligence, liability, or a claim's value. That's the case here.

(A) is wrong because FRE 408 says that statements in conjunction with settlement offers are inadmissible to prove negligence, liability, or a claim's value. So even though Carr's statement would otherwise be admissible as an admission by a party-opponent, the special rule of FRE 408 makes it inadmissible.

(B) is wrong because a limiting instruction would not make the evidence here admissible. FRE 408 makes the statement inadmissible as a statement in connection with a settlement negotiation, and that's true if it's offered to prove liability, not just if it's offered to prove damages. So the limiting instruction wouldn't get around the FRE 408 problem.

(C) is wrong because it misstates the facts — the settlement offer *is* relevant. The settlement offer could be taken to mean that Carr acknowledges his own guilt. Thus, it's relevant to the issue of fault. The problem is that the evidence is barred by the special settlement-offers rule of FRE 408, not that it fails to be relevant to any issue in the case.

2. **No "claim" at all:**

   a. **Incorrect "distractor":**

   Question: A homeowner sued a plumber for damages resulting from the plumber's allegedly faulty installation of water pipes in her basement, causing flooding. At trial, the homeowner was prepared to testify that when she first detected the flooding, she turned off the water and called the plumber at his emergency number for help. The plumber responded, "I'll come by tomorrow and redo the installation for free."

   Is the plumber's response admissible?

   (A) No, because it is an offer in compromise.

   (B) No, because it is hearsay not within any exception.

   (C) Yes, as a subsequent remedial measure.

   (D) Yes, as evidence of the plumber's fault.

   [Q7044]

   Answer: Choice **(A)** is **incorrect**. FRE 408 protects statements concerning a "claim" that is "disputed as to validity or amount." However, in this case there was no pending dispute at the time the statement was made. The homeowner was simply calling for help and had not complained about the plumber's work or in any other way indicated that there was a dispute between the parties. Accordingly, the statement does not qualify as an offer in compromise. (The correct answer is (D); see infra, p. 55.)

3. **Collateral admissions of fact:**

   a. **Speaker denies the claim's validity:**

   Question: In a personal injury case, the plaintiff sued a retail store for injuries she sustained from a fall in the store. The plaintiff alleged that the store negligently allowed its entryway to become slippery due to snow tracked in from the sidewalk. When the plaintiff threatened to sue, the store's manager said, "I know that there was slush on that marble entry, but I think your four-inch-high heels were the real cause of your fall. So let's agree that we'll pay your medical bills, and you release us from any claims you might have." The plaintiff refused the offer. At trial, the plaintiff seeks to testify to the manager's statement that "there was slush on that marble entry."

   Is the statement about the slush on the floor admissible?

   (A) No, because it is a statement made in the course of compromise negotiations.

   (B) No, because the manager denied that the slippery condition was the cause of the plaintiff's fall.

   (C) Yes, as an admission by an agent about a matter within the scope of his authority.

   (D) Yes, because the rule excluding offers of compromise does not protect statements of fact made during compromise negotiations.

   [Q7058]

   Answer: Choice **(A)** is correct. FRE 408 excludes, when offered to prove liability for a disputed claim, evidence of "conduct or statements made in compromise negotiations regarding the claim[.]" Here, there is a disputed claim, and the manager's statement was made in an effort to settle that dispute. As such the entire statement is protected under Rule 408.

   (B) is wrong because the fact that the statement denied that the slipperiness was the cause of the problem does not prevent the overall statement from falling within FRE 408's ban on "conduct or statements made in compromise negotiations regarding [a disputed] claim." Even though the manager's statement contained a large portion of self-serving "it's not our fault," the entire statement is inadmissible because uttered during the course of compromise negotiations.

   (C) is wrong because, although the statement is true as far as it goes, it does not go far enough. The fact that the statement was an admission by an agent about a matter within the scope of his authority only means that the statement is not excluded as hearsay. There is another ground for exclusion, so the statement is inadmissible even though it satisfies the hearsay rule. FRE 408 excludes evidence of conduct or statements made in compromise negotiations, as further discussed in Choice (A) above.

   (D) is wrong because FRE 408 protects not only offers of compromise, but also so-called "collateral statements," or more precisely what 408 calls "conduct or statements made in the course of compromise negotiations regarding [a disputed] claim." The rationale is to allow the parties and counsel to speak freely during settlement negotiations, without having to worry that their statements will be used against them at trial. Here, there is a dispute, and the manager's statement was made in an attempt to settle that dispute. Therefore, the entire statement — including those portions consisting of statements of fact — would be excluded under FRE 408.

C. Offer to pay medical expenses:

Question: Plaintiff is suing Doctor for medical malpractice occasioned by allegedly prescribing an incorrect medication, causing Plaintiff to undergo substantial hospitalization. When Doctor learned of the medication problem, she immediately offered to pay Plaintiff's hospital expenses. At trial, Plaintiff offers evidence of Doctor's offer to pay the costs of his hospitalization.

The evidence of Doctor's offer is

(A) admissible as a nonhearsay statement of a party.

(B) admissible, although hearsay, as a statement against interest.

(C) inadmissible, because it is an offer to pay medical expenses.

(D) inadmissible, because it is an offer to compromise.

[Q3069]

Answer: Choice **(C)** is correct. FRE 409 makes an offer to pay medical expenses related to an injury inadmissible to prove liability for the injury. Although the facts don't state the purpose for which Plaintiff is offering the fact of Doctor's offer to pay expenses, we can assume that the purpose is the obvious one of trying to show liability or responsibility (on the theory that "Doctor wouldn't have offered to pay my hospital expenses unless she believed that she was or might be the cause of my problem.") So it's clearly covered by FRE 409.

(A) is wrong because, while it's true that the offer to pay expenses would not be hearsay (since it's a party admission), there are many reasons other than hearsay for exclusion of statements, and the no-evidence-of-offers-to-pay-for-medical-expenses rule (see Choice (C) above) is one of them.

(B) is wrong because the offer is not hearsay, and in any event is inadmissible for other reasons. First, the out-of-court statement here is "I'll pay your medical expenses." That statement is being offered to supply an inference of liability ("You wouldn't have made the offer unless you thought you might be responsible or liable for my condition.") A statement is hearsay only if it's offered to prove "the truth of the matter asserted therein." Here, there is no matter whose "truth" is asserted in the out-of-court statement; the statement is merely an offer to do something. Therefore, repeating the statement in court couldn't be hearsay. (If Doctor had said, "I'm sorry my negligence caused your hospitalization," then this *would* be a statement containing an assertion of fact, which could make it hearsay.) The statement is instead inadmissible because of FRE 409's ban on proof of offers to pay medical expenses when offered on the issue of liability.

(D) is wrong because Doctor's offer was unilateral and not the product of negotiation. It's true that the fact that a party has offered to settle a claim may not be admitted on the issue of the claim's validity. See FRE 408. But the exclusion only applies to offers, or other statements, made *during the course of settlement negotiations.* The offer here was a unilateral one, not one made during settlement negotiations. (The facts tell us that the offer was made "immediately" once Doctor learned of the problem.) Therefore, it doesn't fall within the exclusion.

Chapter 3
EXAMINATION AND IMPEACHMENT OF WITNESSES

V. PRESENT RECOLLECTION REFRESHED AND OTHER TECHNIQUES

A. **Present recollection refreshed:**

4. **MBE tip:**

   Question: A defendant was charged with burglary. At trial, a police officer testified that, after the defendant was arrested and agreed to answer questions, the officer interrogated him with a stenographer present, but that he could not recall what the defendant had said. The prosecutor presented the officer with a photocopy of the stenographic transcript of the interrogation. The officer, after looking at it, was prepared to testify that he recalled that the defendant admitted to being in the area of the burglary. The defendant objected to the officer's testimony on the ground that it violated the "original document" rule (also known as the "best evidence" rule).

   Should the officer's testimony concerning the defendant's recorded confession be admitted?

   (A) No, because a photocopy cannot be used without a showing that the original is unavailable.

   (B) No, because the stenographer has not testified to the accuracy of the transcript.

   (C) Yes, because a photocopy is a duplicate of the original.

   (D) Yes, because the prosecutor is not attempting to prove the contents of the document.

   [Q7016]

   Answer: Choice **(D)** is correct. The prosecutor is trying to prove what the defendant said, not what the transcript says. Accordingly, FRE 1003, the Best Evidence Rule, is not relevant. (It would be different, for example, if this were a contract and the parties differed over the wording of a clause in the contract — then the B.E.R. *would* apply.) In this case, the copy of the transcript is properly used under FRE 612 to revive the officer's recollection. (Notice, by the way, that neither this choice nor any part of the question uses the phrase "present recollection refreshed," even though that's the doctrine that controls the outcome. It's up to you to recognize that refreshment of recollection is what's occurring, and that it's being done properly here.)

   (A) is wrong because the prosecutor is trying to prove what the defendant said, not what the transcript says. Accordingly, the Best Evidence Rule is not relevant. By the way, even assuming that the B.E.R. applied here, this is not an accurate statement of the law. Under FRE 1003, a duplicate can be admissible without any showing that the original is unavailable. A showing of unavailability is required only if the party is seeking to introduce something other than a duplicate (e.g., oral testimony) to prove the contents of a document. See FRE 1004.

   (B) is wrong because this is not a case of past recollection recorded; if it were, the prosecutor *would* have to show that the stenographer accurately recorded what the defendant said. In this case, the officer is testifying to his *own (present) recollection* of what the defendant said, that recollection having been revived by looking at the transcript. Therefore, the relevant doctrine is "present recollection refreshed." That doctrine is embodied in FRE 612, under which a document used only to refresh the recollection of the witness does not have to be accurate or reliable, because the document is not being admitted into evidence. So here, the copy of the transcript is being properly used to refresh the officer's recollection, and the officer's testimony is the evidence.

(C) is wrong because, although FRE 1003 supports the admission of photocopies with some exceptions, this option assumes that the Best Evidence Rule applies here, which it doesn't. The prosecutor is trying to prove what the defendant said, not what the transcript says. The transcript here is being used to refresh the officer's recollection under Federal Rule of Evidence 612, and Rule 1003 (the FRE's version of the Best Evidence Rule) is not relevant.

VII. IMPEACHMENT — GENERALLY

B. **Impeaching one's own witness:**

Question: In a civil trial for fraud arising from a real estate transaction, the defendant claimed not to have been involved in the transaction. The plaintiff called a witness to testify concerning the defendant's involvement in the fraudulent scheme, but to the plaintiff's surprise the witness testified that the defendant was not involved, and denied making any statement to the contrary. The plaintiff now calls a second witness to testify that the first witness had stated, while the two were having a dinner conversation, that the defendant was involved in the fraudulent transaction.

Is the testimony of the second witness admissible?

(A) No, because a party cannot impeach the party's own witness.

(B) No, because it is hearsay not within any exception.

(C) Yes, but only to impeach the first witness.

(D) Yes, to impeach the first witness and to prove the defendant's involvement.

[Q7019]

Answer: Choice **(C)** is correct. Prior statements that are inconsistent with a witness's present testimony impeach the witness's credibility because they tend to show that the witness's trial testimony is not believable. The prior inconsistent statement was not made under oath, and so does not fit the exemption to the hearsay rule provided by FRE 801(d)(1)(A). There is no other hearsay exception that is satisfied under the facts. Therefore, the statement is admissible only to impeach the witness and not for its truth.

(A) is wrong because, under FRE 607, "[t]he credibility of a witness may be attacked by any party, including the party calling the witness."

(B) is wrong because the prior statement of the witness is inadmissible hearsay under FRE 802 only if offered to prove that the defendant was involved in the transaction. It is not hearsay if offered to impeach the witness whose trial testimony is inconsistent with it. This is because, whether true or not, the statement is probative to show that the witness is not credible—he said one thing at trial and said something else previously.

(D) is wrong because the first part of the statement is correct but the second part is incorrect. The prior inconsistent statement was not made under oath, and so does not fit the exemption to the hearsay rule provided by FRE 801(d)(1)(A). There is no other hearsay exception that is satisfied under the facts. Therefore the statement is admissible only to impeach the witness and not for its truth. Using the statement to prove the defendant's involvement would violate FRE 802, the hearsay rule.

VIII. IMPEACHMENT BY PRIOR CRIMINAL CONVICTION

A. **Federal Rule:**

   2. **Felony:**

      c. **Comparison:**

         Question: The defendant was prosecuted for armed robbery. At trial, the defendant testified in his own behalf, denying that he had committed the robbery. On cross-examination, the prosecutor intends to ask the defendant whether he had been convicted of burglary six years earlier.

         The question concerning the burglary conviction is

         (A) proper if the court finds that the probative value for impeachment outweighs the prejudice to the defendant.

         (B) proper, because the prosecutor is entitled to make this inquiry as a matter of right.

         (C) improper, because burglary does not involve dishonesty or false statement.

         (D) improper, because the conviction must be proved by court record, not by question on cross-examination.

         [Q4044]

         Answer: Choice (A) is correct. Where the witness is an accused (a criminal defendant), FRE 609(a)(1) says that the court "shall" allow impeachment by proof of a less-than-10-year-old felony conviction, "if the court determines that the probative value of admitting this evidence outweighs its prejudicial effect to the accused." Choice (A) exactly matches this standard. It's important to note that the conviction here was for burglary, a crime whose elements do not include "an act of dishonesty or false statement"; if the conviction *were* for such a dishonesty/false-statement crime (whether felony or misdemeanor), FRE 609(a)(2) says that it "shall" be admitted, without any provision for the trial judge to determine that its probative value outweighs its prejudicial effect to the accused.

         (B) is wrong because it ignores the fact that (as described in the analysis of Choice (A) above), where the witness being impeached is a criminal defendant and the crime is not a crime of dishonesty/false-statement, the conviction is admissible only if the trial judge determines that its probative value outweighs its prejudicial effect to the accused. So on the facts here, admission is not "a matter of right" as this choice asserts.

         (C) is wrong because the fact that the crime here (burglary) is not a crime of dishonesty or false statement doesn't prevent its use. Under FRE 609(a), any felony (crime punishable by at least one year in prison), or any felony or misdemeanor involving dishonesty or false statement, can be used to impeach a witness. Where the crime does not involve dishonesty, it's admissible only "if the court determines that the probative value of admitting this evidence outweighs its prejudicial effect to the accused." If it *does* involve dishonesty, admission is mandatory (with no balancing). So the fact that the crime here didn't involve dishonesty or false statement doesn't automatically block its admissibility, as this choice asserts.

         (D) is wrong, because the conviction *can* be proven through intrinsic impeachment (i.e., on cross examination of the witness being impeached). FRE 609(a) allows impeachment on these facts (as analyzed in the treatment of Choice (A) above), and that rule does not impose any requirement that the impeachment occur by means of the court record of the conviction. So impeachment by asking the witness, "Isn't it true that you were convicted ..." is proper.

IX. IMPEACHMENT BY PRIOR BAD ACTS

A. Federal Rule:

1. May bring out on cross:

Question: Powers sued Debbs for battery. At trial, Powers's witness Wilson testified that Debbs had made an unprovoked attack on Powers. On cross-examination, Debbs asks Wilson about a false claim that Wilson had once filed on an insurance policy.

The question is

(A) proper, because the conduct involved untruthfulness.

(B) proper provided that the conduct resulted in conviction of Wilson.

(C) improper, because the impeachment involved a specific instance of misconduct.

(D) improper, because the claim form would be the best evidence.

[Q4040]

Answer: Choice **(A)** is correct. Discrediting testimony is being sought from Wilson's own mouth. This is "intrinsic" impeachment. There are various types of questions that may be used to elicit intrinsic impeachment from a witness. One of these consists of questions about the witness's prior bad acts bearing on his character for truthfulness, even if the bad act(s) did not lead to a conviction. The situation is covered by FRE 608(b), which says in part that "*Specific instances* of the conduct of a witness, for the purpose of attacking ... the witness's *character for truthfulness, other than conviction of crime* as provided in rule 609, may not be proved by extrinsic evidence. They may, however, in the discretion of the court, if *probative of truthfulness or untruthfulness*, be *inquired into on cross-examination* of the witness (1) concerning the witness's character for truthfulness or untruthfulness[.]" This last-quoted sentence from 608(b) applies here: Wilson's own "character for truthfulness" is being attacked, and the attack consists of specific instances of the witness's conduct, other than conviction of a crime, being proved not by extrinsic evidence but instead by being "inquired into on cross-examination of the witness." Notice that it is only because the bad act illustrates Wilson's character for untruthfulness — rather than his character for some other trait, such as violence — that the question falls within the area allowed by 608(b).

(B) is wrong because the conduct didn't have to result in a conviction in order to be usable for impeachment. Prior bad acts of the witness, bearing on his character for untruthfulness, may be inquired into on cross examination, as described in the analysis of Choice (A) above. For such bad acts, there is no requirement that the act have led to a criminal conviction. (For acts that did lead to a criminal conviction, there is a separate provision, FRE 609, that handles admissibility.)

(C) is wrong because the impeachment *can* be in the form of a specific instance of misconduct. The portion of 608(b) quoted in the discussion of Choice (A) above expressly allows use of specific instances of conduct, provided that they are brought up on cross-examination of the witness whose truthfulness is being attacked by the cross-examiner. If you chose this response, you were probably thinking of the rule for *extrinsic* impeachment (i.e., evidence from a new witness or document) by means of bad acts. While the witness's bad character for truthfulness *can* be addressed with extrinsic impeachment, *when the evidence is extrinsic,* FRE 608(a) and (b) together says that *only reputation or opinion testimony may be used.* But the bad-act evidence here is being used on cross of the very witness whose truthfulness is being attacked (i.e., it's "*intrinsic,*" not extrinsic, evidence).

(D) is wrong, because it erroneously applies the Best Evidence Rule to these facts. The B.E.R. only applies when the terms of a writing are being proven, or the witness is testifying relying on a writing. Under those circumstances, the document itself must be introduced, if it's available. The B.E.R. does not apply to these facts because, although the best evidence of a writing is the writing itself, where the issue is "collateral" — here, the claim will only address Wilson's character for truthfulness — the witness's testimony will be admissible without producing the document. FRE 1004.

a. Applies to any witness:

Question: In an automobile negligence action by Popkin against Dwyer, Juilliard testified for Popkin. Dwyer later called Watts, who testified that Juilliard's reputation for truthfulness was bad.

On cross-examination of Watts, Popkin's counsel asks, "Isn't it a fact that when you bought your new car last year, you made a false affidavit to escape paying the sales tax?"

This question is

(A) proper, because it will indicate Watts's standard of judgment as to reputation for truthfulness.

(B) proper, because it bears on Watts's credibility.

(C) improper, because character cannot be proved by specific instances of conduct.

(D) improper, because one cannot impeach an impeaching witness.

[Q2010]

Answer: Choice **(B)** is correct. A witness's credibility may be impeached by evidence of specific instances conduct reflecting on his truthfulness, but only by the cross-examiner's making "inquiry" into those specific instances during the cross-examination of that witness. FRE 608(b). Since Watts is on the stand and being cross-examined, the question about his prior act of dishonesty meets these requirements (it's probative of his general truthfulness, and what Popkin's counsel is doing is merely making "inquiry" into the act). The fact that Watts is a witness called solely to give impeachment testimony, as opposed to substantive or occurrence-type testimony, doesn't matter — *any* witness may be impeached by inquiry into specific past conduct of the witness that is probative of untruthfulness.

(A) is wrong because Watts is not being asked about the reputation testimony, but is instead being impeached on account of his own bad acts. So what Watts's standard is for judging reputation is not what the question is about.

(C) is wrong because there is an exception to the general rule that, for the purpose of attacking a witness's character for truthfulness, specific instances of conduct may not be proved by extrinsic evidence. The judge may, in her discretion, allow such evidence if it is brought out through cross examination of the witness whose credibility is being attacked and if the bad acts are probative of truthfulness or untruthfulness. FRE 608(b). Watts is being cross-examined with evidence of his falsifying an affidavit to avoid paying sales tax on the sale of a new car. The act is probative of untruthfulness and is being brought out on cross-examination. Therefore, the question is proper even though it involves a specific instance of the witness's past conduct.

(D) is wrong because it states a non-existent rule: there is no rule against "impeaching an impeaching witness."

2. Probative of truthfulness:

Question: In a civil trial arising from a car accident at an intersection, the plaintiff testified on direct that he came to a full stop at the intersection. On cross-examination, the defendant's lawyer asked whether the plaintiff claimed that he was exercising due care at the time, and the plaintiff replied that he was driving carefully. At a sidebar conference, the defendant's lawyer sought permission to ask the plaintiff about two prior intersection accidents in the last 12 months where he received traffic citations for failing to stop at stop signs. The plaintiff's lawyer objected.

Should the court allow defense counsel to ask the plaintiff about the two prior incidents?

(A) No, because improperly failing to stop on the recent occasions does not bear on the plaintiff's veracity and does not contradict his testimony in this case.

(B) No, because there is no indication that failing to stop on the recent occasions led to convictions.

(C) Yes, because improperly failing to stop on the recent occasions bears on the plaintiff's credibility, since he claims to have stopped in this case.

(D) Yes, because improperly failing to stop on the recent occasions tends to contradict the plaintiff's claim that he was driving carefully at the time he collided with the defendant.

[Q7012]

Answer: Choice **(A)** is correct. Under FRE 608(b), a witness can be impeached with prior bad acts that bear upon truthfulness. Failing to stop at a stop sign has no bearing on truthfulness. As a general matter, a witness also can be impeached with evidence that contradicts a part of his testimony that bears on an important issue in dispute. However, in this case, the prior bad acts do not contradict the witness's testimony that he stopped on this occasion. Essentially, the defendant is trying to show that the plaintiff is a careless driver. Carelessness is a character trait, and evidence of a person's character is not admissible in a civil case to prove how that person acted on the occasion in question. (FRE 404(a)).

(B) is wrong because, under FRE 608(b), a witness can be impeached with bad acts that do not result in convictions. The reason that the prior acts here are inadmissible is not because there were no convictions, but rather because the acts have no bearing on veracity or contradiction of prior testimony.

(C) is wrong because it's factually incorrect. It's true that under FRE 608(b), a witness can be impeached with prior bad acts that bear upon truthfulness by demonstrating falsity, dishonesty, or the like; so if the prior acts bore on truthfulness, they could be used for impeachment here. But in this case, the plaintiff's prior acts may demonstrate carelessness, but they do not demonstrate dishonesty.

(D) is wrong, because the conclusion does not follow logically from the premise. A person can be acting carefully on one occasion and not another, so the prior acts are not contradictory of the plaintiff's testimony that he was careful in this instance, as this choice asserts. If the plaintiff testified that he had never run a stop sign, then the prior acts *would* contradict his testimony, and would be admissible.

3. **No extrinsic evidence:**

   Question: At a defendant's trial for burglary, his friend supported the defendant's alibi that they were fishing together at the time of the crime. On cross-examination, the friend was asked whether his statement on a credit card application that he had worked for his present employer for the last five years was false. The friend denied that the statement was false.

The prosecutor then calls the manager of the company for which the friend works, to testify that although the friend had been first employed five years earlier and is now employed by the company, there had been a three-year period during which he had not been so employed.

The testimony of the manager is

(A) admissible, in the judge's discretion, because the friend's credibility is a fact of major consequence to the case.

(B) admissible, as a matter of right, because the friend "opened the door" by his denial on cross-examination.

(C) inadmissible, because whether the friend lied in his application is a matter that cannot be proved by extrinsic evidence.

(D) inadmissible, because the misstatement by the friend could have been caused by a misunderstanding of the application form.

[Q3122]

Answer: Choice **(C)** is correct. This choice is correct because the friend cannot be impeached on a collateral issue by extrinsic evidence. The manager's testimony is not relevant to any substantive issue in the case — it bears solely on the friend's credibility. Therefore, the matter is governed by FRE 608(b), which says in part that "Specific instances of the conduct of a witness, for the purpose of attacking or supporting the witness's credibility, other than conviction of crime as provided in Rule 609, may not be proved by extrinsic evidence." In other words, once a lawyer has completed cross-examination of a witness, he must be satisfied with whatever he could bring out on cross tending to show that the witness lied on a collateral matter (i.e., a matter not pertaining to the substantive issues in the case) — the lawyer may not introduce another witness, or document, to prove that the first witness lied. Here, the testimony of the manager is extrinsic evidence of specific conduct by the friend, offered for the purpose of attacking the friend's credibility. Therefore, it is barred by the just-quoted portion of 608(b).

(A) is wrong because there is no discretion to admit extrinsic evidence to impeach on a collateral issue. If the prosecutor had presented the friend with a document tending to show he had lied on his credit card application, *that* would be admissible in the judge's discretion, because the second sentence of Rule 608(b) says that "Specific instances of the conduct of a witness, for the purpose of attacking or supporting the witness's credibility ... may, however, in the discretion of the court, if probative of truthfulness or untruthfulness, be *inquired into on cross-examination* of the witness (1) concerning the witness's character for truthfulness or untruthfulness[.]" But since the testimony here is from witness 2 (the manager) about the credibility of witness 1 (the friend), it's extrinsic evidence governed by the first sentence of 608(b) (quoted in the discussion of Choice (C) above), not the sentence just quoted; therefore, the judge can't use her discretion to admit it.

(B) is wrong because, while the friend may have "opened the door" to being asked further questions about his application on cross, he did not (and could not) open the door to the use of extrinsic evidence to show he was lying. As the discussion of Choice (C) indicates, once a lawyer has completed cross-examination of a witness, he must be satisfied with whatever he could bring out on cross tending to show that the witness lied on a collateral matter (i.e., a matter not pertaining to the substantive issues in the case) — the lawyer may not introduce another witness, or document, to show that the first witness lied. So nothing the friend said could have "opened the door" to this type of extrinsic evidence.

(D) is wrong because whether the friend could have honestly misunderstood the form is irrelevant — the evidence is extrinsic evidence barred because it pertains to a collateral matter, as discussed in the analysis of Choice (C) above.

Question: The plaintiff sued the defendant for breach of a commercial contract in which the defendant had agreed to sell the plaintiff all of the plaintiff's requirements for widgets. The plaintiff called an expert witness to testify as to damages. The defendant seeks to show that the expert had provided false testimony as a witness in his own divorce proceedings.

This evidence should be

(A) admitted only if elicited from the expert on cross-examination.

(B) admitted only if the false testimony is established by clear and convincing extrinsic evidence.

(C) excluded, because it is impeachment on a collateral issue.

(D) excluded, because it is improper character evidence.
[Q3013]

Answer: Choice **(A)** is correct. FRE 608(b) says that "Specific instances of the conduct of a witness, for the purpose of attacking or supporting the witness's credibility, other than conviction of crime as provided in rule 609, *may not be proved by extrinsic evidence.* They may, however, in the discretion of the court, if probative of truthfulness or untruthfulness, be *inquired into on cross-examination of the witness* (1) concerning the witness's character for truthfulness or untruthfulness..." The present use fits the second sentence of FRE 608(b): the giving of false testimony in a prior trial is obviously "probative of untruthfulness." And Choice's (A)'s limitation to matters "elicited from the expert on cross-examination" brings the situation into the second sentence (cross-examination) rather than the first sentence (extrinsic evidence).

(B) is wrong because, as described in Choice (A) above, the prior-bad-act evidence here can only be brought out on cross, making this choice wrong since it does not include this limitation. On the other hand, if the evidence *is* brought out on cross, it need not be supported by "clear and convincing" evidence. It's true that as a judge-made rule, the cross-examiner must have a "good faith basis" for believing that the false-testimony episode actually occurred. But such a good-faith basis, not the possession of clear-and-convincing-evidence, is all that is required for introducing the topic on cross.

(C) is wrong because the defendant's testimony, though "collateral," would be admissible if elicited on cross-examination. If the evidence were being offered "extrinsically" (e.g., by testimony from a different witness who witnessed the false testimony), this choice would be correct — see the first sentence of FRE 608(b), quoted in the discussion of Choice (A) above. But the evidence would be allowed to be brought up ("elicited") on cross of the expert himself, even though it relates solely to credibility rather than to a substantive issue in the case (and thus concerns a "collateral matter").

(D) is wrong, because evidence of a prior bad act by the witness demonstrating the witness's poor character for truthfulness does not fall within the general ban on proof of character traits to show action-in-conformity-therewith-on-the-present-occasion. Instead, FRE 608(b) imposes specific rules governing when such evidence is admissible — as described in Choice (A), such prior-acts-of-lying evidence may be brought out only on cross of the witness whose veracity is in question, not by means of "extrinsic evidence." Therefore, Choice (D) is an incorrect statement of both the rule and the outcome.

Question: PullCo sued Davidson, its former vice president, for return of $230,000 that had been embezzled during the previous two years. Called by PullCo as an adverse witness, Davidson testified that his annual salary had been $75,000, and he denied the embezzlement. PullCo calls banker Witt to show that, during the two-year period, Davidson had deposited $250,000 in his bank account.

Witt's testimony is

(A) admissible as circumstantial evidence of Davidson's guilt.

(B) admissible to impeach Davidson.

(C) inadmissible, because its prejudicial effect substantially outweighs its probative value.

(D) inadmissible, because the deposits could have come from legitimate sources.

[Q3024]

Answer: Choice **(B)** is **incorrect**, because the use of Witt's testimony for impeachment purposes would violate FRE 608(b). FRE 608(b) says that "Specific instances of the conduct of a witness, for the purpose of *attacking or supporting the witness's credibility*, other than conviction of crime as provided in rule 609, *may not be proved by extrinsic evidence*." The evidence here consists of "specific instances" of Davidson's conduct. If the evidence is being offered to "impeach" Davidson as Choice (B) specifies, it is being offered to "attack the witness's credibility," and falls within 608(b), given that there has been no criminal conviction. Therefore, the specific instances of conduct can't be proved by "extrinsic evidence" (which is what separate testimony from Witt would be). Instead, impeachment could only happen by bringing out the instances while Davidson was on the stand (e.g., "Isn't it true that according to bank records you deposited almost twice the amount of your salary?") (The correct answer is (A); see supra, p. 5.)

XI. IMPEACHMENT BY PRIOR INCONSISTENT STATEMENT

A. General rule:

Question: Davidson and Smythe were charged with burglary of a warehouse. They were tried separately. At Davidson's trial, Smythe testified that he saw Davidson commit the burglary. While Smythe is still subject to recall as a witness, Davidson calls Smythe's cellmate, Walton, to testify that Smythe said, "I broke into the warehouse alone because Davidson was too drunk to help."

This evidence of Smythe's statement is

(A) admissible as a declaration against penal interest.

(B) admissible as a prior inconsistent statement.

(C) inadmissible, because it is hearsay not within any exception.

(D) inadmissible, because the statement is not clearly corroborated.

[Q1148]

Answer: Choice **(B)** is correct. Under FRE 613(b), when a witness testifies at trial, evidence of his prior inconsistent statement is admissible to impeach his credibility (if a foundation is laid either before or after the impeachment where the witness has an opportunity to explain or deny the statement and where the opposite party has the opportunity to interrogate the witness). Since Smythe is "still subject to recall as a witness," the foundation can be laid. In addition, some types of prior inconsistent statements are not barred by the hearsay rule and may be admitted as substantive proof of the matters contained in the statement – i.e., those made in an earlier trial or proceeding, where the declarant spoke under oath and subject to perjury penalties. FRE 801(d)(1). Since Smythe's statement was not under oath, it may not be admitted substantively. Therefore, the statement is admissible as a prior inconsistent statement, but only for impeachment purposes. (Note that this answer is correct because Smythe is a non-party in this action. If Smythe were on trial here, his prior statement would be admissible for substantive purposes, as an admission.)

(A) is wrong because the declarant is available. Under FRE 804(b)(3), the requirements for the declaration-against-interest exception are: (1) the declaration must be against the declarant's pecuniary or proprietary interest when made; (2) the declarant must be unavailable; and (3) the declarant must have had first-hand knowledge of the facts asserted in the declaration. The fact pattern indicates that Smythe is still subject to recall as a witness when Walton is testifying about Smythe's prior statement, so he is available.

(C) is wrong because, although it is correct in identifying the statement as hearsay not within any exception, it does not recognize that the statement would still be admissible for impeachment purposes.

(D) is wrong because the statement is admissible, and the requirement of corroboration does not apply in the context of a prior inconsistent statement, but rather, to the hearsay exception of the declaration against interest. FRE 804(b)(3), which provides for the hearsay exception of declaration against interest, states, "a statement tending to expose the declarant to criminal liability and offered to exculpate the accused is not admissible unless corroborating circumstances clearly indicate the trustworthiness of the statement." This is the source of the language in (D), but it does not apply here. If the declarant was unavailable and the exception was applied, then corroboration *would* be required.

B. Special rules from FRE 613:

2. "Extrinsic evidence," and the "explain or deny" and "interrogate" rules:

Question: Perez sued Dawson for damages arising out of an automobile collision. At trial, Perez called Minter, an eyewitness to the collision. Perez expected Minter to testify that she had observed Dawson's automobile for five seconds prior to the collision and estimated Dawson's speed at the time of the collision to have been 50 miles per hour. Instead, Minter testified that she estimated Dawson's speed to have been 25 miles per hour.

Without finally excusing Minter as a witness, Perez then called Wallingford, a police officer, to testify that Minter had told him during his investigation at the accident scene that Dawson "was doing at least 50."

Wallingford's testimony is

(A) admissible as a present sense impression.

(B) admissible to impeach Minter.

(C) inadmissible, because Perez may not impeach his own witness.

(D) inadmissible, because it is hearsay not within any exception.
[Q1034]

Answer: Choice **(B)** is correct. Under FRE 613(b), when a witness testifies at trial, extrinsic evidence of his prior inconsistent statement is admissible to impeach his credibility, so long as the subsequently witness has an opportunity to explain or deny the statement and the opposite party has the opportunity to interrogate the witness about it. Wallingford's testimony as to Minter's statement at the accident scene – "the driver (defendant) was doing at least 50" — is inconsistent with Minter's previous testimony at trial that the defendant's speed was 25 miles per hour. The fact pattern indicates that Minter was not excused as a witness and that therefore there exists the opportunity for him to explain or deny the statement and to be interrogated on it by the opposite party (Dawson).

(A) is wrong because the statement was not made close enough to the time of the accident. FRE 803(1) provides for the hearsay exception of a present sense impression, defined as a statement "describing or explaining an event or condition made *while the declarant was perceiving* the event or condition, or *immediately thereafter.*" Minter's statement was made to the police officer during the investigation of the accident scene so it was not made immediately after viewing the collision.

(C) is wrong because "the credibility of a witness may be attacked by any party, including the party calling the witness." FRE 607.

(D) is wrong because what Minter said to the Officer is not hearsay. The out-of-court statement at issue is Minter's statement to the officer, "Dawson was doing at least 50." But the statement is not being offered to prove that Dawson really was doing at least 50 — it's merely being used to cast doubt on the credibility of Minter's in-court statement that Dawson was doing 25. If the statement to the officer *were* being offered as substantive evidence, i.e., to prove that Dawson really was "doing at least 50," then it *would* be inadmissible hearsay.

3. **Can be used by calling witness:**

   Question: The plaintiff sued the defendant for illegal discrimination, claiming that the defendant fired him because of his race. At trial, the plaintiff called a witness, expecting him to testify that the defendant had admitted the racial motivation. Instead, the witness testified that the defendant said that he had fired the plaintiff because of his frequent absenteeism. While the witness is still on the stand, the plaintiff offers a properly authenticated secret tape recording he had made at a meeting with the witness in which the witness related the defendant's admissions of racial motivation.

   The tape recording is

   (A) admissible as evidence of the defendant's racial motivation and to impeach the witness's testimony.

   (B) admissible only to impeach the witness's testimony.

   (C) inadmissible, because it is hearsay not within any exception.

   (D) inadmissible, because a secret recording is an invasion of the witness's right of privacy under the U.S. Constitution.

   [Q3026]

   Answer: Choice **(B)** is correct. The tape is admissible as a prior inconsistent statement offered to impeach the witness, but inadmissible substantively because of hearsay. First, let's consider the recording's admissibility for impeachment. FRE 613(b) implicitly allows use of extrinsic evidence to show that a witness has made a prior inconsistent statement. ("Extrinsic evidence of a prior inconsistent statement by a witness is not admissible unless the witness is afforded an opportunity to explain or deny the same and the opposite party is afforded an opportunity to interrogate the witness thereon, or the interests of justice otherwise require.") So here, once the witness said on the stand that the defendant had given a non-racial explanation for the firing, the witness's tape-recorded statement that the defendant had given a racial explanation was extrinsic evidence tending to show a prior inconsistent statement by the witness. Consequently, the statement was admissible for impeachment under FRE 613(b), since the witness was still on the stand (and thus had a chance to explain or deny the statement).

Now, let's consider substantive admissibility. Here, the tape recording is "hearsay within hearsay." The outer level is that the witness is making a recorded, and thus out-of-court, statement. The inner level is that the witness is repeating an admission made by the defendant. Here, the inner level is not inadmissible hearsay, because it falls within the exception for admissions introduced against the maker. See FRE 801(d)(2) (A statement is not hearsay if "The statement is offered against a party and is (A) the party's own statement...") But the outer level is hearsay that is not within any exception — the witness is making an out-of-court statement (the witness's words on the recording) offered to demonstrate the truth of the matter asserted (that the defendant made a certain admission to the witness). There is nothing in this statement ("The defendant told me he fired the plaintiff for racial reasons") that falls within any hearsay exception. Thus the statement can't come in for the substantive purpose of demonstrating that the defendant was racially motivated.

(A) is wrong because, as is described in the analysis of Choice (B), the recording is not admissible as "evidence of the defendant's racial motivation," which is a substantive (non-impeachment-of-the-witness) purpose.

(C) is wrong because, as is described in Choice (B), the statement is admissible for impeachment as a prior inconsistent statement of the witness.

(D) is wrong because no violation of the Constitution occurs when a person secretly records a conversation to which he is a party (and in any event, the witness was not a governmental actor, again preventing the recording from possibly being a constitutional violation).

XIV. IMPEACHMENT BY CONTRADICTION; THE "COLLATERAL ISSUE" RULE

B. Collateral issue rule:

2. Disallowed:

Question: Price sued Derrick for injuries Price received in an automobile accident. Price claims Derrick was negligent in exceeding the posted speed limit of 35 m.p.h. Bystander, Price's eyewitness, testified on cross-examination that Derrick was wearing a green sweater at the time of the accident. Derrick's counsel calls Wilson to testify that Derrick's sweater was blue. Wilson's testimony is

(A) admissible as substantive evidence of a material fact.

(B) admissible as bearing on Bystander's truthfulness and veracity.

(C) inadmissible, because it has no bearing on the capacity of Bystander to observe.

(D) inadmissible, because it is extrinsic evidence of a collateral matter.

[Q4014]

Answer: Choice **(D)** is correct. Derrick's counsel is attempting to impeach Bystander with evidence that is not from Bystander's own mouth – in other words, by "extrinsic" evidence. Extrinsic evidence that only discredits a witness, without bearing on any substantive issues in the case, is called "collateral," and in most instances is not admissible. Evidence that discredits the witness by showing that the witness gave incorrect testimony in the present case about an immaterial issue falls into this category of inadmissible extrinsic evidence on collateral matters. The FRE do not specifically recite this rule, but it is a common-law rule that is universally observed by courts following the FRE. Here, the issues in the case involve the speed of Derrick's car, his failing to keep a lookout, and his crossing the center line. The color of his sweater is not a material issue; all Wilson's testimony will serve to do is slightly discredit Bystander by contradiction. So it's a classic illustration of the "no extrinsic evidence on collateral matters" rule.

(A) is wrong because it mischaracterizes the facts: the color of Derrick's sweater is *not* a material fact (it doesn't relate to any of the substantive issues in the case). It is instead a "collateral" matter – relevant only to discredit a witness, Bystander. As such, it will not be admissible, under the common-law rule against extrinsic evidence on collateral matters, applicable as a "gap filler" to cases governed by the FRE.

(B) is wrong because the testimony here could *not* be admitted on the subject of Bystander's truthfulness and veracity. It's true that the testimony has some bearing on Bystander's truthfulness, because it contradicts his testimony (and thus raises the question, "If he could be lying or mistaken on this point, isn't he likely to be lying or mistaken about some really important fact in his testimony?") But because the contradiction about the color of the sweater does not touch on any substantive issue in the case, and does not bear on other issues considered highly important aspects of witness veracity (e.g., presence of bias), its impeachment effect is considered minor, and not worth the trouble of calling a separate witness. Therefore, it falls within the general common-law rule that extrinsic impeachment evidence on a collateral matter is not allowed.

(C) is wrong because it misstates the facts – the testimony *would* (or at least might) bear on Bystander's ability to observe. Any contradiction of witness 1's testimony by witness 2 about a matter that witness 1 said he observed would or might bear on witness 1's ability to observe. But where the contradiction is on a point that does not matter substantively, and is not on some other kind of issue that is considered important (e.g., bias on the part of witness 1), it is excludable based on the common-law rule barring extrinsic evidence (i.e., evidence from a separate witness or document) on a collateral matter.

3. **Allowed:**

    a. **Bias:**

       Question: At the defendant's trial for a gang-related murder, the prosecution introduced, as former testimony, a statement by a gang member who testified against the defendant at a preliminary hearing and has now invoked his privilege against self-incrimination.

       If the defendant now seeks to impeach the credibility of the gang member, which of the following is the court most likely to admit?

       (A) Evidence that the gang member had three misdemeanor convictions for assault.

       (B) Testimony by a psychologist that persons with the gang member's background have a tendency to fabricate.

       (C) Testimony by a witness that at the time the gang member testified, he was challenging the defendant's leadership role in the gang.

       (D) Testimony by a witness that the gang member is a cocaine dealer.
       [Q7034]

       Answer: Choice **(C)** is correct. This is evidence of "bias." It shows that the declarant had a motive to implicate the defendant falsely, because by doing so he would remove the defendant from the position that the witness wanted to have. Evidence of bias is considered important and, generally speaking, it is liberally admitted, although no specific provision in the FRE allows it. (The common law rules of evidence apply to any "gap" in the

FRE, and proof of bias is liberally admitted — and not deemed "collateral" — at common law.) Note, by the way, that the gang member can be impeached even though he is not at trial to testify — FRE 806 allows parties to impeach a hearsay declarant in the same ways that would be permitted if the declarant were to testify, on the theory that a hearsay declarant is essentially a witness in the case.

(A) is wrong because, under FRE 609(a)(2), misdemeanor convictions are not admissible to impeach a witness unless they involved dishonesty or false statement. Assault convictions do not involve dishonesty or false statement. If the misdemeanor convictions had been for, say, lying to a government official, then they *would* have been admissible to impeach the declarant.

(B) is wrong because expert testimony on credibility is usually found inadmissible on the theory that credibility issues are for the jury, not for the imprimatur of an expert. There have been a few cases in which expert testimony on credibility has been permitted, but the question asks for the most likely evidence to be admitted, and this is not the best answer.

(D) is wrong because this is "bad act" evidence, and to be admissible to impeach a witness, FRE 608 says that bad-act evidence must tend to prove that the witness is an untruthful person. If its probative value is substantially outweighed by the risk of prejudice, confusion, and delay, then it must be excluded under Rule 403. Courts have ruled that evidence of drug activity is only minimally probative of truthfulness, and therefore is usually inadmissible to impeach the witness. While it is probably within the trial court's discretion to admit this evidence, at least in some cases, the question asks for the most likely evidence to be admitted, and this is not the best answer.

CHAPTER 4

HEARSAY

I. DEFINITION

B. Definition:

3. **Hearsay may be by the present witness:**

   a. **Statement about what declarant previously said:**

   Question: Pawn sued Dalton for injuries received when she fell down a stairway in Dalton's apartment building. Pawn, a guest in the building, alleged that she caught the heel of her shoe in a tear in the stair carpet. Pawn calls Witt, a tenant, to testify that Young, another tenant, had said to him a week before Pawn's fall: "When I paid my rent this morning, I told the manager he had better fix that torn carpet."

   Young's statement, reported by Witt, is

   (A) admissible, to prove that the carpet was defective.

   (B) admissible, to prove that Dalton had notice of the defect.

   (C) admissible, to prove both that the carpet was defective and that Dalton had notice of the defect.

   (D) inadmissible, because it is hearsay not within any exception.

   [Q2082]

   Answer: Choice **(D)** is correct. Young's statement, "I told the manger he had better fix that torn carpet," is an "out-of-court statement" being offered to "prove the truth of the matter asserted," that Young told the manager about the needed repair and that, therefore, the manager knew of the ripped carpet. In other words, Young's out-of court-statement "I told the manager X" is being offered to show that Young, the declarant, indeed told the manager X. So the statement is inadmissible hearsay if offered for that purpose. FRE 801. (Notice that this would be hearsay whether or not X was itself true.) And there is no other plausible purpose for which it is being offered on these facts.

(A) is wrong because the statement is inadmissible to prove that the carpet was defective, because it is hearsay not within any exception, as discussed in Choice (D). The statement can't tend to prove that the carpet was defective unless the trier first believes that Young made the statement about a defect to the manager; so the statement "Young told me he had told the manager X" would be offered to prove that Young indeed told the manager X, and that would be an offer to prove the truth of the matter asserted.

(B) is wrong because the statement is inadmissible hearsay, as explained in the discussion of (D). Young's statement "I told the manager thus-and-such" is being offered to prove that Young, the declarant, indeed told the manager thus-and-such. So even if the statement is not being offered to prove that Young's statement to the manager was true (and instead offered to merely prove "notice" to the manager of a fact that might or might not be true), Young's statement to Witt that Young had previously made the statement to the manager is inadmissible hearsay.

(C) is wrong because, as discussed in (D), the statement is inadmissible for both these purposes.

D. Illustrations of hearsay on MBE:

Question: At Defendant's trial for sale of drugs, the government called Witness to testify, but Witness refused to answer any questions about Defendant and was held in contempt of court. The government then calls Officer to testify that, when Witness was arrested for possession of drugs and offered leniency if he would identify his source, Witness had named Defendant as his source.

The testimony offered concerning Witness's identification of Defendant is

(A) admissible as a prior inconsistent statement by Witness.

(B) admissible as an identification of Defendant by Witness after having perceived him.

(C) inadmissible, because it is hearsay not within any exception.

(D) inadmissible, because Witness was not confronted with the statement while on the stand.

[Q3193]

Answer: Choice **(C)** is correct. FRE 801(c) defines hearsay as a statement, other than one made by the declarant while testifying at trial, offered in evidence to prove the truth of the matter asserted. Witness's statement naming Defendant as his source was made by Witness after being arrested by Officer, which is to say it was not made when Witness was testifying at trial. The government seeks to offer Officer's repetition of that statement for the truth of the matter asserted in it, i.e., that Defendant was indeed the source for the drugs he is now charged with selling. So the statement is hearsay, and is inadmissible unless some exception applies. No exception applies. For instance, the "prior inconsistent statement" exception doesn't apply for the reason stated in the analysis of Choice (A) below, and the "identification" exception doesn't apply for the reason stated in the analysis of Choice (B) below.

(A) is wrong because Witness has made only one statement. Certain statements by a person who testifies at a trial or hearing, and is subject to cross-examination about the statements, are not hearsay. FRE 801(d)(1) says that where the declarant "testifies at the trial or hearing and is subject to cross-examination" concerning the prior statement, the prior statement is non-hearsay (and thus admissible) if it is "inconsistent with the declarant's testimony, and was given under oath subject to the penalty of perjury at a trial, hearing, or other proceeding." (801(d)(1)(A).) This exclusion obviously doesn't apply here: the declarant is Witness, and he is not "testifying ... subject to cross-examination" at trial. (Merely appearing at the trial and refusing to answer doesn't count as "testifying," certainly not when there is a requirement of being "subject to cross-examination.") And even in the unlikely event Witness's out-of-court statement were viewed as being both "prior" and "inconsistent," it wasn't given "under oath."

(B) is wrong because Witness has refused to testify. Certain statements by a person who testifies at a trial or hearing, and is subject to cross-examination about the statements, are not hearsay. FRE 801(d)(1)(C) says that where the declarant "testifies at the trial or hearing and is subject to cross-examination" concerning the prior statement, the prior statement is non-hearsay (and thus admissible) if it is "one of *identification of a person made after perceiving the person.*" This exclusion doesn't apply here. Witness has not "testified" or been "subject to cross-examination" (see the analysis of Choice (A) for more detail about why).

(D) is wrong because the lack of confrontation doesn't have anything to do with the inadmissibility of the statement. There is no general principle that an out-of-court declaration can't be introduced unless the declarant is "confronted with the statement while on the stand." It's true that in the case of a prior inconsistent statement from a testifying witness, FRE 613(b) says that extrinsic evidence of the prior statement is inadmissible "unless the witness is afforded an opportunity to explain or deny the same and the opposite party is afforded an opportunity to interrogate the witness thereon, or the interests of justice otherwise require." But this provision doesn't come close to applying, since Witness is not a testifying witness, and the prior statement is not a "prior inconsistent statement."

It's also true that in some cases, the *defendant's* Confrontation Clause rights will constitutionally prevent an out-of-court declaration from being admitted against him. But Choice (D) refers to *Witness*'s right to "confront" the statement while on the stand, not the defendant's right to confront the witness. In summary, Witness had no right to be "confronted with the statement while on the stand."

Question: In a jurisdiction without a Dead Man's Statute, Parker's estate sued Davidson claiming that Davidson had borrowed from Parker $10,000, which had not been repaid as of Parker's death. Parker was run over by a truck. At the accident scene, while dying from massive injuries, Parker told Officer Smith to "make sure my estate collects the $10,000 I loaned to Davidson."

Smith's testimony about Parker's statement is

(A) inadmissible, because it is more unfairly prejudicial than probative.

(B) inadmissible, because it is hearsay not within any exception.

(C) admissible as an excited utterance.

(D) admissible as a statement under belief of impending death.
[Q3081]

Answer: Choice **(B)** is correct. First, let's look at whether the statement was hearsay. It's clearly an out-of-court declaration. And, the statement includes Parker's assertion that he's owed $10,000 by Davidson, offered to prove that Davidson does indeed owe this money. So the statement easily fits within the definition of hearsay — out-of-court statement offered to prove the truth of the matter asserted. Now, does some exception apply? No. The two most plausible ones are the excited utterance exception (not applicable because the statement doesn't relate to the exciting event — see the discussion of Choice (C)) and the dying declaration exception (not applicable because the statement doesn't relate to the cause of impending death — see the discussion of Choice (D)).

(A) is wrong because even if the statement were more prejudicial than probative, it would be inadmissible hearsay not within any exception. Apart from the hearsay problem (see the discussion of Choice (B) above), the statement here is not all that prejudicial, so it's unlikely that the statement's probative value would be found to be "*substantially* outweighed" by the prejudicial effect, as FRE 403's balancing test requires.

(C) is wrong because FRE 803(2)'s excited-utterance exception applies to "a statement *relating to a startling event or condition* made while the declarant was under the stress of excitement caused by the event or condition." As you can see from the italicized phrase, the statement has to relate to the startling event. Parker's comment here relates solely to the debt, not to the startling event (the truck accident).

(D) is wrong because Parker's comment did not concern the cause or circumstance of his death. FRE 803(b)(2)'s dying-declaration exception applies to (in a civil case or homicide prosecution) "a statement made by a declarant while believing that death was imminent, *concerning the cause or circumstances of what the declarant believed to be impending death.*" Since Parker's statement related only to the collection of the debt, not to the truck accident that was about to cause his death, it doesn't qualify.

Question: While crossing Spruce Street, Pesko was hit by a car that she did not see. Pesko sued Dorry for her injuries.

At trial, Pesko calls Williams, a police officer, to testify that, ten minutes after the accident, a driver stopped him and said, "Officer, a few minutes ago I saw a hit-and-run accident on Spruce Street involving a blue convertible, which I followed to the drive-in restaurant at Oak and Third," and that a few seconds later Williams saw Dorry sitting alone in a blue convertible in the drive-in restaurant's parking lot.

Williams' testimony about the driver's statement should be

(A) admitted as a statement of recent perception.

(B) admitted as a present sense impression.

(C) excluded, because it is hearsay not within any exception.

(D) excluded, because it is more prejudicial than probative.

[Q4041]

Answer: Choice **(C)** is correct, because the statement here is inadmissible hearsay. The statement here *is* hearsay because it's an out-of-court statement offered to prove the truth of its assertion. The out-of-court declarant is the driver, saying that the driver saw a hit-and-run accident on Spruce Street involving a blue convertible later found at Oak and Third, and the driver's statement is being offered to prove that the driver saw a hit-and-run accident on Spruce Street involving a blue convertible later found at Oak and Third. (Otherwise, the fact that Williams found Dorry sitting in the blue convertible at Oak and Third would be meaningless — you have to believe the truth of the driver's assertion in order for Williams' own testimony to be relevant.)

(For why (B) is wrong, i.e., why this doesn't qualify for the present-sense-impression exception, see p. 67.)

II. SPECIAL ISSUES

B. "Truth of matter asserted":

1. Verbal acts:

Question: In a suit based on a will, inheritance of $1 million depended upon whether the wife had survived her husband when both died in the crash of a small airplane. An applicable statute provided that, for purposes of distributing an estate after a common disaster, there was a rebuttable presumption that neither spouse had survived the other. A witness was called to testify that as she approached the plane she heard what she thought was a woman's voice saying, "I'm dying," although by the time the two occupants were removed from the wreckage they were both dead.

Is the witness's testimony admissible?

(A) No, because the matter is governed by the presumption that neither spouse survived the other.

(B) No, because the witness's testimony is too speculative to support a finding.

(C) Yes, because the hearsay rule does not apply to statements by decedents in actions to determine rights under a will.

(D) Yes, because it is relevant and not otherwise prohibited.

[QA001]

Answer: Choice **(D)** is correct. The witness is testifying as to what she heard someone say outside of the courtroom. But this is not hearsay, because although the witness is recounting an out-of-court statement, that statement is not being offered to prove the truth of the matter asserted therein, i.e., that the declarant was, in fact, dying. Rather, the statement is being offered to prove that only that it was made, because that fact has independent legal significance. As such it is classified as a verbal act, i.e., an operative fact that gives rise to legal consequences. Thus, the statement does not constitute hearsay as defined by FRE 801(c) and, therefore, is not barred by FRE 802. And it is relevant as it helps establish that the wife survived the husband.

(A) is wrong because under the majority common law "bursting bubble" rule, which is followed by FRE 301, a presumption disappears when sufficient counterproof is offered about the presumed fact. Here the testimony of the witness, although not conclusive, is sufficient to rebut the presumption that neither spouse survived the other and to support a jury finding that the wife outlived the husband. Therefore, the presumption is no longer controlling, and the witness's testimony is admissible. In any event, regardless of how (or even whether) the bursting bubble rule applies, the witness's testimony would be admissible — in all jurisdictions, the party who does not benefit from a presumption is always entitled to submit otherwise-competent evidence rebutting the existence of the presumed fact.

(B) is wrong because the testimony is not "too speculative." A witness need not be absolutely certain of matters about which the witness testifies. Here the testimony is based on the perception and memory of a lay witness, and thus satisfies the FRE 701 standard that the testimony be "(a) rationally based on the perception of the witness, and (b) helpful to a clear understanding of the witness's testimony or the determination of a fact in issue."

(C) is wrong because it presumes that the statement is hearsay. But the statement is not hearsay under FRE 801(c), because it is not being offered to prove the truth of the matter asserted. Instead, the statement is an operative fact being offered to prove that the woman was alive at the time she made the statement; so the mere existence of the statement (regardless of its "truth value") is relevant on the issue of whether the speaker survived her husband, even if by only a few minutes.

2. **Effect on hearer/reader:**

   Question: Park sued Officer Dinet for false arrest. Dinet's defense was that, based on a description he heard over the police radio, he reasonably believed Park was an armed robber. Police radio dispatcher Brigg, reading from a note, had broadcast the description of an armed robber on which Dinet claims to have relied.

   The defendant offers the following items of evidence:

   I. Dinet's testimony relating the description he heard.

   II. Brigg's testimony relating the description he read over the radio.

   III. The note containing the description Brigg testifies he read over the radio.

   Which of the following are admissible on the issue of what description Dinet heard?

   (A) I and II only.

   (B) I and III only

   (C) II and III only.

   (D) I, II, and III.

   [Q1032]

   Answer: Choice **(D)** is correct. All three items are admissible because the statement presented in each is not hearsay, and there is no other problem with the items. Hearsay is an out-of-court statement offered to prove "the truth of the matter asserted." FRE 801(c). Here, the matter being asserted in the out-of-court statement is the description of an armed robber. The purpose for which all three items in question are being used is not to show that the description is in fact true (that the robber really had that description), but to show that Officer Dinet had a *reasonable belief* that Park was an armed robber based on the description he heard. Where a statement is offered to show the effect of that statement on the listener — and the effect did not depend on whether the statement was true — the statement will not be hearsay. That principle applies here: the reasonableness of the Officer's belief did not depend on whether the robber really had that description, so none of the three versions of the description is being offered to show the truth of the matter asserted, i.e., that the robber really had the description that was broadcast.

   Question: Plaintiff sued Defendant under an age discrimination statute, alleging that Defendant refused to hire Plaintiff because she was over age 65. Defendant's defense was that he refused to employ Plaintiff because he reasonably believed that she would be unable to perform the job. Defendant seeks to testify that Employer, Plaintiff's former employer, advised him not to hire Plaintiff because she was unable to perform productively for more than four hours a day.

   The testimony of Defendant is

   (A) inadmissible, because Defendant's opinion of Plaintiff's abilities is not based on personal knowledge.

   (B) inadmissible, because Employer's statement is hearsay not within any exception.

   (C) admissible as evidence that Plaintiff would be unable to work longer than four hours per day.

(D) admissible as evidence of Defendant's reason for refusing to hire Plaintiff.

[Q3078]

Answer: Choice **(D)** is correct. Hearsay is a statement offered to prove "the truth of the matter asserted." FRE 801(c). The matter being "asserted" in the out-of-court declaration is "Plaintiff can't work productively more than 4 hours per day." So if the statement were being offered to prove that Plaintiff couldn't in fact work more than 4 hours per day, it would be hearsay (and not within any exception). However, Plaintiff can properly claim that this is *not* the purpose of introducing the former employer's statement. Plaintiff can say, "I'm offering this statement not to show that the former employer was speaking truthfully or accurately — I have no idea whether Plaintiff could or couldn't work productively — but rather to explain that at the moment I declined to hire her, my having heard this statement, not my desire to avoid hiring someone over 65, was my motivation." A court would agree — where the out-of-court statement is offered to show its effect on the listener rather than its truth, that's a non-hearsay purpose.

(A) is wrong because Defendant's opinion of Plaintiff's abilities is not rendered inadmissible by the fact that it is not based on personal knowledge. It's true that there are some types of testimony that are not admissible because not based on personal knowledge. But here, Defendant's opinion is not being offered to show that that opinion was "true." Rather, it's being offered to show that the opinion — whether "true" or not — was not based on forbidden age discrimination. Therefore, the fact that the opinion was not based on Defendant's personal experience does not make it inadmissible.

(B) is wrong because Employer's statement is not offered for the truth of the matter asserted in it, and therefore cannot be hearsay. The matter asserted in the statement is that Plaintiff was incapable of working productively for more than four hours in a day. If the statement was offered to prove that Plaintiff in fact was incapable of working more than this amount, the statement would indeed be inadmissible hearsay. But that's not why it's being offered — it's being offered merely to prove that Defendant's reason for not hiring Plaintiff was this advice from Employer (whether that advice was based on real facts or not) rather than an age-discriminatory motive. And, as outlined in the discussion of Choice (D), that's not hearsay.

(C) is wrong because if the statement was offered for this purpose, it would be inadmissible hearsay. The out of court statement includes the sub-statement "Plaintiff can't work more than four hours productively." If the statement were offered to prove that Plaintiff indeed couldn't work more than four hours productively, the statement would be being offered to prove the truth of the (or a) matter asserted in it. This would make the statement hearsay. However, as further explained in Choice (D) above, it wasn't offered for this purpose.

D. **Multiple hearsay:**

1. **FRE provision:**

   c. **Split of outcomes on the MBE:**

   Question: The plaintiff, who is executor of her late husband's estate, has sued the defendant for shooting the husband from ambush. The plaintiff offers to testify that the day before her husband was killed, he described to her a chance meeting with the defendant on the street in which the defendant said, "I'm going to blow your head off one of these days."

   The witness's testimony concerning her husband's statement is

   (A) admissible, to show the defendant's state of mind.

   (B) admissible, because the defendant's statement is that of a party-opponent.

(C) inadmissible, because it is improper evidence of a prior bad act.

(D) inadmissible, because it is hearsay not within any exception.

[Q3045]

Answer: Choice **(D)** is correct. The plaintiff's testimony would be hearsay within hearsay, and the "outer level" is not within any exception. The FRE defines hearsay as "a statement, other than one made by the declarant while testifying at the trial or hearing, offered in evidence to prove the truth of the matter asserted." FRE 801(c). Anytime the evidence in question consists of an out-of-court statement by *A* repeating another out-of-court statement by *B*, you have to analyze *both A*'s statement and *B*'s statement — if *either* statement is hearsay not falling within any exception, the combined statement cannot come in.

Here, the "inner" level (the defendant's statement to the plaintiff's husband) is an admission being used against a party-opponent, so it falls within the admissions exception to the hearsay rule. But the "outer" level (the husband's statement to the plaintiff, "Here's what the defendant told me...") is hearsay not within any exception. First, notice that the statement ("The defendant told me he'd blow my head off one day") is being offered to prove the matter asserted: it's being offered to prove that the defendant indeed made the threat — if the defendant hadn't made the threat, the evidence would be of no probative value in the case. (The statement is also being offered for the additional not-really-hearsay inference that if the defendant made a threat to kill the husband by shooting, that's evidence tending to show that the fatal shooting of the husband by someone unknown was done by the defendant. But this "secondary" purpose doesn't detract from the fact that the primary purpose — to prove that the defendant made the threat — is a hearsay purpose.) Now, let's look at whether the husband's statement falls within any exception. It doesn't. For instance, it doesn't fall within the state-of-mind exception, because the husband wasn't saying, "I'm scared of the defendant because he threatened to kill me..." — it's offered for the pure purpose of showing that the defendant made the threat, and that purpose doesn't qualify for state-of-mind, excited-utterance, or any other exception.

(A) is wrong because the state-of-mind exception doesn't solve the problem that the husband's statement to the plaintiff is, separately, hearsay. It's true that the defendant's statement alone might well be admissible as evidence of the defendant's state of mind vis-à-vis the husband, under FRE 803(3) (covering declarant's "then existing state of mind, emotion, sensation, or physical condition"). But the problem (as further discussed in Choice (D) above) is that what's offered is what the husband said out of court that the defendant told him out of court. So if the husband's statement (the "outer" statement) is hearsay not within an exception, the fact that the defendant's statement (the "inner" statement) falls within a hearsay exception doesn't help. Here, the statement by the husband is hearsay not within any exception, as shown by the analysis in Choice (D). Therefore, the combined statements of the husband and the defendant can't come in.

(B) is wrong because the admissibility of statements made by, and offered against, a party-opponent doesn't solve the combined hearsay-on-hearsay problem present here. It's true that the defendant's statement, if made directly to the testifying witness (the plaintiff) could be repeated by her on the stand, since then it would be a statement made by a party opponent admitted against that opponent, a non-hearsay use under FRE 801(d)(2)(A). But the problem (as further discussed in Choice (D) above) is that what's offered is what the husband said out of court that the defendant told him out of court. So if the husband's statement (the "outer" statement) is hearsay not within an exception, the fact that the defendant's statement (the "inner" statement) is a non-hearsay admission doesn't help.

(C) is wrong because it mischaracterizes the evidence, and it also doesn't address the hearsay within hearsay issue. First, the answer choice characterizes the evidence incorrectly, as proof of a prior bad act, when it is being offered as a statement. Secondly, it does not address the pivotal issue: the hearsay problem presented by the husband's statement (the "outer" statement).

Question: The plaintiff was injured when the ladder on which she was standing collapsed without warning. Immediately following the accident, the plaintiff was taken to a hospital where she remained for approximately six hours. At the trial of the plaintiff's action against the manufacturer of the ladder, the plaintiff's attorney offered a properly authenticated record from the hospital. After examining the record, the defendant's attorney, outside the presence of the jury, moved to exclude a portion of the record which read: "History: Ladder collapsed. Patient fell."

The motion to exclude that portion of the record should be

(A) granted, if, but only if, it can be excluded without causing any physical damage to the record.

(B) granted, because it has no bearing on the plaintiff's medical condition.

(C) denied, if the history was taken for the purpose of diagnosis or treatment.

(D) granted, since hospital personnel are not experts in determining the causes of accidents.

[Q5081]

Answer: Choice **(C)** is correct. This is a multiple-level hearsay problem: the hospital record is an out-of-court statement (the "outer" level), and it contains another out-of-court statement, namely, the plaintiff's statement that she fell when the ladder collapsed (the "inner" level). Since the inner level is being offered for the truth of the matter asserted therein (that the plaintiff fell when the ladder collapsed), both levels must meet some exclusion to the hearsay rule. (See FRE 805, saying that "hearsay included within hearsay is not excluded ... if *each part* of the combined statements conforms with an exception to the hearsay rule[.]") Fortunately for the plaintiff, FRE 803(4) and (6), taken together, permit the introduction of both levels. First, FRE 803(6)'s business-records provision grants an exception for a "record ... of conditions ... made at or near the time ... from information transmitted by, a person with knowledge, if kept in the course of a regularly conducted business activity, and if it was the regular practice of that business activity to make the ... record[.]" Here, the various facets of this rule are satisfied since: (a) the hospital regularly made such patient-intake records; (b) the record here was made at or near the time of the patient's fall; (c) the information was "transmitted by a person with knowledge" (the plaintiff); and (d) the particular record was "kept in the course of a regularly conducted business activity" (the running of the hospital).

Next, 803(4) gives a hearsay exception for the plaintiff's own statement, since that statement was "made for the purposes of medical diagnosis or treatment and describing medical history, or past or present symptoms . . . or the inception or general character of the cause or external source thereof insofar as reasonably pertinent to diagnosis or treatment." That is, the plaintiff was trying to get treatment, and was describing her present symptoms, as well as the "cause or external source" of those symptoms (the falling ladder). So each level of the hospital record is supported by its own hearsay exception.

(A) is wrong because there is no need to exclude the portion about the ladder, due to the availability of the two hearsay exceptions discussed above.

(B) is wrong because the sentence is admissible under the two hearsay exceptions discussed in (C). It's true that 803(4)'s exception for "statements [made] for purposes of medical diagnosis or treatment" requires that the statement be "reasonably pertinent to diagnosis or treatment." But a terse statement about how an injury was caused — especially if not accompanied by any statements about fault — will generally satisfy the "reasonably pertinent" requirement, and the "ladder collapsed" statement here pretty clearly meets that requirement.

(D) is wrong because the statements in the record were not statements of opinion (and, indeed were not statements by the hospital personnel), so the fact that they were not made by experts in accident causation is irrelevant.

CHAPTER 5
HEARSAY EXCEPTIONS AND EXCLUSIONS

I. ADMISSIONS

B. Personal admissions:

Question: In an accident case, the defendant testified in his own behalf that he was going 30 m.p.h. On cross-examination, the plaintiff's counsel did not question the defendant with regard to his speed. Subsequently, the plaintiff's counsel calls a police officer to testify that, in his investigation following the accident, the defendant told him he was driving 40 m.p.h.

The officer's testimony is

(A) admissible as a prior inconsistent statement.

(B) admissible as an admission.

(C) inadmissible, because it lacks a foundation.

(D) inadmissible, because it is hearsay not within any exception.

[Q4015]

Answer: Choice **(B)** is correct. The plaintiff is offering the defendant's out-of-court statement to prove that the defendant was speeding. Since the statement is being offered to prove the truth of its assertion, the statement is hearsay. However, the statement will be admissible under the admission exclusion to the hearsay rule. FRE 801(d)(2)(A) gives a hearsay exclusion for a statement that is offered against a party and is "the party's own statement[.]" Since the statement was made by the defendant, and is being offered against the defendant, it meets the requirements of the just-quoted rule.

(A) is wrong because there is no basis on which to admit a prior inconsistent statement. The basic problem with the evidence here concerns hearsay, which is an out-of-court statement offered to prove the truth of its assertion. Here, if the defendant's out-of-court statement is offered to prove that the defendant was, in fact, speeding, the statement will have to be admissible *substantively* — that is, to prove that the defendant was, in fact, speeding. The out-of-court statement won't work as a substantively-admissible prior inconsistent statement, though, because although FRE 801(d)(1)(A) does give a hearsay exclusion for a prior statement of a testifying witness where the statement is "inconsistent with the declarant's testimony," that exclusion applies only where the prior statement was "given *under oath* subject to the penalty of perjury at a *trial, hearing or other proceeding, or in a deposition.*" Since the defendant's prior statement during the officer's investigation was not made under oath or at a proceeding or deposition, it doesn't qualify. A second problem is that the defendant isn't the testifying witness.

Now, let's examine whether the statement can be used simply to *impeach* the defendant (in other words, call into question his truthfulness), rather than to prove substantively that the defendant really was speeding. Here, the plaintiff's counsel is trying to impeach the defendant by "extrinsic" evidence (i.e., evidence that doesn't come from the mouth of the impeached witness). But FRE 613(b) says that "Extrinsic evidence of a prior inconsistent statement by a witness is not admissible unless the witness is afforded an opportunity to explain or deny the same[.]" Since the plaintiff's counsel already had the defendant on cross and dismissed him without asking him about the prior statement, counsel has failed to comply with this rule, so the statement can't be used for impeachment except under the admission theory discussed in Choice (B).

(C) is wrong because the absence of a foundation doesn't matter here. That's because the statement is admissible as an admission by a party opponent under FRE 801(d)(2)(A), and admissions do not need any foundation to qualify under that Rule.

(D) is wrong because it fails to realize that the testimony will be admissible as an admission, for the reasons discussed in Choice (B) above.

2. **Question may not say "admission":**

    Question: A defendant was on trial for perjury for having falsely testified in an earlier civil case that he knew nothing about a business fraud. In the perjury trial, the defendant again testified that he knew nothing about the business fraud. In rebuttal, the prosecutor called a witness to testify that after the civil trial was over, the defendant admitted to the witness privately that he had known about the fraud.

    Is the witness's testimony in the perjury trial admissible?

    (A) Yes, but only to impeach the defendant's testimony.

    (B) Yes, both to impeach the defendant's testimony and as substantive evidence of the perjury.

    (C) No, because it is hearsay not within any exception.

    (D) No, because it relates to the business fraud and not to the commission of perjury.
    [QA076]

    Answer: Choice **(B)** is correct. First, let's consider the statement's admissibility as substantive evidence of the perjury. The witness is testifying about an out-of-court statement. If the statement is offered to prove the truth of its contents, i.e., that the declarant knew about the fraud, this would meet the hearsay definition of FRE 801(c). But the declarant is the defendant in this case, and the declarant's statement is being offered against him. Consequently, the statement is a party admission and, therefore, FRE 801(d)(2)(A) says that it is deemed not hearsay. Since it is not hearsay, it is admissible to prove the truth of its contents (i.e., as substantive evidence of the perjury).

    The statement is also admissible to impeach the declarant's testimony, since it is a prior statement that is inconsistent with the declarant/defendant's testimony at the present (perjury) trial. Rule 613, which deals with prior inconsistent statements, makes them generally admissible for impeachment, subject to some exceptions that are not relevant here. In fact, where, as here, the prior inconsistent statement was made by one who is a party opponent in the present proceeding, Rule 613(b) allows use of "extrinsic evidence" (which is what the prosecutor's witness's statement is) of the prior inconsistent statement even if the maker of the prior statement (here, the defendant) is not given an opportunity to "explain or deny" the prior statement.

    (A) is wrong because although the testimony is certainly admissible to impeach the defendant's testimony, it can *also* be used substantively as an admission by a party-opponent under FRE 801(d)(2)(A), as the analysis of Choice (B) demonstrates.

(C) is wrong because under FRE 801(d)(2)(A), a statement of a party-opponent that is offered against that party is deemed to be not hearsay.

(D) is wrong because although the statement made to the witness does relate to the prior business fraud, it also relates to the present perjury charge. That's because the prior statement demonstrates that the defendant in fact *did* know about the fraud, despite his testimony in two trials that he did not know of it. Thus the statement is relevant to prove that the defendant's trial testimony was knowingly false and hence constituted perjury.

Question: A homeowner sued a plumber for damages resulting from the plumber's allegedly faulty installation of water pipes in her basement, causing flooding. At trial, the homeowner was prepared to testify that when she first detected the flooding, she turned off the water and called the plumber at his emergency number for help. The plumber responded, "I'll come by tomorrow and redo the installation for free."

Is the plumber's response admissible?

(A) No, because it is an offer in compromise.

(B) No, because it is hearsay not within any exception.

(C) Yes, as a subsequent remedial measure.

(D) Yes, as evidence of the plumber's fault.

[Q7044]

Answer: Choice **(D)** is correct. This is a party admission, admissible as a hearsay exclusion under Rule 801(d)(2)(A). A statement made by a party (the plumber) cannot be excluded as hearsay when offered against that party by the opponent. Moreover, the statement is probative — a person who makes a statement like this is likely to think he is at fault, and this is probative evidence that indeed he is at fault.

(A) is wrong because FRE 408 protects statements concerning a "claim" that is "disputed as to validity or amount." However, in this case there was no pending dispute at the time the statement was made. For more about this, see p. 28.

(B) is wrong because FRE 801(d)(2)(A) exempts statements made by a party, used against the party, from the definition of hearsay. In this case, the plumber is a party and the statement is being offered against him. In this context, the statement is not hearsay.

(C) is wrong because, although this option correctly states that the statement is admissible, it misstates the reason why this is so. FRE 407 excludes evidence of measures taken that, had they been taken prior to the event that caused the injury, would have made the injury or harm less likely to occur. Here, no "measure" was taken at all. The plaintiff wants to introduce a statement, not any action that would have made the injury less likely to occur. Therefore Rule 407 is inapplicable.

Question: The defendant was prosecuted for homicide. He testified that he shot in self-defense. In rebuttal, a police officer testified that he came to the scene in response to a telephone call from the defendant. The officer offers to testify that he asked, "What is the problem here, sir?" and the defendant replied. "I was cleaning my gun and it went off accidentally."

The offered testimony is

(A) admissible, as an excited utterance.

(B) admissible, to impeach the defendant and as evidence that he did not act in self-defense.

(C) inadmissible, because of the defendant's privilege against self-incrimination.

(D) inadmissible, because it tends to exculpate without corroboration.

[Q1049]

Answer: Choice **(B)** is correct. First, let's consider whether it's admissible substantively, i.e., to prove that the defendant did not act in self-defense. The police officer's testimony that the defendant had told him, "I was cleaning my gun and it went off accidentally," is an "out-of-court statement" offered to "prove the truth of the matter asserted," so it would on its face be hearsay if it's being used as evidence that the defendant did not act in self-defense. However, admissions of a party-opponent are treated as non-hearsay statements and are admissible under FRE 801(d)(2)(A). Next, once a statement is available substantively because it's non-hearsay (or falls within a hearsay exception), it can also be used for impeachment purposes. (A separate provision, FRE 613(b), allows for impeachment by a prior inconsistent statement, but use of this provision is necessary only when the witness is a non-party — if the witness that is the target of impeachment is a party, as here, then it's simpler to use FRE 801(d)(2)(A) to get the statement in for both impeachment and substantive purposes.)

(A) is wrong because the fact that a statement is an excited utterance matters only if the statement is hearsay. As described in Choice (B), under the FRE admissions by a party opponent are hearsay "exclusions" — i.e., non-hearsay — so the statement was never hearsay in the first place, and does not need a hearsay exception in order to be admitted. Furthermore, it's doubtful that the defendant's statement would qualify as an excited utterance even if offered by rather than against him (so that the statement was not a non-hearsay party-admission). FRE 803(2) defines the excited-utterance hearsay exception this way: "a statement relating to a startling event or condition made *while the declarant was under the stress of excitement* caused by the event or condition." Here, there's no affirmative indication that the statement was being uttered under the stress of excitement from the shooting (though we don't know for sure).

(C) is wrong because application of the Fifth Amendment privilege of self-incrimination that "no person...shall be compelled in any criminal case to be a witness against himself..." applies only where there is some element of compulsion that brought about (or threatens to bring about) the statement. So statements at a trial or other proceeding (e.g., a grand jury hearing or deposition) where the defendant is required to testify are covered. Similarly, statements made in response to custodial interrogation are covered if the *Miranda* warnings weren't given, because *Miranda* is a method of preventing Fifth Amendment violations. But the defendant's out-of-court statement here did not fall into either of these two categories. In particular, it is not covered by the *Miranda* anti-self-incrimination policy, because the defendant was not in custody at the time he made the statement, and no other element of compulsion was present. (Also, even a statement by a defendant that was given in custody in violation of *Miranda* may be used to impeach the defendant's contrary trial testimony; *Harris v. N.Y.* (1971).)

(D) is wrong because the principle cited does not apply in the context of admissions, but rather, to the declaration-against-interest hearsay exception. FRE 804(b)(3), which provides for that exception, says that "a statement tending to expose the declarant to criminal liability and offered to exculpate the accused is not admissible unless corroborating circumstances clearly indicate the trustworthiness of the statement." But the quoted language applies where *A* inculpates himself and simultaneously exculpates *B*, the accused — here, where the defendant is trying to exculpate himself, neither the general declaration-against-interest exception nor the corroborating-circumstances exception to it applies.

C. **Adoptive:**

2. **Silence:**

   a. **"Partners in crime":**

   Question: Defendant is on trial for participating in a drug sale. The prosecution calls Witness, an undercover officer, to testify that, when Seller sold the drugs to Witness, Seller introduced Defendant to Witness as "my partner in this" and Defendant shook hands with Witness but said nothing.

   Witness's testimony is

   (A) inadmissible, because there is no evidence that Seller was authorized to speak for Defendant.

   (B) inadmissible, because the statement of Seller is hearsay not within any exception.

   (C) admissible as a statement against Defendant's penal interest.

   (D) admissible as Defendant's adoption of Seller's statement.

   [Q3179]

   Answer: Choice **(D)** is correct. FRE 801(2)(B) codifies the common-law notion of an adoptive admission: a statement is not hearsay if it is "offered against a party and is ... (B) a statement of which the party has manifested an adoption or belief in its truth." The applicable test for adoption is whether, taking into account all circumstances, *A*'s conduct or silence justifies the conclusion that he knowingly agreed to the accuracy of *B*'s statement. Here, it's clear that Defendant adopted Seller's statement. Seller introduced Defendant to Witness as "my partner." Defendant clearly heard and understood the statement, and it was the sort of statement that would, if untrue, have called for a denial by Defendant rather than a shaking of hands.

   (A) is wrong because Defendant did not need to authorize Seller to speak for him. It's true that one way *A*'s statement can be used as an admission against *B* is if *B* authorized *A* to speak for him. (See FRE 801(d)(2)C).) But another way for *A*'s statement to be used as an admission against *B* is if *B* has "manifested an adoption or belief in [the statement's] truth." (FRE 801(d)(2)(B)). That's what happened here, as described more fully in the discussion of Choice (D) above.

   (B) is wrong because the statement here was admissible as an admission against Defendant, because Defendant adopted it. (See the discussion in Choice (D).) Consequently, the statement was rendered non-hearsay by FRE 801(d)(2)(B).

   (C) is wrong because Defendant is not the declarant. A statement against interest is one made by a person (the declarant), now unavailable as a witness, against that person's pecuniary, proprietary, or penal interest when made. FRE 804(b)(3) treats statements against interest as an exception to the hearsay rule. However, there is no doctrine by which a statement made by *A* against *B*'s interest can be admitted against *B* based on *B*'s adoption of the statement. Since the declarant was *A*, the statement would have to be against *A*'s (not *B*'s) interest for it to fall within the statement-against-interest exception. And that's not what this choice specifies. (Also, even if the statement *were* somehow treated as if it were made or authorized by Defendant, the exception wouldn't apply because Defendant is present at trial and thus not unavailable.)

b. Analyze surrounding circumstances:

i. Statements made while declarant is in police custody:

Question: Alex and Sam were arrested for holding up a gas station. They were taken to police headquarters and placed in a room for interrogation. As a police officer addressing both started to give them the *Miranda* warnings prior to the questioning, Alex said, "Look, Sam planned the damned thing and I was dumb enough to go along with it. We robbed the place — what else is there to say?" Sam said nothing. Sam was escorted into another room and a full written confession was then obtained from Alex.

If Sam is brought to trial on an indictment charging him with robbery, the fact that Sam failed to object to Alex's statement and remained silent after Alex had implicated him in the crime should be ruled

(A) admissible because his silence was an implied admission by Sam that he had participated in the crime.

(B) admissible because a statement of a participant in a crime is admissible against another participant.

(C) inadmissible because, under the circumstances, there was no duty or responsibility on Sam's part to respond.

(D) inadmissible because whatever Alex may have said has no probative value in a trial against Sam.

[Q2007]

Answer: Choice **(C)** is correct. What's more important here, Choice **(A)** is **incorrect**. The prosecutor is attempting to admit Alex's statement against Sam. This is hearsay — it's Alex's statement, made out of court, offered to show the truth of the matter asserted (that "Sam planned the damn thing.") If it's admissible at all, it will have to be under a hearsay exclusion or exception. The only plausible exclusion or exception is the one for an admission offered against a party opponent, in which the party "manifested an adoption or belief in its truth." FRE 801(d)(2)(B). Here, it could be argued that by his silence, Sam adopted Alex's statement. However, under the case law interpreting FRE 801(d)(2)(B), an adoption by silence will only be deemed to occur if the person heard the accusatory statement, was capable of denying the statement, and a reasonable person under these circumstances *would have denied the statement were it not true.* Here, the fact that Sam was in police custody makes it unlikely that a reasonable person under the same circumstances would have denied the statement, since he could reasonably feel that he didn't want to say anything in the presence of police. For this reason, (A) is wrong — this was not a party admission by means of the party's adoption of another's statement.

(B) is wrong because it misstates the law. It's true that an admission by one conspirator is admissible against the other(s) if it was made during the course and in furtherance of the conspiracy. FRE 801(d)(2)(E). But here, Alex and Sam were in police custody by the time of the statement, at which point the conspiracy had presumably ended. So nothing Alex said can be admissible against Sam under the conspiracy exception.

(D) is wrong because Alex's comment *is* of probative value in Sam's trial. "Probative value" is another way of referring to "logical relevance." That is, a piece of evidence is logically relevant if it tends to prove or disprove a material fact. The comment of Alex, a co-conspirator of Sam's, that Sam planned the hold up, would clearly make it more likely that Sam, in fact, took part in the crime. Thus, the statement may be inadmissible, but it won't be because it's irrelevant.

II. SPONTANEOUS, EXCITED, OR CONTEMPORANEOUS UTTERANCES (INCLUDING STATEMENTS ABOUT PHYSICAL OR MENTAL CONDITION)

B. **Statements made for purposes of medical diagnosis or treatment:**

1. **Past symptoms:** The statement may be about *past* pain or past symptoms.

2. **Cause:** The statement may include references to the *cause* of the bodily condition.

> **Question:** A plaintiff sued a ladder manufacturer for injuries he suffered to his neck and back when a rung of the ladder on which he was standing gave way. When the plaintiff's back and neck continued to be very sore after more than two weeks, his treating physician sent him to an orthopedist for an evaluation. Though the orthopedist did not treat the plaintiff, he diagnosed an acute cervical strain. At trial, the plaintiff called the orthopedist to testify that in response to the orthopedist's inquiry about how the plaintiff had injured his back, the plaintiff told him, "I was standing near the top of a 15-foot ladder when I abruptly fell, landing hard on my back, after which the ladder toppled onto my neck."

Should the statement be admitted?

(A) Yes, because the plaintiff is present and can be cross-examined about it.

(B) Yes, because it was made for the purpose of medical diagnosis or treatment.

(C) No, because it was not made to a treating physician.

(D) No, because it relates to the inception or the cause of the injury rather than the plaintiff's physical condition.

[QA040]

> **Answer:** Choice **(B)** is correct. The witness orthopedist is testifying about an out-of-court statement to prove the truth of the contents of that statement. So the statement meets the definition of hearsay under FRE 801(c). (Although the declarant was a party to the case, the statement is being offered by that party, so is not a party admission within FRE 801(d)(2)(A).) But this hearsay statement fits within the exception codified at FRE 803(4) for statements made for the purpose of medical diagnosis that describe "medical history, or past or present symptoms, pain, or sensations, or the *inception or general character of the cause or external source thereof*" when pertinent to diagnosis or treatment. Both of these requirements are met: the plaintiff's statement relates to the cause of his injury, and the cause of his injury is relevant to the orthopedist's diagnosis. Moreover, Rule 803(4) allows not only statements made to treating physicians, but also statements made to other doctors for evaluation or diagnosis. So the fact that the orthopedist never treated the plaintiff doesn't affect admissibility of the statement. And, by the way, this exception applies regardless of whether or not the declarant is unavailable to testify at trial.

> (A) is wrong because the choice gives an incorrect reason for the correct outcome. The statement is an admissible statement for purposes of medical diagnosis or treatment under FRE 803(4). While it is true that the plaintiff is present and presumably could be cross-examined about the statement, this exception to the hearsay rule does not depend on the declarant's being present — the statement would be admissible even if the plaintiff were not present to testify or be cross-examined.

> (C) is wrong because FRE 803(4) does not require that the statement be made to a treating physician — the Rule also admits statements made to a non-treating doctor for purposes of diagnosis. The Rule is specifically designed to admit statements such as this, where an injured party is seeking a diagnosis and opinion from a medical specialist.

(D) is wrong because FRE 803(4) expressly permits the introduction of statements concerning the cause of injury when that information is pertinent to diagnosis or treatment. Thus it is admissible under FRE 803(4). (If the statement related to *fault* — e.g., "I fell when D tripped over the base of the ladder" — then the part of the statement relating to fault would likely *not* be covered by the 803(4) exception.)

a. Does not cover fault:

Question: In a civil action for personal injury, Payne alleges that he was beaten up by Dabney during an altercation in a crowded bar. Dabney's defense is that he was not the person who hit Payne. To corroborate his testimony about the cause of his injuries, Payne seeks to introduce, through the hospital records custodian, a notation in a regular medical record made by an emergency room doctor at the hospital where Payne was treated for his injuries. The notation is: "Patient says he was attacked by Dabney."

The notation is

A) inadmissible, unless the doctor who made the record is present at trial and available for cross-examination.

(B) inadmissible as hearsay not within any exception.

(C) admissible as hearsay within the exception for records of regularly conducted activity.

(D) admissible as a statement made for the purpose of medical diagnosis or treatment.

[Q1139]

Answer: Choice **(D)** is **incorrect**. The statement does not fall under the purpose-of-medical-diagnosis-or-treatment exception because the identification of the attacker was not pertinent to the diagnosis or treatment of Payne's injuries. Under FRE 803(4), statements for purposes of medical diagnosis or treatment describing pain or "the inception or general character of the cause or external source thereof" are admissible if *"reasonably pertinent to diagnosis or treatment."* Payne's statements to his doctor that he was attacked and how he was attacked might well be admissible under FRE 803(4) on the theory that they were "reasonably pertinent to diagnosis or treatment." However, a statement identifying his attacker will not help in treatment or diagnosis in any way, and is therefore inadmissible under this exception. (The answer is (B), hearsay not within any exception.)

C. Declaration of present mental, emotional, or physical condition:

1. State of mind directly in issue:

Question: In a prosecution of Dale for murdering Vera, Dale testified that the killing had occurred in self defense when Vera tried to shoot him. In rebuttal, the prosecution seeks to call Walter, Vera's father, to testify that the day before the killing, Vera told Walter that she loved Dale so much she could never hurt him.

Walter's testimony is

(A) admissible within the hearsay exception for statements of the declarant's then existing state of mind.

(B) admissible, because Vera is unavailable as a witness.

(C) inadmissible as hearsay not within any exception.

(D) inadmissible, because Vera's character is not an issue.

[Q1171]

Answer: Choice **(A)** is correct. When the mental state of a declarant is directly at issue in a case, statements of the declarant's then existing state of mind are admissible under FRE 803(3) to prove the declarant's mental state pre-dating or post-dating the statement. Here, Vera's statement, that she loved Dale and she could never hurt him, is being offered to prove the truth of the matter asserted, that she could not hurt him, and that therefore, the next day, it is unlikely that she would have been the first aggressor in the encounter with Dale. This evidence would counter Dale's claim that he acted in self-defense.

(B) is wrong because the declarant's availability is immaterial when a statement is being offered under the exception for a then existing state of mind under FRE 803(3).

(C) is wrong because the statement is admissible under the then existing state of mind hearsay exception provided by FRE 803(3), as explained in the discussion of Choice A.

(D) is wrong because (1) the statement is admissible and (2) it does not reflect on Vera's "character," but rather, her state of mind, as further discussed in (A).

2. **Proof of subsequent event:**

   a. **Most common on MBE:**

   Question: Defendant is on trial for robbing a bank in State A. She testified that she was in State B at the time of the robbery. Defendant calls her friend, Witness, to testify that two days before the robbery Defendant told him that she was going to spend the next three days in State B.

   Witness's testimony is

   (A) admissible, because the statement falls within the present sense impression exception to the hearsay rule.

   (B) admissible, because a statement of plans falls within the hearsay exception for then-existing state of mind.

   (C) inadmissible, because it is offered to establish an alibi by Defendant's own statement.

   (D) inadmissible, because it is hearsay not within any exception.
   [Q3051]

   Answer: Choice **(B)** is correct. The out-of-court statement here is "I'm going to spend the next three days in State B," offered to show that the declarant in fact spent the next three days there. So at least in a loose sense, the declaration is being offered to prove the "truth" of the matter asserted. But FRE 803(3) gives a hearsay exception for "A statement of the declarant's then existing state of mind ... (such as intent, *plan* [or] motive...)" So to the extent that the statement here is a statement by Defendant of the fact that she currently plans to do act X, it fits within this exception as a statement of then-existing plan. (Once it comes in, it's allowable for the further inference that if Defendant planned to do act X, she probably did act X as planned.)

   (A) is wrong because Defendant's statement wasn't an effort to describe an event she was perceiving. FRE 803(1)'s implementation of the present-sense-impression exception gives an exception for "A statement describing or explaining *an event or condition* made while the declarant was perceiving the event or condition, or immediately thereafter." Defendant's plan to make a trip is not an "event or condition" that Defendant was perceiving, so the exception doesn't apply.

   (C) is wrong because there is no special rule against "establish[ing] an alibi by [a] defendant's own statement." This is one of those cases where the examiners try to trick you into believing that there is a "rule" on a particular subject when there isn't. There is simply no special rule preventing a defendant from offering his own prior statement that furnishes an alibi.

(D) is wrong because the statement falls within the then-existing-state-of-mind hearsay exception. See the analysis of Choice (B) for an explanation of why this is so.

Question: Prine sued Dover for an assault that occurred March 5 in California. To support his defense that he was in Utah on that date, Dover identifies and seeks to introduce a letter he wrote to his sister a week before the assault in which he stated that he would see her in Utah on March 5.

The letter is

(A) admissible, within the state of mind exception to the hearsay rule.

(B) admissible, as a prior consistent statement to support Dover's credibility as a witness.

(C) inadmissible, because it lacks sufficient probative value.

(D) inadmissible, because it is a statement of belief to prove the fact believed.

[Q2192]

Answer: Choice **(A)** is correct. A statement is admissible to prove that a plan, design, or intention of the declarant was in fact carried out by the declarant, under the hearsay exception for a statement concerning a declarant's present mental, emotional or physical condition. FRE 803(3). That provision allows for the introduction of a statement showing that the declarant had the intent to take a certain action, in order to prove that the declarant did in fact eventually take that action where whether that act took place is an issue in the case. Here, Dover's stated intention to meet his sister in Utah on March 5 is admissible to prove that he in fact was in Utah on March 5; therefore, it is evidence that he did not commit an assault in California on that same day.

(B) is wrong because the general rule is that evidence offered to bolster the character of a witness is not admissible. Under FRE 801(d)(1)(b), a statement consistent with the declarant's testimony may only be "offered to rebut an express or implied charge against the declarant of recent fabrication or improper influence or motive." The fact pattern does not indicate that those circumstances occurred here.

(C) is wrong because the letter is admissible and it, in fact, has sufficient probative value. It makes the factual proposition that Dover was not in California on March 5 more likely than it would be without the evidence.

(D) is wrong because the letter is admissible and the concept stated does not apply. It's true that FRE 803(3) provides for an exception for the declarant's then existing mental, emotional or physical condition, "but not including a statement of memory or belief to prove the fact remembered or believed unless it relates to the…declarant's will." But, here, the letter is not a statement of belief about past actions or events. It is a stated intention to do something in the future, as explained in the discussion of (A).

3. **Statements of memory or belief:**

   Question: Pamela sued Driver for damages for the death of Pamela's husband Ronald, resulting from an automobile collision. At trial, Driver calls Ronald's doctor to testify that the day before his death, Ronald, in great pain, said, "It was my own fault; there's nobody to blame but me."

   The doctor's testimony should be admitted as

(A) a statement against interest.

(B) a dying declaration.

(C) a statement of Ronald's then existing state of mind.

(D) an excited utterance.

[Q2183]

Answer: (C) is **incorrect**. It's true that 803(3) gives an exception for a statement of the declarant's then existing state of mind. But the state-of-mind exception does not apply to statements of memory or belief about past actions or events, and that's what's being offered here — Ronald's statement is about who caused the accident, and as of the time he spoke, that was a "statement of memory or belief to prove the fact remembered or believed." (The correct choice is (A), statement against interest; see infra, p. 85.)

Question: A pastor was a well-known clergyman. A large daily newspaper printed an article by a journalist in its employ. The article accused the pastor of misusing church funds. The pastor commenced a defamation action against the newspaper. An issue in the case was whether the journalist, at the time he wrote the article, acted without malice in charging that the pastor had misused church funds. (For this purpose, it was relevant whether the journalist genuinely believed that the misuse had occurred.)

The newspaper's attorney called a bartender, who worked in a bar near the newspaper's office. The bartender stated that on the day after the journalist's article appeared in the newspaper, the journalist told him, "When I wrote that piece on the pastor, I believed every word of it." On objection by the pastor's attorney, the bartender's testimony should be

(A) admitted as evidence that the article was published without malice.

(B) admitted as a declaration of the journalist's state of mind.

(C) admitted as a self-serving declaration.

(D) excluded as hearsay not falling within any exception.

[Q5024]

Answer: Choice **(D)** is correct. Hearsay is defined as an out-of-court statement offered to prove the truth of the matter asserted in that statement. Since the newspaper can only be offering the journalist's statement "When I wrote the article, I believed it" in order to prove that when the journalist wrote the article, he believed in it, the statement is indeed being offered to prove the truth of the matter asserted therein. So it's hearsay, and it's not admissible unless some exception applies. No exception applies; most notably, the exception for state of mind (discussed in Choice (B) below) does not apply.

(A) is wrong because if the out-of-court statement by the journalist were admitted as evidence of with whether the article was published without malice, the statement would be being admitted to prove the truth of the matter asserted therein, and would thus be hearsay not falling within any exception.

(B) is wrong because the choice's reference to the admissibility of the declarant's "declaration of [his] state of mind" could only be a reference to FRE 803(3)'s exception for "A statement of the declarant's *then existing state of mind* ... but not including a *statement of memory or belief to prove the fact remembered or believed* unless it relates to the ... the declarant's will." Here, the journalist's statement was not about his present belief as of the moment of the statement, but rather about what he remembered his mental state to have been at the moment in the past when he wrote the article. So the statement falls within 803(3)'s inapplicability to "a statement of memory ... to prove the fact remembered." (The "fact remembered" was the journalist's prior mental state.) As the idea is often put, 803(3) does not cover "backward looking statements."

(C) is wrong because there is no rule allowing a party to put in a self-serving statement made by that party (or in this case, made by an employee that party). Indeed, one of the main purposes of the hearsay rule is to prevent a party from putting in statements made out of court by that party, for fear that these may be self-serving attempts to "manufacture evidence."

D. Excited utterance:

1. Requirements:

Question: A defendant was charged with aggravated assault. At trial, the victim testified that the defendant beat her savagely, but she was not asked about anything said during the incident. The prosecutor then called a witness to testify that when the beating stopped, the victim screamed: "I'm dying-don't let [the defendant] get away with it!"

Is the testimony of the witness concerning the victim's statement admissible?

(A) No, because it is hearsay not within any exception.

(B) No, because the victim was not asked about the statement.

(C) Yes, as a statement under belief of impending death, even though the victim did not die.

(D) Yes, as an excited utterance.

[Q7037]

Answer: Choice **(D)** is correct. FRE 803(2) admits a hearsay statement that would otherwise be barred under Rule 802 where the statement "relat[es] to a startling event or condition made while the declarant was under the stress of excitement caused by the event or condition." In this case, the assault was a startling event, and the victim made the statement immediately after the beating, trying to identify the perpetrator. Thus, all the admissibility requirements of Rule 803(2), the excited utterance exception, are met.

(A) is wrong because, although the statement is hearsay, it is admissible under FRE 803(2), the excited utterance exception, as described in Choice (D) below.

(B) is wrong because the statement fits under the FRE 803(2)'s exception to the hearsay rule for excited utterances. Under the hearsay exceptions in Rule 803, there is no requirement that the declarant be made available to testify. In this case, the victim's statement would have been admissible even if she had not been available at trial. Nor is there any requirement that the declarant under an FRE 803 exception be asked about the hearsay statement.

(C) is wrong because, while the declarant does not have to die for a statement to be admissible as a dying declaration under FRE 804(b)(2), this statement fails to satisfy that exception for at least two reasons. First, the declarant has to be unavailable, as the dying declaration is one of the "declarant unavailable" exceptions of Rule 804. Here, the victim testified and so obviously is not unavailable. Second, a dying declaration is admissible only in homicide prosecutions and civil cases. This is a criminal case for aggravated assault.

3. Relate to the startling event:

Question: In a jurisdiction without a Dead Man's Statute, Parker's estate sued Davidson claiming that Davidson had borrowed from Parker $10,000, which had not been repaid as of Parker's death. Parker was run over by a truck. At the accident scene, while dying from massive injuries, Parker told Officer Smith to "make sure my estate collects the $10,000 I loaned

SPONTANEOUS, EXCITED, OR CONTEMPORANEOUS UTTERANCES

to Davidson."

Smith's testimony about Parker's statement is

(A) inadmissible, because it is more unfairly prejudicial than probative.

(B) inadmissible, because it is hearsay not within any exception.

(C) admissible as an excited utterance.

(D) admissible as a statement under belief of impending death.

[Q3081]

Answer: Choice **(C)** is **incorrect**. That's because FRE 803(2)'s excited-utterance exception applies to "a statement *relating to a startling event or condition* made while the declarant was under the stress of excitement caused by the event or condition." So the statement has to relate to the startling event. Parker's comment here relates solely to the debt, not to the startling event (the truck accident). (The correct answer is (B), hearsay not within any exception. See *supra*, p. 46.)

6. **Need for inference:**

   Question: Daggett was prosecuted for murder of Vales, whose body was found one morning in the street near Daggett's house. The state calls Witt, a neighbor, to testify that during the night before the body was found he heard Daggett's wife scream, "You killed him! You killed him!"

   Witt's testimony is

   (A) admissible as a report of a statement of belief.

   (B) admissible as a report of an excited utterance.

   (C) inadmissible, because it reports a privileged spousal communication.

   (D) inadmissible on spousal immunity grounds, but only if the wife objects.

   [Q1106]

   Answer: Choice **(B)** is correct. The wife's statement is hearsay, an "out-of-court statement" offered to "prove the truth of the matter asserted" — that Daggett was the killer. FRE 801. FRE 803(2) provides for the excited utterance exception to the hearsay rule — "a statement relating to a startling event or condition made while the declarant was under the stress of excitement caused by the event or condition." The screamed exclamation, "You killed him! You killed him!" would qualify — the fact that there was a scream strongly suggests that Daggett's wife was responding to some event that (1) startled her, (2) convinced her that her husband had been killed (the event), and (3) induced her to make the statement (showing causation between the startling event, and the statement).

   (A) is wrong because it relies on a concept that doesn't exist. There is no hearsay exception provided for a "statement of belief." Indeed, FRE 803(3) indicates just the contrary, since it gives a hearsay exception for "A statement of the declarant's then existing state of mind ... but *not* including a statement of memory or belief to prove the fact remembered or believed[.]"

   (C) is wrong because the evidence would not be barred by the confidential spousal communications privilege. If the wife thought her husband was dead, she could not have been intending to communicate with him (barring communications with the other world, which are presumably not protected by the privilege).

(D) is wrong because the evidence is not barred by the adverse testimony privilege. The privilege applies only to testimony against the spouse of the declarant. So there are two problems here: (1) the husband (the declarant's spouse) is not on trial; and (2) this out-of-court startled exclamation would not be deemed to be "testimonial" for purposes of the adverse-testimony privilege, even if it were used by the prosecution against the husband.

E. Present sense impression:

Question: Penn sues Duke's Bar for injuries suffered in an automobile accident caused by Chase, who had been a patron of Duke's Bar. Penn claims that Chase was permitted to drink too much liquor at Duke's Bar before the accident.

Wood, a patron of Duke's Bar, testified that on the night of the accident Chase was drunk. Wood then proposed to testify that he remarked to his companion, "Chase is so drunk he can't even stand up."

Wood's remark to his companion is

(A) admissible as an excited utterance.

(B) admissible as a prior consistent statement.

(C) admissible as a statement by Wood regarding a condition he observed, made while he was observing it.

(D) inadmissible if there was no evidence that Wood had expertise in determining drunkenness.

[Q8056]

Answer: Choice **(C)** is correct, because it correctly implies that Wood's remark will be admissible under the "present sense impression" hearsay exception. Under FRE 803(1), a statement is admissible under this exception if it was made while the declarant was perceiving an event/condition (or immediately thereafter), and it describes or explains the event/condition. That's what Wood's statement does. Note that Wood's statement is hearsay even though he's repeating it himself. A hearsay statement is an out-of-court statement offered to prove the truth of its assertion. Here, Wood's statement is offered to prove that Chase was drunk, so it's hearsay. However, since it fits the present sense impression hearsay exception, it will be admissible.

(A) is wrong because the facts here do not show that Wood was excited when he made the comment. In order to be admissible under the "excited utterance" exception to the hearsay rule, an out-of-court statement must meet the requirements in FRE 803(2). It must have been made while declarant was under the stress of excitement, it must have been due to a startling event or condition, and it must relate to the event or condition. Under these facts, the key word is "remarked." An excited utterance would require some evidence that the declarant was under stress of excitement when the statement was made; simply "remarking" would not qualify.

(B) is wrong because the statement here does not satisfy the prior consistent statement hearsay exclusion under the FRE. Under FRE 801(d)(1), a prior consistent statement of a currently-testifying declarant is admissible only if it is offered to rebut a charge (express or implied) against the witness of improper motive/influence or recent fabrication. That's clearly not the case here — there's no indication that Wood's testimony has been attacked on grounds of either improper motive or recent fabrication. FRE 801(d)(1) is both extremely narrow *and* a popular MBE distractor.

(D) is wrong because the appearance of drunkenness is a subject which is appropriate for lay opinion testimony. As a general rule, lay witnesses cannot offer opinion testimony. However, under FRE 701, where the opinion testimony is helpful to understanding witness's testimony or determining a fact in issue, and is rationally based on witness's first-hand knowledge, such lay opinion testimony will be helpful. One common use of lay-opinion is where it is a kind of shorthand summary of various small observations by the witness that would be hard to set out in detail. Thus "he looked drunk" or "he seemed worried" or "he was driving very fast" are all typically admissible as short-hand summaries of perceptions by lay witnesses.

1. **Immediacy:**

   Question: While crossing Spruce Street, Pesko was hit by a car that she did not see. Pesko sued Dorry for her injuries.

   At trial, Pesko calls Williams, a police officer, to testify that, ten minutes after the accident, a driver stopped him and said, "Officer, a few minutes ago I saw a hit-and-run accident on Spruce Street involving a blue convertible, which I followed to the drive-in restaurant at Oak and Third," and that a few seconds later Williams saw Dorry sitting alone in a blue convertible in the drive-in restaurant's parking lot.

   Williams' testimony about the driver's statement should be

   (A) admitted as a statement of recent perception.

   (B) admitted as a present sense impression.

   (C) excluded, because it is hearsay not within any exception.

   (D) excluded, because it is more prejudicial than probative.

   [Q4041]

   Answer: Choice **(B)** is **incorrect**, because the required immediacy between the thing being sensed and the statement about it is missing. The driver is the declarant, and he is talking about something he saw "a few minutes ago." For present-sense impression, virtually no time must pass between the sensing and the statement about what is being sensed. (The correct answer is (C); see *supra*, p. 47.)

3. **Declarant must perceive:**

   Question: In a personal injury action by the plaintiff against the defendant, the plaintiff claimed that the accident occurred because the defendant, who was operating a blue Ford sedan, was driving at an excessive rate of speed. At the trial, the plaintiff's attorney called a witness on the plaintiff's direct case. The witness testified that after hearing a broadcast on a police radio on the day of the accident, she looked out of her window and saw the defendant's blue Ford sedan strike the plaintiff's red convertible on Main Street. The witness said that she did not have a present recollection of what she had heard on the police radio, but that she made a written note of it immediately following the broadcast. The plaintiff's attorney showed her a piece of paper which had been marked for identification, and the witness said that she now remembered that she had heard a police dispatcher saying that officers were in pursuit of a blue Ford sedan which was traveling down Main Street at an excessive rate of speed.

   If the defendant's attorney objects to the testimony of the witness regarding what she heard on the police radio, the court should hold that her testimony is

   (A) inadmissible as hearsay, not within any exception.

   (B) admissible as a sense impression.

   (C) admissible as a past recollection recorded.

(D) admissible as present recollection refreshed.

[Q5068]

Answer: Choice **(A)** is correct. Hearsay is an out-of-court statement offered to prove the truth of the matter asserted in that statement. Since the statement by the dispatcher that a blue sedan was traveling at an excessive speed was made out of court, and since it was offered to prove that the defendant's blue sedan was traveling at an excessive speed, it is hearsay. No exception applies, as is analyzed below.

(B) is wrong because the "present sense impression" exception (given by FRE 803(1)), applies only to "A statement describing or explaining an event or condition *made while the declarant was perceiving the event or condition,* or immediately thereafter." The declarant would have to be the police dispatcher. But the dispatcher is extremely unlikely to have been perceiving the fact that "officers [are] in pursuit of a blue Ford sedan ... traveling ... at an excessive rate of speed" — rather, the dispatcher was almost certainly repeating information that the officers had themselves radioed to him, and he therefore did not have the requisite present sense impression.

(C) is wrong because the "past recollection recorded" exception (given by FRE 803(5)) allows a witness to read from a written record that satisfies various requirements. But here, the witness is not reading from the memorandum, she has instead used it to refresh her recollection, and that use does not qualify for the past recollection recorded exception.

(D) is wrong because the use here does not qualify for the present recollection refreshed doctrine. A witness may refresh her recollection while testifying by examining almost anything which will have that effect. She may then testify from her refreshed recollection, but *only if her testimony is otherwise admissible.* Since the statement to which the witness is attempting to testify is hearsay (the dispatcher's statement about the speed at which the officers were chasing the car), it is inadmissible, and is not made admissible by the fact that the witness properly refreshed her recollection by looking at a writing.

IV. PAST RECOLLECTION RECORDED

A. **Exception under the FRE:**

1. **Four requirements:**

    Question: A plaintiff sued a defendant for wrongful death arising out of a traffic collision between the plaintiff's decedent and the defendant. At trial, the investigating traffic officer authenticated a tape recording of her shift-end dictation of comments used in preparing the written report of her factual findings. She testified that the tape recording was accurate when made and that she currently had no clear memory of the details of the investigation.

    Is the tape recording admissible as evidence?

    (A) Yes, under the past recollection recorded exception to the hearsay rule.

    (B) Yes, under the public records exception to the hearsay rule.

    (C) No, because it is hearsay and is a police report being offered against the defendant in a wrongful death case.

    (D) No, because the police report itself is the best evidence.

    [QA048]

    Answer: Choice **(A)** is correct. The tape recording is evidence of an oral out-of-court statement that is being offered to prove the truth of the contents of that statement. Thus it is hearsay under FRE 801(c). But it also satisfies the requirements of FRE 803(5), the past recollection recorded exception to the hearsay rule. Under that rule, a record is admissible "concerning a matter about which a witness once had knowledge but now has insufficient recollection to enable the witness to testify fully and accurately, shown to have been made or adopted by the witness when the matter was fresh in the witness's memory and to reflect that knowledge correctly[.]" So here all four requirements of FRE 803(5) are met: (1) we know that the "witness once had knowledge" requirement is satisfied because we're told that she was the investigating officer, and was dictating an account of what she had learned first-hand; (2) we know she "now has insufficient recollection to enable [her] to testify fully and accurately" because we're explicitly told in the facts that she "currently ha[s] no clear memory of the details"; (3) we know that she "made [the record] when the matter was fresh in [her] memory" from the fact that she made the tape recording at the end of the very shift in which she learned the underlying facts to which the recording pertained; and (4) we know the record "reflects [the witness's] knowledge correctly" because the facts tell us that the witness "testified that the tape recording was accurate when made." Accordingly, under FRE 803(5), the recording is admissible evidence (in the sense that it can be played for the jury, although not taken into the jury room as an exhibit).

(B) is wrong because although the officer's formal written report would qualify as a public record under FRE 803(8), the informal dictated comments she made to help her prepare the report would not. To be admissible under 803(8), the material must fall within one of clauses (A), (B), or (C) of 803(8). Let's see why none of these clauses applies:

Clause (A) of 803(8) covers reports of "the activities of the [public] office or agency." The clause is interpreted to refer to records of the internal activities of the agency, not to its inquiries into events occurring in the outside world. So the recording here does not qualify, since it's not about the police department, but about real-world non-police activities.

Clause (B) of 803(8) covers "matters observed pursuant to duty imposed by law as to which matters there was a duty to report, excluding, however, in criminal cases matters observed by police officers and other law enforcement personnel[.]" (B) is generally interpreted to cover only material that is "more concrete and simple than interpretive or evaluative" (see M&K, §8.50, p. 862), so it would not apply to the dictated notes here, which clearly have an evaluative component (Who caused the accident, which the officer didn't personally witness?).

Clause (C) of 803(8) covers "factual findings resulting from an investigation made pursuant to authority granted by law[.]" ((C) goes on to say that such findings may be used only "in civil actions and proceedings and against the Government in criminal cases"; since this is a civil action, this limit does not bar the use here.) But (C) by its terms covers "factual *findings*," and the preliminary, informal tape-recording here would not be construed to have produced such "factual findings" (a phrase that has the connotation of final and formal conclusions), especially given that the traffic officer knew that she would later use her recording in order to prepare her eventual "written report of her factual findings." (The written report is a document that *would* satisfy clause (C).)

So none of the three clauses of 803(8) applies.

(C) is wrong because although the tape recording is hearsay, it fits the hearsay exception of FRE 803(5) as a past recollection recorded. This choice's reference to a "police report being offered against the defendant in a wrongful death case" is an attempt to trick you into thinking that the prohibition in 803(8), clause (C), applies. As is covered in more detail in the analysis of Choice (B) above, 803(8)'s public-records hearsay exception says, in clause (C), that "factual findings resulting from an investigation made pursuant to authority granted by law" are admissible only in civil actions and against the government in criminal cases, not against the accused in a criminal case. And there is some (though weak) authority that where factual findings by law enforcement officials are prohibited by 803(8) clause (C) (i.e., where the findings are proposed to be used by the government against the accused), not only can't Rule 803(8) be used, but neither can other exceptions, like past recollection recorded. But even in a court following this minority authority, the 803(8), clause (C) prohibition wouldn't apply here, since the prohibition doesn't apply to any civil case, even one involving wrongful death.

(D) is wrong because the tape recording was made prior to the written report and was used as a basis for the written report. The recording is not being offered to prove the content of the written report, so its admission does not violate the best evidence/original document rule of FRE 1002. (If the officer gave courtroom testimony that the previous day, she had listened to the recording and here is what it said, then this testimony *would* violate the original document rule of FRE 1002, because the recording itself would have to be offered as the best evidence of what the recording's contents were.)

Question: At the defendant's trial for theft, a man called as a witness by the prosecutor testified to the following: (1) that from his apartment window, he saw thieves across the street break the window of a jewelry store, take jewelry, and leave in a car; (2) that the witness's wife telephoned the police and relayed to them the license number of the thieves' car as the witness looked out the window with binoculars and read it to her; and (3) that the witness has no present memory of the number, but that immediately afterward he listened to a playback of the police tape recording giving the license number (which belongs to the defendant's car) and verified that she had relayed the number accurately.

Playing the tape recording for the jury would be

(A) proper, because it is recorded recollection.

(B) proper, because it is a public record or report.

(C) improper, because it is hearsay not within any exception.

(D) improper, because the witness's wife lacked firsthand knowledge of the license number.

[Q3040]

Answer: Choice **(A)** is correct. The events satisfy all the requirements of FRE 803(5)'s exception for recorded recollection (sometimes called "past recollection recorded"). These requirements are: (1) the memorandum must relate to something of which the witness once had firsthand knowledge; (2) the record must have been made by, or adopted by, the witness when the matter was fresh in the witness's memory; (3) there must currently be some impairment of the witness's memory of the events; and (4) there must be evidence that the record correctly reflects the witness's original knowledge. The tape satisfies all these elements: (1) the tape relates to something of which the witness once had first-hand knowledge, since the witness personally saw the events, including the license number; (2) the tape was made when the matter was fresh in the witness's memory, and although he didn't make it he adopted it by listening to the playback and verifying that his wife had relayed the license number correctly; (3) there is presently an impairment of the witness's memory, since he has said that he has no present memory of the license plate number; and (4) the witness's listening to it and concluding that it was accurately satisfies the requirement that the tape correctly reflects his original knowledge.

(B) is wrong because the witness is not a public official who had a duty to make the report. There is indeed an exception to the hearsay rule for public records and reports. This exception is codified in FRE 803(8), which allows the admission of "records, reports [or] statements ... of public offices or agencies" "setting forth ... (B) matters *observed pursuant to duty imposed by law* as to which matters there was a *duty to report*, excluding, however, in criminal cases matters observed by police officers and other law enforcement personnel[.]" But the public records exception does not apply in this case because the witness (the one who made the "observation") was not a public official, nor was the report he made to the police of the break-in part of an official duty. (And even if the witness *was* a police officer, the last clause quoted above starting with "excluding" would prevent the report from coming in against the defendant in the defendant's criminal trial.)

(C) is wrong because the tape recording of the call to the police falls within the past recollection recorded exception. (See the discussion of Choice (A) for why this is so.)

(D) is wrong because the witness's wife did not have to have first-hand knowledge of the license number in order for the recorded recollection exception to apply. It's true that the witness's wife was the one who "made" the recording (in the sense that she was the one who spoke the license number on to the tape). But the requirements of FRE 803(5)'s past recollection recorded exception do not require that witness be the one who physically made the record. All that 803(5) requires in this respect is that the record be one that is "made *or adopted* by the witness when the matter was fresh in the witness's memory," and that the witness have had first-hand knowledge. Here, when the witness immediately listened to the playback and pronounced the relayed number correct, the witness adopted the record; since he had the first-hand knowledge about the license number, the first-hand knowledge requirement is also satisfied.

3. **Distinguish from present recollection refreshed:**

   Question: Carr ran into and injured Pedersen, a pedestrian. With Carr in his car was Walter Passenger. Pedersen has sued Carr for negligence.

   On the evening of the day of the accident, Walter Passenger wrote a letter to his sister in which he described the accident. When Walter says he cannot remember some details of the accident, Pedersen's counsel seeks to show him the letter to assist him in his testimony on direct examination.

   The trial judge should rule this

   (A) permissible under the doctrine of present recollection refreshed.

   (B) permissible under the doctrine of past recollection recorded.

   (C) objectionable because the letter was not a spontaneous utterance.

   (D) objectionable because the letter is a self-serving declaration in so far as the witness, Walter, is concerned.

   [Q4031]

   Answer: Choice **(B)** is **incorrect**. The record here (the letter) is not being introduced as evidence, as it would be if past recollection recorded were being used. Instead, the item is being used to refresh the witness's memory, but will not itself become evidence. Therefore, this is present recollection refreshed, not past recollection recorded. That makes **(A)** correct. (Under the doctrine of present recollection refreshed, *any* item may be used to refresh the witness's memory, including leading questions, documents, or objects. If the witness, having seen the refreshing object, can testify from memory, the item will not be considered evidence.)

V. RECORDS OF REGULARLY CONDUCTED ACTIVITY (a/k/a "BUSINESS RECORDS")

B. Various requirements:

2. Regular practice:

a. **Ad hoc or special-occasion documents don't qualify:**

Question: A plaintiff sued her employer, alleging that poor working conditions had caused her to develop a stomach ulcer. At trial, the plaintiff's medical expert testified to the cause of the plaintiff's ulcer and stated that his opinion was based in part on information in a letter the plaintiff's personal physician had written to the plaintiff's employer, explaining why the plaintiff had missed work.

When offered to prove the cause of the plaintiff's condition, is the letter from the plaintiff's doctor admissible?

(A) No, because it is hearsay not within any exception.

(B) No, because the plaintiff's physician is not shown to be unavailable.

(C) Yes, because it was relied upon by the plaintiff's medical expert.

(D) Yes, under the business records exception to the hearsay rule.

[Q7100]

Answer: Choice **(D)** is **incorrect**, because the doctor's letter does not qualify under FRE 803(6) as a business record. It is not a medical record prepared in the ordinary course of regularly conducted activity. Rather, it is a letter written by the doctor on an ad hoc occasion. Thus, the letter lacks the earmarks of regularity that are critical for admissibility under the business records exception to the hearsay rule. (The **correct** answer is (A) — this is hearsay not within any exception.)

(B) is wrong because this fact would only be relevant if the hearsay were offered under FRE 804 as one of the "unavailability-dependent" exceptions to the hearsay rule. None of those exceptions are pertinent here. Furthermore, if the hearsay qualified as a hearsay exception under Rule 803 (e.g., if it were a business record), then the doctor's availability would be completely irrelevant, because unavailability need not be shown for those exceptions. But the letter does not qualify under any of the Rule 803 exceptions. In particular, it is not a business record because it was not prepared in the ordinary course of regularly conducted activity.

(C) is wrong because the letter is hearsay if offered to prove that the plaintiff's condition was as indicated in the letter, and the expert's reliance on it doesn't overcome this problem. FRE 703 does allow an expert to rely on hearsay in reaching a conclusion, so long as other experts in the field would reasonably rely on such information. But Rule 703 distinguishes between expert reliance on the hearsay and admitting the hearsay at trial for the jury to consider. Here, the letter itself is being offered as evidence as to cause, and the letter is hearsay. The expert reliance does not overcome the general rule that hearsay or other otherwise-inadmissible evidence will not be admissible when offered only because the expert relied upon it.

4. Timeliness:

Question: Plaintiff sued Defendant for injuries sustained in an automobile collision. During Plaintiff's hospital stay, Doctor, a staff physician, examined Plaintiff's X rays and said to Plaintiff, "You have a fracture of two vertebrae, C4 and C5." Intern, who was accompanying Doctor on her rounds, immediately wrote the diagnosis on Plaintiff's hospital record. At trial, the hospital records custodian testifies that Plaintiff's hospital record was made and kept in the ordinary course of the hospital's business.

The entry reporting Doctor's diagnosis is

(A) inadmissible, because no foundation has been laid for Doctor's competence as an expert.

(B) inadmissible, because Doctor's opinion is based upon data that are not in evidence.

(C) admissible as a statement of then-existing physical condition.

(D) admissible as a record of regularly conducted business activity.

[Q3173]

Answer: Choice **(D)** is correct. FRE 803(6) gives a hearsay exception for "A ... *record* ... of acts, events, conditions, opinions, or *diagnoses*, made at or near the time by, or *from information transmitted by,* a *person with knowledge,* if *kept in the course of a regularly conducted business activity,* and if it was the *regular practice* of that business activity to make the ... record ..., all as shown by the testimony of the custodian or other qualified witness, or by certification..." The record here qualifies: (1) it's a record of a diagnosis; (2) made "at or near the time" of the diagnosis; (3) from information transmitted by a person with knowledge (Doctor); and (4) kept as part of the hospital's regularly conducted business activity (since the custodian has testified that the record was "made and kept in the ordinary course of the hospital's business.") Notice that there is no problem with the fact that Doctor didn't write the record himself — the fact that he spoke the words and Intern wrote them down means that the record was made "from information transmitted by" a person with knowledge (Doctor).

(A) is wrong because establishment of Doctor's expertise is not necessary for admissibility of the record. Doctor is not giving testimony here, so he's not an "expert witness," and the foundation required for expert testimony is therefore not required.

(B) is wrong because what's at issue is the admissibility of the record, not the admissibility of data that is not in evidence. When a record containing an opinion is admissible as an exception to the hearsay rule, the fact that the data on which the maker of the record relied is not in evidence is irrelevant. (By the way, even if Doctor were on the stand repeating his diagnosis, the underlying data still wouldn't have to be in evidence, or even admissible — see FRE 703: "The facts or data in the particular case upon which an expert bases an opinion or inference may be those perceived by or made known to the expert at or before the hearing. If of a type reasonably relied upon by experts in the particular field in forming opinions or inferences upon the subject, the facts or data *need not be admissible in evidence* in order for the opinion or inference to be admitted.")

(C) is wrong because the entry records Doctor's statements, not Plaintiff's. Statements *by a patient* regarding the patient's physical condition made to a treating physician fall within the exception in FRE 803(3) for "A statement of the declarant's then existing state of mind, emotion, sensation, or physical condition." But the statement here wasn't made by the patient (Plaintiff) — it was made by the treating doctor. And it's clear that statements by a treating doctor to the patient who has the physical condition don't qualify for the 803(3) exception.

5. *No requirement of unavailability:*

Question: A plaintiff sued his insurance company for the full loss of his banquet hall by fire. The insurance company defended under a provision of the policy limiting liability to 50 percent if "flammable materials not essential to the operation of the business were stored on the premises and caused a fire." The insurance company called the keeper of the city fire inspection records to identify a report prepared and filed by the fire marshal as required by law, indicating that shortly before the fire, the fire marshal had cited the plaintiff for storing gasoline at the banquet hall.

Is the report admissible?

(A) No, because it is hearsay not within any exception.

(B) No, because the proceeding is civil, rather than criminal.

(C) Yes, as a public record describing matters observed as to which there was a duty to report.

(D) Yes, as a record of regularly conducted activity, provided the fire marshal is unavailable.

[QA061]

Answer: Choice **(D)** is **incorrect**, because it incorrectly states how the regularly-conducted-activity exception works. This choice is correct in suggesting that the hearsay exception for records of regularly conducted activity contained in FRE 803(6) (a/k/a the "business records" exception) would likely apply to this report. But the choice is incorrect in stating that the exception will apply only if the fire marshall is unavailable to testify. The 803(6) business-records exception, like all the exceptions contained in FRE 803, does not require a showing of the unavailability of the declarant (here, the fire marshal). For the correct answer, see p. 76.

C. **Person supplying info:**

2. **Consumer complaints or reports:**

Question: Plaza Hotel sued Plaza House Hotel for infringement of its trade name. To establish a likelihood of name confusion, Plaintiff Plaza Hotel offers a series of memoranda which it had asked its employees to prepare at the end of each day listing instances during the day in which telephone callers, cab drivers, customers, and others had confused the two names.

The memoranda should be

(A) excluded, because they are more unfairly prejudicial and confusing than probative.

(B) excluded, because they are hearsay not within any exception.

(C) admitted, because they are records of regularly conducted business activity.

(D) admitted, because they are past recollection recorded.

[Q2200]

Answer: Choice **(C)** is **incorrect**. The series of memoranda are "out-of-court statements" offered to "prove the truth of the matter asserted," that the name confusion actually occurred. FRE 803(6) provides for the business record hearsay exception if the entries (a) are made in the routine of a business, (b) are made by, or from information transmitted by, a person with personal knowledge of the matter recorded, who is acting pursuant to a business duty to make the report or record (or whose statement meets some other hearsay exception); (c) are made "at or near the time" of the matter recorded; and (d) are not untrustworthy due to sources, methods or circumstances. There are two reasons why the memos here don't qualify: (1) requirement (b) is not met, because the consumers who are making the "I'm confused" statements aren't acting pursuant to any business duty, and their statements don't fall within any other hearsay exception; and (2) requirement (d) is not met, because the circumstances (anticipation of litigation), and the Hotel's strong self-interest, make the records untrustworthy. (The **correct** answer is (B) — this is hearsay not within any exception.)

H. **Absence of entry:**

1. **FRE 803(7):**

Question: A large daily newspaper printed an article by a reporter who worked for it, accusing a well-known local businessman of misusing corporate funds. The businessman commenced a defamation action against the newspaper. As a defense, the newspaper asserted the businessman's non-compliance with a state law that limited damages for defamation unless a demand for retraction is made.

The newspaper attorney offered the testimony of an editor employed by the paper. The editor testified that it was his job to note retraction demands in an office file, and that as a matter of company policy and practice all such demands were promptly reported to him for that purpose and promptly noted by him. He said that on the morning of trial, he had searched the file for notes of any retraction demand made by the businessman, and found none.

If the newspaper's attorney offers the file in evidence, the businessman's objection should be

(A) sustained, since the absence of a notation cannot be used as evidence that an event did not occur.

(B) sustained, since the file is self-serving.

(C) overruled, if the file itself is admissible as a business record.

(D) overruled, since the editor used the file to refresh his recollection.

[Q5025]

Answer: Choice **(C)** is correct. FRE 803(7) gives a hearsay exception for "evidence that a matter is *not included in the ... records ...* kept in accordance with [the business records exception], to *prove the nonoccurrence or nonexistence of the matter*[.]" This exception applies perfectly here: the editor has kept a business record of all retraction demands received by the newspaper, and is submitting here evidence that no retraction demand from the businessman is included in that business record. So this can be used to show that no such retraction demand was received by the paper.

(A) is simply wrong as a matter of law: where a record is kept that satisfies the business records exception, absence of a notation *can* be used as evidence that an event did not occur, as further described in (C) above.

(B) is wrong because the fact that evidence is self-serving is not, alone, sufficient to make it inadmissible.

(D) is wrong because, although almost anything may be used by a witness to refresh his recollection, the fact that a document was so used is not sufficient to permit its admission into evidence.

VI. PUBLIC RECORDS AND REPORTS

A. **Public records and reports:**

 1. **Federal Rule:**

 b. **Matters observed under duty:**

 Question: A plaintiff sued his insurance company for the full loss of his banquet hall by fire. The insurance company defended under a provision of the policy limiting liability to 50 percent if "flammable materials not essential to the operation of the business were stored on the premises and caused a fire." The insurance company called the keeper of the city fire inspection records to identify a report prepared and filed by the fire marshal as required by law, indicating that shortly before the fire, the fire marshal had cited the plaintiff for storing gasoline at the banquet hall.

Is the report admissible?

(A) No, because it is hearsay not within any exception.

(B) No, because the proceeding is civil, rather than criminal.

(C) Yes, as a public record describing matters observed as to which there was a duty to report.

(D) Yes, as a record of regularly conducted activity, provided the fire marshal is unavailable.

[QA061]

Answer: Choice **(C)** is correct. The report is an out-of-court written statement offered to prove the truth of its contents, so it meets the hearsay definition of FRE 801(c). Nevertheless, it is admissible because it falls within the hearsay exception for "public records and reports" codified at FRE 803(8). Under Clause (B) of this rule, a report made by a public official or agency concerning "matters observed pursuant to duty imposed by law as to which matters there was a duty to report" is admissible, "unless the sources of information or other circumstances indicate lack of trustworthiness." All of the requirements embedded in Clause (B) are met: (1) The fire marshal is a public official; (2) we know that the report concerned a matter that the marshal "observed," since the fact that he issued the citation indicates that he observed gasoline being stored in the banquet hall; and (3) we know that the report concerned something "as to which there was a duty to report," because the facts tell us that the report was prepared and filed "as required by law." As to the "lack of trustworthiness" proviso, there is no suggestion of any reason to believe that the report's contents are untrustworthy. Thus, the report meets the requirements of the FRE 803(8) public records exception to the hearsay rule, making it admissible.

(A) is wrong because this report is admissible as a public record under FRE 803(8). See the analysis of Choice (C) for why this is so.

(B) is wrong because the fact that this is a civil case does not make the report inadmissible. Public records are admissible in both civil and criminal cases. In fact, they are more broadly admissible in civil cases than in criminal cases, because law enforcement reports are generally not admissible against criminal defendants. See the analysis of Choice (C) for why the report here is admissible as a public record.

(D) is wrong because it incorrectly states how the regularly-conducted-activity exception works. This choice is correct in suggesting that the hearsay exception for records of regularly conducted activity contained in FRE 803(6) (commonly called the "business records" exception) would likely apply to this report. But the choice is incorrect in stating that the exception will apply only if the fire marshal is unavailable to testify. The 803(6) business-records exception, like all the exceptions contained in FRE 803, does not require a showing of the unavailability of the declarant (here, the fire marshal).

c. **Investigative reports:**

Question: A plaintiff sued a defendant for wrongful death arising out of a traffic collision between the plaintiff's decedent and the defendant. At trial, the investigating traffic officer authenticated a tape recording of her shift-end dictation of comments used in preparing the written report of her factual findings. She testified that the tape recording was accurate when made and that she currently had no clear memory of the details of the investigation.

Is the tape recording admissible as evidence?

(A) Yes, under the past recollection recorded exception to the hearsay rule.

(B) Yes, under the public records exception to the hearsay rule.

(C) No, because it is hearsay and is a police report being offered against the defendant in a wrongful death case.

(D) No, because the police report itself is the best evidence.

[QA048]

Answer: Choice **(B)** is **incorrect** because although the officer's formal written report would qualify as a public record under FRE 803(8), the informal dictated comments she made to help her prepare the report would not. To be admissible under 803(8), the material must fall within one of clauses (A), (B), or (C) of 803(8). Let's see why none of these clauses applies:

Clause (A) of 803(8) covers reports of "the activities of the [public] office or agency." The clause is interpreted to refer to records of the internal activities of the agency, not to its inquiries into events occurring in the outside world. So the recording here does not qualify, since it's not about the police department, but about real-world non-police activities.

Clause (B) of 803(8) covers "matters observed pursuant to duty imposed by law as to which matters there was a duty to report, excluding, however, in criminal cases matters observed by police officers and other law enforcement personnel[.]" (B) is generally interpreted to cover only material that is "more concrete and simple than interpretive or evaluative" (see M&K, §8.50, p. 862), so it would not apply to the dictated notes here, which clearly have an evaluative component (Who caused the accident, which the officer didn't personally witness?).

Clause (C) of 803(8) covers "factual findings resulting from an investigation made pursuant to authority granted by law[.]" ((C) goes on to say that such findings may be used only "in civil actions and proceedings and against the Government in criminal cases"; since this is a civil action, this limit does not bar the use here.) But (C) by its terms covers "factual *findings*," and the preliminary, informal tape-recording here would not be construed to have produced such "factual findings" (a phrase that has the connotation of final and formal conclusions), especially given that the traffic officer knew that her recording would be used by her later in order to prepare her eventual "written report of her factual findings." (The written report is a document that *would* satisfy clause (C).) So none of the three clauses of 803(8) applies.

(The correct answer is (A), admissible as past recollection recorded; see *supra*, p. 68.)

D. Absence of public record:

Question: In a civil action for misrepresentation in the sale of real estate, the parties contested whether the defendant was licensed by the State Board of Realtors, a public agency established by statute to license real estate brokers. The defendant testified she was licensed. On rebuttal, the plaintiff offers a certification, bearing the seal of the secretary of the State Board of Realtors. The certification states that the secretary conducted a thorough search of the agency's records and all relevant databases, and that this search uncovered no record of a license ever having been issued to the defendant. The certification is signed by the secretary.

Is the certification that there was no record of a license issuance admissible?

(A) No, because it is hearsay not within any exception.

(B) No, because the writing was not properly authenticated.

(C) Yes, for the limited purpose of impeaching the defendant.

(D) Yes, to prove the nonexistence of a public record.

[Q7065]

Answer: Choice **(D)** is correct. The certification is hearsay, but it qualifies under FRE 803(10), the hearsay exception for a certification offered to prove the absence of a public record. The certification is offered for the proper inference that if a license had been issued, it would have been recorded in the public record. Thus, the fact that there was no record found is probative evidence that a license was never issued. To be admissible, the certification must be prepared by a public official and must on its face indicate that a diligent search of the records was conducted. This certification satisfies the requirements of the exception.

(A) is wrong because the certification qualifies under FRE 803(10), the hearsay exception for a certification offered to prove the absence of a public record, as further discussed in Choice (D) above.

(B) is wrong because no extrinsic evidence of authenticity is required to admit a domestic public document bearing a government seal under FRE 902(1). Here, the certification is from a public agency of the United States and bears the agency's seal. Therefore, it is self-authenticating under Rule 902(1), and is admissible under FRE 803(10), the hearsay exception for a certification offered to prove the absence of a public record.

(C) is wrong because the certification qualifies under FRE 803(10), the hearsay exception for a certification offered to prove the absence of a public record. The certification can be offered for its truth, that there was no record of any issuance of a license to the defendant. Therefore its admissibility is not limited to impeachment; it can be used both for impeachment and as substantive proof of the disputed fact.

VII. LEARNED WRITINGS AND COMMERCIAL PUBLICATIONS

A. Learned writings:

1. Text of FRE 803(18):

   Question: Post sued Dean for personal injury alleged to have been caused by Dean's negligence. A major issue at trial was whether Post's disability was caused solely by trauma or by a preexisting condition of osteoarthritis.

   Post called Dr. Cox, who testified that the disability was caused by trauma. On cross-examination, Dr. Cox testified that a medical textbook entitled *Diseases of the Joints* was authoritative and that she agreed with the substance of passages from the textbook that she was directed to look at, but that the passages were inapplicable to Post's condition because they dealt with rheumatoid arthritis rather than with the osteoarthritis that Post was alleged to have.

   Dean then called his expert, Dr. Freed, who testified that, with reference to the issue being litigated, there is no difference between the two kinds of arthritis. Dean's counsel then asks permission to read to the jury the textbook passages earlier shown to Dr. Cox.

   The judge should rule the textbook passages

   (A) admissible only for the purpose of impeaching Cox.

   (B) admissible as substantive evidence if the judge determines that the passages are relevant.

   (C) inadmissible, because they are hearsay not within any exception.

   (D) inadmissible, because Cox contended that they are not relevant to Post's condition.

   [Q4042]

Answer: Choice **(B)** is correct. This choice correctly recognizes that there's a hearsay problem with this evidence. Hearsay is an out-of-court statement offered to prove the truth of its assertion. Here, the out-of-court declarant is the author of the treatise. It's being offered to prove that Post's injuries may not have been caused by Dean's negligence. Thus, the treatise is hearsay, and it will have to fit some hearsay exception or exclusion to be admissible. Choice (B) correctly recognizes that the learned treatise hearsay exception will make the passages admissible. Under FRE 803(18), a learned treatise can be read into evidence (it *cannot* be admitted as an exhibit) if an expert witness relies on it on direct examination, or it's called to his attention on cross-examination, or it's established as reliable authority by witness's testimony or admission, other expert testimony, or judicial notice. (The judge still must determine that the passages are relevant to some issue in the case, as this choice also recognizes.)

(A) is wrong because it is too restrictive. While the evidence will be admissible to impeach Cox, it will also be substantively admissible under FRE 803(18)'s learned-treatises hearsay exception, as further discussed in Choice (B) above.

(C) is wrong, because the evidence here, although hearsay, *is* admissible under the learned treatises exception to the hearsay rule, FRE 803(18), as further discussed in Choice (B) above.

(D) wrong, because Cox's acknowledgment of relevance is not a requirement for admissibility. Under FRE 803(18), a learned treatise can be read into evidence if an expert witness relies on it on direct examination, or it's called to his attention on cross-examination, or it's established as reliable authority by witness's testimony or admission, other expert testimony, or judicial notice. Thus, under these facts, as long as the treatise is established as reliable authority, it can be read into evidence even if Cox thinks it's pure drivel.

2. **Details:**

   e. **Not admitted as exhibit:**

      i. **MBE tip:**

      Question: In a civil trial for professional malpractice, the plaintiff sought to show that the defendant, an engineer, had designed the plaintiff's flour mill with inadequate power. The plaintiff called an expert witness who based his testimony solely on his own professional experience but also asserted, when asked, that the book Smith on Milling Systems was a reliable treatise in the field and consistent with his views. On cross-examination, the defendant asked the witness whether he and Smith were ever wrong. The witness answered, "Nobody's perfect." The defendant asked no further questions. The defendant called a second expert witness and asked, "Do you accept the Smith book as reliable?" The second witness said, "It once was, but it is now badly out of date." The plaintiff requested that the jury be allowed to examine the book and judge for itself the book's reliability.

      Should the court allow the jury to examine the book?

      (A) No, because the jury may consider only passages read to it by counsel or witness.

      (B) No, because the plaintiff's expert in testifying did not rely on the treatise but on his own experience.

      (C) Yes, because an expert has testified that the treatise is reliable.

      (D) Yes, because the jury is the judge of the weight and credibility to be accorded both written and oral evidence.

      [Q7005]

Answer: Choice **(A)** is correct. FRE 803(18), the learned treatise exception, provides that if the court finds a publication to be a reliable authority, then "statements" in it may be read into evidence, but that the publication may not be received as an exhibit (which is what would have to happen if the jury were to "examine the book" as the question asks). Thus, the jury is not allowed to bring learned treatises into the jury room — there is a concern that if juries were allowed unrestricted access to the whole publication, they might rely on parts of the publication that are not germane to the case. Moreover, the intent of the rule is that juries need to be guided through the pertinent parts of the publication by the testifying experts.

(B) is wrong because FRE 803(18), the learned treatise exception, allows statements from a treatise to be read into evidence where the treatise is "called to the attention of an expert witness" and is found to be reliable by the court. The rule does not require that an expert rely on the treatise. In this case, the publication was called to the attention of the defendant's expert.

(C) is wrong because it's not enough that one expert testifies that the treatise is reliable. FRE 803(18) allows statements from a treatise to be read into evidence when the treatise is "*established as a reliable authority* by the testimony or admission of the witness or by other expert testimony or by judicial notice." In this case, one expert testified that the publication was reliable, but the other expert contests that assertion. The decision on reliability is for the court; it is not correct to say that the court should find the publication reliable simply because one expert has found it to be so. In addition, the rule allows "statements" from a learned treatise to be read into evidence, but does not allow the publication to be received as an exhibit (which would be required if the jury were to "examine the book" as the question asks).

(D) is wrong because, although the statement is true so far as it goes, it does not mean that the jury gets to consider any evidence that the parties wish to present. FRE 803(18), the learned treatise exception, requires the judge to determine that the publication is reliable before it can be considered by the jury. In addition, the rule allows "statements" from a learned treatise to be read into evidence, but does not allow the publication to be received as an exhibit (and since the question is asking whether the court should allow the jury to "examine the book," this should only happen if the book was received as an exhibit).

X. DYING DECLARATIONS

B. Requirements in detail:

1. Awareness of imminent death:

a. Declarant wrongly believes he'll live:

Question: The defendant is charged with the murder of the victim. The prosecutor introduced testimony of a police officer that the victim told a priest, administering the last rites, "I was stabbed by [the defendant]. Since I am dying, tell him I forgive him." Thereafter, the defendant's attorney offers the testimony of a witness that the day before, when the victim believed he would live, he stated that he had been stabbed by Jack (not the defendant), an old enemy.

The testimony of this witness is

(A) admissible under an exception to the hearsay rule.

(B) admissible to impeach the dead declarant.

(C) inadmissible because it goes to the ultimate issue in the case.

(D) inadmissible because it is irrelevant to any substantive issue in the case.

[Q4022]

Answer: Choice **(B)** is correct. The victim's statement about the defendant was hearsay, but was properly admitted under FRE 804(b)(2)'s "dying declaration" exception, because it was made by a person now unavailable to testify, believing he was about to die, concerning personal knowledge of the cause of death, and the statement is offered at either a criminal homicide trial or a civil wrongful death suit. Since that statement came in, his prior inconsistent statement (about Jack) can be used to impeach his credibility, since hearsay declarants *can* be impeached. Note that this impeaching evidence would not be admissible *substantively,* since it does not fulfill the requirements of 801(d)(1)(A)'s prior-inconsistent-statement hearsay exclusion — the prior inconsistent statement is only admissible substantively if the statement was made under oath, at a prior proceeding, subject to perjury, with the declarant now being the testifying witness; here, the victim's statement about Jack was not made under oath or at a proceeding.

(A) is wrong because the witness's testimony does not fit an exception to the hearsay rule; it's inadmissible hearsay. In particular, the statement does not fit the most obvious exception, the "dying declaration" exception to the hearsay rule, because the victim did not have an impending sense of death when he made the statement. FRE 804(b)(2). The rationale behind the exception is that no one wants to die with a lie on his lips; where a person thinks he's going to *live*, this is not applicable. (Also, the statement will not be admissible *substantively* as a prior inconsistent statement, for the reasons discussed in Choice (B) above.)

(C) is wrong because the FRE do not condition the admissibility of a statement on whether it addresses an "ultimate issue." See FRE 704(a).

(D) is wrong, because the testimony *is* relevant to a substantive issue in the case. A piece of evidence is logically relevant if it tends to prove or disprove a material fact. FRE 401. If the victim's prior statement about Jack is true, it will tend to prove that the victim was lying about the defendant's stabbing him, and thus make it less likely that the defendant is guilty of murder. As a result, it's *extremely* relevant!

2. **Actual death:**

   a. **Don't overlook "unavailability" requirement:**

   Question: A defendant was charged with aggravated assault. At trial, the victim testified that the defendant beat her savagely, but she was not asked about anything said during the incident. The prosecutor then called a witness to testify that when the beating stopped, the victim screamed: "I'm dying-don't let [the defendant] get away with it!"

   Is the testimony of the witness concerning the victim's statement admissible?

   (A) No, because it is hearsay not within any exception.

   (B) No, because the victim was not asked about the statement.

   (C) Yes, as a statement under belief of impending death, even though the victim did not die.

   (D) Yes, as an excited utterance.

   [Q7037]

   Answer: Choice **(C)** is **incorrect**. While the declarant does not have to die for a statement to be admissible as a dying declaration under FRE 804(b)(2), this statement fails to satisfy that exception for at least two reasons. First, the declarant has to be unavailable, as the dying declaration is one of the "unavailability-dependent" exceptions of Rule 804. Here, the victim testified and so obviously is not unavailable. Second, a dying declaration is admissible only in homicide prosecutions and civil cases. This is a criminal case for aggravated assault. (The correct answer is (D); for why the excited-utterance exception applies, see *supra*, p. 64.)

3. **No non-homicide prosecutions:**

   a. **Usable in civil cases**

   Question: A pedestrian died from injuries caused when a driver's car struck him. The executor of the pedestrian's estate sued the driver for wrongful death. At trial, the executor calls a nurse to testify that two days after the accident, the pedestrian said to the nurse, "The car that hit me ran the red light." Fifteen minutes thereafter, the pedestrian died.

   As a foundation for introducing evidence of the pedestrian's statement, the executor offers to the court a doctor's affidavit that the doctor was the intern on duty the day of the pedestrian's death and that several times that day the pedestrian had said that he knew he was about to die.

   Is the affidavit properly considered by the court in ruling on the admissibility of the pedestrian's statement?

   (A) No, because it is hearsay not within any exception.

   (B) No, because it is irrelevant since dying declarations cannot be used except in prosecutions for homicide.

   (C) Yes, because though hearsay, it is a statement of then-existing mental condition.

   (D) Yes, because the judge may consider hearsay in ruling on preliminary questions.

   [Q3147]

   Answer: Choice **(D)** is correct. FRE 104(a) says that "Preliminary questions concerning ... the admissibility of evidence shall be determined by the court.... In making its determination it is *not bound by the rules of evidence* except those with respect to privileges." The pedestrian's statement to the nurse is admissible if, and only if, the statement qualified for the dying-declaration exception. That exception requires that the declarant knew or believed that he was about to die. The affidavit is relevant to that issue. It's true that the affidavit is hearsay (it's an out-of-court statement offered to prove the truth of the matter asserted, i.e., that the pedestrian really knew or believed he was dying). And this hearsay does not fall within any exception. But under 104(a), the judge may consider this inadmissible hearsay in making her preliminary ruling on the admissibility of the pedestrian's statement to the nurse.

   (A) is wrong because even though the affidavit is hearsay not within any exception, it may still be considered on the preliminary matter of the admissibility of the statement to the nurse. As described in Choice (D) above, the fact that the affidavit is hearsay not within any exception does not prevent the court from using it to resolve a preliminary question about the admissibility of other evidence.

   (B) is wrong because (1) dying declarations are admissible in civil cases; and (2) the admissibility of the affidavit is irrelevant to whether it can be considered on the preliminary question here. First, FRE 804(b)(2) gives a hearsay exception for, "In a prosecution for homicide *or in a civil action or proceeding*, a statement made by a declarant while believing that the declarant's death was imminent, concerning the cause or circumstances of what the declarant believed to be impending death." So the proposition asserted in Choice (B) — that dying declarations can't be used except in homicide prosecutions —is simply incorrect as a matter of law. Furthermore, even if this statement of law were true, it would be irrelevant — as described in the discussion of Choice (D) above, the judge may consider inadmissible material in ruling on an evidentiary question.

(C) is wrong because: (1) the affidavit is the "outer level" of a two-level hearsay statement, and that outer level doesn't qualify for the then-existing-state-of-mind exception; and (2) the affidavit's admissibility doesn't matter here anyway. First, notice that we have hearsay-within-hearsay. The "outer" level is the doctor's affidavit (a statement made out of court, repeating some other statement). The "inner" level is the pedestrian's statement to the doctor. Each must satisfy a hearsay exception. It's true that the inner statement arguably qualifies for the then-existing-state-of-mind exception (though even this is far from clear, since under FRE 803(3) "A statement of ... belief to prove the fact ... believed" does not qualify for the exception.) But the *outer* statement is not a statement about *the declarant's* then-existing state of mind — for this purpose, the declarant is the doctor, and he's not summarizing his own then-existing state of mind (except insofar as he's making a statement of what he currently remembers the pedestrian to have said, which is inadmissible since FRE 803(3) denies the state-of-mind exception for "a statement of memory ... to prove the fact remembered"). Since one of the two levels is inadmissible hearsay, the entire statement-within-a-statement is inadmissible. Nonetheless, as described in Choice (D) above, the statement need not be admissible to be considered by the judge in making a preliminary admissibility ruling.

5. **Relating to circumstances of killing:**

    Question: In a jurisdiction without a Dead Man's Statute, Parker's estate sued Davidson claiming that Davidson had borrowed from Parker $10,000, which had not been repaid as of Parker's death. Parker was run over by a truck. At the accident scene, while dying from massive injuries, Parker told Officer Smith to "make sure my estate collects the $10,000 I loaned to Davidson."

    Smith's testimony about Parker's statement is

    (A) inadmissible, because it is more unfairly prejudicial than probative.

    (B) inadmissible, because it is hearsay not within any exception.

    (C) admissible as an excited utterance.

    (D) admissible as a statement under belief of impending death.

    [Q3081]

    Answer: Choice **(D)** is **incorrect**, because Parker's comment did not concern the cause or circumstance of his death. FRE 803(b)(2)'s dying-declaration exception applies to (in a civil case or homicide prosecution) "a statement made by a declarant while believing that death was imminent, *concerning the cause or circumstances of what the declarant believed to be impending death.*" Since Parker's statement related only to the collection of the debt, not to the truck accident that was about to cause his death, it doesn't qualify. (The correct answer is (B); see *supra*, p. 46.)

XI. DECLARATIONS AGAINST INTEREST

A. **Generally:**

1. **Text of Federal Rule:**

    Question: The defendant, a man, has been charged with murdering the victim. The defendant defends on the grounds that the murder was really committed by a particular woman, who has since died. The defendant offers a properly authenticated photocopy of a transcript of a deposition in a civil suit brought against the woman by the victim's family for the victim's death, in which the woman said, "Yes, I killed him because I hated him." The civil suit was brought because the woman was known to have quarreled with and disliked the victim. Upon proper objection by the prosecution, the statement should be

(A) admitted as a declaration against interest.

(B) admitted as former testimony by a person now unavailable.

(C) inadmissible as hearsay not within any exception.

(D) inadmissible, because the original rather than a photocopy must be offered.

[Q6001]

Answer: Choice **(A)** is correct. First, this is hearsay: the declarant's statement "I killed him" is being offered to show that she did indeed kill him. But FRE 804(b)(3) (one of the declarant-unavailable exceptions) gives a hearsay exception for a statement by a now-unavailable witness which "was at the time of its making so far contrary to the declarant's pecuniary or proprietary interest, or so far tended to subject the declarant to civil or criminal liability . . . that a reasonable person in the declarant's position would not have made the statement unless believing it to be true." The woman's statement in the deposition qualifies, since: (1) her subsequent death of course makes her unavailable; (2) the statement, viewed as of the time she made it, potentially subjected her to such civil and criminal liability that she would be unlikely to have made it unless she believed it was true. 804(b)(3) adds a further requirement, that a statement "tending to expose the declarant to criminal liability and offered to exculpate the accused is not admissible unless corroborating circumstances clearly indicate the trustworthiness of the statement." Here, the fact that the woman was known to have quarreled with and disliked the victim, and the fact that the victim's family chose to bring civil suit against the woman, supply the required corroborating circumstances to indicate the statement's trustworthiness.

(B) is wrong because, although there is indeed an exception for former testimony given under oath at a trial or other proceeding, the exception applies only if "the party against whom the testimony is now offered . . . had an opportunity and similar motive to develop the testimony by direct, cross, or redirect examination." See FRE 804(b)(1). Since the "party against whom the testimony is now offered" is the government, the statement could qualify only if the government had the opportunity and similar motive to "develop" (i.e., undermine) the woman's testimony in the earlier civil suit; since the prosecution was not part of that suit, this requirement was not satisfied.

(C) is wrong because, while the statement is indeed hearsay, the declaration-against-interest exception applies, as described in Choice (A) above.

(D) is wrong because, although the Best Evidence Rule does indeed sometimes require an original, FRE 1003 says that "a duplicate is admissible to the same extent as an original unless (1) a genuine issue is raised as to the authenticity of the original or (2) in the circumstances it would be unfair to admit to duplicate in lieu of the original." There is no indication on these facts that either of these problems is present.

Question: Pamela sued Driver for damages for the death of Pamela's husband Ronald, resulting from an automobile collision. At trial, Driver calls Ronald's doctor to testify that the day before his death, Ronald, in great pain, said, "It was my own fault; there's nobody to blame but me."

The doctor's testimony should be admitted as

(A) a statement against interest.

(B) a dying declaration.

(C) a statement of Ronald's then existing state of mind.

(D) an excited utterance.

[Q2183]

Answer: Choice **(A)** is correct. There are three requirements for the declaration-against-interest exception to the hearsay rule: (1) the declarant must be unavailable; (2) the declaration must have been against the declarant's pecuniary or proprietary interest when made; and (3) the circumstances must be such that declarant would not have made the statement unless he believed it to be true. All of these requirements are fulfilled regarding the statement made by the now-deceased Ronald: (1) he's dead and thus unavailable; (2) he exposed himself to tort liability by acknowledging responsibility for the accident; and (3) there is no apparent reason why he'd acknowledge responsibility if he didn't think he was in fact at fault.

B. **Meaning of "against interest":**

5. **Unavailability:**

Question: Davidson and Smythe were charged with burglary of a warehouse. They were tried separately. At Davidson's trial, Smythe testified that he saw Davidson commit the burglary. While Smythe is still subject to recall as a witness, Davidson calls Smythe's cellmate, Walton, to testify that Smythe said, "I broke into the warehouse alone because Davidson was too drunk to help."

This evidence of Smythe's statement is

(A) admissible as a declaration against penal interest.

(B) admissible as a prior inconsistent statement.

(C) inadmissible, because it is hearsay not within any exception.

(D) inadmissible, because the statement is not clearly corroborated.

[Q1148]

Answer: Choice **(A)** is **incorrect**, because the declarant is available. FRE 804(b)(3), giving a hearsay exception for declarations against pecuniary or penal interest, requires that the declarant be "unavailable as a witness[.]" The fact pattern indicates that Smythe is still subject to recall as a witness when Walton is testifying about Smythe's prior statement, so Smythe is "available." (The correct choice is (B), prior inconsistent statement, substantively admissible under FRE 801(d)(1); see *supra*, p. 39.)

XIII. PRIOR STATEMENTS OF AVAILABLE WITNESS

A. **Prior inconsistent statements:**

1. **Proceeding:**

a. **MBE tip:**

Question: The defendant is charged with the murder of the victim. The prosecutor introduced testimony of a police officer that the victim told a priest, administering the last rites, "I was stabbed by [the defendant]. Since I am dying, tell him I forgive him." Thereafter, the defendant's attorney offers the testimony of a witness that the day before, when the victim believed he would live, he stated that he had been stabbed by Jack (not the defendant), an old enemy.

The testimony of this witness is

(A) admissible under an exception to the hearsay rule.

(B) admissible to impeach the dead declarant.

(C) inadmissible because it goes to the ultimate issue in the case.

(D) inadmissible because it is irrelevant to any substantive issue in the case.

[Q4022]

Answer: Choice **(B)** is correct. The victim's statement about the defendant was hearsay, but was properly admitted under FRE 804(b)(2)'s "dying declaration" exception, because it was made by a person now unavailable to testify, believing he was about to die, concerning personal knowledge of the cause of death, and the statement is offered at either a criminal homicide trial or a civil wrongful death suit. Since that statement came in, his prior inconsistent statement (about Jack) can be used to impeach his credibility, since hearsay declarants *can* be impeached. Note that this impeaching evidence would not be admissible *substantively*, since it does not fulfill the requirements of 801(d)(1)(A)'s prior-inconsistent-statement hearsay exclusion — the prior inconsistent statement is only admissible substantively if the statement was made under oath, at a prior proceeding, subject to perjury, with the declarant now being the testifying witness; here, the victim's statement about Jack was not made under oath or at a proceeding.

(A) is wrong because the witness's testimony does not fit an exception to the hearsay rule; it's inadmissible hearsay. In particular, the statement does not fit the most obvious exception, the "dying declaration" exception to the hearsay rule, because the victim did not have an impending sense of death when he made the statement. FRE 804(b)(2). The rationale behind the exception is that no one wants to die with a lie on his lips; where a person thinks he's going to *live*, this is not applicable. (Also, the statement will not be admissible *substantively* as a prior inconsistent statement, for the reasons discussed in Choice (B) above.)

(C) is wrong because the FRE do not condition the admissibility of a statement on whether it addresses an "ultimate issue." See FRE 704(a).

(D) is wrong because the testimony *is* relevant to a substantive issue in the case. A piece of evidence is logically relevant if it tends to prove or disprove a material fact. FRE 401. If the victim's prior statement about Jack is true, it will tend to prove that the victim was lying about the defendant's stabbing him, and thus make it less likely that the defendant is guilty of murder. As a result, it's *extremely* relevant!

Chapter 6
CONFRONTATION AND COMPULSORY PROCESS

[OMITTED]

Chapter 7
PRIVILEGES

II. THE ATTORNEY-CLIENT PRIVILEGE

A. Generally:

1. Client:

Question: Pace sues Def Company for injuries suffered when Pace's car collided with Def Company's truck. Def's general manager prepared a report of the accident at the request of the company's attorney in preparation for the trial, and delivered the report to the attorney. Pace demands that the report be produced.

Will production of the report be required?

(A) Yes, because business reports are not generally privileged.

(B) No, because it is privileged communication from the client to the attorney.

(C) No, because such reports contain hearsay.

(D) No, because such reports are self-serving.

[Q8044]

Answer: Choice **(B)** is correct. A communication is subject to attorney-client privilege if it is a communication from the client to the attorney, made in confidence, concerning legal representation. A corporation is subject to the same privilege as an individual, and the general manager would be within the scope of the privilege under the modern "performance of duties" test, under which the privilege extends to any employee's communication if it was within his duties, and it was offered to advance the legal interests of the corporation. So the communication here is within the attorney-client privilege. A companion "work product immunity," in force as a matter of common-law in nearly all jurisdictions, gives an immunity from discovery or other "production" for materials that would be inadmissible at trial due to the attorney-client privilege.

(A) is not the best response because it does not correctly characterize the facts and law. A communication of *any* kind, business report or not, is subject to attorney-client privilege if it is a communication from the client to the attorney, made in confidence, concerning legal representation. Here, the report fits this description – the general manager made the report about the accident, intended that it be read only by the attorney, and it was made in preparation for trial. And apart from admissibility at trial, the "work product immunity" for direct client-attorney communication prevents the client (Def Co.) from having to produce it in discovery.

(C) is not the best response because (1) because it ignores the central reason the report will be non-producible: it is covered by the work-product immunity; and (2) it falsely asserts that because the report is or might be inadmissible, it need not be produced. As to (1), what makes the report non-producible is the attorney-client privilege and companion "work product immunity," not the presence of hearsay. As to (2), even materials that would not be admissible at trial because they contain hearsay are producible in discovery, if they are reasonably likely to lead to discoverable evidence. (And it's not so clear that the report wouldn't be admissible if it were not for the attorney-client work-product immunity problem; for instance, the report and the statements in it might all be admissible as non-hearsay admissions by a party-opponent or its agents.)

(D) is wrong because the self-serving nature of the report won't prevent the opposite party (the adversary of the report's author) from offering it. If Def Co. were offering the report as a business record under FRE 803(6), the fact that the "source of information or the method or circumstances of preparation indicate lack of trustworthiness" (803(6)) would be fatal. But where the adversary of the preparer of the record or report is offering it, the report can come in as admission, as to which its self-serving nature wouldn't matter.

B. **Professional relationship:**

   3. *Fee arrangements not covered by privilege:*

   Question: A defendant was on trial for tax evasion. The IRS, seeking to establish the defendant's income by showing his expenditures, called on the defendant's attorney to produce records showing only how much the defendant had paid his attorney in fees.

   Should the demand for the attorney's fee records be upheld?

   (A) Yes, because it calls for relevant information not within the attorney-client privilege.

   (B) Yes, because the attorney-client privilege cannot be invoked to conceal evidence of a crime.

   (C) No, because the records are protected by the attorney-client privilege.

   (D) No, because the records are protected by the attorney work-product doctrine.

   [QA098]

   Answer: Choice (A) is correct. The attorney-client privilege applies only to confidential communications made for the purpose of facilitating legal representation of the client. Courts have uniformly held that the details of fee arrangements, including the amount paid by the defendant in fees, are not communications made for the purpose of facilitating representation, and are therefore not covered by the privilege. See M&K, §5.19, p. 356.

   (B) is wrong because it gives an incorrect explanation of the correct outcome. The attorney-client privilege *can* be invoked even where it conceals evidence of a *past* crime. (The examiners are trying to make you think of the "crime or fraud" exception, by which communications are not covered by the privilege if they are made for the purpose of accomplishing or concealing a *future* crime or fraud.)

   (C) is wrong because the attorney-client privilege applies only to confidential communications made for the purpose of facilitating legal representation of the client. The amount the defendant paid in legal fees does not qualify as such a communication, as is described in the analysis of Choice (A).

   (D) is wrong because the work-product doctrine provides a qualified immunity for only those materials prepared by an attorney or client in anticipation of litigation, such as witness statements, investigative reports, or trial memoranda. Documents showing the amount a client has paid or will pay to his attorney for legal representation are not deemed to be prepared "in anticipation of litigation," so they are outside the protection of the work-product doctrine.

III. PHYSICIAN-PATIENT PRIVILEGE

A. **No federal privilege:**

   Question: Mary Webb, a physician, called as a witness by the defendant in the case *Parr v. Doan*, was asked to testify to statements made by Michael Zadok, her patient, for the purpose of obtaining treatment from Dr. Webb.

Which of the following is the best basis for excluding evidence of Zadok's statements in a jurisdiction with a doctor-patient privilege?

(A) An objection by Dr. Webb asserting her privilege against disclosure of confidential communications made by a patient.

(B) An objection by Parr's attorney on the grounds of the doctor-patient privilege.

(C) A finding by the trial judge that Zadok had left the office without actually receiving treatment.

(D) The assertion of a privilege by Zadok's attorney, present at the trial as a spectator at Zadok's request, and allowed by the trial judge to speak.

[Q8018]

Answer: Choice **(D)** is correct. When the jurisdiction recognizes the doctor-patient privilege (which the federal courts do not, by the way, as a matter of federal common law, outside of the psychotherapist-patient area) the privilege belongs only to the patient. This choice correctly recognizes that the privilege belongs to the patient, and that the patient may designate an agent (here, his lawyer) to assert the privilege in litigation.

(A) is incorrect because a doctor simply does not have a privilege against disclosure of confidential communications made by a patient. The doctor-patient privilege rests exclusively with the patient. The patient might authorize the doctor to assert it on the patient's behalf, but that's not what (A) says — this choice refers to "her privilege" (meaning Dr. Webb's privilege), and it's not hers.

(B) is incorrect because the privilege is held only by the patient, and cannot be asserted by a third party who happens to be a litigant.

(C) is incorrect because (1) the applicability of the doctor-patient privilege does not depend on whether the patient actually received treatment, but whether the doctor-patient relationship existed at the time the confidential communication was made (so the privilege can exist in the absence of receiving actual treatment); and (2) in any event, the privilege belongs to, and can only be asserted by, the patient, and there's no evidence in this choice about whether Zadok is asserting it.

IV. THE PRIVILEGE AGAINST SELF-INCRIMINATION

G. Negative inference allowed in civil cases:

A plaintiff sued an individual defendant for injuries suffered in a collision between the plaintiff's car and the defendant's truck while the defendant's employee was driving the truck. The plaintiff sought discovery of any accident report the employee might have made to the defendant, but the defendant responded that no such report existed. Before trial, the defendant moved to preclude the plaintiff from asking the defendant in the presence of the jury whether he destroyed such a report, because the defendant would then invoke his privilege against self-incrimination.

Should the court allow the plaintiff to ask the defendant about the destruction of the report?

(A) No, because a report that was prepared in anticipation of litigation is not subject to discovery.

(B) No, because no inference may properly be drawn from invocation of a legitimate privilege.

(C) Yes, because a party in a civil action may not invoke the privilege against self-incrimination.

(D) Yes, because the defendant's destruction of the report would serve as the basis of an inference adverse to the defendant.

[QA068]

Answer: Choice **(D)** is correct. If a party destroys evidence, it is proper for the jury to draw an inference that the evidence was adverse to that party. It's true that the Supreme Court has held that in a *criminal* case, neither the judge nor the prosecution can encourage a jury to draw an inference of guilt from a defendant's invocation of her privilege against self-incrimination; *Griffin v. California* (1965). But it's proper for the jury to draw an adverse inference in a *civil* case from a party's assertion of that privilege against self-incrimination. Thus, the court should allow the question to be asked, because it is proper regardless of how the defendant responds.

(A) is wrong because although it is true that a report prepared in anticipation of litigation may qualify as work product, the work-product immunity is not absolute. Documents that are work product are still subject to discovery upon a showing of substantial need and the inability to obtain the substantial equivalent of the materials by other means. Moreover, a claim of work-product immunity must be asserted before, and ruled on by, the court — a party cannot simply destroy the material and claim work-product protection. Finally, here the plaintiff would not be asking the defendant to produce the report for the jury to see; the plaintiff would only ask whether such a report had been destroyed.

(B) is wrong because although the Supreme Court has held that neither the judge nor the prosecution can encourage a jury to draw an inference of guilt from a defendant's invocation of her privilege against self-incrimination in a *criminal* case, *Griffin v. California* (1965), it is proper for the jury to draw an adverse inference in a *civil* case from a party's assertion of the privilege against self-incrimination.

(C) is wrong because the privilege against self-incrimination may be asserted in both civil and criminal cases.

CHAPTER 8
REAL AND DEMONSTRATIVE EVIDENCE, INCLUDING WRITINGS

II. AUTHENTICATION

B. **Methods of authentication:**

 1. **Real evidence:**

    a. **Distinctive characteristics:**

C. **Authentication of writings and recordings:**

 5. **Signature or handwriting:**

    b. **Non-expert:**

       Question: When a man entered a bank and presented a check for payment, the bank teller recognized the signature on the check as a forgery because the check was drawn on the account of a customer whose handwriting she knew. The bank teller called the police. Before the police arrived, the man picked up the check from the counter and left.

The man was charged with attempting to cash a forged check. At trial, the prosecutor called the bank teller to testify that the signature on the check was forged.

Is the bank teller's testimony admissible?

(A) Yes, because a bank teller is by occupation an expert on handwriting.

(B) Yes, because it is rationally based on the bank teller's perception and is helpful to the jury.

(C) No, because the bank teller was at fault in allowing loss of the original by failing to secure the check.

(D) No, because it is not possible for either the jury or an expert to compare the signature on the missing check with a signature established as genuine.

[QA085]

Answer: Choice **(B)** is correct. The witness teller, who has not been qualified as a handwriting expert, is offering her lay opinion as to the genuineness of the signature on the check. FRE 701 allows lay opinion testimony in general when it is "rationally based on the perception of the witness" *and* is "helpful to a clear understanding of the witness's testimony or the determination of a fact in issue". Additionally, FRE 901(b)(2) provides that the authenticity of a document can be established by "[n]onexpert opinion as to the genuineness of handwriting, based upon familiarity not acquired for purposes of the litigation." This requirement is met here, since the facts tell us that the witness/teller already, at the time of the episode, knew the signature of the bank customer on whose account the check was drawn. This knowledge made it possible for her to recognize the signature on the check as a forgery, and to testify with first-hand knowlege that the signature on the check presented was different from the signature of the owner of the account. Thus, the testimony is permitted.

(A) is wrong because there is nothing in the fact pattern to suggest that the bank teller is an expert on handwriting — merely working as a bank teller would not give a person such expertise.

(C) is wrong because it misstates the application of the original document rule. This choice is premised on a plausible idea: that because what's being proved is the contents of a writing (namely, the signature on a check), the original of that writing must be produced. FRE 1002's implementation of the original documents rule (a/k/a the Best Evidence Rule) indeed says that "To prove the contents of a writing ... the original writing ... is required, except as otherwise provided in these rules[.]" So if the original of the check had been available to the prosecution, the prosecution's failure to present that original, and to have the teller testify about the check's contents instead, would indeed have been a violation of FRE 1002. But FRE 1004(1) grants an exception to the original documents rule where "All originals are lost or have been destroyed, unless the proponent lost or destroyed them in bad faith." The proponent here is the prosecution (not the bank teller), so even if the teller had acted in bad faith in not securing the check, the FRE 1004(1) exception would still have applied. In any event, on the facts here, there is no evidence that the teller behaved in bad faith (or was even "at fault") by not securing the check before the defendant could grab it and run away with it.

(D) is wrong because having an expert (or even the jury members themselves) compare an exemplar established as genuine with the disputed signature is not the only way to establish whether a signature is forged or authentic. It's true that FRE 901(b)(3) permits authentication of a document via "comparison by the trier of fact or by expert witnesses with specimens which have been authenticated." However, this is not the only method authorized by FRE 901. FRE 901(b)(2) permits authentication by "[n]onexpert opinion as to the genuineness of handwriting, based upon familiarity not acquired for purposes of the litigation." The testimony here satisfies that method, since the teller got her familiarity with the real account-holder's signature in a way that pre-dated the litigation.

c. **Exemplars:**

Question: Parker sues Dix for breach of a promise made in a letter allegedly written by Dix to Parker. Dix denies writing the letter.

Which of the following would NOT be a sufficient basis for admitting the letter into evidence?

(A) Testimony by Parker that she is familiar with Dix's signature and recognizes it on the letter.

(B) Comparison by the trier of fact of the letter with an admitted signature of Dix.

(C) Opinion testimony of a nonexpert witness based upon familiarity acquired in order to authenticate the signature.

(D) Evidence that the letter was written in response to one written by Parker to Dix.

[Q1162]

Answer: Choice **(C)** is correct (i.e., the choice is not an acceptable method of authentication). FRE 901(b)(2) allows "nonexpert opinion as to the genuineness of handwriting, based upon familiarity *not acquired for purposes of the litigation.*" The fact pattern indicates that the nonexpert acquired familiarity in order to authenticate the signature; therefore, this would not serve as a sufficient basis for admitting the letter into evidence.

(A) is wrong because a nonexpert who is already familiar with a signature may testify as to its genuineness as provided by FRE 901(b)(2) and discussed in the explanation to (C). It is irrelevant that the nonexpert is a party to the litigation.

(B) is wrong because handwriting may be authenticated by the use of exemplars, in which case it is up to the jury to compare the exemplar with the offered writing to determine its genuineness.

(D) is wrong because evidence that the letter (relying on its contents and other circumstances) was written as a reply to one already authenticated is a method of authentication falling under the category of "distinctive characteristics and the like." FRE 901(b)(4).

7. **Phone conversation:**

b. **Incoming calls:**

Question: Defendant is on trial for extorting $10,000 from Victim. An issue is the identification of the person who made a telephone call to Victim. Victim is prepared to testify that the caller had a distinctive accent like Defendant's, but that he cannot positively identify the voice as Defendant's. Victim recorded the call but has not brought the tape to court, although its existence is known to Defendant.

Victim's testimony is

(A) inadmissible, because Victim cannot sufficiently identify the caller.

(B) inadmissible, because the tape recording of the conversation is the best evidence.

(C) admissible, because Defendant waived the "best evidence" rule by failing to subpoena the tape.

(D) admissible, because Victim's lack of certainty goes to the weight to be given Victim's testimony, not to its admissibility.

[Q3110]

Answer: Choice **(D)** is correct. According to the FRE, authentication is the condition precedent to admissibility that is satisfied by evidence sufficient to support a finding that the matter in question is what its proponent claims. FRE 901(a). Since the prosecution is trying to establish that the voice on the phone was Defendant's, Victim's testimony that he believes the voice was victim's will have to be authenticated. FRE 901(b)(5) gives, as an illustration of proper authentication, "Identification of a voice, whether heard firsthand or through mechanical or electronic transmission or recording, by opinion based upon hearing the voice at any time under circumstances connecting it with the alleged speaker." Since Victim has heard Defendant's voice and knows that that voice has a distinctive accent, his proposed testimony (which states that the voice had a similar distinctive accent) meets this requirement. There is no requirement that the giver of the opinion must be positive in the identification — the witness is permitted to say merely that the voice was similar, for instance having a similar distinctive accent. At that point, the jury is free to give very little weight to the evidence — the point is that the lack of certainty doesn't make the tentative identification inadmissible.

(A) is wrong because, for the reasons stated in the treatment of Choice (D) above, the fact that Victim cannot conclusively identify the voice as being Defendant's does not prevent the tentative identification from being admissible.

(B) is wrong because the Best Evidence Rule (B.E.R.) does not apply here. The B.E.R. states that if the terms of a writing or a recording are to be proved, the original must be produced. The Rule does not apply to events that have by happenstance been recorded — it applies only where the *terms of the recording, per se, are what are being sought to be proved*. See FRE 1002 (making the rule applicable "to prove the content of a writing, recording, or photograph[.]") Here, the extortion happened in a live phone call. The prosecution is proving the contents of that live phone call. The fact that Victim happened to have made a tape of the call, therefore, does not mean that the prosecution is attempting to "prove the contents" of this incidentally-created tape. So the B.E.R. doesn't apply. (It would be different if the extortion occurred when someone sent a threatening tape to Victim — then the recording *would* be subject to the B.E.R., because the prosecution's case would require it to show what the contents of the tape were.)

(C) is wrong because the Best Evidence Rule (B.E.R.) wouldn't be waived by a failure to subpoena, and in any case, the Rule is not applicable to these facts. The B.E.R., like any evidentiary requirement, can be waived by the non-proponent party. But that waiver would have to take the form of a failure to object at trial. The opponent's mere failure to subpoena the tape would not serve as a waiver. In any event, the B.E.R. doesn't apply to these facts, because the contents of the recording are not what's being proved, as discussed in Choice (B) above.

Question: In a narcotics conspiracy prosecution against Daly, the prosecutor offers in evidence a tape recording of a telephone call allegedly made by Daly. A lay witness is called to testify that the voice on the recording is Daly's. Her testimony to which of the following would be the LEAST sufficient basis for admitting the recording?

(A) She had heard the same voice on a similar tape recording identified to her by Daly's brother.

(B) She had heard Daly speak many times, but never over the telephone.

(C) She had, specifically for the purpose of preparing to testify, talked with Daly over the telephone at a time after the recording was made.

(D) She had been present with Daly when he engaged in the conversation in question but had heard only Daly's side of the conversation.

[Q8060]

Answer: Choice **(A)** is the best response, because under this alternative, the lay witness is not *personally familiar* with Daly's voice, and thus the recording wouldn't be admissible with this testimony alone. The rule is that a voice can be authenticated by any person who recognizes it. Under FRE 901(b)(5), *"Identification of a voice, whether heard firsthand or through mechanical or electronic transmission or recording, [can be accomplished] by opinion based upon hearing the voice at any time under any circumstances connecting it with the alleged speaker."* Here, the only thing linking the lay witness and Daly's voice is an assurance by Daly's brother that a recorded voice was Daly's; the witness herself has no personal familiarity with it. (Thus, if Daly's brother were lying or mistaken, the lay witness's testimony would be useless.) Since (A) states the only basis on which the lay witness *couldn't* authenticate the tape, of these four choices, it's the best response.

(B) is wrong because the fact that the witness had never heard Daly speak over the telephone would be irrelevant. Under FRE 901(b)(5), "Identification of a voice, whether heard firsthand or through mechanical or electronic transmission or recording, [can be accomplished] by opinion based upon hearing the voice at any time under any circumstances connecting it with the alleged speaker." Here, the lay witness satisfies this requirement because she had heard the voice many times. The rule doesn't require that the witness be familiar with the voice in the form in which it must be authenticated (here, a tape recording).

(C) is wrong because the lay witness could authenticate the recording on this basis, since any person who recognizes a voice can authenticate it. FRE 901(b)(5) (quoted in full in (A) above) allows lay testimony identifying a voice based upon "hearing the voice *at any time under any circumstances.*" This language means that familiarity acquired in anticipation of litigation does not disqualify the witness. (This makes the situation different from handwriting, as to which 901(b)(2) allows lay testimony only if "based on familiarity not acquired for purposes of the litigation.")

(D) is wrong because it represents possibly the *best* basis on which the lay witness *could* authenticate the recording. Not only would she be able to recognize the voice, but she'd be familiar with the very conversation that was recorded. Nothing in 901(b)(5) would come close to ruling out an identification of the speaker on a tape as having been the person whose side of the taped conversation the witness heard in person.

D. Self-authentication;

1. Federal Rules:

Question: At the trial of the case of *Smith v. Jones,* which of the following is LEAST likely to be admitted into evidence for the purpose of determining whether a certain letter was written by Jones?

(A) A sample of Jones's signature, together with the testimony of a handwriting expert that the letter was signed by the same person who created the sample.

(B) A sample of Jones's signature submitted to the jury together with the letter in question.

(C) The testimony of a layperson who stated that he saw Jones sign the letter in question.

(D) Testimony that the letterhead on the letter in question was Jones's.

[Q5048]

Answer: Choice **(D)** is correct. Under common law, self-identifying statements are not sufficient to establish the source of a writing. FRE 902 creates some exceptions to this rule, but letterheads are not among them.

(A) is wrong because an expert may state an opinion concerning the authorship of a particular writing based upon a comparison of the writing in question with an exemplar of the defendant's writing. See FRE 901(b)(2), giving as an illustration of proper authentication "comparison by ... expert witnesses with specimens which have been authenticated."

(B) is wrong because the trier of fact may form a conclusion about the authorship of a particular writing based upon its own comparison of that writing with an exemplar of the defendant's handwriting.

(C) is wrong because any person may testify to what he has seen, if what he has seen is relevant to the facts in issue.

III. THE "BEST EVIDENCE RULE" FOR RECORDED COMMUNICATIONS

B. Communications covered:

4. Other "real" evidence not covered:

Question: Plaintiff sued Defendant for injuries suffered in a car accident allegedly caused by brakes that had been negligently repaired by Defendant. At a settlement conference, Plaintiff exhibited the brake shoe that caused the accident and pointed out the alleged defect to an expert, whom Defendant had brought to the conference. No settlement was reached. At trial, the brake shoe having disappeared, Plaintiff seeks to testify concerning the condition of the shoe.

Plaintiff's testimony is

(A) admissible, because Defendant's expert had been able to examine the shoe carefully.

(B) admissible, because Plaintiff had personal knowledge of the shoe's condition.

(C) inadmissible, because the brake shoe was produced and examined as a part of settlement negotiations.

(D) inadmissible, unless Plaintiff establishes that the disappearance was not his fault.

[Q3102]

Answer: Choice **(B)** is correct. Where a witness has personal knowledge about a fact, the witness is ordinarily entitled to testify about that fact. Here, Plaintiff has personal knowledge about the condition of the shoe, and is therefore entitled to testify about that condition, unless some other rule blocks the testimony. There is no such other rule that applies here.

(A) is wrong because the fact that Defendant's expert was able to examine the shoe carefully is irrelevant. Even if the Defendant's expert had *not* been able to examine the shoe, the Plaintiff would still have been permitted to testify about his personal knowledge of the condition.

(C) is wrong because the fact that a physical object was present during settlement negotiations does not mean that testimony about the object becomes inadmissible. It is true that FRE 408 makes inadmissible settlement offers, as well as "conduct and statements made in" settlement negotiations. But FRE 408 carefully states that the rule "does not require the exclusion of any evidence otherwise discoverable merely because it is presented in the course of compromise negotiations." The fact that the shoe was presented to the other side during settlement negotiations falls within the last sentence of 408 quoted above, making testimony about the shoe admissible.

(D) is wrong because Plaintiff does not bear the burden of establishing that the disappearance was not his fault. If the item had been a *document*, and its "contents" were sought to be proved, the fact that the person seeking to testify about the contents was responsible in bad faith for the document's disappearance would cause the testimony to be excluded. (See FRE 1004: "The original is not required, and other evidence of the contents of a writing ... is admissible if (1) All originals are lost or have been destroyed, unless the proponent lost or destroyed them in bad faith.") But no such rule applies to items of physical evidence that are not writings, recordings, or photographs (i.e., to items that are not subject to the Best Evidence Rule). The court probably has discretion to exclude testimony about an item of real evidence whose disappearance has been shown to have been procured by the intentional wrongdoing of the proponent of the testimony. But even so, it certainly is not the case that the burden would be placed on the party who will be testifying to make an affirmative showing that that party was not responsible for the disappearance.

Question: Poole sued Darrel for unlawfully using Poole's idea for an animal robot as a character in Darrel's science fiction movie. Darrel admitted that he had received a model of an animal robot from Poole, but he denied that it had any substantial similarity to the movie character. After the model had been returned to Poole, Poole destroyed it.

In order for Poole to testify to the appearance of the model, Poole

(A) must show that he did not destroy the model in bad faith.

(B) must give advance notice of his intent to introduce the oral testimony.

(C) must introduce a photograph of the model if one exists.

(D) need do none of the above, because the "best evidence rule" applies only to writings, recordings, and photographs.

[Q2012]

Answer: Choice **(D)** is correct. Under FRE 1002, the best evidence rule applies only to writings recordings, and photographs. Since the Best Evidence Rule doesn't apply to models, the original model need not be produced and Poole may testify to its appearance without adhering to any of the requirements laid out in Choices (A), (B), and (C).

C. **Proving the contents:**

2. **Incidental record:**

b. **Photo, recordings, etc.:**

Question: At a trial of a contract dispute, the plaintiff offered to testify to what the defendant said in a private conversation between the two of them, which the plaintiff had secretly recorded on an audiotape that she did not offer in evidence.

Is the plaintiff's testimony admissible?

(A) Yes, because the plaintiff has personal knowledge of the statement of a party-opponent.

(B) Yes, because the original document rule does not apply to audiotapes.

(C) No, because the statement must be proved by introduction of the audiotape itself.

(D) No, because of the plaintiff's deception, even if the recording was not illegal.

[QA034]

Answer: Choice **(A)** is correct. The witness is recounting an out-of-court statement and is offering that statement, it appears, to prove the truth of the contents of that statement; so it meets the hearsay definition of FRE 801(c). Nevertheless, it is not hearsay because the declarant was a party to the case, and this admission is being offered against the declarant party. Consequently, it meets the requirements of a party admission set forth in FRE 801(d)(2)(A).

There is no Best Evidence Rule (*a/k/a* original document rule) problem here caused by the fact that the witness is testifying to the contents of a statement that also happen to be contained in a recording without offering the recording itself. FRE 1002, which codifies the Best Evidence Rule, only requires introduction of an available original of a writing or recording when the witness is attempting to testify *as to the contents of that writing or recording*. Had the witness testified that she had only learned of the defendant's statements by listening to an audiotape, and stated that "on the tape the defendant said X", this *would* invoke FRE 1002. But the witness is testifying from her personal knowledge of what the defendant said and is not making any reference to the fact of the recording. The collateral fact that an audiotape also exists that contains that conversation does not invoke FRE 1002. And the fact that introduction of the recording might be "better evidence" of what the defendant actually said is irrelevant, since FRE 1002 does not require offering the best evidence of a proposition.

(B) is wrong because it gives the wrong reason for the correct result. The original document rule, FRE 1002, applies to writings, *recordings*, and photographs. (Instead, the reason the original document rule doesn't apply here is because the plaintiff will testify to what she heard directly from the defendant, not about what she heard on the audiotape. Therefore, she would not be attempting to prove the contents of the audiotape, making the original document rule inapplicable.)

(C) is wrong because FRE 1002 requires a recording to be introduced only when its contents are being proved. Here the plaintiff is offering to testify about what she heard directly from the defendant, not about what she heard on the audiotape. The fact that an audiotape was contemporaneously made does not mean that the tape has to be produced, since the plaintiff has independent knowledge of what the defendant said. If the problem were changed so that the plaintiff only learned of the defendant's statements by listening to an audiotape, then the audiotape would have to be produced.

(D) is wrong because there is no rule automatically barring evidence obtained by deception. Moreover, the evidence obtained by deception (the secretly recorded audiotape) was not in fact offered. Some state and federal statutes do regulate secret recordings of conversations, and violation of such statutes sometimes means that recordings obtained in violation thereof must be excluded. But the recording was not offered in evidence in this problem — only the statements made by the defendant were offered, and they would be admissible irrespective of whether a contemporaneous recording was made.

Question: Defendant is on trial for extorting $10,000 from Victim. An issue is the identification of the person who made a telephone call to Victim. Victim is prepared to testify that the caller had a distinctive accent like Defendant's, but that he cannot positively identify the voice as Defendant's. Victim recorded the call but has not brought the tape to court, although its existence is known to Defendant.

Victim's testimony is

(A) inadmissible, because Victim cannot sufficiently identify the caller.

(B) inadmissible, because the tape recording of the conversation is the best evidence.

(C) admissible, because Defendant waived the "best evidence" rule by failing to subpoena the tape.

(D) admissible, because Victim's lack of certainty goes to the weight to be given Victim's testimony, not to its admissibility.

[Q3110]

Answer: Choice **(B)** is **incorrect**, because the Best Evidence Rule (B.E.R.) does not apply here. The B.E.R. states that if the terms of a writing or a recording are to be proved, the original must be produced. The Rule does not apply to events that have by happenstance been recorded — it applies only where the *terms of the recording, per se, are what are being sought to be proved.* See FRE 1002 (making the rule applicable "to prove the content of a writing, recording, or photograph[.]") Here, the extortion happened in a live phone call. The prosecution is proving the contents of that live phone call. The fact that Victim happened to have made a tape of the call, therefore, does not mean that the prosecution is attempting to "prove the contents" of this incidentally-created tape. So the B.E.R. doesn't apply. (It would be different if the extortion occurred when someone sent a threatening tape to Victim — then the recording *would* be subject to the B.E.R., because the prosecution's case would require it to show what the contents of the tape were.) (The correct answer is (D). See *supra*, p. 93.)

Question: A plaintiff sued a defendant for wrongful death arising out of a traffic collision between the plaintiff's decedent and the defendant. At trial, the investigating traffic officer authenticated a tape recording of her shift-end dictation of comments used in preparing the written report of her factual findings. She testified that the tape recording was accurate when made and that she currently had no clear memory of the details of the investigation.

Is the tape recording admissible as evidence?

(A) Yes, under the past recollection recorded exception to the hearsay rule.

(B) Yes, under the public records exception to the hearsay rule.

(C) No, because it is hearsay and is a police report being offered against the defendant in a wrongful death case.

(D) No, because the police report itself is the best evidence.

[QA048]

Answer: Choice **(D)** is **incorrect** because the tape recording was made prior to the written report and was used as a basis for the written report. The recording is not being offered to prove the content of the written report, so its admission does not violate the best evidence/original document rule of FRE 1002. (If the officer gave courtroom testimony that the previous day, she had listened to the recording and here is what it said, then this testimony *would* violate the original document rule of FRE 1002, because the recording itself would have to be offered as the best evidence of what the recording's contents were.)

The correct choice is (A), admissible as past recollection recorded; see *supra*, p. 68.

E. Duplicates:

1. Federal:

a. "Duplicate" defined:

Question: Plaintiff Construction Co. sued Defendant Development Co. for money owed on a cost-plus contract that required notice of proposed expenditures beyond original estimates.

Defendant asserted that it never received the required notice. At trial Plaintiff calls its general manager, Witness, to testify that it is Plaintiff's routine practice to send cost overrun notices as required by the contract. Witness also offers a photocopy of the cost overrun notice letter to Defendant on which Plaintiff is relying, and which he has taken from Plaintiff's regular business files.

On the issue of giving notice, the letter copy is

(A) admissible, though hearsay, under the business record exception.

(B) admissible, because of the routine practices of the company.

(C) inadmissible, because it is hearsay not within any exception.

(D) inadmissible, because it is not the best evidence of the notice.

[Q3077]

Answer: Choice **(D)** is **incorrect**, because even though the Best Evidence Rule applies, the duplicate copy is admissible. FRE 1002's version of the Best Evidence Rule (called "Requirement of Original"), says that in proving the terms of a writing, the original writing must ordinarily be produced. So on the face of this rule, since the contents of the letter are being proved, FRE 1002 seems to require use of the original. But FRE 1003 says that "A *duplicate is admissible* to the same extent as an original unless (1) a genuine question is raised as to the authenticity of the original or (2) in the circumstances it would be unfair to admit the duplicate in lieu of the original." Since Defendant has not raised a genuine question about the authenticity of the original, and since it would be not be unfair to admit the duplicate (Plaintiff obviously couldn't possess the original any more if its story of having sent it to Defendant is true), FRE 1003 allows use of the copy here. (The correct answer is (B); see *supra*, p. 23.)

IV. SUMMARIES OF VOLUMINOUS WRITINGS

A. **Summaries generally:**

Question: A lawyer worked steadily on a case for a client over five-year period, with the billing agreed to be on particular amount charge per hour worked. The lawyer kept regular timesheets showing, for any day on which he worked on the matter, how long he worked and which of various activities (phone calls, letter-writing, etc.) he performed on that day. In the lawyer's suit against the client for non-payment, the lawyer did not offer into evidence the actual timesheets. Instead, in preparation for trial, the lawyer used the timesheets to create a summary showing, for each week, how much time the lawyer spent on each of the activity types. Then, at trial, the lawyer offered these weekly summaries, together with his testimony about how he had prepared them. If the client properly objects, the judge should hold that the summaries are

(A) inadmissible for any purpose, because the underlying timesheets from which they were prepared were not offered into evidence.

(B) inadmissible as substantive evidence, but usable as non-admitted materials to refresh the lawyer's present recollection.

(C) admissible as substantive evidence of hours worked, if the underlying timesheets were made available to the client prior to trial.

(D) admissible as substantive evidence only if the underlying timesheets were lost through no fault of the lawyer.

[Q6002]

Answer: Choice **(C)** is correct. FRE 1006 says that "the contents of voluminous writings, recordings or photographs which cannot conveniently be examined in court may be presented in the form of a chart, summary, or calculation." The individual timesheets here meet the "voluminous writings" standard, since they would be almost daily over a five-year timeframe, a stack that would be hard for the judge or jury to examine in court. FRE 1006 also says that "the originals, or duplicates, shall be made available for examination or copying, or both, by other parties at reasonable time and place." So the fact that the underlying timesheets were made available to the client prior to trial, as specified in this choice, is a necessary condition for the summaries' admission under FRE 1006. By the way, the summaries: (1) become evidence (i.e., they're not just non-evidentiary testimonial aids); and (2) substitute for the underlying originals, which means that those originals must be independently admissible. Here, the underlying timesheets are hearsay, but they fall within FRE 803(6)'s business records exception.

(A) is wrong because the summary-of-voluminous-writings provision of FRE 1006 applies as described in Choice (C) above, and that provision does not require that the underlying writings being summarized be offered into evidence (although they may be).

(B) is wrong because, under FRE 1006, the summaries can come in as substantive evidence, as described in Choice (C) above.

(D) is wrong because the summaries can come in under FRE 1006 even if the underlying timesheets have not been lost. If you picked this choice, you may be thinking of FRE 1004(1), under which the B.E.R. can be satisfied by something other than the original writing or a duplicate thereof (e.g., a summary) if "all originals are lost or have been destroyed, unless the proponent lost or destroyed them in bad faith[.]" But FRE 1006 provides an independent means of getting summaries into evidence (one that does not depend on loss of originals), and that means 1006 is available here as discussed in Choice (C) above.

CHAPTER 9

OPINIONS, EXPERTS, AND SCIENTIFIC EVIDENCE

I. FIRST-HAND KNOWLEDGE AND LAY OPINIONS

A. First-hand knowledge required:

3. *No requirement that evidence not be "speculative":*

Question: In a suit based on a will, inheritance of $1 million depended upon whether the wife had survived her husband when both died in the crash of a small airplane. An applicable statute provided that, for purposes of distributing an estate after a common disaster, there was a rebuttable presumption that neither spouse had survived the other. A witness was called to testify that as she approached the plane she heard what she thought was a woman's voice saying, "I'm dying," although by the time the two occupants were removed from the wreckage they were both dead.

Is the witness's testimony admissible?

(A) No, because the matter is governed by the presumption that neither spouse survived the other.

(B) No, because the witness's testimony is too speculative to support a finding.

(C) Yes, because the hearsay rule does not apply to statements by decedents in actions to determine rights under a will.

(D) Yes, because it is relevant and not otherwise prohibited.

[QA001]

Answer: (B) is **incorrect**, because the testimony is not "too speculative." A witness need not be absolutely certain of matters about which the witness testifies. Here the testimony is based on the perception and memory of a lay witness, and thus satisfies the FRE 701 standard that the testimony be "(a) rationally based on the perception of the witness, and (b) helpful to a clear understanding of the witness's testimony or the determination of a fact in issue." (The correct answer is (D). For analysis of all the choices, see *supra*, p. 48.)

C. Opinion on "ultimate issue":

Question: On trial for murdering her husband, Defendant testified she acted in self-defense. Defendant calls Expert, a psychologist, to testify that under hypnosis Defendant had described the killing, and that in Expert's opinion Defendant had been in fear for her life at the time of the killing.

Is Expert's testimony admissible?

(A) Yes, because Expert was able to ascertain that Defendant was speaking truthfully.

(B) Yes, because it reports a prior consistent statement by a witness (Defendant) subject to examination concerning it.

(C) No, because reliance on information tainted by hypnosis is unconstitutional.

(D) No, because it expresses an opinion concerning Defendant's mental state at the time of the killing.

[Q3095]

Answer: Choice **(D)** is correct. FRE 704(b) says that "No expert witness testifying with respect to the mental state or condition of a defendant in a criminal case may state an opinion or inference as to whether the defendant did or did not have the mental state or condition constituting an element of the crime charged or of a defense thereto. Such ultimate issues are matters for the trier of fact alone." The proposed testimony here — that Defendant had the mental state required for a defense (the defense of self-defense) — falls squarely within this prohibition.

(A) is wrong because the statement is not admissible, whether or not Expert believed that Defendant was speaking truthfully. As described in Choice (D) above, FRE 704(b) bars the proposed testimony. Additionally, the vast majority of courts have rejected the admission of statements made under hypnosis. This is true whether the statement is offered as substantive evidence or for its bearing on the credibility of the witness's live testimony at trial.

(B) is wrong because, as described in Choice (D), the statement is expressly barred by FRE 704(b). If it weren't barred by 704(b), it might well be admissible under FRE 801(d)(1)(B), which defines as non-hearsay, and thus allows, prior statements by a witness, where "The declarant testifies at the trial or hearing and is subject to cross-examination concerning the statement, and the statement is ... (B) consistent with the declarant's testimony and is offered to rebut an express or implied charge against the declarant of recent fabrication or improper influence or motive..." It's not clear from the facts here that the prosecution is making an "express or implied charge" that Defendant has "recently fabricated" her assertion that she acted in fear for her life, but if the court were convinced that there was such a charge, and if FRE 704(b) didn't intervene, the statement here would be admissible under 801(d)(1)(B).

(C) is wrong because use of the hypnosis-induced out-of-court statement by Defendant would not violate his constitutional rights. If hypnosis-induced testimony were introduced *against* a criminal defendant, this usage might conceivably violate the defendant's criminal rights. (If the statement were induced from a third-party witness who was not available for cross-examination at trial, for instance, use of the testimony might violate the defendant's Confrontation Clause rights.) But use by a criminal defendant could never violate the constitution — whose rights would be violated? (The state itself, in the form of the prosecution, does not have "constitutional rights" vis-à-vis the defendant.)

II. EXPERT WITNESSES

B. Illustration:

Question: The plaintiff sued the defendant for personal injuries suffered in a train-automobile collision. The plaintiff called an eyewitness, who testified that the train was going 20 miles per hour. The defendant then offered the testimony of an experienced police accident investigator who described his extensive training and experience in examining high-speed accidents including ones involving trains. The investigator explained that he examined the physical evidence, including the types of damage inflicted on the metal structure of the car, and that such physical evidence is typically relied upon by investigators trying to determine the speed at which a collision occurred. The investigator then stated that it was his opinion that the train was going between 5 and 10 miles per hour at the moment of the collision.

This testimony by the investigator is

(A) improper, because there cannot be both lay and expert opinion on the same issue.

(B) improper, because the investigator is unable to establish the speed with a sufficient degree of scientific certainty.

(C) proper, because the investigator has demonstrated sufficient expertise to express an opinion on speed.

(D) proper, because the plaintiff first introduced opinion evidence as to speed.

[Q3117]

Answer: Choice **(C)** is correct. FRE 702 imposes five requirements that expert testimony must meet in order to be admissible: (1) it must be the case that *scientific, technical, or other specialized knowledge* will *assist* the trier of fact to *understand the evidence or to determine a fact in issue*; (2) the witness must be qualified as an expert by *knowledge, skill, experience, training, or education*; (3) the testimony must be *based upon sufficient facts or data*; (4) the testimony must be the *product of reliable principles and methods*; and (5) the witness must have *applied these principles and methods reliably to the facts of the case*. The proposed testimony by the investigator meets these requirements: (1) The investigator's testimony about the speed of the train will help the trier of fact to understand the evidence in the case. (2) The facts state that the police accident investigator is experienced and has received training. (3) The investigator's testimony is based on his examination of the physical evidence, and he has stipulated that these types of physical data are the ones examined in such matters. (4) There is no indication that the investigator's methodology is not the product of reliable principles and methods. (5) The investigator made his conclusion about the train's speed after applying his training and experience to the physical evidence of the case. Having satisfied all five requirements, the accident investigator's testimony is proper and admissible.

(A) is wrong because there is simply no principle that says that "there cannot be both lay and expert opinion on the same issue." (For instance, it is perfectly proper for one side to put on lay eyewitness opinion testimony about the approximate speed of the train, and for the other to put on expert scientific opinion on the same subject.)

(B) is wrong because there is no principle that scientific or other expert testimony must reach its conclusion with any particular degree of "scientific certainty." All that is required is that the conclusion be sufficiently "reliable." For the reasons discussed in Choice (C), this reliability standard is satisfied here. To the extent that this choice is referring to the fact that the investigator is testifying merely that the speed falls within a range, instead of giving a single number, the existence of a range does not pose a problem. (Indeed, use of a range is probably more, not less, reliable, since it's less likely to give a false impression of precision.)

(D) is wrong because the only requirements for expert testimony are those discussed in the analysis of Choice (C) above. There is no requirement that the other side have first introduced some sort of opinion evidence on the issue.

C. **Basis for expert's opinion:**

1. **Inadmissible evidence:**

    b. **Proponent and expert can't disclose:**

    Question: A plaintiff sued her employer, alleging that poor working conditions had caused her to develop a stomach ulcer. At trial, the plaintiff's medical expert testified to the cause of the plaintiff's ulcer and stated that his opinion was based in part on information in a letter the plaintiff's personal physician had written to the plaintiff's employer, explaining why the plaintiff had missed work.

    When offered to prove the cause of the plaintiff's condition, is the letter from the plaintiff's doctor admissible?

    (A) No, because it is hearsay not within any exception.

    (B) No, because the plaintiff's physician is not shown to be unavailable.

    (C) Yes, because it was relied upon by the plaintiff's medical expert.

    (D) Yes, under the business records exception to the hearsay rule.

    [Q7100]

    Answer: Choice **(A)** is correct. The doctor's letter is not a business record under FRE 803(6), because it was not prepared in the ordinary course of regularly conducted activity. In addition, it cannot be admitted simply because an expert relies upon it. Rule 703 does allow an expert to rely on hearsay (or other otherwise-inadmissible evidence) in reaching a conclusion, so long as other experts in the field would reasonably rely on such information. But the rule distinguishes between expert reliance on the hearsay and admitting the hearsay at trial for the jury to consider. Generally speaking, hearsay will not be admissible when offered only because the expert relied upon it — FRE 703 says that "Facts or data that are otherwise inadmissible *shall not be disclosed to the jury* by the proponent of the opinion or inference unless the court determines that their probative value in assisting the jury to evaluate the expert's opinion *substantially outweighs* their prejudicial effect." Here, that strict balancing test is not met, since the expert's opinion is not so hard to understand, and the substantive point on which the letter is being offered is the ultimate point in the case. There is no other exception that appears even close to being applicable (and none is listed in the possible answers), so the letter is inadmissible hearsay.

(B) is wrong because this fact would only be relevant if the hearsay were offered under FRE 804 as one of the "unavailability-dependent" exceptions to the hearsay rule. None of those exceptions are pertinent here. Furthermore, if the hearsay qualified as a hearsay exception under Rule 803 (e.g., if it were a business record), then the doctor's availability would be completely irrelevant, because unavailability need not be shown for those exceptions. But the letter does not qualify under any of the Rule 803 exceptions. In particular, it is not a business record because it was not prepared in the ordinary course of regularly conducted activity.

(C) is wrong because the letter is hearsay if offered to prove that the plaintiff's condition was as indicated in the letter, and the expert's reliance on it doesn't overcome this problem. FRE 703 does allow an expert to rely on hearsay in reaching a conclusion, so long as other experts in the field would reasonably rely on such information. But Rule 703 distinguishes between expert reliance on the hearsay and admitting the hearsay at trial for the jury to consider. As discussed in Choice (A), the expert reliance here does not overcome the general rule that hearsay or other otherwise-inadmissible evidence will not be admissible when offered only because the expert relied upon it.

(D) is wrong because the doctor's letter clearly does not qualify under FRE 803(6) as a business record. It is not a medical record prepared in the ordinary course of regularly conducted activity. Rather, it is a letter written by the doctor on an ad hoc occasion. Thus, the letter lacks the earmarks of regularity and reliability that are critical for admissibility under the business records exception to the hearsay rule.

Question: Phillips purchased a suit of thermal underwear manufactured by Makorp from synthetic materials. While he was attempting to stamp out a fire, Phillips's thermal underwear caught fire and burned in a melting fashion up to his waist. He suffered a heart attack a half hour later. In a suit against Makorp, Phillips alleged that negligence and breach of warranty caused both the burn and the heart attack. Phillips testified to the foregoing.

Dr. Jones, a physician, having listened to Phillips's testimony, is called by Phillips and asked whether, assuming the truth of such testimony, Phillips's subsequent heart attack could have resulted from the burns. His opinion is

(A) admissible as a response to a hypothetical question.

(B) admissible because the physician's expertise enables him to judge the credibility of Phillips's testimony.

(C) inadmissible, because a hypothetical question may not be based on prior testimony.

(D) inadmissible, because an expert's opinion may not be based solely on information provided by lay persons.

[Q8079]

Answer: Choice **(A)** is the best response because it correctly identifies that the testimony here is admissible as a response to a hypothetical question. Expert testimony is appropriate where the court determines that "scientific, technical, or other specialized knowledge will assist the trier of fact to understand the evidence or to determine a fact in issue." FRE 702. Here, physician's testimony will address the causation issue — whether or not flaming underwear could cause a heart attack. Physician's status as an expert entitles him to offer opinion evidence that would be inadmissible coming from a lay witness, and to rely on information unavailable to a lay witness. The related issue is whether Physician may rely on the testimony presented at trial. The answer is yes: FRE 703 says that "The facts or data in the particular case upon which an expert bases an opinion ... may be those perceived by or *made known to the expert at* or before the hearing." So data supplied "at" the hearing — whether in the form of testimony of other witnesses or a hypothetical posed by the questioner (here, it's a combination of both) — may be the basis for the expert opinion.

(B) is wrong because Jones's status as a physician wouldn't give him expert status in determining credibility. As a threshold matter, credibility itself is not a "fact," and expert testimony is only available to assist the trier of fact to understand evidence or to determine a fact in issue. FRE 702. Beyond that, a physician's expertise gives him the ability to offer opinion testimony on medical matters; it's irrelevant to assessing the credibility of testimony, since one's status as a doctor doesn't make him a better judge of witness credibility than anyone else.

(C) is wrong because it states an incorrect rule. FRE 703 says that "The facts or data in the particular case upon which an expert bases an opinion ... may be those perceived by or *made known to the expert at* or before the hearing." This language allows the expert to offer an opinion based on the "data" included in a hypothetical question. And the hypothetical question for this purpose can be based on prior trial testimony and on the assumption that that prior testimony is truthful. (That's in fact a very common way for a proponent of expert testimony to proceed.)

(D) is wrong because it states an incorrect rule. An expert may base her opinion on "[t]he facts or data ... made known to the expert at or before the hearing." FRE 703. Neither this nor any other provision prevents the expert from basing her opinion solely on information provided by lay persons.

CHAPTER 10
BURDENS OF PROOF, PRESUMPTIONS, AND OTHER PROCEDURAL ISSUES

II. PRESUMPTIONS

B. **Effect of presumptions in federal civil cases:**

1. **How this works:**

    Question: In a suit based on a will, inheritance of $1 million depended upon whether the wife had survived her husband when both died in the crash of a small airplane. An applicable statute provided that, for purposes of distributing an estate after a common disaster, there was a rebuttable presumption that neither spouse had survived the other. A witness was called to testify that as she approached the plane she heard what she thought was a woman's voice saying, "I'm dying," although by the time the two occupants were removed from the wreckage they were both dead.

    Is the witness's testimony admissible?

    (A) No, because the matter is governed by the presumption that neither spouse survived the other.

    (B) No, because the witness's testimony is too speculative to support a finding.

    (C) Yes, because the hearsay rule does not apply to statements by decedents in actions to determine rights under a will.

    (D) Yes, because it is relevant and not otherwise prohibited.

    [QA001]

Answer: Choice **(A)** is **incorrect**, because the witness's testimony is admissibility to rebut the existence of the presumed fact. Under the majority common law "bursting bubble" rule, which is followed by FRE 301, a presumption disappears when sufficient counterproof is offered about the presumed fact. Here the testimony of the witness, although not conclusive, is sufficient to rebut the presumption that neither spouse survived the other and to support a jury finding that the wife outlived the husband. Following the witness's testimony, the party who originally had the burden of persuasion on the survival issue (whichever party that was) still had that burden, as if the presumption had never existed. In any event, regardless of how (or even whether) the bursting bubble rule applies, the witness's testimony would be admissible — in all jurisdictions, the party who does not benefit from a presumption is always entitled to submit otherwise-competent evidence rebutting the existence of the presumed fact. (The correct answer is (D); see *supra*, p. 48.)

a. **Instructions to jury:**

Question: In litigation on a federal claim, Plaintiff had the burden of proving that Defendant received a notice. Plaintiff relied on the presumption of receipt by offering evidence that time notice was addressed to Defendant, properly stamped, and mailed. Defendant, on the other hand, testified that she never received the notice.

Which of the following is correct?

(A) The jury must find that the notice was received.

(B) The jury may find that the notice was received.

(C) The burden shifts to Defendant to persuade the jury of nonreceipt.

(D) The jury must find that the notice was not received, because the presumption has been rebutted and there is uncontradicted evidence of nonreceipt.

[Q1091]

Answer: Choice **(B)** is correct. Under FRE 301, once the opponent of the presumption comes up with enough evidence of the presumed fact's non-existence that a jury could reasonably find that the presumed fact does not exist, the presumption disappears from the case in the sense that there is no effect on the burden of persuasion. When this happens, the court may instruct the jury that it *may* infer the existence of the presumed fact from proof of the basic fact, but the jury is not required to so infer. In this case, Defendant's testimony, "I never got the notice," is enough to entitle a reasonable jury to find that the presumed fact (receipt) does not exist. Therefore, the presumption of receipt has disappeared and the plaintiff still has the burden of persuasion regarding the issue of receipt of the notice. But notwithstanding the disappearance of the presumption, the jury is still entitled to conclude that notice was received from proof of the basic fact that notice was given. Therefore, this choice is accurate in saying that the jury may infer, but is not required to infer, that the notice was received.

(A) is wrong because, as noted in the explanation of (B), once the presumption disappears from the case, the court may instruct the jury that it *may* infer the existence of the presumed fact from proof of the basic facts, but it is *not required* that the jury do so.

(C) is wrong because, as explained in (B), the presumption has no effect on the burden of persuasion; it "remains throughout the trial upon the party on whom it was originally cast" (FRE 301) which, in this case, is the plaintiff.

(D) is wrong because, as discussed in (B), the jury may infer the existence of the presumed fact from proof of the basic fact (i.e., jury may find that the notice was received) even though the presumption has disappeared from the case.

III. JUDGE-JURY ALLOCATION

B. Issues of fact:

1. Technical exclusionary rule:

   a. Rules of evidence not binding:

   Question: A pedestrian died from injuries caused when a driver's car struck him. The executor of the pedestrian's estate sued the driver for wrongful death. At trial, the executor calls a nurse to testify that two days after the accident, the pedestrian said to the nurse, "The car that hit me ran the red light." Fifteen minutes thereafter, the pedestrian died.

   As a foundation for introducing evidence of the pedestrian's statement, the executor offers to the court a doctor's affidavit that the doctor was the intern on duty the day of the pedestrian's death and that several times that day the pedestrian had said that he knew he was about to die.

   Is the affidavit properly considered by the court in ruling on the admissibility of the pedestrian's statement?

   (A) No, because it is hearsay not within any exception.

   (B) No, because it is irrelevant since dying declarations cannot be used except in prosecutions for homicide.

   (C) Yes, because though hearsay, it is a statement of then-existing mental condition.

   (D) Yes, because the judge may consider hearsay in ruling on preliminary questions.

   [Q3147]

   Answer: Choice **(D)** is correct. FRE 104(a) says that "Preliminary questions concerning ... the admissibility of evidence shall be determined by the court.... In making its determination it is *not bound by the rules of evidence* except those with respect to privileges." The pedestrian's statement to the nurse is admissible if, and only if, the statement qualified for the dying-declaration exception. That exception requires that the declarant knew or believed that he was about to die. The affidavit is relevant to that issue. It's true that the affidavit is hearsay (it's an out-of-court statement offered to prove the truth of the matter asserted, i.e., that the pedestrian really knew or believed he was dying). And this hearsay does not fall within any exception. But under 104(a), the judge may consider this inadmissible hearsay in making her preliminary ruling on the admissibility of the pedestrian's statement to the nurse.

   (A) is wrong because even though the affidavit is hearsay not within any exception, it may still be considered on the preliminary matter of the admissibility of the statement to the nurse. As described in Choice (D) above, the fact that the affidavit is hearsay not within any exception does not prevent the court from using it to resolve a preliminary question about the admissibility of other evidence.

   (B) is wrong because (1) dying declarations are admissible in civil cases; and (2) the admissibility of the affidavit is irrelevant to whether it can be considered on the preliminary question here. First, FRE 804(b)(2) gives a hearsay exception for, "In a prosecution for homicide *or in a civil action or proceeding*, a statement made by a declarant while believing that the declarant's death was imminent, concerning the cause or circumstances of what the declarant believed to be impending death." So the proposition asserted in Choice (B) — that dying declarations can't be used except in homicide prosecutions — is simply incorrect as a matter of law. Furthermore, even if this statement of law were true, it would be irrelevant — as described in the discussion of Choice (D) above, the judge may consider inadmissible material in ruling on an evidentiary question.

(C) is wrong because (1) the affidavit is the "outer level" of a two-level hearsay statement, and that outer level doesn't qualify for the then-existing-state-of-mind exception; and (2) the affidavit's admissibility doesn't matter here anyway. First, notice that we have hearsay-within-hearsay. The "outer" level is the doctor's affidavit (a statement made out of court, repeating some other statement). The "inner" level is the pedestrian's statement to the doctor. Each must satisfy a hearsay exception. It's true that the inner statement arguably qualifies for the then-existing-state-of-mind exception (though even this is far from clear, since under FRE 803(3) "A statement of ... belief to prove the fact ... believed" does not qualify for the exception.) But the *outer* statement is not a statement about *the declarant's* then-existing state of mind — for this purpose, the declarant is the doctor, and he's not summarizing his own then-existing state of mind (except insofar as he's making a statement of what he currently remembers the pedestrian to have said, which is inadmissible since FRE 803(3) denies the state-of-mind exception for "a statement of memory ... to prove the fact remembered"). Since one of the two levels is inadmissible hearsay, the entire statement-within-a-statement is inadmissible. Nonetheless, as described in Choice (D) above, the statement need not be admissible to be considered by the judge in making a preliminary admissibility ruling.

Question: In a prosecution of Drew for forgery, the defense objects to the testimony of West, a government expert, on the ground of inadequate qualifications. The government seeks to introduce a letter from the expert's former criminology professor, stating that West is generally acknowledged in his field as well qualified.

On the issue of the expert's qualifications, the letter may be considered by

(A) the jury, without regard to the hearsay rule.

(B) the judge, without regard to the hearsay rule.

(C) neither the judge nor the jury, because it is hearsay not within any exception.

(D) both the judge and the jury, because the letter is not offered for a hearsay purpose.
[Q2015]

Answer: Choice **(B)** is correct. Questions of whether a person is qualified to be a witness (whether expert or lay) are to be decided by the judge. In doing so, the judge may take into account inadmissible evidence (except with respect to privileges). FRE 104(a).

(A), (C), and (D) are wrong because each is inconsistent with the above explanation.

Question: In a prosecution of the defendant for murder, the government seeks to introduce a properly authenticated note written by the victim that reads: "[the defendant] did it." In laying the foundation for admitting the note as a dying declaration, the prosecution offered an affidavit from the attending physician that the victim knew she was about to die when she wrote the note.

The admissibility of the note as a dying declaration is

(A) a preliminary fact question for the judge, and the judge must not consider the affidavit.

(B) a preliminary fact question for the judge, and the judge may properly consider the affidavit.

(C) a question of weight and credibility for the jury, and the jury must not consider the affidavit.

(D) a question of weight and credibility for the jury, and the jury may properly consider the affidavit.

[Q1005]

Answer: Choice **(B)** is correct. Both parts of this answer are true. As to the first part, before a declaration can be found to be an admissible "dying declaration," some preliminary questions of fact must be answered. In particular, it must be determined whether the declarant was indeed aware of her impending death. Under the FRE, the jury decides issues like this, of conditional relevance, but it is the judge who makes the initial decision of admissibility, in determining whether a reasonable jury could find that the preliminary fact exists: "When the relevancy of evidence depends upon the fulfillment of a condition of fact, the court shall admit it upon, or subject to, the introduction of evidence sufficient to support a finding of the fulfillment of the condition." FRE 104(b). In other words, if the judge decides that there is enough evidence that a jury could reasonably find that there was an awareness of impending death, he will let the jury hear the declaration (even though he may personally believe that it is less likely than not that there was such awareness).

As to the second part, the judge's ability to consider the affidavit, FRE 104(a) says that "Preliminary questions concerning … the admissibility of evidence shall be determined by the court… In making its determination it is not bound by the rules of evidence except those with respect to privileges." The affidavit is relevant to the issue of whether the declarant was aware of her impending death. It's true that the affidavit is hearsay (it's an out-of-court statement offered to prove the truth of the matter asserted, i.e., that the victim knew or believed she was dying). And this hearsay does not fall within any exception. But under 104(a), the court may consider this inadmissible hearsay to make his preliminary ruling on the admissibility of the note.

(A) is wrong because, although it correctly states that the admissibility of the note is a preliminary fact question for the judge, it incorrectly states that the judge must not consider the affidavit. As described in the discussion of Choice (B) above, the judge may consider inadmissible hearsay when resolving a preliminary question about the admissibility of other evidence.

(C) is wrong because, although it is true that the jury must not consider the affidavit, the admissibility of the note is not a question for the jury. It will be up to the jury to determine what weight and credibility to give the evidence of the note once it has been admitted.

(D) is wrong because the jury cannot consider the affidavit (it is hearsay) and also because the admissibility of the note is not a question for the jury. It will be up to the jury to determine what weight and credibility to give the evidence of the note once it has been admitted.

CHAPTER 11

JUDICIAL NOTICE

II. ADJUDICATIVE FACTS

A. **General rule:**

2. **Immediate verification:**

a. **"Cannot reasonably be questioned" is tough standard:**

Question: In a federal civil trial, the plaintiff wishes to establish that, in a state court, the defendant had been convicted of fraud, a fact that the defendant denies.

Which mode of proof of the conviction is LEAST likely to be permitted?

(A) A certified copy of the judgment of conviction, offered as a self-authenticating document.

(B) Testimony of the plaintiff, who was present at the time of the sentence.

(C) Testimony by a witness to whom the defendant made an oral admission that he had been convicted.

(D) Judicial notice of the conviction, based on the court's telephone call to the clerk of the state court, whom the judge knows personally.

[Q3167]

Answer: Choice **(D)** is correct. FRE 201(b) allows judicial notice of a fact that is "not subject to reasonable dispute" because it is either "(1) generally known within the territorial jurisdiction of the trial court" or "(2) capable of accurate and ready determination by resort to *sources whose accuracy cannot reasonably be questioned*." The fact here would be very unlikely to fall within category (1), since even the federal judge seems not to know it. So the only hope is category (2). The clerk of the state court might be a reasonably accurate source, but not a "source whose accuracy cannot reasonably be questioned." For instance, the clerk might be relying on a faulty memory, or might have some hidden motive to intentionally misstate the facts. In any event, the custom in most courts (including ones following FRE 201) is not to take judicial notice of the determinations of courts other than the court which is doing the noticing.

(A) is wrong because a certified copy would be permitted under FRE 902(4). FRE 902 lists a number of categories of documents that are self-authenticating. One of these is 902(4)'s category of "certified copies of public records," defined to include "a copy of an official record or report ... certified as correct by the custodian or other person authorized to make the certification." A certified copy of a record of conviction would clearly fall within this definition.

(B) is wrong because testimony of someone who heard the sentence be issued would be a good means of authentication. FRE 901(b) gives a number of illustrations of acceptable methods of authentication, i.e., of (in FRE 901(a)'s language) "evidence sufficient to support a finding that the matter in question is what its proponent claims." Since the claim is that there has been a conviction, authentication consists of evidence sufficient to find that the conviction really occurred. The first illustration given in FRE 901(b) is (1), "Testimony of witness with knowledge" — the text of (1) recognizes authentication by means of "testimony that a matter is what it is claimed to be." So here, the plaintiff's testimony, from his own personal knowledge, that a sentence of conviction was pronounced, will qualify.

(C) is wrong because the defendant's statement would be admissible as an admission. The testimony here is a classic admission by a party-opponent. Under FRE 801(d)(2), an out-of-court statement is admissible (as an exclusion to the hearsay rule) if it is "offered against a party and is (1) the party's own statement..." Since the "oral admission" by the defendant that he had been convicted is a statement by the defendant being offered against him, the testimony by the witness is admissible.

B. **Must take if requested, and may take without a request:**

2. **Discretionary notice:**

Question: In contract litigation between Pixley and Dill, a fact of consequence to the determination of the action is whether Pixley provided Dill with a required notice at Dill's branch office "in the state capital." Pixley introduced evidence that he gave notice at Dill's office in the city of Capitan. Although Capitan is the state's capital, Pixley failed to offer proof of that fact.

Which of the following statements is most clearly correct with respect to possible judicial notice of the fact that Capitan is the state's capital?

(A) The court may take judicial notice even though Pixley does not request it.

(B) The court may take judicial notice only if Pixley provides the court with an authenticated copy of the statute that designates Capitan as the capital.

(C) If the court takes judicial notice, the burden of persuasion on the issue of whether Capitan is the capital shifts to Dill.

(D) If the court takes judicial notice, it should instruct the jury that it may, but is not required to, accept as conclusive the fact that Capitan is the capital.

[Q2007]

Answer: Choice **(A)** is correct. First, the location of the state capital is a fact that is *"generally known"* within the relevant community. FRE 201(b). So the fact that Capitan is the capital is appropriate for judicial notice. Second, FRE 201(c) provides that "A court may take judicial notice, whether requested or not." So the court may take notice here without a request from either party.

(B) is wrong because judicial notice of an appropriate fact may be taken without submission of formal evidence that the fact is true.

(C) is wrong because, in a civil case, once there is judicial notice, the issue is decided and the jury does not weigh the evidence in order to come to its own conclusion. See FRE 201: the judge "shall instruct the jury to accept as conclusive any fact judicially noticed."

(D) is wrong because in a civil case the jury is required to accept as conclusive the judicially noticed fact, as discussed in (C).

C. Instructions, and jury's right to disregard:

2. Criminal:

a. On appeal:

Question: A defendant was charged in federal court with selling a controlled substance (heroin) in interstate commerce. At trial, the prosecutor introduced evidence that the defendant obtained the substance from a supplier in Kansas City and delivered it in Chicago. The defendant denied that the substance in question was heroin, but he introduced no contrary evidence on the issue of transportation.

Which of the following instructions regarding judicial notice may the judge legitimately give the jury?

(A) "If you find that the defendant obtained the drugs in Kansas City and delivered them to Chicago, I instruct you to find that the substance was sold in an interstate transaction."

(B) "If you find that the defendant obtained the drugs in Kansas City and delivered them to Chicago, then the burden of persuasion is on the defendant to establish that the transaction was not interstate."

(C) "If you find that the defendant obtained the drugs in Kansas City and delivered them to Chicago, then you may, but you are not required to, find that the transaction was interstate in nature."

(D) "I instruct you that there is a presumption that the substance was sold in an interstate transaction, but the burden of persuasion on that issue is still on the government."

[Q7049]

Answer: Choice **(C)** is correct. This instruction complies with FRE 201(g), which states that in a criminal case, "the court shall instruct the jury that it may, but is not required to, accept as conclusive any fact judicially noticed." In other words, a judicially-noticed fact in a criminal case allows the court to instruct on a permissible inference, but nothing more.

(A) is wrong because under FRE 201(g), a judge may not instruct a jury to find a fact in a criminal case, even if it is a fact that is subject to judicial notice. Such an instruction would violate the accused's Sixth Amendment right to a trial by jury on all elements of the crime. A judicially-noticed fact in a criminal case allows the court to instruct on a permissible inference, but nothing more.

(B) is wrong because the government has the burden of proving all elements of a crime beyond a reasonable doubt. Under FRE 201(g), a judicially-noticed fact in a criminal case cannot shift that constitutionally mandated burden of proof.

(D) is wrong because, under FRE 201(g), a judicially-noticed fact in a criminal case does not create a presumption. In civil cases, a judicially-noticed fact is conclusive; in a criminal case, because of the accused's constitutional right to trial by jury, the judicially-noticed fact can be brought to the attention of the jury, but the jury is free to reject it. Any instruction about a "presumption" is inappropriate in these circumstances — in a criminal case, the court may instruct on a permissible inference, but may not mention the idea of a presumption.

REAL PROPERTY

REAL PROPERTY Q&A BY TOPIC

Headings in this Q&A material are the same as in the *Steve Emanuel's Bootcamp for the MBE: Real Property* subject-matter outline, and are presented in the same order as in that outline. Therefore, to locate questions on any topic, check the topic in the subject-matter outline, then look under the same heading in this book. Some questions are reprinted multiple times; when that occurs, one version of the question usually includes a discussion of all four choices, whereas the other version(s) typically discuss just one particular wrong choice. Occasionally, in the interests of clarity we have chosen to use a heading here that was not present in the subject-matter outline; when that happens, we indicate this by putting the header in italics.

Questions from the Self-Assessment Test that is part of your materials are reprinted here in full, as are many questions that were not part of the Self-Assessment Test. Questions from the 200-Question Simulated MBE are not reprinted or referred to here (a book with the questions and answers to the Simulated MBE is also part of your materials).

References to "Stoebuck & Whitman" are to Stoebuck & Whitman, *The Law of Property* Hornbook (West, 2000). References to "Rest." and "Rest. 2d" are to the *First* and *Second Restatements of Property*, respectively. References to "Rest. 3d (Serv.)" and "Rest. 3d (Mort.)" are to the *Restatement Third of Property: Servitudes* and the *Restatement Third of Property: Mortgages*, respectively.

CHAPTER 1
ADVERSE POSSESSION

IV. "HOSTILE" POSSESSION

B. Boundary disputes:

Question: Twenty-five years ago a seller conveyed Lot 1 to a buyer by a warranty deed. The seller at that time also executed and delivered an instrument in the proper form of a deed, purporting to convey Lot 2 to the buyer. The seller thought she had title to Lot 2 but did not; therefore, no title passed by virtue of the Lot 2 deed. Lot 2 consisted of three acres of brushland adjoining the west boundary of Lot 1. The buyer has occasionally hunted rabbits on Lot 2, but less often than annually. No one else came onto Lot 2 except occasional rabbit hunters.

Twenty years ago, the buyer planted a row of evergreens in the vicinity of the opposite (east) boundary of Lot 1 and erected a fence just beyond the evergreens to the east. In fact both the trees and the fence were placed on Lot 3, owned by a neighbor, which bordered the east boundary of Lot 1. The buyer was unsure of the exact boundary, and placed the trees and the fence in order to establish his rights up to the fence. The fence is located ten feet within Lot 3.

Now, the buyer has had his property surveyed and the title checked and has learned the facts.

The period of time to acquire title by adverse possession in the jurisdiction is 15 years.

The buyer consulted his lawyer, who properly advised that, in an appropriate action, the buyer would probably obtain title to

(A) Lot 2 but not to the ten-foot strip of Lot 3.

(B) the ten-foot strip of Lot 3 but not to Lot 1.

(C) both Lot 2 and the ten-foot strip of Lot 3.

(D) neither Lot 2 nor the ten-foot strip of Lot 3.

[Q1063]

Answer: Choice **(B)** is correct. Courts generally hold that one who possesses an adjoining landowner's land, under the mistaken belief that he has only possessed up to the boundary of his own land, meets the requirement of "hostile" possession and can become an owner by adverse possession. This is especially likely where the possessor has both planted and fenced in the land in question, since such actions are very likely to bring home to the record owner that the possessor is asserting an adverse claim. So the buyer is highly likely to be found to have gained title to the 10-foot strip of Lot 3 by adverse possession. On the other hand, the buyer has not met the requirement for "continuous" possession of Lot 2. The requirement of "continuous" position does not mean that the possessor must be physically on the property 100% of the time. However, a court would almost certainly require more than the very occasional rabbit-hunting at issue here in order to conclude that the buyer had "continuously" occupied Lot 2.

(A), (C), and (D) are wrong because they are inconsistent with the above analysis.

2. **Family members, with one allowing the other to occupy:**

    Question: A man and a woman, who were cousins, acquired title in fee simple to a property, as equal tenants in common, by inheritance from their aunt. During the last 15 years of her lifetime, the aunt had allowed the man to occupy an apartment in the house on the property, to rent the other apartment in the house to various tenants, and to retain the rent. The man made no payments to the aunt, and since the aunt's death 7 years ago, he has made no payments to the woman (his cousin). For those 22 years, the man has paid the real estate taxes on the property, kept the building on the property insured, and maintained the building. At all times, the woman has lived in a distant city and has never had anything to do with the aunt, the man, or the property.

    Recently, the woman needed money for the operation of her business and demanded that the man join her in selling the property. The man refused.

    The period of time to acquire title by adverse possession in the jurisdiction is 10 years. There is no other applicable statute.

    The woman brought an appropriate action against the man for partition. The man asserted all available defenses and counterclaims.

    In that action, the court should

    (A) deny partition and find that title has vested in the man by adverse possession.

    (B) deny partition, confirm the tenancy in common, but require an accounting to determine if either the woman or the man is indebted to the other on account of the rental payment, taxes, insurance premiums, and maintenance costs.

    (C) grant partition and require, as an adjustment, an accounting to determine if either the man or the woman is indebted to the other on account of the rental payments, taxes, insurance premiums, and maintenance costs.

(D) grant partition to the woman and the man as equal owners, but without an accounting.

[Q3025]

Answer: Choice **(C)** is correct. Either co-tenant has the right, at any time, to demand partition. During the course of partition, the court will order an accounting, to determine whether either party owes the other money for rents collected, taxes paid, etc. It is not clear what substantive rules will govern that analysis — for instance, jurisdictions differ on whether a co-tenant who occupies the premises himself must account for the imputed value of rent received beyond his pro rata share. But the one thing that we can be sure of is that the court will require an accounting, and that's what this choice specifies.

(A) is wrong because the man never occupied the property in a "hostile" manner.

(B) is wrong because the court would grant partition, for the reason described in the discussion of (C).

(D) is wrong because a court would conduct an accounting to determine if either party has an obligation to pay money to the other.

V. CONTINUITY OF POSSESSION

A. **Continuity of possession:**

2. **Temporary or seasonal gaps in possession:**

    Question: Brown owned Blackacre, a tract of undeveloped land. Blackacre abuts Whiteacre, a tract of land owned by Agency, the state's governmental energy agency. At Whiteacre, Agency has operated a waste-to-electricity recycling facility for 12 years. Blackacre and Whiteacre are in a remote area and Whiteacre is the only developed parcel of real estate within a ten-mile radius. The boundary line between Blackacre and Whiteacre had never been surveyed or marked on the face of the earth.

    During the past 12 years, some of the trucks bringing waste to the Agency facility have dumped their loads so that the piles of waste extend from Whiteacre onto a portion of Blackacre. However, prior to the four-week period during each calendar year when the Agency facility is closed for inspection and repairs, the waste piles are reduced to minimal levels so that during each of the four-week closures no waste was, in fact, piled on Blackacre. Neither Brown nor any representative of Agency knew the facts about the relation of the boundary line to the waste piles.

    The time for acquiring title by adverse possession in the jurisdiction is ten years.

    Last year, Brown died, and his son, Silas, succeeded him as the owner of Blackacre. Silas became aware of the facts, demanded that Agency stop using Blackacre for the piling of waste, and, when Agency refused his demand, brought an appropriate action to enjoin any such use of Blackacre in the future.

    If Agency prevails in that action, it will be because

    (A) the facts constitute adverse possession and title to the portion of Blackacre concerned has vested in Agency.

    (B) Brown's failure to keep himself informed as to Agency's use of Blackacre and his failure to object constituted implied consent to the continuation of that use.

(C) the interest of the public in the conversion of waste to energy overrides any entitlement of Silas to equitable remedies.

(D) the power of eminent domain of the state makes the claim of Silas moot.

[Q2089]

Answer: Choice **(A)** is correct. Agency will win on an adverse possession claim if its possession was open, notorious, visible, hostile and continuous. The requirement of hostility would likely be deemed satisfied, because in a boundary dispute an owner who openly occupies the adjacent parcel under the mistaken belief it is his own is typically found to meet the hostility requirement. The only other requirement that is seriously in issue here is whether Agency's possession was "continuous," in the light of the annual four-week period in which there was no trespass. A court would likely hold that this brief respite each year did not prevent the possession from being continuous, because Agency was treating Blackacre exactly the same way it treated its own adjacent portion of Whiteacre — doing annual cleanup that happened to have the unanticipated effect of removing the trespass. It is not certain that a court would conclude that the continuity requirement was met, but adverse possession is the only one of the choices that would plausibly yield a victory for Agency.

(B) is wrong because the only way in which Brown could be found to have given an implied consent to Agency's use would be if Brown's silence was found to have created either a license or an easement. A license is by its nature a revocable right of use, so even if Brown's silence had created a license by implication, Brown or his successor would be entitled to revoke the license at will, and Silas's suit would constitute such a revocation. As for an easement, easements must generally satisfy the statute of frauds. It is true that an easement by "estoppel" can be created, but this occurs only when the owner of the servient tenement allows a use of his land while he knew or should have known that the user would change position in reliance; here there has been no meaningful reliance by Agency, so this theory would not work.

(C) is wrong because Agency can win only if it obtained legal title to the part of Blackacre in question, and not degree of "public interest" in waste-conversion could ever give Agency title to the property by operation of law.

(D) is wrong because it concerns the wrong area of law. Agency is not trying to obtain title to the relevant portion of Blackacre through eminent domain (i.e. it is not trying to obtain title by paying just compensation). Instead, it is acting under "color of title" as if it already owned the portion of Blackacre concerned. Hence, the problem calls for an adverse possession analysis, not an eminent domain analysis.

CHAPTER 2

FREEHOLD ESTATES

II. THE FEE SIMPLE

A. **Fee simple absolute:**

2. **Words to create:**

b. **Abolished:**

Question: Six years ago, Oscar, owner of Blackacre in fee simple, executed and delivered to Albert an instrument in the proper form of a warranty deed, purporting to convey Blackacre to "Albert and his heirs." At that time, Albert was a widower who had one child, Donna.

Three years ago, Albert executed and delivered to Bea an instrument in the proper form of a warranty deed, purporting to convey Blackacre to "Bea." Donna did not join in the deed. Bea was and still is unmarried and childless.

The only possibly applicable statute in the jurisdiction states that any deed will be construed to convey the grantor's entire estate, unless expressly limited.

Last month, Albert died, never having remarried. Donna is his only heir. Blackacre is now owned by

(A) Donna, because Albert's death ended Bea's life estate *pur autre vie*.

(B) Bea in fee simple pursuant to Albert's deed.

(C) Donna and Bea as tenants in common of equal shares.

(D) Donna and Bea as joint tenants, because both survived Albert.

[Q3187]

Answer: Choice **(B)** is correct. A literal reading of the grant "to Albert and his heirs" would suggest that Albert's heirs took something. But a gift "to A and his heirs" has always been interpreted to mean the grant of a fee simple interest to A, with A's heirs taking nothing. Consequently, Albert had the ability to convey that same fee simple to Bea, which he did, and the fact that Donna did not join the deed is irrelevant (she had no interest to convey or not convey). Then, when Albert conveyed to "Bea," under the statute ("any deed will be construed to convey the grantor's entire estate, unless expressly limited"), the entire interest Albert had (i.e., the fee simple) passed to Bea.

(A), (C), and (D) are wrong, because each choice incorrectly suggests that Donna received an interest as Albert's "heir."

B. Fee simple defeasible:

2. Determinable:

f. Distinguish from restrictive covenant:

Question: A grantor executed an instrument in the proper form of a warranty deed purporting to convey a tract of land to his church. The granting clause of the instrument ran to the church "and its successors forever, so long as the premises are used for church purposes." The church took possession of the land and used it as its site of worship for many years. Subsequently, the church wanted to relocate and entered into a valid written contract to sell the land to a buyer for a substantial price. The buyer wanted to use the land as a site for business activities and objected to the church's title. The contract contained no provision relating to the quality of title the church was bound to convey. There is no applicable statute. When the buyer refused to close, the church sued the buyer for specific performance and properly joined the grantor as a party.

Is the church likely to prevail?

(A) No, because the grantor's interest prevents the church's title from being marketable.

(B) No, because the quoted provision is a valid restrictive covenant.

C) Yes, because a charitable trust to support religion will attach to the proceeds of the sale.

D) Yes, because the grantor cannot derogate from his warranty to the church.

[Q7018]

Answer: Choice **(A)** is correct. The warranty deed conveyed a fee simple determinable title to the church, and the grantor retained the future interest (a possibility of reverter).

Such a reverter becomes possessory immediately upon the occurrence of the limitation. A title is unmarketable when a reasonable person would not purchase it. This buyer plans to use the land as a site for business purposes, which would cause the limitation to occur and the title to be forfeited automatically to the grantor. That possibility is easy enough to render the title unmarketable.

(B) is incorrect. Although this answer correctly states that the church is unlikely to prevail, it misstates the legal basis for this conclusion. The quoted provision creates a fee simple determinable title in the church (because the title in this case will be automatically forfeited to the grantor if the land is not used for church purposes), not a restrictive covenant. A restrictive covenant involves a promise regarding the use of the land and is not the title itself (though the existence of a restrictive covenant barring non-church uses would, like the determinable fee here, be enough to render title unmarketable).

(C) is wrong because it cites an irrelevant fact. The "so long as ..." clause created a possibility of reverter, making the church's title unmarketable. The clause will not create a trust for the benefit of religion, as this choice asserts (and even if it did, that wouldn't prevent the possibility of reverter from operating to divest the buyer of title if he were forced to close on the sale).

(D) is wrong because it's gibberish. The choice seems to be asserted that the grantor can't have a possibility of reverter because such an interest would be inconsistent with the warranty deed that grantor gave. But that's flatly untrue — the warranty deed just asserts that whatever title grantor is conveying, he has (and in this case, he gave a lesser interest than he had, i.e., reserved a possibility of reverter to himself).

3. **Fee simple subject to condition subsequent:**

   c. *Distinguishing fee simple subject to condition precedent:*

   Question: A landowner owned land in fee simple. A small house on the land was occupied, with the landowner's oral permission, rent-free, by the landowner's son and the son's college classmate. The son was then 21 years old.

   The landowner, by properly executed instrument, conveyed the land to "my beloved son, his heirs and assigns, upon the condition precedent that he earn a college degree by the time he reaches the age of 30. If, for any reason, he does not meet this condition, then the land shall become the sole property of my beloved daughter, her heirs and assigns." At the time of the conveyance, the son and the classmate attended a college located several blocks from the land. Neither had earned a college degree.

   One week after the delivery of the deed to the son, the son recorded the deed and immediately told the classmate that he, the son, was going to begin charging the classmate rent since "I am now your landlord." There is no applicable statute.

   The son and the classmate did not reach agreement, and the son served the appropriate notice to terminate whatever tenancy the classmate had. The son then sought, in an appropriate action, to oust the classmate.

   Who should prevail?

   (A) The son, because the conveyance created a fee simple subject to divestment in the son.

   (B) The son, because the landowner's conveyance terminated the classmate's tenancy.

   (C) The classmate, because the landowner's permission to occupy preceded the landowner's conveyance to the son.

   (D) The classmate, because he is a tenant of the landowner, not of the son.

[Q1173]

Answer: Choice **(D)** is correct. The conveyance to the son was a gift of a fee simple subject to the condition precedent that the son get a college degree prior to turning 30. Until the son got the degree, the conveyance did not create any present possessory interest in him (and the possessory interest remained in the landowner, with an executory interest in the daughter ready to spring out of the landowner if the son turned 30 without getting the degree). Therefore, the classmate continued to be a tenant of the landowner, not of the son, with the result that the son did not have the right to terminate the classmate's tenancy or oust him.

(A) is wrong because the phrase "upon the condition precedent..." in the landowner-to-son conveyance made the gift a fee simple subject to a condition precedent, not a fee simple subject to divestment. (If the gift had read, "to my son and his heirs, but if my son turns 30 without having obtained a college degree, then to my daughter," then the son *would* indeed have had a fee simple subject to divestment, and the son would have won the case, making this choice correct.)

(B) is wrong because a conveyance by the owner will not normally terminate a tenancy, even where the conveyance is a transfer of a fee simple absolute or a fee simple subject to divestment; furthermore, in this case the conveyance was of a fee simple subject to a condition precedent, so it was even further from terminating the classmate's tenancy.

(C) is wrong because the fact that the permission to occupy was both oral and rent-free establishes that it was a tenancy at will (or else a license); therefore, it could be terminated at any time by either party acting unilaterally. Consequently, although this choice correctly states the result that the classmate wins, it does not correctly state the reason this is so.

IV. THE LIFE ESTATE

B. Duties and powers of life tenant:

2. Duties:

a. No waste:

i. Demolition and rebuilding:

Question: Alice owned a commercial property, Eastgate, consisting of a one-story building rented to various retail stores and a very large parking lot. Two years ago, Alice died and left Eastgate to her nephew, Paul, for life, with remainder to her godson, Richard, his heirs and assigns. Paul was 30 years old and Richard was 20 years old when Alice died. The devise of Eastgate was made subject to any mortgage on Eastgate in effect at the time of Alice's death.

When Alice executed her will, the balance of the mortgage debt on Eastgate was less than $5,000. A year before her death, Alice suffered financial reverses; and in order to meet her debts, she had mortgaged Eastgate to secure a loan of $150,000. The entire principal of the mortgage remained outstanding when she died. As a result, the net annual income from Eastgate was reduced not only by real estate taxes and regular maintenance costs, but also by the substantial mortgage interest payments that were due each month.

Paul was very dissatisfied with the limited benefit that he was receiving from the life estate. When, earlier this year, Acme, Inc., proposed to purchase Eastgate, demolish the building, pay off the mortgage, and construct a 30-story office building, Paul was willing to accept Acme's offer. However, Richard adamantly refused the offer, even though Richard, as the remainderman, paid the principal portion of each monthly mortgage amortization payment. Richard was independently wealthy and wanted to convert Eastgate into a public park when he became entitled to possession.

When Acme realized that Richard would not change his mind, Acme modified its proposal to a purchase of the life estate of Paul. Acme was ready to go ahead with its building plans, relying upon a large life insurance policy on Paul's life to protect it against the economic risk of Paul's death. Paul's life expectancy was 45 years.

When Richard learned that Paul had agreed to Acme's modified proposal, Richard brought an appropriate action against them to enjoin their carrying it out.

There is no applicable statute.

The best argument for Richard is that

(A) Acme cannot purchase Paul's life estate, because life estates are not assignable.

(B) the proposed demolition of the building constitutes waste.

(C) Richard's payment of the mortgage principal has subrogated him to Paul's rights as a life tenant and bars Paul's assignment of the life estate without Richard's consent.

(D) continued existence of the one-story building is more in harmony with the ultimate use as a park than the proposed change in use.

[Q2179]

Answer: Choice **(B)** is correct. Ordinarily, a life tenant may not demolish a structure on the premises, even in order to build a bigger structure at his own expense that would render the future interest more valuable; such a demolition is classified as waste. Courts have recognized a narrow exception where changes in the character of the neighborhood have deprived the property in its present form of "reasonable productivity or usefulness," but this would probably not be found to have occurred here, since the structure is being used for retail stores and produces meaningful rent. (The problem is the substantial mortgage that eats up the rents, not the lack of any reasonably-productive use.) It is not certain that Richard would win with this argument (since Paul might succeed in establishing the no-reasonably-productive-use-in-present-form exception), but this is the only one of the four listed arguments that might plausibly produce a victory for Richard.

(A) is wrong because life estates are completely assignable, without the consent of the holder of the future interest; the assignee simply receives a life estate *pur autre vie*.

(C) is wrong because Richard's payment of the mortgage principal does not change his rights; even without such payments he would be entitled to veto a demolition and replacement of the premises unless the narrow exception described in (B) applied.

(D) is wrong because the maintenance of "harmony" with the use envisioned by the future interest holder is not a relevant factor in the decision about whether the proposed use violates the latter's rights; the issue is whether the proposed use would or would not constitute "waste," and harmony with the future holder's desires is not part of the waste analysis.

b. **Current operating expenses:**

ii. **Taxes:**

Question: Ody, owner of Profitacre, executed an instrument in the proper form of a deed, purporting to convey Profitacre "to Leon for life, then to Ralph in fee simple." Leon, who is Ody's brother and Ralph's father, promptly began to manage Profitacre, which is valuable income-producing real estate. Leon collected all rents and paid all expenses, including real estate taxes. Ralph did not object, and this state of affairs continued for five years until 2007. In that year, Leon executed an instrument in the proper form of a deed, purporting to convey Profitacre to Mona. Ralph, no admirer of Mona, asserted his right to ownership of Profitacre. Mona asserted her ownership and said that if Ralph had any rights he was obligated to pay real estate taxes, even though Leon had been kind enough to pay them in the past. Income from Profitacre is ample to cover expenses, including real estate taxes.

In an appropriate action to determine the rights of the parties, the court should decide

(A) Leon's purported deed forfeited his life estate, so Ralph owns Profitacre in fee simple.

(B) Mona owns an estate for her life, is entitled to all income, and must pay real estate taxes; Ralph owns the remainder interest.

(C) Mona owns an estate for the life of Leon, is entitled to all income, and must pay real estate taxes; Ralph owns the remainder interest.

(D) Mona owns an estate for the life of Leon and is entitled to all income; Ralph owns the remainder interest, and must pay real estate taxes.

[Q2138]

Answer: Choice **(C)** is correct. When Leon, the life tenant, purported to convey the fee simple to Mona, this conveyance had the effect of conveying all of Leon's interest in the property, i.e., his life tenancy. Therefore, Mona had a life estate *pur autre vie*, i.e., an estate for the life of Leon. Once Mona stepped into Leon's shoes as life tenant, she had the right to collect all income from the property, but also the obligation to pay all current operating expenses including real estate taxes. Ralph always had a remainder interest following Leon's life estate, and Ralph's interest was not changed in any way by Leon's conveyance of his own interest to Mona.

(A) is wrong because a life tenant's attempt to convey a fee simple does not cause the life estate to be forfeited; such a conveyance merely transfers to the grantee the entirety of the grantor's interest (i.e., the life tenancy).

(B) is wrong because what Mona received is precisely what Leon had, namely an estate for the life of Leon.

(D) is wrong because real estate taxes are the responsibility of the life tenant, not the remainderman.

c. **Payment of mortgage:**

i. **No personal obligation:**

Question: A testator owned in fee simple a farm of 300 acres. He died and by will duly admitted to probate devised the farm to his surviving widow, for life with remainder in fee simple to his three children, two daughters and a son. All three children survived the testator.

At the time of the testator's death, there existed a mortgage on the farm that the testator had given ten years before to secure a loan for the purchase of the farm. At his death, there remained unpaid $40,000 in principal, payable in installments of $4,000 per year for the next ten years. In addition, there was due interest at the rate of 10% per annum, payable annually with the installment of principal. The widow took possession and out of a gross income of $50,000 per year realized $25,000 net after paying all expenses and charges except the installment of principal and interest due on the mortgage.

The daughters wanted the three children, including the son, to each contribute one-third of the amounts needed to pay the mortgage installments. The son objected, contending that the widow should pay all of these amounts out of the profits she had made in operation of the farm. When foreclosure of the mortgage seemed imminent, the son sought legal advice.

If the son obtained sound advice relating to his rights, he was told that

(A) his only protection would lie in instituting an action for partition to compel the sale of the life estate of the widow and to obtain the value of the son's one-third interest in remainder.

(B) he could obtain appropriate relief to compel the widow personally to pay the sums due because the income is more than adequate to cover these amounts.

(C) he could be compelled personally to pay his share of the amounts due because discharge of the mortgage enhances the principal.

(D) he could not be held personally liable for any amount but that his share in remainder could be lost if the mortgage installments are not paid.

[Q1107]

Answer: Choice **(D)** is correct. The general rule about personal liability for mortgage payments as between present and future interests is that neither party has personal liability, except to the extent that party is receiving net operating income from the property. Since the son as remainderman gets no operating income from the property, he has no personal liability to make any mortgage payments. However, if neither he nor anyone else makes all required mortgage payments, the property will presumably be lost to foreclosure, in which case the son's remainder interest will be lost. Therefore, the son has the right (which he may well want to exercise), but not the obligation, to contribute his one-third share of whatever mortgage payments that the widow is unable or unwilling to make.

(A) is wrong because the holder of a future interest generally does not have the right to bring a partition action to compel the sale of the possessory estate (here, the widow's life estate).

(B) is wrong because it overstates the widow's obligation; the widow probably does have a personal obligation to pay her fairly-allocated share of the mortgage payments (based on the relative value of the widow's life estate versus the remainder), up to the amount of net income she's receiving, but this choice incorrectly suggests that she would be personally liable to pay the *entire* installments rather than just her share if the net income were large enough.

(C) is wrong because the son, as a remainderman, has no personal liability to make mortgage payments at all (since he is not getting any operating income out of which to pay them).

CHAPTER 3
FUTURE INTERESTS

II. POSSIBILITY OF REVERTER; RIGHT OF RE-ENTRY

A. **Possibility of reverter and right of re-entry:**

   1. **Possibility of reverter:**

      a. **Can pass by will or by inheritance:**

         Question: Thirty years ago, a landowner conveyed land by warranty deed to a church (a charity) "so long as the land herein conveyed is used as the site for the principal religious edifice maintained by said church."

         Twenty years ago, the landowner died intestate, survived by a single heir.

         One year ago, the church dissolved and its church building situated on the land was demolished.

There is no applicable statute. The common law Rule Against Perpetuities is unmodified in the jurisdiction.

In an appropriate action, the landowner's heir and the attorney general, who is the appropriate official to assert public interests in charitable trusts, contest the right to the land.

In such action, who will prevail?

(A) The landowner's heir, as successor to the landowner's possibility of reverter.

(B) The landowner's heir, because a charity cannot convey assets donated to it.

(C) The attorney general, because *cy pres* should be applied to devote the land to religious purposes to carry out the charitable intent of the landowner.

(D) The attorney general, because the landowner's attempt to restrict the church's fee simple violated the Rule Against Perpetuities.

[QA007]

Answer: Choice **(A)** is correct. The landowner's conveyance to the church was a fee simple determinable, because it conveyed the land only "so long as" the property was used for a religious edifice. When a grantor conveys a fee simple determinable and the grant remains silent about what happens should the terminating event occur, then the grantor is deemed to retain a possibility of reverter; therefore, the landowner retained a possibility of reverter here. The church's fee simple ended automatically upon the demolition of the church building. Since a possibility of reverter can pass by will or inheritance, when the landowner died his heir was entitled to possession of the land.

(B) is wrong because it misstates the facts. The church did not convey the land; it simply demolished the church building. When it did that, its right to possession ended automatically because it had a fee simple determinable. The heir is entitled to possession of the land because he inherited the landowner's possibility of reverter.

(C) is wrong because the *cy pres* doctrine does not apply to these facts. The primary use of the equitable doctrine of *cy pres* is to reform a charitable gift to approximate as closely as possible the grantor's intent when the grantor's stated intent has become impossible or impractical to pursue. The *cy pres* doctrine will not be used to override the grantor's intent, only to further it. Here, the terms of the conveyance to the church specifically demonstrate the landowner's intent to limit the church's use of the property. Moreover, the landowner has used a form of conveyance (a fee simple determinable) that automatically terminates the church's interest in the property should it not comply with the landowner's intended use of the property. Since using the *cy pres* doctrine would thwart rather than further the landowner's intent, the doctrine will not be applied.

(D) is wrong because a possibility of reverter is not subject to the Rule Against Perpetuities. Since the Rule Against Perpetuities can only be violated when the interest might vest later than lives in being plus 21 years, any conveyance that vests at the time it is created cannot violate the Rule. A possibility of reverter vests at the time it is created; thus, the Rule Against Perpetuities does not apply to it.

i. Conflict between will and inheritance:

Question: Twenty years ago, a landowner who owned Blackacre, a one-acre tract of land, duly delivered a deed of Blackacre "to School District so long as it is used for school purposes." The deed was promptly and properly recorded. Five years ago, the landowner died, leaving Sonny as his only heir at law. The landowner left a duly probated will, by which he left "all my Estate" to his friend, who was a doctor.

Last month, School District closed its school on Blackacre and for valid consideration duly executed and delivered a quitclaim deed of Blackacre to a developer, who planned to use the land for commercial development. The developer has now brought an appropriate action to quiet title against the son, the doctor and School District.

The only applicable statute is a provision in the jurisdiction's probate code which provides that any property interest which is descendible is devisable.

In such action, the court should find that title is now in

(A) the developer.

(B) the son.

(C) the doctor.

(D) School District.

[Q1200]

Answer: Choice **(C)** is correct. When the landowner conveyed to School District, School District got a fee simple determinable (a fee simple that would automatically end if the property ever ceased to be used for school purposes). The landowner retained a possibility of reverter, which is what the grantor retains following a fee simple determinable, if the fee simple determinable doesn't specify what happens upon failure of the condition. In virtually all states, a possibility of reverter can be inherited under the intestacy statute (i.e., it is "descendible"). The probate provision here tells us that if the interest is descendible, it is also devisable (i.e., can be left by will). Since we know that the possibility of reverter is descendible, we therefore know that it is also devisable. Since the landowner left a will devising his entire estate to the doctor, the reverter will pass by devise (i.e., by the will), not by inheritance. That's because of the basic rule that where a particular item of property is covered by a valid bequest in a will, the item will pass by will rather than by intestacy. Therefore, the reverter goes to the doctor under the will.

(A) is wrong because once School District closed its school, its interest in Blackacre was automatically extinguished, and there was nothing left to pass to the developer via the quitclaim deed.

(B) is wrong because the son's status as heir (i.e., as taker under the intestacy statute) was irrelevant given that the reverter here was bequeathed under the will, and was therefore not available to be passed by inheritance.

(D) is wrong because once School District closed its school, its interest was automatically extinguished.

IV. REMAINDERS

C. Contingent remainders:

1. Condition precedent

Question: A testator owned a tract of land in fee simple. By will duly admitted to probate after his death, the testator devised the land to "any wife who survives me with remainder to such of my children as are living at her death."

The testator was survived by his widow and by three children, who were an accountant, a lawyer, and a doctor. Thereafter, the lawyer died and by will duly admitted to probate devised his entire estate to his friend. The accountant and the doctor were the lawyer's heirs at law.

Later the widow died. In an appropriate lawsuit to which the accountant, the doctor, and the friend are parties, title to the land is at issue.

In such lawsuit, judgment should be that title to the property is in

(A) the accountant, the doctor, and the friend, because the earliest vesting of remainders is favored and reference to the surviving wife's death should be construed as relating to time of taking possession.

(B) the accountant, the doctor, and the friend, because the provision requiring survival of children violates the Rule Against Perpetuities since the surviving wife might have been a person unborn at the time of writing of the will.

(C) the accountant and the doctor, because the lawyer's remainder must descend by intestacy and is not devisable.

(D) the accountant and the doctor, because the remainders were contingent upon surviving the life tenant.

[Q2187]

Answer: Choice **(D)** is correct. The terms of the bequest made it clear that only a child who survived the testator's wife would take. Each child had a contingent remainder as of the testator's death. When the lawyer died before his mother (the widow) died, the lawyer's contingent remainder was nullified without ever becoming vested, leaving nothing to pass to the lawyer's friend by devise. At the widow's death, the contingent remainders in the accountant and the doctor vested (and, simultaneously, became possessory).

(A) is wrong for the same reason (D) is right: the remainders were intended by the testator to be contingent unless and until the remaindermen survived the widow, at which time they would vest. So when the lawyer died, his contingent remainder was destroyed by his failing to have survived the widow, and he had no interest to pass to the friend.

(B) is wrong because under the common law approach to the Rule against Perpetuities, the time for evaluating a will is when the testator *dies*, *not* when the will was *executed*. At the time the testator died, his widow (and, indeed, his children as well) were necessarily already in existence, and could therefore serve as measuring lives. So there was no risk that the remainder to the testator's children would vest beyond "measuring lives plus 21 years," making the gift to those children valid contingent remainders.

(C) is wrong as a matter of law: some remainders can indeed descend by intestacy. *Example*: O bequeaths "to A for life, then to B." Assume B is living at O's death, but dies intestate before A, and with C as his heir at law. At B's death, the vested remainder in B passes by intestacy to C, and C will have a fee simple once B dies.

a. *Implied condition of survival:*

Question: Theresa owned Blueacre, a tract of land, in fee simple. Theresa wrote and executed, with the required formalities, a will that devised Blueacre to "my daughter, Della, for life with remainder to my descendants *per stirpes*." At the time of writing the will, Theresa had a husband and no descendants living other than her two children, Della and Seth.

Theresa died and the will was duly admitted to probate. Theresa's husband predeceased her. Theresa was survived by Della, Seth, four grandchildren, and one great-grandchild. Della and Seth were Theresa's sole heirs at law.

Della and Seth brought an appropriate action for declaratory judgment as to title of Blueacre. Guardians *ad litem* were appointed and all other steps were taken so that the judgment would bind all persons interested whether born or unborn.

In that action, if the court rules that Della has a life estate in the whole of Blueacre and that the remainder is contingent, it will be because the court chose one of several possible constructions and that the chosen construction

(A) related all vesting to the time of writing of the will.

(B) related all vesting to the death of Theresa.

(C) implied a condition that remaindermen survive Della.

(D) implied a gift of a life estate to Seth.

[Q3181]

Answer: Choice **(C)** is correct, because if no condition that the remaindermen survive Della was implied, the remainder would be vested rather than contingent. A remainder is contingent if it is subject to a condition precedent (other than the mere expiration of the preceding estate) that must be satisfied before the remainder can become a present interest. A common type of condition precedent is the requirement that the holder of the remainder survive the holder of the previous estate (often a life estate), and that is what we might have here. There are two most plausible interpretations of what Theresa meant by "my descendants": (1) "all of my descendants existing and identifiable at the moment of my own death" (when the remainder is being created); or (2) "all of my descendants in existence when the remainder becomes possessory" (i.e., all descendants who survive Della). If interpretation (1) is chosen by the court, the remainder would be vested, because at the moment of Theresa's death we would know everyone who was to take, and if any pre-deceased Della, their heirs could take. If interpretation (2) is chosen, we would not know who takes until Della dies, at which point we would look to which descendants of Theresa survived Della; in that event, the remainder would be contingent (because at the moment when Theresa created the interest by dying, we don't know who will take). So it is only if the court selects interpretation (2) (imputing a condition that the remaindermen must survive Della in order to take) that the remainder would be deemed contingent.

(A) is wrong because if vesting occurred at the moment the will was written, the remainder would be vested, not contingent. This choice is referring to the possibility that the court would conclude that the bequest's reference to "my descendants" meant "anyone who is my descendant viewed as of the moment when I am writing this will." If this were the interpretation, then at the moment of the will-writing, we would know everyone who could take (they're all identifiable, and their remainder interests would vest immediately even though the remainder would not become possessory until Della died). In that event, the remainders would be vested, not contingent.

(B) is wrong because if all vesting were related to Theresa's death, the remainder would be vested, not contingent. The vesting/contingent determination is to be made at the moment the interest (the remainder) is created. That moment of creation is Theresa's death. Saying that "all vesting is [related] to the death of Theresa," as this choice does, is equivalent to saying that to be a "descendant," a person just has to survive Theresa, not Della. On that scenario, at the moment of Theresa's death, the remaindermen would be fully identifiable, and would be certain to take once Della dies. So on this analysis, the remainder would be vested (because fully identified as of the moment of creation of the interest, and certain to take), not contingent.

(D) is wrong because an interpretation giving a remainder life estate to Seth wouldn't automatically make that remainder contingent. Even in the unlikely event the court implied a life estate remainder to Seth, we still wouldn't know whether that remainder was vested or contingent, since we don't know whether there was a requirement that Seth survive Della (it would be contingent if there were a survival requirement, vested if there were not). In other words, reading in a remainder for life to Seth doesn't fully answer the vested/contingent remainder — of the four choices, only the choice that implies a survival-of-Della condition (Choice (C)) does that.

2. **Unborn or unascertained:**

   a. **Remainder "to A and her heirs or assigns" is vested:**

   Question: A grantor owned a tract of land in fee simple. By warranty deed he conveyed the land to his nephew for life "and from and after the death of my nephew to my niece, her heirs and assigns."

   Subsequently the niece died, devising all of her estate to the niece's boyfriend. The niece was survived by a cousin, her sole heir-at-law.

   Shortly thereafter the nephew died, survived by the grantor, the niece's boyfriend, and the niece's cousin.

   Title to the land now is in

   (A) the grantor, because the contingent remainder never vested and the grantor's reversion was entitled to possession immediately upon the nephew's death.

   (B) the boyfriend, because the vested remainder in the niece was transmitted by her will.

   (C) the cousin, because she is the niece's heir.

   (D) either the grantor or the cousin, depending upon whether the destructibility of contingent remainders is recognized in the applicable jurisdiction.

   [Q1151]

   Answer: Choice **(B)** is correct. The remainder to "my niece, her heirs and assigns" was a remainder to the niece in fee simple. Since the niece was alive and identifiable at the time of the grantor's deed, the remainder to the niece was vested. A vested remainder can be left by will. Therefore, the remainder passed by the will to the boyfriend.

   (A) is wrong because the remainder was never contingent, not even for an instant.

   (C) is wrong because a vested remainder can be passed by will, and the will here devised the remainder to the boyfriend; therefore, the fact that the niece's cousin was the niece's heir at law is irrelevant.

   (D) is wrong because the remainder here was vested, not contingent; therefore, the doctrine of destructibility of contingent remainders is irrelevant.

V. EXECUTORY INTERESTS

A. **Executory interests:**

   2. **Can be assigned:**

   Question: A landowner died, validly devising his land to his wife "for life or until remarriage, then to" their daughter. Shortly after the landowner's death, his daughter executed an instrument in the proper form of a deed, purporting to convey the land to her friend. A year later, the daughter died intestate, with her mother, the original landowner's wife, as her sole heir. The following month, the wife remarried. She then executed an instrument in the proper form of a deed, purporting to convey the land to her new husband as a wedding gift.

   Who now owns what interest in the land?

   (A) The daughter's friend owns the fee simple.

   (B) The wife owns the fee simple.

   (C) The wife's new husband has a life estate in the land for the wife's life, with the remainder in the daughter's friend.

(D) The wife's new husband owns the fee simple.

[Q7023]

Answer: Choice **(A)** is correct. The landowner's wife had a determinable life estate, evidenced by the words "for life" and "until remarriage" in the landowner's will. The daughter had a vested remainder (following the determinable life estate) and an executory interest (following the remarriage contingency). Both of the daughter's interests could be assigned to the friend. On the remarriage of the landowner's wife, the wife's life estate ended and it automatically went to the holder of the future interest, who at that time was the daughter's friend.

(B) is incorrect, because the landowner's wife had a determinable life estate, evidenced by the words "for life" and "until remarriage" — a fee simple estate has no such words of special limitation.

(C) is incorrect, because the landowner's wife had a determinable life estate. Had she not remarried, her life estate would have been transferable; however, the words of limitation regarding remarriage terminated her life estate immediately upon her remarriage, and her estate automatically went to the holder of the future interest.

(D) is incorrect, because the wife's new husband got nothing, for the reason discussed in Choice (C).

VI. THE RULE AGAINST PERPETUITIES (RAP)

B. Applicability of Rule to various estates:

3. Reversion (RAP does not apply):

Question: Thirty years ago, a landowner conveyed land by warranty deed to a church (a charity) "so long as the land herein conveyed is used as the site for the principal religious edifice maintained by said church."

Twenty years ago, the landowner died intestate, survived by a single heir.

One year ago, the church dissolved and its church building situated on the land was demolished.

There is no applicable statute. The common law Rule Against Perpetuities is unmodified in the jurisdiction.

In an appropriate action, the landowner's heir and the attorney general, who is the appropriate official to assert public interests in charitable trusts, contest the right to the land.

In such action, who will prevail?

(A) The landowner's heir, as successor to the landowner's possibility of reverter.

(B) The landowner's heir, because a charity cannot convey assets donated to it.

(C) The attorney general, because *cy pres* should be applied to devote the land to religious purposes to carry out the charitable intent of the landowner.

(D) The attorney general, because the landowner's attempt to restrict the church's fee simple violated the Rule Against Perpetuities.

[QA007]

Answer: Choice **(D)** is **incorrect** because a possibility of reverter is not subject to the Rule Against Perpetuities. Since the Rule Against Perpetuities can only be violated when the interest might vest later than lives in being plus 21 years, any conveyance that vests at the time it is created cannot violate the Rule. A possibility of reverter vests at the time it is created; thus, the

Rule Against Perpetuities does not apply to it. (The correct choice is (A), because the landlowner automatically retained a possibility of reverter, which passed by intestacy to the heir; see *supra*, p. 125.)

5. **Options to purchase land:**

    c. **Right of first refusal (RAP may apply):**

    Question: A grantor owned two tracts of land, one of 15 acres and another of five acres. The two tracts were a mile apart.

    Fifteen years ago, the grantor conveyed the smaller tract to a grantee. The grantor retained the larger tract. The deed to the grantee contained, in addition to proper legal descriptions of both properties and identifications of the parties, the following:

    I, the grantor, bind myself and my heirs and assigns that in the event that the larger tract that I now retain is ever offered for sale, I will notify the grantee and his heirs and assigns in writing, and the grantee and his heirs and assigns shall have the right to purchase the larger tract for its fair market value as determined by a board consisting of three qualified expert independent real estate appraisers.

    With appropriate references to the other property and the parties, there followed a reciprocal provision that conferred upon the grantor and her heirs and assigns a similar right to purchase the smaller tract, purportedly binding the grantee and his heirs and assigns.

    Ten years ago, a corporation acquired the larger tract from the grantor. At that time, the grantee had no interest in acquiring the larger tract and by an appropriate written document released any interest he or his heirs or assigns might have had in the larger tract.

    Last year, the grantee died. The smaller tract passed by the grantee's will to his daughter. She has decided to sell the smaller tract. However, because she believes the corporation has been a very poor steward of the larger tract, she refuses to sell the smaller tract to the corporation even though she has offered it for sale in the local real estate market.

    The corporation brought an appropriate action for specific performance after taking all of the necessary preliminary steps in its effort to exercise its rights to purchase the smaller tract.

    The daughter asserted all possible defenses.

    The common law Rule Against Perpetuities is unmodified in the jurisdiction.

    If the court rules for the daughter, what is the reason?

    (A) The provision setting out the right to purchase violates the Rule Against Perpetuities.

    (B) The grantee's release 10 years ago operates as a waiver regarding any right to purchase that the corporation might have.

    (C) The two tracts of land were not adjacent parcels of real estate, and thus the right to purchase is in gross and is therefore unenforceable.

    (D) Noncompliance with a right to purchase gives rise to a claim for money damages, but not for specific performance.

    [QA040]

    Answer: Choice **(A)** is correct. Each of the original parties granted a reciprocal right of first refusal to the other and the other's heirs and assigns. A right of first refusal provides that if the owner ever decides to sell the property, the one holding the right of first refusal has the right to purchase it. A right of first refusal is therefore a conditional option to purchase, and it is analyzed for Rule Against Perpetuities (RAP) issues like other purchase options that are "in gross" (i.e., not associated with a lease). Courts are split as to whether to apply the RAP to rights of first refusal or other options in gross. We don't know here that the RAP will definitely be applied to such interests, but we do know that *if* it's applied, the daughter will win (and the question is asking what the reason will be if the daughter wins). Why will the daughter win? Because the RAP invalidates an interest unless it can be said with certainty at the time of creation that that interest will vest or fail to vest within 21 years. Here, the right of first refusal extended to the heirs and assigns of the original parties, so the decision to exercise the right *might* occur more than 21 years after a life in being at the time the right was granted. (For instance, the grantor's great-grandchild might try to exercise the right as against the grantee's great-grandchild.) The RAP in this jurisdiction is unmodified by statute — therefore, the right of first refusal is deemed void as of the time it was created, and the court will not wait to see whether anyone tries to exercise that right more than 21 years after a life in being. Consequently, the right is already invalid, even though only 15 years have passed since the right was created.

(B) is wrong because the fact that the grant*ee* chose not to exercise *his* right of first refusal has no effect on whether the grant*or* can exercise the reciprocal right of first refusal regarding the land originally owned by the grantee. That is, even if the grantee's decision not to exercise the right 10 years ago was a waiver of any subsequent right of first refusal on the part of the grantee or his heirs (which it almost certainly was), there would be no reason why that decision should act as a waiver by the grantor or her heirs as to the reciprocal right held by them.

(C) is wrong because it misstates the effect of the fact that the option is "in gross." An option "in gross" is an option that is not associated with a lease to the option-holder of the property to which the option applies. So the right of first refusal here is indeed an option in gross, as the choice suggests. But the choice is wrong for two reasons: (1) an option in gross is enforceable as long as the time period during which it can be enforced is not longer than the RAP period (i.e., not longer than lives in being plus 21 years); and (2) the fact that the parcels are not adjacent is irrelevant to the analysis. (That is, even if the two parcels *were* adjacent, the option would still be in gross because there is no lease.)

(D) is wrong because it misstates the remedies for breach of a right of first refusal. A holder of a purchase option is entitled to a decree of specific performance, under which the other party will be compelled to make the sale in return for the payment of the option's strike price. A right of first refusal is a conditional option to purchase. Once the condition is satisfied (by the other party's decision to sell), the holder of the option has the same right to a decree of specific performance as would the holder of an unconditional purchase option.

i. Say that Rule is relevant:

Question: Aris was the owner in fee simple of adjoining lots known as Lot 1 and Lot 2. He built a house which he took up residence on Lot 1. Thereafter, he built a house on Lot 2, which he sold, house and lot, to Baker. Consistent with the contract of sale and purchase, the deed conveying Lot 2 from Aris to Baker contained the following clause:

> In the event Baker, his heirs or assigns, decide to sell the property hereby conveyed and obtain a purchaser ready, willing, and able to purchase Lot 2 and the improvements thereon on terms and conditions acceptable to Baker, said Lot 2 and improvements shall be offered to Aris, his heirs or assigns, on the same terms and conditions. Aris, his heirs or assigns, as the case may be, shall have ten days from said offer to accept said offer and thereby to exercise said option.

Three years after delivery and recording of the deed and payment of the purchase price, Baker became ill and moved to a climate more compatible with his health. Baker's daughter orally offered to purchase the premises from Baker at its then fair market value. Baker declined his daughter's offer but instead deeded Lot 2 to his daughter as a gift.

Immediately thereafter, Baker's daughter sold Lot 2 to Charles at the then fair market value of Lot 2. The sale was completed by the delivery of deed and payment of the purchase price. At no time did Baker or his daughter offer to sell Lot 2 to Aris.

Aris learned of the conveyance to Baker's daughter and the sale by Baker's daughter to Charles one week after the conveyance of Lot 2 from Baker's daughter to Charles. Aris promptly brought an appropriate action against Charles to enforce rights created in him by the deed of Aris to Baker. Aris tendered the amount paid by Charles into the court for whatever disposition the court deemed proper. The common-law Rule Against Perpetuities is unmodified by statute.

Which of the following will determine whether Aris will prevail?

I. The parol evidence rule.

II. The Statute of Frauds.

III. The type of recording statute of the jurisdiction in question.

IV The Rule Against Perpetuities.

(A) I only.

(B) IV only.

(C) I and IV only.

(D) II and III only.

[Q1033]

Answer: The correct choice is **(B)**. Item IV, the Rule Against Perpetuities, is relevant. That's true because if the Rule applies, the right of first refusal is completely unenforceable, even if Baker's daughter's offer triggered the first-refusal clause. By its terms, the right of first refusal here has no time limit, and applies to the "heirs or assigns" of both original parties to the conveyance; therefore, it could easily vest beyond any of the measuring lives — Baker's and Aris' — plus 21 years.

Item I, the parol evidence rule, is not relevant because that rule applies only to oral statements or other writings between the two contracting parties (here, Baker and Aris) made before or simultaneously with the signing of the written agreement, not to post-contract statements by either party (let alone to a post-contract statement by one party to a non-party). The only statements not included in the original contractual writing at issue in this case are the ones in the oral conversation between Baker and his daughter, and the parol evidence rule is irrelevant to these both because they occurred after the contract was signed and because they were between a party and a non-party.

Item II, the Statute of Frauds, is not relevant because the applicability of the statute does not matter to any issue in the case. If the controversy were between Baker and his daughter, with the daughter claiming that Baker and the daughter had reached an oral contract for him to convey the property to her, then the statute would be relevant (since if it applied it would provide a defense for Baker). But the right of first refusal clause that is at issue here is triggered any time Baker "decides" to sell and obtains a ready, willing, and able purchaser, and even an oral third-party purchase offer that would not be enforceable because of the Statute can therefore serve as a trigger for the clause. So whether the Statute of Frauds would apply to agreement between Baker and his daughter is irrelevant.

Item III, the nature of the recording act, is not relevant, because no matter what type of recording act the jurisdiction has, Charles will not be protected by it. That's because the deed from Aris to Baker disclosed the right of first refusal, and that deed is in Charles' chain of title. Therefore, Charles had constructive notice of the right of refusal, preventing him from being a bona fide purchaser (which virtually all recording acts require him to be in order to get the act's protection).

6. Restrictive covenants and equitable servitudes:

Question: Twenty-five years ago, a man who owned a 45-acre tract of land conveyed 40 of the 45 acres to a developer by warranty deed. The man retained the rear five-acre portion of the land and continues to live there in a large farmhouse.

The deed to the 40-acre tract was promptly and properly recorded. It contained the following language:

"It is a term and condition of this deed, which shall be a covenant running with the land and binding on all owners, their heirs and assigns, that no use shall be made of the 40-acre tract of land except for residential purposes."

Subsequently, the developer fully developed the 40-acre tract into a residential subdivision consisting of 40 lots with a single-family residence on each lot.

Although there have been multiple transfers of ownership of each of the 40 lots within the subdivision, none of them included a reference to the quoted provision in the deed from the man to the developer, nor did any deed to a subdivision lot create any new covenants restricting use.

Last year, a major new medical center was constructed adjacent to the subdivision. A doctor who owns a house in the subdivision wishes to relocate her medical offices to her house. For the first time, the doctor learned of the restrictive covenant in the deed from the man to the developer. The applicable zoning ordinance permits the doctor's intended use. The man, as owner of the five-acre tract, however, objects to the doctor's proposed use of her property.

There are no governing statutes other than the zoning code. The common law Rule Against Perpetuities is unmodified in the jurisdiction.

Can the doctor convert her house in the subdivision into a medical office?

(A) No, because the owners of lots in the subdivision own property benefitted by the original residential covenant and have the sole right to enforce it.

(B) No, because the man owns property benefitted by the original restrictive covenant and has a right to enforce it.

(C) Yes, because the original restrictive covenant violates the Rule Against Perpetuities.

(D) Yes, because the zoning ordinance allows the doctor's proposed use and preempts the restrictive covenant.

[QA087]

Answer: (C) is **incorrect** because the Rule Against Perpetuities does not apply to a restrictive covenant or equitable servitude. The Rule Against Perpetuities fosters the policy against restraining alienation of fee simple estates in land. Thus, it voids only those future interests that are not capable of vesting within 21 years of a life in being. An equitable servitude is not a future interest; thus, RAP does not apply. (The correct answer is (C); see p. 159 *infra* for a full discussion.)

D. Special situations:

2. "Unborn widow":

a. Unborn widow in cases where gift is by will:

Question: A testator owned a tract of land in fee simple. By will duly admitted to probate after his death, the testator devised the land to "any wife who survives me with remainder to such of my children as are living at her death."

The testator was survived by his widow and by three children, who were an accountant, a lawyer, and a doctor. Thereafter, the lawyer died and by will duly admitted to probate devised his entire estate to his friend. The accountant and the doctor were the lawyer's heirs at law.

Later the widow died. In an appropriate lawsuit to which the accountant, the doctor, and the friend are parties, title to the land is at issue.

In such lawsuit, judgment should be that title to the property is in

(A) the accountant, the doctor, and the friend, because the earliest vesting of remainders is favored and reference to the surviving wife's death should be construed as relating to time of taking possession.

(B) the accountant, the doctor, and the friend, because the provision requiring survival of children violates the Rule Against Perpetuities since the surviving wife might have been a person unborn at the time of writing of the will.

(C) the accountant and the doctor, because the lawyer's remainder must descend by intestacy and is not devisable.

(D) the accountant and the doctor, because the remainders were contingent upon surviving the life tenant.

[Q2187]

Answer: Choice **(B)** is **incorrect**, because under the common law approach to the Rule against Perpetuities, the time for evaluating a will is when the testator *dies*, *not* when the will was *executed*. At the time the testator died, his widow (and, indeed, his children as well) were necessarily already in existence, and could therefore serve as measuring lives. So there was no risk that the remainder to the testator's children would vest beyond "measuring lives plus 21 years," making the gift to those children valid contingent remainders. (The correct answer is (D); see *supra*, p. 127 for a full discussion.)

CHAPTER 4

CONCURRENT OWNERSHIP

II. JOINT TENANCY

C. **Severance:**

1. **Conveyance by one joint tenant:**

   a. **Most important on MBE:**

   Question: By warranty deed, Marta conveyed Blackacre to Beth and Christine "as joint tenants with right of survivorship." Beth and Christine are not related. Beth conveyed all her interest to Eugenio by warranty deed and subsequently died intestate. Thereafter, Christine conveyed to Darin by warranty deed.

   There is no applicable statute, and the jurisdiction recognizes the common-law joint tenancy.

   Title to Blackacre is in

   (A) Darin.

(B) Marta.

(C) Darin and Eugenio.

(D) Darin and the heirs of Beth.

[Q2001]

Answer: Choice **(C)** is correct. When Beth conveyed her interest to Eugenio, this act caused a severance, destroying the joint tenancy immediately and leaving Eugenio and Christine as tenants in common. When Christine conveyed her interest to Darin, he stepped into Christine's shoes, becoming a tenant in common with Eugenia.

Choices (A), (B), and (D) are wrong because they are inconsistent with the above analysis.

b. **Motive irrelevant:**

Question: A brother and sister owned a large tract of land in fee simple as joint tenants with rights of survivorship. While the sister was on an extended safari in Kenya, the brother learned that there were very valuable coal deposits within the land, but he made no attempt to inform his sister. Thereupon, the brother conveyed his interest in the land to his wife, who immediately reconveyed that interest to the brother. The common-law joint tenancy is unmodified by statute.

Shortly thereafter, the brother was killed in an automobile accident. His will, which was duly probated, specifically devised his one-half interest in the property to his wife.

The sister then returned from Kenya and learned what had happened. The sister brought an appropriate action against the brother's wife, who claimed a one-half interest in the property, seeking a declaratory judgment that she, the sister, was the sole owner of the land.

In this action, who should prevail?

(A) The brother's wife, because the brother and sister were tenants in common at the time of the brother's death.

(B) The brother's wife, because the brother's will severed the joint tenancy.

(C) The sister, because the joint tenancy was reestablished by the brother's wife's reconveyance to the brother.

(D) The sister, because the brother breached his fiduciary duty as her joint tenant.

[Q1047]

Answer: Choice **(A)** is correct. When the brother conveyed his interest in the property to his wife, this conveyance acted as an immediate severance, transforming the joint tenancy into a tenancy in common between the wife and the sister. When the wife immediately reconveyed to the brother, the brother and sister were tenants in common. When the brother died, his interest as a tenant in common passed back to his wife, making her a tenant in common with the sister.

(B) is wrong because the joint tenancy was severed before the brother's will took effect (at the moment the brother conveyed to his wife).

(C) is wrong because once the joint tenancy was broken by the conveyance from the brother to his wife, it could only be reestablished by a new conveyance joined in by both tenants in common, i.e., the wife and the sister (or, later, the brother and sister).

(D) is wrong because a conveyance by either joint tenant severs the joint tenancy regardless of whether the conveying joint tenant had or breached any fiduciary obligation to the other.

4. **Creditors of deceased joint tenant take nothing:**

Question: A brother and sister owned a parcel as joint tenants, upon which was situated a two-family house. The brother lived in one of the two apartments and rented the other apartment to a tenant. The brother got in a fight with the tenant and injured him. The tenant obtained and properly filed a judgment for $10,000 against the brother.

The statute in the jurisdiction reads: Any judgment properly filed shall, for ten years from filing, be a lien on the real property then owned or subsequently acquired by any person against whom the judgment is rendered.

The sister, who lived in a distant city, knew nothing of the tenant's judgment. Before the tenant took any further action, the brother died. The common-law joint tenancy is unmodified by statute.

The sister then learned the facts and brought an appropriate action against the tenant to quiet title to the land.

The court should hold that the tenant has

(A) a lien against the whole of the property, because he was a tenant of both the brother and the sister at the time of the judgment.

(B) a lien against the brother's undivided one-half interest in the land, because his judgment was filed prior to the brother's death.

(C) no lien, because the sister had no actual notice of the tenant's judgment until after the brother's death.

(D) no lien, because the brother's death terminated the interest to which the tenant's lien attached.

[Q1090]

Answer: Choice **(D)** is correct. Since the tenant's judgment was only against the brother, the tenant's judgment lien was only against the brother's real property, not the sister's real property. That real property consisted of the brother's joint tenancy interest. At the moment of the brother's death, that joint tenancy interest ceased to exist, and there was nothing left for the judgment lien to be a lien against.

(A) is wrong because the basis for the tenant's judgment (and thus for his judgment lien) was the brother's having injured him in the fight; since this had nothing to do with the tenant's having been a tenant of both brother and sister, it did not create any lien against the sister's interest in the property.

(B) is wrong because it inaccurately characterizes the brother's interest: it was a joint tenancy, not an "undivided one-half interest" (a phrase that would be used to describe a tenancy in common). Therefore, the fact that the judgment was filed while the brother was still alive is irrelevant, because the brother's joint tenancy ceased to exist at the moment he died.

(C) is wrong because it cites an irrelevant factor; even if the sister had had actual notice of the judgment while the brother was still alive, there would be no lien after the brother died for the reasons described in the discussion of (D).

III. TENANCY IN COMMON

A. **Tenancy in common:**

5. **Conveyance by one co-tenant:**

b. **Grant of mortgage or judgment lien:**

Question: A mother owned a two-family apartment house on a small city lot not suitable for partition-in-kind. Upon the mother's death, her will devised the property to "my son and my daughter."

A week ago, a creditor of the son obtained a money judgment against the son, and properly filed the judgment in the county where the property is located. A statute in the jurisdiction provides: any judgment properly filed shall, for ten years from filing, be a lien on the real property then owned or subsequently acquired by any person against whom the judgment is rendered.

The son needed cash, but the daughter did not wish to sell the property. The son commenced a partition action against the daughter and the creditor.

Assume that the court properly ordered a partition by judicial sale.

After the sale, the creditor's judgment will be a lien on

(A) all of the property.

(B) only a one-half interest in the property.

(C) all of the proceeds of sale of the property.

(D) only the portion of the proceeds of sale due the son.

[Q1066]

Answer: Choice **(D)** is correct. The mother's will had the effect of giving the property to the son and the daughter as tenants in common, with a undivided one-half interest going to each. (A conveyance "to *A* and *B*," without further specification, creates a tenancy in common with equal shares.) At the time the creditor got his money judgment against the son, that judgment became a lien only against real property owned by the son, and the son's real property consisted of his undivided one-half interest. When the partition by judicial sale occurred, the son's interest in the property became sole ownership of one-half of the proceeds, and the creditor's lien became a lien solely on that share of the proceeds.

Choices (A), (B), and (C) are wrong because they are inconsistent with the above analysis.

IV. RELATIONS BETWEEN CO-TENANTS

B. **Payments made by one tenant:**

3. **Duties if whole title is acquired:**

   Question: Alpha and Beta owned Greenacre, a large farm, in fee simple as tenants in common, each owning an undivided one-half interest. For five years Alpha occupied Greenacre and conducted farming operations. Alpha never accounted to Beta for any income but Alpha did pay all real estate taxes when the taxes were due and kept the buildings located on Greenacre insured against loss from fire, storm, and flood. Beta lived in a distant city and was interested only in realizing a profit from the sale of the land when market conditions produced the price Beta wanted.

   Alpha died intestate survived by Hera, Alpha's sole heir. Thereafter Hera occupied Greenacre but was inexperienced in farming operations. The result was a financial disaster. Hera failed to pay real estate taxes for two years. The appropriate governmental authority held a tax sale to recover the taxes due. At such sale Beta was the only bidder and obtained a conveyance from the appropriate governmental authority upon payment of an amount sufficient to discharge the amounts due for taxes, plus interest and penalties, and the costs of holding the tax sale. The amount paid was one-third of the reasonable market value of Greenacre.

   Thereafter Beta instituted an appropriate action against Hera to quiet title in and to recover possession of Greenacre. Hera asserted all defenses available to Hera.

Except for the statutes related to real estate taxes and tax sales, there is no applicable statute.

In this lawsuit, Beta is entitled to a decree quieting title so that Beta is the sole owner in fee simple of Greenacre

(A) because Beta survived Alpha.

(B) because Hera defaulted in the obligations undertaken by Alpha.

(C) unless Hera pays Beta one-half of the reasonable market value of Greenacre.

(D) unless Hera pays Beta one-half of the amount Beta paid for the tax deed.

[Q3131]

Answer: Choice **(D)** is correct because, by buying the tax debt, Beta was deemed to have acted on Hera's behalf, and is required to hold Hera's former interest in trust, subject to redemption. First, note that Beta and Hera were tenants in common. (Because Alpha and Beta were tenants in common, not joint tenants, Alpha's interest passed to Hera when Alpha died.) Tenants in common (like joint tenants) owe each other a fiduciary duty of fair dealing and good faith. One aspect of that duty is that when one co-tenant buys an outstanding interest, she holds that interest on behalf of the other co-tenant(s). So here, when Beta bought the tax deed, she was deemed to have bought on behalf of Hera as well as herself. Thus Hera received, in effect, an option to contribute (after the fact) to the tax sale, and Beta got a lien to make sure that if Hera didn't exercise that option, Beta would own the property free and clear. So now, Hera can choose either to pay her one-half share of the amount Beta paid at the tax sale (at which point Beta and Hera would each own 1/2 the tax debt and would in effect retire it), or to forfeit Hera's undivided one-half interest. (Hera is not personally liable for the one-half — the only sanction against her if she doesn't pay is to lose her one-half interest in the property.)

(A) is wrong, because there is no right of survivorship with a tenancy in common, so Beta's surviving Alpha did not make her sole owner.

(B) is wrong, because Hera's failure to pay her share of the taxes did not automatically divest Hera of her one-half interest. All Hera's failure to pay the taxes did was to give Beta the right to pay them off and then demand reimbursement from Hera, as described in Choice (D).

(C) is wrong, because under the duty of fair dealing, Beta's original right to purchase at the tax sale was shared by Hera. When one co-tenant buys an outstanding interest in the property, the purchaser in a sense buys on behalf of all other co-tenants (see the discussion of Choice (D) above). What Beta bought here was not the whole property, but the government's tax lien on the property. At that point, Beta succeeded to the government's lien position. Hera had a right to "redeem" her interest in the property from that lien, by paying her share of the tax debt represented by that lien. Hera was not required to pay the value of Hera's interest in the entire property, because Beta did not own the whole property outright. (In other words, what Hera had the right to do was analogous to her right to pay off her share of an outstanding mortgage.)

C. Partition:

2. Accounting:

Question: A man and a woman, who were cousins, acquired title in fee simple to a property, as equal tenants in common, by inheritance from their aunt. During the last 15 years of her lifetime, the aunt had allowed the man to occupy an apartment in the house on the property, to rent the other apartment in the house to various tenants, and to retain the rent.

The man made no payments to the aunt, and since the aunt's death 7 years ago, he has made no payments to the woman (his cousin). For those 22 years, the man has paid the real estate taxes on the property, kept the building on the property insured, and maintained the building. At all times, the woman has lived in a distant city and has never had anything to do with the aunt, the man, or the property.

Recently, the woman needed money for the operation of her business and demanded that the man join her in selling the property. The man refused.

The period of time to acquire title by adverse possession in the jurisdiction is 10 years. There is no other applicable statute.

The woman brought an appropriate action against the man for partition. The man asserted all available defenses and counterclaims.

In that action, the court should

(A) deny partition and find that title has vested in the man by adverse possession.

(B) deny partition, confirm the tenancy in common, but require an accounting to determine if either the woman or the man is indebted to the other on account of the rental payment, taxes, insurance premiums, and maintenance costs.

(C) grant partition and require, as an adjustment, an accounting to determine if either the man or the woman is indebted to the other on account of the rental payments, taxes, insurance premiums, and maintenance costs.

(D) grant partition to the woman and the man as equal owners, but without an accounting.

[Q3025]

Answer: Choice **(C)** is correct. Either co-tenant has the right, at any time, to demand partition. During the course of partition, the court will order an accounting, to determine whether either party owes the other money for rents collected, taxes paid, etc. It is not clear what substantive rules will govern that analysis — for instance, jurisdictions differ on whether a co-tenant who occupies the premises himself must account for the imputed value of rent received beyond his pro rata share. But the one thing that we can be sure of is that the court will require an accounting, and that's what this choice specifies.

(A) is wrong because the man never occupied the property in a "hostile" manner.

(B) is wrong because the court would grant partition, for the reason described in the discussion of (C).

(D) is wrong because a court would conduct an accounting to determine if either party has an obligation to pay money to the other.

CHAPTER 5

LANDLORD AND TENANT

III. TORT LIABILITY OF LANDLORD AND TENANT

B. **Landlord's liability:**

1. **Common law:**

h. **Assignment of interest by L:**

Question: Les leased a barn to his neighbor, Tom, for a term of three years. Tom took possession of the barn and used it for his farming purposes. The lease made Les responsible for structural repairs to the barn, unless they were made necessary by actions of Tom.

One year later, Les conveyed the barn and its associated land to Lottie "subject to the lease to Tom." Tom paid the next month's rent to Lottie. The next day a portion of an exterior wall of the barn collapsed because of rot in the interior structure of the wall. The wall had appeared to be sound, but a competent engineer, on inspection, would have discovered its condition. Neither Lottie nor Tom had the barn inspected by an engineer. Tom was injured as a result of the collapse of the wall.

Les had known that the wall was dangerously weakened by rot and needed immediate repairs, but had not told Tom or Lottie. There is no applicable statute.

Tom brought an appropriate action against Les to recover damages for the injuries he sustained. Lottie was not a party.

Which of the following is the most appropriate comment concerning the outcome of this action?

(A) Tom should lose, because Lottie assumed all of Les's obligations by reason of Tom's attornment to her.

(B) Tom should recover, because there is privity between lessor and lessee and it cannot be broken unilaterally.

(C) Tom should recover, because Les knew of the danger but did not warn Tom.

(D) Tom should lose, because he failed to inspect the barn.

[Q2036]

Answer: Choice **(C)** is correct. A landlord generally does not have tort liability for accidents that arise out of a dangerous condition on the property. For example, a landlord has no duty to inspect the property to discover dangerous conditions. But the landlord does have liability if he *knows* of the danger, or is in possession of facts that would reasonably have led a person in his position to know of the danger, and the tenant does not know of the danger. Les met this requirement because the facts tell us that he had "known that the wall was dangerously weakened by rot and needed immediate repairs." When Les assigned to Lottie, Les remained liable until Lottie actually discovered the condition and had a reasonable opportunity to fix it. Since Lottie had only owned the property for one day before the accident, and had not learned of the condition, liability had not yet passed to Lottie, and thus remained with Les, at the moment of the accident.

(A) is wrong because, while Lottie took "subject to" the lease, she did not assume Les's obligations to Tom, and her receipt of a payment from Tom did not change this. By the rule discussed in the prior paragraph, Lottie would not become liable for the condition until she learned of it and had time to fix it (unless she expressly assumed liability for conditions not known to her, which didn't happen here).

(B) is wrong because a landlord is liable to the tenant for failing to disclose a known dangerous condition. That liability persists regardless of whether landlord and tenant remain in privity of estate (and ends only when the successor on the landlord side becomes liable, which could only have been when the successor learned of the condition and had a chance to fix it).

(D) is wrong because, where a landlord is actually aware of a dangerous condition, and the tenant is not aware, the landlord is liable regardless of whether the tenant could have (or

IV. TENANT'S DUTIES

B. Fixtures:

1. Factors:

a. Contrary lease provision:

Question: A little more than five years ago, Len completed construction of a single-family home located on Homeacre, a lot that Len owned. Five years ago, Len and Tina entered into a valid five-year written lease of Homeacre that included the following language: "This house is rented as is, without certain necessary or useful items. The parties agree that Tina may acquire and install such items as she wishes at her expense, and that she may remove them if she wishes at the termination of this lease."

Tina decided that the house needed, and she paid cash to have installed, standard-sized combination screen/storm windows, a freestanding refrigerator to fit a kitchen alcove built for that purpose, a built-in electric stove and oven to fit a kitchen counter opening left for that purpose, and carpeting to cover the plywood living room floor.

Last month, by legal description of the land, Len conveyed Homeacre to Pete for $200,000. Pete knew of Tina's soon-expiring tenancy, but did not examine the written lease. As the lease expiration date approached, Pete learned that Tina planned to vacate on schedule, and learned for the first time that Tina claimed and planned to remove all of the above-listed items that she had installed.

Pete promptly brought an appropriate action to enjoin Tina from removing those items.

The court should decide that Tina may remove

(A) none of the items.

(B) only the refrigerator.

(C) all items except the carpet.

(D) all of the items.

[Q3011]

Answer: Choice **(D)** is correct. The easiest way to get this answer is to apply the general principle that even something that would otherwise be a non-removable fixture may be removed if the lease so specifies. The lease provision referring to "certain necessary or useful items," and saying that the tenant may remove them at the end of the lease, is such a provision, and would therefore be enforced.

By the way, even without this lease provision, it is doubtful whether any of the items here would be non-removable fixtures. When courts determine whether an item is a fixture, the main factors they consider are (1) whether its removal would seriously damage the item or the real estate; (2) whether the item is "firmly embedded" in the real estate; and (3) whether the item is "peculiarly adapted or fitted" to the real estate. All of these factors here cut in favor of non-fixture status: all of items appear to be capable of being removed without significantly damaging either the item or the real estate, none appears to be "firmly embedded" in the real estate, and none appears to have been "peculiarly adapted or fitted" to the real estate (since even the "built-in" stove and oven were probably mass-produced items, and thus not peculiarly-adapted-or-fitted).

VI. TRANSFER AND SALE BY LESSOR; ASSIGNMENT AND SUBLETTING BY LESSEE

A. **Generally allowed:**

  1. **Distinguish assignment from sublease:**

     a. **Significance:**

        i. **Question might not say "sublease":**

           Question: By a writing, a homeowner leased his house to a tenant for a term of three years, ending December 31 of last year, at the rent of $1,000 per month. The lease provided that the tenant could sublet and assign.

           The tenant lived in the house for one year and paid the rent promptly. After one year, the tenant leased the house to his cousin for one year at a rent of $1,000 per month.

           The cousin took possession of the house and lived there for six months but, because of her unemployment, paid no rent. After six months, on June 30 the cousin abandoned the house, which remained vacant for the balance of that year. The tenant again took possession of the house at the beginning of the third and final year of the term but paid the homeowner no rent.

           At the end of the lease term, the homeowner brought an appropriate action against both the tenant and the cousin to recover $24,000, the unpaid rent.

           In such action the homeowner is entitled to a judgment

           (A) against the tenant individually for $24,000, and no judgment against the cousin.

           (B against the tenant individually for $18,000, and against the cousin individually for $6,000.

           (C) against the tenant for $12,000, and against the tenant and the cousin jointly and severally for $12,000.

           (D) against the tenant individually for $18,000, and against the tenant and the cousin jointly and severally for $6,000.
           [Q3085]

           Answer: Choice **(A)** is correct. An "assignment" is the transfer by the lessee of his entire interest in the leased premises. If something less, even a term one day less, is transferred, the transfer is not an assignment, but a "sublease." With a sublease, there is a relationship between the lessee and the sublessee, but there is no relationship, no privity of estate, between the lessor and sublessee. Since there is no privity of estate between the two, *the lessor cannot sue the sublessee for rent.* (By contrast, in an assignment the assignee becomes liable to the assignor for rent unless/until the assignee re-assigns.) Here, the tenant's lease of the house to the cousin was a sublease, because it was for a shorter time (1 year) than remained on the original lease (2 years). On the other hand, the creation of the sublease did not release the tenant from his original liability to the homeowner for the full rent (only a release executed by the homeowner could do that). Therefore, the tenant is responsible to the homeowner for the full unpaid 24 months, and the cousin is not responsible to the homeowner for anything.

           (B), (C), and (D) are incorrect because each is inconsistent with the above analysis.

Question: A landlord leased an apartment to a tenant by written lease for two years ending on the last day of a recent month. The lease provided for $700 monthly rental. The tenant occupied the apartment and paid the rent for the first 15 months of the lease term, until he moved to a new job in another city. Without consulting the landlord, the tenant moved a friend into the apartment and signed an informal writing transferring to the friend his "lease rights" for the remaining nine months of the lease. The friend made the next four monthly $700 rental payments to the landlord. For the final five months of the lease term, no rent was paid by anyone, and the friend moved out with three months left on the lease term. The landlord was on an extended trip abroad, and did not learn of the default and the vacancy until last week. The landlord sued the tenant and the friend, jointly and severally, for $3,500 for the last five months' rent.

What is the likely outcome of the lawsuit?

(A) Both the tenant and the friend are liable for the full $3,500, because the tenant is liable on privity of contract and the friend is liable on privity of estate as assignee.

(B) The friend is liable for $1,400 on privity of estate, which lasted only until he vacated, and the tenant is liable for $2,100 on privity of contract and estate for the period after the friend vacated.

(C) The friend is liable for $3,500 on privity of estate and the tenant is not liable, because the landlord's failure to object to the friend's payment of rent relieved the tenant of liability.

(D) The tenant is liable for $3,500 on privity of contract and the friend is not liable, because a sublessee does not have personal liability to the original landlord.

[Q7004]

Answer: Choice **(A)** is correct. An assignment arises when a tenant transfers all or some of the leased premises to another for the remainder of the lease term, retaining no interest in the assigned premises. In this case, prior to the agreement with the friend, the tenant had privity of contract with the landlord because of the lease. The tenant also had privity of estate because the tenant was in possession of the apartment. Subsequently, an assignment arose when the tenant transferred the premises to the friend for the remainder of the lease term of nine months. The friend was then in privity of estate with the landlord as to all promises that run with the land, including the covenant to pay rent. (When the friend moved out, this did not end the privity of estate, because the friend did not assign to someone else, and simply abandoned the premises. See Rest. 2d (Landlord & Tenant), § 16.1, Illustr. 24.) The tenant was not released by the landlord, however, and thus remained liable on privity of contract.

(B) is incorrect, because the friend entered privity of estate with the landlord when he received the assignment, and this privity of estate remained with the friend until the end of the lease because the friend made no assignment. Therefore, the friend remained liable on privity of estate for the period after he vacated. Furthermore, because the landlord never released the tenant, the tenant remained liable for the full $3,500 on privity of contract.

(C) is incorrect, because the landlord never released the tenant, thereby keeping the tenant liable on privity of contract based on the original lease. (There was no express release, and a release would not be implied merely because the landlord accepted rent from the friend.)

(D) is incorrect, because this choice assumes that the friend was a sublessee, which he was not. A sublease arises when a tenant transfers the right of possession to all or some of the leased premises to another for a time less than the remaining time of the lease, or when the tenant retains some other interest in the premises. Here, the tenant transferred all the remaining time of the lease to the friend and retained no other interest. Accordingly, this was an assignment and not a sublease. As an assignee, the friend was in privity of estate with the landlord as to all promises that run with the land, including the covenant to pay rent.

B. Running of benefit and burden:

1. Purchase options in leases:

b. Split on exercise apart from lease:

Question: Lanny, the owner of Whiteacre in fee simple, leased Whiteacre to Ten for a term of ten years by a properly executed written instrument. The lease was promptly and properly recorded. It contained an option for Ten to purchase Whiteacre by tendering $250,000 as purchase price any time "during the term of this lease." One year later, Ten, by a properly executed written instrument, purported to assign the option to Oscar, expressly retaining all of the remaining term of the lease. The instrument of assignment was promptly and properly recorded.

Two years later, Lanny contracted to sell Whiteacre to Jones and to convey a marketable title "subject to the rights of Ten under her lease." Jones refused to close because of the outstanding option assigned to Oscar.

Lanny brought an appropriate action against Jones for specific performance.

If judgment is rendered in favor of Lanny, it will be because the relevant jurisdiction has adopted a rule on a key issue as to which various state courts have split.

Which of the following identifies the determinative rule or doctrine upon which the split occurs, and states the position favorable to Lanny?

(A) In a contract to buy, any form of "subject to a lease" clause that fails to mention expressly an existing option means that the seller is agreeing to sell free and clear of any option originally included in the lease.

(B) Marketable title can be conveyed so long as any outstanding option not mentioned in the purchase contract has not yet been exercised.

(C) Options to purchase by lessees are subject to the Rule Against Perpetuities.

(D) Options to purchase contained in a lease cannot be assigned separately from the lease.
[Q2013]

Answer: Choice **(D)** is correct. Courts disagree about whether a purchase option embodied in a lease may be assigned independently of the lease. Since Lanny is arguing that his title is marketable, the position that purchase options cannot be assigned independently of the lease is favorable to Lanny (because that position, if upheld, would certainly mean that Oscar could not exercise the option, and might even mean that Ten had rendered the option invalid by purporting to assign it independently of the lease).

(A) is wrong because, even if the contract's "subject to a lease" language meant what this choice says it means (that Lanny is committing to sell free and clear of any option), Lanny would still lose: he would not in fact be able to sell free and clear of the purchase option now purportedly held by Oscar.

(B) is wrong because the existence of a purchase option renders title unmarketable, even though the option has not yet been exercised. (If the rule were otherwise, the buyer would be paying full dollar for property that might be "called away" from him by exercise of the option at any time, perhaps at a below-market price.)

(C) is wrong because: (1) purchase options embodied in leases are typically not subjected to the Rule against Perpetuities; and (2) even if the option here *were* subject to the Rule, the option would not thereby be rendered invalid (since the option must be exercised during the lease term, and the lease terms falls within "lives in being plus 21 years").

E. **Agreement by the parties about transfer:**

1. **Generally enforced**

    a. **Condemnation awards:**

    Question: Six years ago, a landlord and a tenant entered into a 10-year commercial lease of land. The written lease provided that, if a public entity under the power of eminent domain condemned any part of the land, the lease would terminate and the landlord would receive the entire condemnation award. Thereafter, the city condemned approximately two-thirds of the land.

    The tenant notified the city and the landlord that an independent appraisal of the value of the tenant's possessory interest established that it substantially exceeded the tenant's obligation under the lease and that the tenant was entitled to share the award. The appraisal was accurate.

    In an appropriate action among the landlord, the tenant, and the city as to the right of the tenant to a portion of the condemnation award, for whom will the court likely find?

    (A) The landlord, because the condemnation superseded and canceled the lease.

    (B) The landlord, because the parties specifically agreed as to the consequences of condemnation.

    (C) The tenant, because the landlord breached the landlord's implied warranty of quiet enjoyment.

    (D) The tenant, because otherwise the landlord would be unjustly enriched.

    [QA070]

    Answer: Choice **(B)** is correct. The lease between the landlord and the tenant specifically addressed what would happen if a public entity condemned any part of the land under its power of eminent domain. That agreement between the parties controls. Thus, the court will find for the landlord: the lease will terminate and the landlord will receive the entire condemnation award.

    (A) is wrong because the specific terms of the lease supersede the condemnation, not vice versa. If the lease had been silent on the issue of condemnation, then the result would have depended on whether the condemnation was of all the property, or of just part. (With a total condemnation and a lease silent on this point, the leasehold and all the tenant's duties under the lease would have been terminated, and the tenant would have been entitled to share in the condemnation award only to the extent that the fair market value of his leasehold exceeded his obligations under the lease. Had the city condemned just part of the property, in most courts the tenant would have been required to continue paying the full rent, but would have been entitled to a portion of the condemnation award to compensate him for the portion of the leasehold no longer available to him.) However, this "default" rule for handling a condemnation award will, in all courts, not be applied if the parties have specified a different treatment, as they did here.

    (C) is wrong because it misstates the law. The taking of all or part of the leased land, or the taking of some interest in it — say an easement — by eminent domain does not constitute a breach of the landlord's covenant of quiet enjoyment of the premises because it occurs through no fault of the landlord.

    (D) is wrong because there has been no unjust enrichment. Had the lease not provided for the consequences of condemnation, the lease would have remained in force, and the tenant would, to prevent unjust enrichment of the landlord, have gotten either a pro-rata reduction of rent, some portion of the award (if the lease was below-market), or both. But the fact that the parties expressly agreed that the landlord would keep the entire award means that there is no unjust enrichment when the agreed-upon outcome is enforced.

CHAPTER 6
EASEMENTS AND SERVITUDES

II. CREATION OF EASEMENTS

E. **Easement by prescription:**

2. **Adverse use:**

Question: Oxnard owned Goldacre, a tract of land, in fee simple. At a time when Goldacre was in the adverse possession of Amos, Eric obtained the oral permission of Oxnard to use as a road or driveway a portion of Goldacre to reach adjoining land, Twin Pines, which Eric owned in fee simple. Thereafter, during all times relevant to this problem, Eric used this road between Goldacre regularly for ingress and egress between Twin Pines and a public highway.

Amos quit possession of Goldacre before acquiring title by adverse possession. Without any further communication between Oxnard and Eric, Eric continued to use the road for a total period, from the time he first began to use it, sufficient to acquire an easement by prescription. Oxnard then blocked the road and refused to permit its continued use. Eric brought suit to determine his right to continue use of the road. Eric should

(A) win, because his use was adverse to Amos and once adverse it continued adverse until some affirmative showing of a change.

(B) win, because Eric made no attempt to renew permission after Amos quit possession of Goldacre.

(C) lose, because his use was with permission.

(D) lose, because there is no evidence that he continued adverse use for the required period after Amos quit possession.

[Q4015]

Answer: Choice **(C)** is correct, because it correctly identifies the reason Eric will lose: his use of Goldacre was not "adverse," i.e., non-permissive. The key facts here are that Eric had oral permission from Oxnard *originally* to use the road across Goldacre, and Amos quit possession of Goldacre before acquiring title by adverse possession. What does this mean? That Eric's use of Goldacre was never adverse to the interests of the landowner, and that Amos never had any enforceable rights to Goldacre. In order to gain an easement by prescription, one's use of another's property must be actual, open and notorious, continuous for the statutory period, exclusive, and hostile and adverse (non-permissive). Here, the facts specifically state that Eric had Oxnard's oral permission to use the road across Goldacre. The red herring here is the presence of Amos. However, Amos is merely in possession of Goldacre. The facts state that he quit possession before he acquired title to it. Thus, the elements of an easement by prescription would apply to Eric vis-à-vis Oxnard, *not* Eric vis-à-vis Amos.

(A) is wrong because it focuses on the wrong fact. Here, it doesn't matter if Eric's use is adverse to Amos, because Amos is not the landowner — *Oxnard* is. Eric's use is not adverse to Oxnard, because the facts state that Oxnard granted Eric oral permission to use the road across Goldacre. An easement by prescription requires use of another's property that is actual, open and notorious, continuous for the statutory period, exclusive, and hostile and adverse. "Hostile and adverse" means non-permissive in this context. Here, since Eric's use was with the permission of the landowner the entire time, his use was *never* adverse. Since (A) does not recognize this, it's not the best response.

(B) is wrong because it falsely suggests that Amos's quitting possession of Goldacre is relevant. It is not, because an easement by prescription is gained by adverse use against the *landowner*, not the *possessor*. Eric could only gain an easement by prescription if his use of Goldacre *as against Oxnard* was actual, open and notorious, continuous for the statutory period, exclusive, and non-permissive.

(D) is wrong because it focuses on a basically irrelevant fact. What matters is whether Eric had the requisite open and hostile use *as against the true owner*, Oxnard. If Eric hadn't originally gotten permission from Oxnard, his time of use of the driveway while Amos was in adverse possession of the overall tract would count against Oxnard. So the problem is not that Eric didn't use the driveway long enough once Amos left, it's that Eric's entire use of the driveway (even when Amos was there) wasn't adverse as against Oxnard.

III. SCOPE OF EASEMENTS

B. Development of dominant estate:

2. Remedy for misuse is injunction or damages, not forfeiture:

Question: A large tract of land was owned by a religious order. On the land, the order erected a large residential building where its members reside. The land is surrounded by rural residential properties and its only access to a public way is afforded by an easement over a strip of land 30 feet wide. The easement was granted to the order by deed from a neighbor, who owned one of the adjacent residential properties. The order built a driveway on the strip, and the easement was used for 20 years without incident or objection.

Last year, as permitted by the applicable zoning ordinance, the order constructed a 200-bed nursing home and a parking lot on their land, using all of the land that was available for such development. The nursing home was very successful, and on Sundays visitors to the nursing home overflowed the parking facilities on the land and parked all along the driveway from early in the morning through the evening hours. After two Sundays of the resulting congestion and inconvenience, the neighbor erected a barrier across the driveway on Sundays preventing any use of the driveway by anyone seeking access to the order's land. The order objected.

The neighbor brought an appropriate action to terminate the easement.

The most likely result in this action is that the court will hold for

(A) the neighbor, because the order excessively expanded the use of the dominant tenement.

(B) the neighbor, because the parking on the driveway exceeded the scope of the easement.

(C) the order, because expanded use of the easement does not terminate the easement.

(D) the order, because the neighbor's use of self help denies her the right to equitable relief.
[Q2021]

Answer: Choice **(C)** is correct. The expanded use of the easement here — especially the parking along the driveway at all hours — probably does represent excessive use going beyond the intended scope of the easement. However, a court would almost certainly limit the remedy to an injunction against further violations, or to damages for the two past violations, and would not order a forfeiture of the easement. That's because forfeitures are drastic remedies, and will be awarded in excessive-use situations only if no other remedy will be adequate, which would not be the case for the violations here.

(A) is wrong because, while the order has indeed probably excessively expanded their use of the easement, the court would not order the easement forfeited as a remedy, for the reasons stated above.

(B) is wrong for the same reason (A) is wrong.

(D) is wrong because a court would not grant the neighbor the extreme remedy of forfeiture whether or not she had used self-help.

IV. REPAIR AND MAINTENANCE OF EASEMENTS

B. Dominant owner has right to maintain:

Question: Two adjacent, two-story, commercial buildings were owned by a landowner. The first floors of both buildings were occupied by various retail establishments. The second floors were rented to various other tenants. Access to the second floor of each building was reached by a common stairway located entirely in Building l. While the buildings were being used in this manner, the landowner sold Building 1 to an accountant by warranty deed which made no mention of any rights concerning the stairway. About two years later the landowner sold Building 2 to a lawyer. The stairway continued to be used by the occupants of both buildings. The stairway became unsafe as a consequence of regular wear and tear. The lawyer entered upon the accountant's building and began the work of repairing the stairway. The accountant demanded that the lawyer discontinue the repair work and vacate the accountant's building. When the lawyer refused, the accountant brought an action to enjoin the lawyer from continuing the work.

Judgment should be for

(A) the accountant, because the lawyer has no rights in the stairway.

(B) the accountant, because the lawyer's rights in the stairway do not extend beyond the normal life of the existing structure.

(C) the lawyer, because the lawyer has an easement in the stairway and an implied right to keep the stairway in repair.

(D) the lawyer, because the lawyer has a right to take whatever action is necessary to protect himself from possible tort liability to persons using the stairway.

[Q1029]

Answer: Choice **(C)** is correct. At the time of the conveyance by the landowner to the lawyer, the lawyer received an implied easement to use the stairs for access to Building 2. (The three requirements for an easement by implication were met here: (1) the land was "severed" from common ownership when the landowner kept Building 2 while selling Building 1; (2) the use of the stairway for access to Building 2 existed prior to this severance; and (3) the easement was and is reasonably necessary to enjoyment of Building 2.) The holder of the easement (the lawyer) therefore had an implied right to maintain the property used in the easement, given that the maintenance was compatible with the intended use of the easement and did not unreasonably interfere with the servient owner's (the accountant's) use of the servient estate.

(A) is wrong because the lawyer *does* have rights in the stairway, namely an implied easement.

(B) is wrong because the lawyer as easement holder has the right to maintain or repair the structure indefinitely, not just for the normal life of the original staircase.

(D) is wrong because it misstates the reason for the lawyer's repair right, which is that the lawyer has an implied easement; if the lawyer did not have an implied easement, he would probably not face tort liability for failing to correct the stairway danger on property belonging to another, at least if he asked the owner (the accountant) to do the work and the owner refused.

Question: Maria is the owner and possessor of Goodacre, on which there is a lumber yard. Maria conveyed to Reliable Electric Company the right to construct and use an overhead electric line across Goodacre to serve other properties. The conveyance was in writing, but the writing made no provision concerning the responsibility for repair or maintenance of the line. Reliable installed the poles and erected the electric line in a proper and workmanlike manner. Neither Maria nor Reliable took any steps toward the maintenance or repair of the line after it was built. Neither party complained to the other about any failure to repair. Because of the failure to repair or properly maintain the line, it fell to the ground during a storm. In doing so, it caused a fire in the lumber yard and did considerable damage. Maria sued Reliable Electric Company to recover for damages to the lumber yard. The decision should be for

(A) Maria, because the owner of an easement has a duty to so maintain the easement as to avoid unreasonable interference with the use of the servient tenement by its lawful possessor.

(B) Maria, because the owner of an easement is absolutely liable for any damage caused to the servient tenement by the exercise of the easement.

(C) Reliable Electric Company, because the possessor of the servient tenement has a duty to give the easement holder notice of defective conditions.

(D) Reliable Electric Company, because an easement holder's right to repair is a right for his own benefit, and is therefore inconsistent with any duty to repair for the benefit of another.

[Q4187]

Answer: Choice **(A)** is correct. Reliable has an expressly-created easement for constructing and using overhead electric lines. Since Reliable was given the right to use Maria's land, it's the "dominant" tenement holder (and Maria is the "servient" tenement holder, since it's her land that's burdened by the easement). The rule on maintaining easements is that the dominant tenement holder has both the *right* and the *duty* to use reasonable care to maintain the easement. Thus, Reliable would have the *right* to enter Maria's land and repair the line and poles, as necessary, and Maria could not object to this interference. However, Reliable also had the duty to use reasonable care to maintain the equipment so it did not pose an unreasonable danger to Maria's land, and the utility, by failing to maintain the line at all, did not fulfill that duty. As a result, Maria will be able to recover for damages to the lumber yard.

(B) is wrong because although it arrives at the correct result, it misstates the responsibility of the dominant tenement holder. There is no doctrine that states that an easement owner is strictly liable for damage caused to the servient tenement by the exercise of the easement. Instead, the dominant holder merely has the obligation to use reasonable care to maintain the easement in such a way that it does not damage the servient property. If the accident had happened without the lack of due care by Reliable (which is not the way it happened), Reliable would not be liable to Maria.

(C) is wrong because it misstates the duty of the servient tenement holder, and arrives at the wrong result. In general, the dominant holder has the obligation to use reasonable care to maintain the easement so that it does not pose unreasonable risk to the servient parcel. This obligation includes an obligation to inspect. So the mere fact that Maria didn't give notice of the problem doesn't save Reliable from liability. (Indeed, an electric utility ought to be able to recognize maintenance issues more easily than a non-utility customer.)

(D) is wrong because it fails to recognize Reliable Electric's duty to Maria. The holder of an easement has both the *right* and the *duty* to take reasonable steps to maintain the easement.

1. **Limited right to contribution:**

    Question: Beach owned a tract of land called Blackacre. An old road ran through Blackacre from the abutting public highway. The road had been used to haul wood from Blackacre. Without Beach's permission and with no initial right, Daniel, the owner of Whiteacre, which adjoined Blackacre, traveled over the old road for a period of 15 years to obtain access to Whiteacre, although Whiteacre abutted another public road. Occasionally, Daniel made repairs to the old road.

    The period of time to acquire rights by prescription in the jurisdiction is ten years.

    After the expiration of 15 years, Beach conveyed a portion of Blackacre to Carrol. The deed included the following clause: "together with the right to pass and repass at all times and for all purposes over the old road." Carrol built a house fronting on the old road. After the conveyance, Beach has used the road once or twice per year. Daniel almost never uses the road anymore.

    The road was severely damaged by a spring flood, and Carrol made substantial repairs to the road. Carrol asked Daniel and Beach to contribute one-third each to the cost of repairing the flood damage. They both refused, and Carrol brought an appropriate action to compel contribution from Beach and Daniel.

    In this action, Carrol will

    (A) lose as to both defendants.

    (B) win as to both defendants.

    (C) win as to Beach, but lose as to Daniel.

    (D) win as to Daniel, but lose as to Beach.
    [Q2191]

    Answer: Choice **(A)** is correct. Carrol is the owner of the dominant tenement (i.e., the owner of the easement), and Beach is the owner of the servient tenement. Beach, as the servient owner, has no obligation to contribute one-third of Carrol's repair expenditures. Beach may have *some* obligation of reimbursement, based on the intensity and frequency of his bridge use versus Carrol's, but certainly not a one-third-of-total-cost obligation, since Beach clearly does not represent one-third of the total usage of the bridge. As to Daniel, he may well have obtained an easement by prescription. But even if he has done so, he, too, has no obligation to reimburse Carrol for one-third of the latter's expenditures, because Daniel, like Beach, rarely makes use of the bridge, and has at most an obligation to reimburse for his small pro rata share of total usage.

    Choices (B), (C), and (D) are wrong because they are inconsistent with the above analysis.

V. TRANSFER AND SUBDIVISION OF EASEMENTS

B. Transfer of benefit:

1. Transfer of easements appurtenant:

a. Deed to dominant parcel is silent:

Question: Olwen owned 80 acres of land, fronting on a town road. Two years ago, Olwen sold to Buck the back 40 acres. The 40 acres sold to Buck did not adjoin any public road. Olwen's deed to Buck expressly granted a right-of-way over a specified strip of Olwen's retained 40 acres, so Buck could reach the town road. The deed was promptly and properly recorded.

Last year, Buck conveyed the back 40 acres to Sam. They had discussed the right-of-way over Olwen's land to the road, but Buck's deed to Sam made no mention of it. Sam began to use the right-of-way as Buck had, but Olwen sued to enjoin such use by Sam.

The court should decide for

(A) Sam, because he has an easement by implication.

(B) Sam, because the easement appurtenant passed to him as a result of Buck's deed to him.

(C) Olwen, because Buck's easement in gross was not transferable.

(D) Olwen, because Buck's deed failed expressly to transfer the right-of-way to Sam.

[Q2055]

Answer: Choice **(B)** is correct. What we have here is an easement appurtenant, because the easement is for the benefit of a particular parcel (the back 40 acres). An easement appurtenant passes to the new holder of the dominant tenement automatically, even if the deed to the dominant tenement does not mention the easement.

(A) is wrong, because the easement here is an express easement, not one by implication. Furthermore, even if the easement here *were* an easement by implication, it would automatically pass together with the dominant tenement.

(C) is wrong because the easement here is appurtenant, not in gross. That is, it is clear from the surrounding circumstances that the easement is being used to benefit a particular parcel (the back 40 acres), not to benefit Buck irrespective of Buck's ownership of those 40 acres. So while many courts indeed hold that an easement in gross is not transferable if the document creating it is silent on the issue, this principle won't apply to the facts here.

(D) is wrong because, as described in the answer to (B) above, an easement appurtenant will pass together with the dominant tenement, even if the deed conveying the dominant tenement does not mention the easement.

VI. TERMINATION OF EASEMENTS

A. Abandonment:

2. Intent plus conduct:

a. Mere non-use not enough:

Question: In 1960, Owens, the owner in fee simple of Barrenacres, a large, undeveloped tract of land, granted an easement to the Water District "to install, inspect, repair, maintain, and replace pipes" within a properly delineated strip of land twenty feet wide across Barrenacres. The easement permitted the Water District to enter Barrenacres for only the stated purposes. The Water District promptly and properly recorded the deed. In 1961, the Water District installed a water main which crossed Barrenacres within the described strip; the Water District has not since entered Barrenacres.

In 1965, Owens sold Barrenacres to Peterson, but the deed, which was promptly and properly recorded, failed to refer to the Water District easement. Peterson built his home on Barrenacres in 1965, and since that time he has planted and maintained, at great expense in money, time, and effort, a formal garden area which covers, among other areas, the surface of the twenty-foot easement strip.

In 2006, the Water District proposed to excavate the entire length of its main in order to inspect, repair, and replace the main, to the extent necessary. At a public meeting, at which Peterson was present, the Water District announced its plans and declared its intent to do as little damage as possible to any property involved. Peterson objected to the Water District plans.

Peterson asked his attorney to secure an injunction against the Water District and its proposed entry upon his property. The best advice that the attorney can give is that Peterson's attempt to secure injunctive relief will be likely to

(A) succeed, because Peterson's deed from Owens did not mention the easement.

(B) succeed, because more than forty years have passed since the Water District last entered Barrenacres.

(C) fail, because the Water District's plan is within its rights.

(D) fail, because the Water District's plan is fair and equitable.

[Q4045]

Answer: Choice **(C)** is correct. The Water District has a valid easement as to Barrenacres. While there are several bases on which an easement can be terminated, the only ones that apply to an easement in gross under these circumstances are: (1) a release, in writing; (2) abandonment; (3) adverse use by the servient tenement holder, for the statutory period; or (4) estoppel. The facts here indicate that none of these have been satisfied, so the easement is still in force. (There is no "statute of limitations" on easements, because they are interests in land — so unless one of the events listed above occurs, the easement lasts forever.) Given that the Water District holds the easement, is it acting within its rights? Yes — the general rule is that the dominant tenement holder has both the right and the duty to take reasonable steps to maintain the easement. That's what the Water District is doing.

(A) is wrong because it does not state a basis on which Peterson can prevail. While the deed itself does not mention the easement, Peterson was on constructive notice of the easement when he took, since it appeared in his "chain of title." You're told that the easement was properly and timely recorded, and, as such, Peterson took subject to it, since an easement is considered an interest in property. Since constructive notice is sufficient to give Peterson notice of the easement, the fact that the easement did not appear on his own deed is not enough for him to succeed.

(B) is not wrong because the passage of 40 years or more doesn't cause an easement to be extinguished. Easements are interests in land — so unless one of the events listed in (C) above occurs, the easement lasts forever.

(D) is wrong because the fact it cites is irrelevant. Even assuming that the statement that the plan is "fair and equitable" is correct, that fact wouldn't make a difference to the outcome here. That's because, even if the plan were fair and equitable, if it wasn't within the Water District's rights, it would be impermissible. In fact, the dominant estate holder (here, the Water District) has both the right and the duty to maintain the easement, and *this* is the basis of its right to excavate the pipe. As long as the Water District is within its rights in doing so, any damage done to the property would not be actionable.

VII. LICENSES

A. Definition:

2. Illustrations:

Question: A hockey fan had a season ticket for a professional hockey team's games at the team's home arena, in Section B, Row 12, Seat 16. During the intermission between the first and second periods of a game between the team and a visiting club, the fan solicited signatures for a petition urging that the coach of the home team be fired.

The arena and the team are owned by a privately owned corporation. As evidenced by many prominently displayed signs, the corporation prohibits all solicitations anywhere within the arena at any time and in any manner. The corporation notified the fan to cease her solicitation of signatures.

The fan continued to seek signatures on her petition during the team's next three home games at the arena. Each time, the corporation notified the fan to cease such solicitation. The fan announced her intention to seek signatures on her petition again during the team's next home game at the arena. The corporation wrote a letter informing the fan that her season ticket was canceled and tendering a refund for the unused portion. The fan refused the tender and brought an appropriate action to establish the right to attend all home games.

In this action, the court will decide for

(A) the corporation, because it has a right and obligation to control activities on realty it owns and has invited the public to visit.

(B) the corporation, because the fan's ticket to hockey games created only a license.

(C) the fan, because, having paid value for the ticket, her right to be present cannot be revoked.

(D) the fan, because she was not committing a nuisance by her activities.

[Q3031]

Answer: Choice **(B)** is correct. A ticket to a sporting event or other public function is considered a license rather than an easement. A license is a right to use the licensor's land that is revocable at the will of the licensor. Because the fan held only a license, that interest was revocable at the will of the licensor. (The fact that this was a *season* ticket makes no difference — the court could look at this as either a single extended license or a series of individual-game licenses, but in either event the license(s) would be revocable at the will of the licensor.)

Choice (A) is wrong because, although the corporation may have a right and obligation to control activities on realty it owns, its right to revoke the fan's season tickets arises from the fact that it has issued the fan only a license.

Choice (C) is wrong because the fan's interest was a license, and the fact that the licensee pays value for the license does not change the license's revocability. (Under principles of unjust enrichment, the licensor would have to refund any unexpired portion of the advance payment, which is what the corporation did here.)

Choice (D) is wrong because the fact that this was a license meant that the corporation had the right to revoke the license, whether the fan was a "nuisance" or not.

3. Oral agreement must produce a license, not an easement:

Question: A landowner orally gave his neighbor permission to share the use of the private road on the landowner's land so that the neighbor could have more convenient access to the neighbor's land. Only the landowner maintained the road. After the neighbor had used the road on a daily basis for three years, the landowner conveyed his land to a grantee, who immediately notified the neighbor that the neighbor was not to use the road. The neighbor sued the grantee seeking a declaration that the neighbor had a right to continue to use the road.

Who is likely to prevail?

(A) The grantee, because an oral license is invalid.

(B) The grantee, because the neighbor had a license that the grantee could terminate at any time.

(C) The neighbor, because the grantee is estopped to terminate the neighbor's use of the road.

(D) The neighbor, because the neighbor's use of the road was open and notorious when the grantee purchased the land.

[Q7098]

Answer: Choice **(B)** is correct. A license is permission to use the land of another. It is ordinarily revocable, and is not subject to the Statute of Frauds. In this case, because the neighbor had the landowner's permission to use the road and did not expend any money, property, or labor pursuant to the agreement (i.e., the neighbor did substantially rely on the continued availability of the license), the neighbor had a license that was revocable — and effectively revoked — by the grantee.

(A) is incorrect because, while this option correctly states that the grantee will prevail, it misstates the reason why this is so. A license (unlike an easement) is not subject to the Statute of Frauds; it may be oral, written, or implied.

(C) is incorrect because for estoppel to apply to make a license (which is ordinarily revocable) irrevocable, the neighbor must have expended money, property, or labor pursuant to the agreement. In this case, the landowner alone maintained the road. The neighbor's use of the land by permission, without expense, was therefore a revocable license that was effectively revoked by the grantee.

(D) is incorrect. An open and notorious use of the road suggests a claim for an easement by prescription. However, the use was with permission, which prevents a prescriptive claim. (Also, the use was for just three years, making it extremely unlikely that the statutory period for adverse possession-type claims could have run.) Instead, the neighbor's use of the land was a license that was effectively revoked by the grantee.

4. **Distinguished from lease:**

    Question: Adam owned Blackacre. Adam entered into a written three-year lease of Blackacre with Bertha. Among other provisions, the lease prohibited Bertha from "assigning this lease, in whole or in part, and from subletting Blackacre, in whole or in part." In addition to a house, a barn, and a one-car garage, Blackacre's 30 acres included several fields where first Adam, and now Bertha, grazed sheep.

    During the following months, Bertha:

    I. By a written agreement allowed her neighbor Charles exclusive use of the garage for storage, under lock and key, of his antique Packard automobile for two years, charging him $240.

II. Told her neighbor Doris that Doris could use the fields to practice her golf as long as she did not disturb Bertha's sheep.

Which, if any, of Bertha's actions constituted a violation of the lease?

(A) I only.

(B) II only.

(C) Both I and II.

(D) Neither I nor II.

[Q3196]

Answer: Choice **(A)** is correct, because Bertha's agreement with Charlie was a subletting of Blackacre, but her agreement with Doris was merely a license or easement. A sublease is a lease executed by the lessee of land or premises to a third person, conveying the same interest the lessee enjoys (as to all or part of the property) but for a shorter term than that for which the lessee holds. When Bertha allowed Charles to use the garage to store his car, this was a sublease because Bertha gave Charles the exclusive use of a defined piece of property, the garage, for a defined term that was less than the time remaining on the master lease. The fact that the arrangement applied to only part of the premises did not prevent it from being a sublease. Therefore, the arrangement violated the no-subleases provision of the master lease.

Bertha's arrangement with Doris, by contrast, was merely a license, not a sublease. A sublease requires that the sublessor gives the sublessee the *exclusive* right to use part of the property for a defined period of time shorter than the time remaining on the master lease. Since Doris could only golf when and if this wouldn't interfere with the sheep, Doris' rights weren't exclusive, preventing the arrangement from being a sublease, and thus preventing it from violating the no-subleases clause of the lease.

Choices (B), (C), and (D) are wrong because they are inconsistent with the above analysis.

IX. EQUITABLE SERVITUDES / RESTRICTIVE COVENANTS

C. Plaintiff's parcel must be intended to be benefitted:

Question: Ollie owned a large tract of land known as Peterhill. During Ollie's lifetime, Ollie conveyed the easterly half (East Peterhill), situated in the municipality of Hawthorn, to Abel, and the westerly half (West Peterhill), situated in the municipality of Sycamore, to Betty. Each of the conveyances, which were promptly and properly recorded, contained the following language:

> "The parties agree for themselves and their heirs and assigns that the premises herein conveyed shall be used only for residential purposes; that each lot created within the premises herein conveyed shall contain not less than five acres; and that each lot shall have not more than one single-family dwelling. This agreement shall bind all successor owners of all or any portion of Peterhill and any owner of any part of Peterhill may enforce this covenant."

After Ollie's death, Abel desired to build houses on one-half acre lots in the East Peterhill tract as authorized by current applicable zoning and building codes in Hawthorn. The area surrounding East Peterhill in Hawthorn was developed as a residential community with homes built on one-half acre lots. West Peterhill was in a residential area covered by the Sycamore zoning code, which allowed residential development only on five-acre tracts of land.

In an appropriate action brought by Betty to enjoin Abel's proposed construction on one-half acre lots, the court will find the quoted restriction to be

(A) invalid, because of the change of circumstance in the neighborhood.

(B) invalid, because it conflicts with the applicable zoning code.

(C) valid, but only so long as the original grantees from Ollie own their respective tracts of Peterhill.

(D) valid, because the provision imposed an equitable servitude.

[Q3163]

Answer: Choice **(D)** is correct. Where a promise regarding land use is a negative one — i.e., one forbidding certain uses — the promise is called an "equitable servitude." An equitable servitude is not enforceable by the owner of a particular parcel unless the original parties intended to benefit that particular parcel. The language in the deeds from Ollie to Abel and from Ollie to Betty specifically provides that "any owner of any part of Peterhill may enforce the covenant"; the fact that Betty's parcel was part of Peterhill shows it was intended to be benefitted by the restriction. Since Betty's parcel was intended to be benefitted, and since equitable servitudes are generally enforceable, Betty wins.

(A) is wrong because the change in local land use does not mean that the court will not enforce the servitude. There can be extreme circumstances in which a change of land use throughout an entire neighborhood might lead a court to conclude that it should no longer enforce an equitable servitude; but the mere fact that uses inconsistent with the servitude are now prevalent in adjacent parcels would not be enough. That's especially true where, as here, some of the parcels near plaintiff (i.e., any parcel on the West Peterhill side of the municipal line) are used in a way that is consistent with the restriction.

(B) is wrong, because the fact that a use forbidden by a servitude is allowed by local zoning codes won't cause a court to refuse enforcement of an otherwise-valid restriction unless the *entire area* in question has changed in such a way that enforcement would be of little value. So where, as here, use patterns on the West Peterhill side are still five-acres, the fact that the zoning code of East Peterhill is inconsistent with five-acre-minimums would not induce the court to relax the enforcement of the servitude.

(C) is wrong, because courts will enforce an equitable servitude against a subsequent owner of burdened land who took with actual or constructive notice. So if, for instance, Abel sold to Cathy, Cathy would be deemed to have constructive notice of the restriction (it's in her chain of title). Consequently, Betty could get an injunction against Cathy even though Cathy was not an "original grantee."

C. Running of benefit and burden:

Question: A developer owned five adjoining rectangular lots, numbered 1 through 5 inclusive, all fronting on Main Street. All of the lots are in a zone limited to one- and two-family residences under the zoning ordinance. Two years ago, the developer conveyed Lots 1, 3, and 5. None of the three deeds contained any restrictions. Each of the new owners built a one-family residence.

One year ago, the developer conveyed Lot 2 to a doctor. The deed provided that each of the doctor and the developer, their respective heirs and assigns, would use Lots 2 and 4 respectively only for one-family residential purposes. The deed was promptly and properly recorded. The doctor built a one-family residence on Lot 2.

Last month, the developer conveyed Lot 4 to a woman who operated a pharmacy. The deed contained no restrictions. The deed from the developer to the doctor was in the title report examined by the pharmacist's lawyer. The pharmacist obtained a building permit and commenced construction of a two-family residence on Lot 4.

The doctor, joined by the owners of Lots 1, 3, and 5, brought an appropriate action against the pharmacist to enjoin the proposed use of Lot 4, or, alternatively, damages caused by the pharmacist's breach of covenant.

Which is the most appropriate comment concerning the outcome of this action?

(A) All plaintiffs should be awarded their requested judgment for injunction because there was a common development scheme, but award of damages should be denied to all.

(B The doctor should be awarded appropriate remedy, but recovery by the other plaintiffs is doubtful.

(C) Injunction should be denied, but damages should be awarded to all plaintiffs, measured by diminution of market value, if any, suffered as a result of the proximity of the pharmacist's two-family residence.

(D) All plaintiffs should be denied any recovery or relief because the zoning preempts any private scheme of covenants.

[Q3055]

Answer: Choice **(B)** is correct. The plaintiff owner of a parcel can't gain enforcement of either a covenant at law or an inequitable servitude against a defendant who is the "downstream" owner of a burdened parcel (i.e., one who took after the burden was imposed), unless: (1) there was an intent by the original parties to benefit the parcel now owned by the plaintiff; and (2) the defendant was on actual or constructive notice of the nature of the restriction at the time she took. In the case of the suit by the doctor on behalf of Lot 2, both of these requirements are satisfied: (1) the developer-to-doctor deed made it clear that both Lots 2 and 4 were being both burdened and benefited by mutual single-family-only restrictions (so the requisite intent to benefit Lot 2 is present); and (2) the pharmacist was on constructive (and probably actual) notice of the restriction on the lot she was buying at the time she bought because it was mentioned in the developer-to-doctor deed that was part of the pharmacist's title report (and, indeed, from this the pharmacist knew that that restriction was intended to benefit Lot 2). Therefore, the doctor will likely be entitled to his choice of an injunction and damages (i.e., to recover on the equitable servitude or, alternatively, for breach of covenant at law).

The owners of Lots 1, 3, and 5, by contrast, cannot satisfy either of these requirements: (1) nothing indicates that at the time the developer conveyed these three lots, he was intending (then or ever) to create any equitable restrictions on any of his five lots, so the present owners of the three lots cannot show that their parcels were ever intended to be benefited; and (2) the pharmacist, at the time she took, was not on notice that Lots 1, 3, and 5 were to be benefited by any restriction on the parcel she was buying. So these owners are unlikely to get any relief against the pharmacist.

(A) is wrong because there was no common development scheme at the time Lots 1, 3, and 5 were conveyed. It's true that had there been in place, at the time Lots 1, 3, and 5 were conveyed, a "plan of development" (say, a filed subdivision plat) showing an intent to keep the whole development single-family residential, the owners of Lots 1, 3, and 5 might succeed with an "implied reciprocal servitude" argument, that the developer implicitly promised them that he'd burden his remaining lots consistently with this plan and that the pharmacist should have known of this promise and be required to honor it. But the facts do not indicate that any such plan existed at the time the developer sold Lots 1, 3, and 5.

(C) is wrong because, as noted in the analysis of Choice (B), owners cannot recover damages (i.e., recover on a covenant at law) unless they can show that there was an intent to give their parcels the benefit of the restrictive promise, an intent which is absent as to Lots 1, 3, and 5. The fact that the developer later developed such a purpose to burden his lots doesn't help —

there must have been an intent-to-burden at the time when the developer still owned the lots in question.

(D) is wrong because, the existence of a zoning scheme that allows the activity in question doesn't trump a stricter scheme of covenants. If the zoning scheme was stricter, it would prevail (landowners can't by mutual agreement cause strict zoning rules to be relaxed). But the converse is not true — indeed, the whole idea of restrictive covenants is that they can be used to forbid uses that are allowed by the zoning rules.

1. **Requirement of notice:**

    b. **Constructive:**

    Question: Twenty-five years ago, a man who owned a 45-acre tract of land conveyed 40 of the 45 acres to a developer by warranty deed. The man retained the rear five-acre portion of the land and continues to live there in a large farmhouse.

    The deed to the 40-acre tract was promptly and properly recorded. It contained the following language:

    "It is a term and condition of this deed, which shall be a covenant running with the land and binding on all owners, their heirs and assigns, that no use shall be made of the 40-acre tract of land except for residential purposes."

    Subsequently, the developer fully developed the 40-acre tract into a residential subdivision consisting of 40 lots with a single-family residence on each lot.

    Although there have been multiple transfers of ownership of each of the 40 lots within the subdivision, none of them included a reference to the quoted provision in the deed from the man to the developer, nor did any deed to a subdivision lot create any new covenants restricting use.

    Last year, a major new medical center was constructed adjacent to the subdivision. A doctor who owns a house in the subdivision wishes to relocate her medical offices to her house. For the first time, the doctor learned of the restrictive covenant in the deed from the man to the developer. The applicable zoning ordinance permits the doctor's intended use. The man, as owner of the five-acre tract, however, objects to the doctor's proposed use of her property.

    There are no governing statutes other than the zoning code. The common law Rule Against Perpetuities is unmodified in the jurisdiction.

    Can the doctor convert her house in the subdivision into a medical office?

    (A) No, because the owners of lots in the subdivision own property benefitted by the original residential covenant and have the sole right to enforce it.

    (B) No, because the man owns property benefitted by the original restrictive covenant and has a right to enforce it.

    (C) Yes, because the original restrictive covenant violates the Rule Against Perpetuities.

    (D) Yes, because the zoning ordinance allows the doctor's proposed use and preempts the restrictive covenant.

    [QA087]

    Answer: Choice **(B)** is correct. The language in the deed between the man and the developer restricted the developer's use of the land to residential purposes. Thus, it was a restrictive covenant (also called an equitable servitude, because it will be enforced in equity by an injunction or decree of specific performance). If it had been the *developer* who wished to convert a house into a medical office, he would have been prevented from doing so as a matter of contract law, since he and the man were the parties to the deed. But here, it's the doctor (who was remote to the original deal between the man and the developer) who wants to make the house a medical officer. However, the man can enforce the covenant even against the doctor, because the deed met the four requirements for the burden of the covenant to run with the land: (1) the covenant must be in writing; (2) the parties must intend that the covenant run with the land; (3) the covenant must "touch and concern" the burdened property; and (4) the person to be burdened must have been on notice of the restriction when he took.

As to (1), the deed was in writing. As to (2), the parties expressly stated that it would run with the land (i.e., bind successors). As to (3), courts have held that restrictions on the use of property "touch and concern" the land because the obligations are tied to ownership or occupancy of the parcel. As to (4), the doctor had "record notice" (a form of "constructive notice") because the facts say that the deed was promptly and properly recorded, and was part of the doctor's chain of title. (That is, if the doctor had checked back in the deed records, he would have seen that his development was created by virtue of the transfer from the man to the developer, and would have seen the restriction in the man-to-developer deed. So the fact that the doctor did not have "actual" knowledge of the restriction at the time he took is irrelevant.) Thus, all conditions for the running of the burden of the residential restriction are satisfied, so that the man has the right to enforce the restriction and the doctor will not be able to convert her home into an office.

(A) is wrong because the covenant also benefitted the 5 acres retained by the man, so he has a right to enforce it as well. It's true that the benefit of the covenant runs to the subdivision property owners, because the promise was in writing, the original parties intended to benefit successors, and the promise "touches and concerns" the land because it deals with how the land can be used. Thus, the subdivision property owners could also enforce the covenant. But their right to do so does not limit the man's right — since the man was retaining (as the developer knew) the 5 acres, and would continue to live there, it was clear from context that both parties intended for the man to receive the benefits of the restriction.

(C) is wrong because the Rule Against Perpetuities does not apply to a restrictive covenant. The Rule Against Perpetuities fosters the policy against restraining alienation of fee simple estates in land. Thus, it voids only those future interests that are not capable of vesting within 21 years of a life in being. An equitable servitude is not a future interest; thus, the Rule Against Perpetuities does not apply.

(D) is wrong because the zoning ordinance, while permitting the proposed use, does not preempt a valid restrictive covenant. The restrictive covenant, as the more restrictive of the two in terms of its limitations, prevails.

Question: In 2000, Oscar, owner of a 100-acre tract, prepared and duly recorded a subdivision plan called Happy Acres. The plan showed 100 one-acre lots, and said that these lots would be "single-family, no mobile homes allowed."

In 2001, Oscar sold 60 of the lots to individual purchasers. Each deed referred to the recorded plan and also contained the following clause: "No mobile homes shall be erected on any lot within Happy Acres." Sarah was one of the original purchasers from Oscar.

In 2006, Oscar sold the remaining 40 lots to Max by a deed which referred to the plan and contained the restriction relating to mobile homes. Max sold the 40 lots to individual purchasers, whose deeds from Max did not include the mobile-home restriction. One of those purchasers was Joe, who did not know of the no-mobile-homes restriction in any prior deeds within Happy Acres. Joe then placed a mobile home on his lot. Sarah now brings an action against

Joe to force him to remove the mobile home. The result of this action will be in favor of

(A) Sarah, because the restrictive covenant in her deed runs with the land.

(B) Sarah, because the presence of the mobile home may adversely affect the market value of her land.

(C) Joe, because his deed did not contain the restrictive covenant.

(D) Joe, because he is not a direct but a remote grantee of Oscar.

[Q4033]

Answer: Choice **(A)** is correct. A restrictive covenant will normally run with the land, i.e., be enforceable by subsequent grantees of the benefitted parcels, and against subsequent grantees of the burdened parcels, if the original parties intended that it run. The existence of the filed subdivision plat with the restriction, and the fact that Oscar took the trouble to insert the restriction in all his deeds, establish that he and his grantees intended the burden and benefit of the restriction to run. Meanwhile, Joe, as a subsequent grantee, will only be bound by the restrictive covenant if he was on actual or constructive notice when he took. "Constructive" notice includes "record" notice. Here, Joe was on record notice of the restriction. That's true because although Joe's deed did not itself refer to the no-mobile-homes restriction, that restriction was present in a prior recording in his chain of title (the Oscar-Max deed). And a purchaser is deemed to be on record notice of any restrictions in his chain of title. Intuitively, this makes sense — Joe's lawyer could have and should have found the Oscar-to-Max deed, and noticed the restriction. (Or, the lawyer could have and should have noticed that the lot was part of a filed subdivision plat that contained the restriction.)

(B) is wrong because the fact it cites is irrelevant to the issues here. The mere fact that the presence of mobile homes would adversely affect the value of Sarah's land does not mean that Sarah has a legally cognizable right to forbid their presence. As a general principle, the owner of land may put the land to any lawful use he chooses, without regard to the impact on the market value of other, neighboring properties. Thus, even if (B) were true, it would not provide a sound basis for Sarah to prevail.

(C) is wrong because it does not correctly cite the rule on restrictive covenants (or "equitable servitudes," as they are also called). Restrictive covenants will bind subsequent purchasers of the land as long as the original parties intended that the agreement will run with the land, and the subsequent purchaser had actual or constructive notice of the restriction. Here, Joe had constructive notice (namely, record notice) of the restriction, as further explained in (A). Therefore, the fact that Joe's own deed did not contain the covenant is irrelevant.

(D) is wrong because as long as the restriction was intended to run with the land, the fact that the person sought to be bound is a remote grantee of the original, covenanting party — here, Oscar – is irrelevant. That's what the fact that the covenant or restriction "runs with the land" *means* — the restriction binds remote grantees who take with actual or constructive (including record) notice.

c. **Check for notice:**

Question: Able, owner of Blackacre and Whiteacre, two adjoining parcels, conveyed Whiteacre to Baker and covenanted in the deed to Baker that when he, Able, sold Blackacre he would impose restrictive covenants to prohibit uses that would compete with the filling station that Baker intended to construct and operate on Whiteacre. The deed was not recorded.

Baker constructed and operated a filling station on Whiteacre and then conveyed Whiteacre to Dodd, who continued the filling station use. The deed did not refer to the restrictive covenant and was promptly and properly recorded.

Able then conveyed Blackacre to Egan, who knew about Able's covenant with Baker to impose a covenant prohibiting the filling station use but nonetheless completed the transaction when he noted that no such covenant was contained in Able's deed to him. Egan began to construct a filling station on Blackacre.

Dodd brought an appropriate action to enjoin Egan from using Blackacre for filling station purposes.

If Dodd prevails, it will be because

(A) Egan had actual knowledge of the covenant to impose restrictions.

(B) Egan is bound by the covenant because of the doctrine of negative reciprocal covenants.

(C) business-related restrictive covenants are favored in the law.

(D) Egan has constructive notice of the possibility of the covenant resulting from the circumstances.

[Q1165]

Answer: Choice (A) is correct. Dodd can win only if Egan is found to have been bound by Able's promise to Baker that Able would impose a restriction on Blackacre when he sold it. A subsequent purchaser of a use-restricted parcel can be bound by the restriction only if he had some sort of *notice* of the restriction at the time he took. Egan did not have *record* notice of the restriction because (1) the restriction was not contained in the Able-to-Egan deed by which Egan took Blackacre; and (2) even if the Able-to-Baker deed to Whiteacre was held to be within Egan's chain of title (which it wouldn't be), that wouldn't give Egan notice, because the Able-to-Baker deed was not recorded, so Egan couldn't have discovered the restriction by tracing back title to Whiteacre in the public records. Therefore, the only way Egan could have received the required notice (and thus lose) is if he had actual notice or some form of *constructive* notice not involving record notice. (A), by referring specifically to Egan's "actual knowledge" of the restriction, is the only choice that satisfies the notice-to-Egan requirement. And as we know from the statement of facts, Egan indeed had such actual knowledge.

(B) is wrong because, while the doctrine of negative reciprocal covenants might apply to restrict Whiteacre, Egan wouldn't be bound by that restriction if he didn't have some form of notice, and this choice does not refer to the notice problem.

(C) is wrong because, like (B), it fails to refer to the key point, notice to Egan.

(D) is wrong because, while Egan might indeed lose if he had constructive notice of the possibility of the restriction, such constructive notice was not present in the facts here: the mere fact that Able sold Whiteacre to Baker and that Baker put a filling station on the property would not suggest to a reasonable purchaser of the adjacent Blackacre parcel that Able would likely have restricted Blackacre by giving Baker a non-compete. (Otherwise any purchaser of a commercially-zoned parcel would have to check into the facts surrounding his seller's sale of any other nearby parcel, to make sure that the seller didn't give a non-compete, too large a burden on buyers to make sense.)

D. Developer's building plan:

1. Plan filed without restriction:

Question: A fee-simple landowner lawfully subdivided his land into 10 large lots. The recorded subdivision plan imposed no restrictions on any of the 10 lots. Within two months after recording the plan, the landowner conveyed Lot 1 to a buyer, by a deed that contained no restriction on the lot's use. There was then a lull in sales. Two years later, the real estate market in the state had generally improved and, during the next six months, the landowner sold and conveyed eight of the remaining nine lots. In each of the eight deeds of conveyance, the landowner included the following language: "It is a term and condition of this conveyance, which shall be a covenant running with the land for the benefit of each of the 10 lots [with an appropriate reference to the recorded subdivision plan], that for 15 years from the date of recording of the plan, no use shall be made of the premises herein conveyed except for single-family residential purposes." The buyer of Lot 1 had actual knowledge of what the landowner had done. The landowner included the quoted language in part because the zoning ordinance of the municipality had been amended a year earlier to permit professional offices in any residential zone. Shortly after the landowner's most recent sale, when he owned only one unsold lot, the buyer of Lot 1 constructed a one-story house on Lot 1 and then conveyed Lot 1 to a doctor. The deed to the doctor contained no reference to any restriction on the use of Lot 1. The doctor applied for an appropriate certificate of occupancy to enable her to use a part of the house on Lot 1 as a medical office. The landowner, on behalf of himself as the owner of the unsold lot, and on behalf of the other lot owners, sued to enjoin the doctor from carrying out her plans and to impose the quoted restriction on Lot 1.

Who is likely to prevail?

(A) The doctor, because Lot 1 was conveyed without the inclusion of the restrictive covenant in the deed to the first buyer and the subsequent deed to the doctor.

(B) The doctor, because zoning ordinances override private restrictive covenants as a matter of public policy.

(C) The landowner, because the doctor, as a successor in interest to the first buyer, is estopped to deny that Lot 1 remains subject to the zoning ordinance as it existed when Lot 1 was first conveyed by the landowner to the first buyer.

(D) The landowner, because with the first buyer's knowledge of the facts, Lot 1 became incorporated into a common scheme.

[Q7061]

Answer: Choice **(A)** is correct. To be binding, a restrictive covenant must be placed on property *at the time it is conveyed.* Here, neither the deed to the first buyer nor the deed to the doctor contains the restrictive covenant. The burden cannot be attached to Lot 1 at a later time by someone who has no interest in Lot 1, even if that person (here, the landowner) purports to be acting on behalf of the entire subdivision. Therefore, the doctor may proceed with her plan to use part of the property as a medical office.

(B) is incorrect, because although this option correctly concludes that the doctor will prevail, it misstates the reason why this is so. Zoning ordinances do not automatically override a private restrictive covenant. The stricter of either the zoning ordinance or the covenant will prevail. In this case, the doctor will prevail because the restrictive covenant was not in the deed to the first buyer of Lot 1, nor was it in the deed to the doctor.

(C) is incorrect. Public land use controls and private land use controls are separate issues. Zoning may be changed. In this case, the zoning was changed a year after the first buyer purchased Lot 1. The doctor's use of Lot 1 is governed by the zoning in existence during the time of the doctor's ownership, and the previous zoning of the property is irrelevant. The doctor may proceed with her plan to use part of the property as a medical office, because the restrictive covenant was not in the deed to the first buyer of Lot 1, nor was it in the deed to the doctor.

(D) is incorrect. To be binding, a restrictive covenant must be placed on property at the time when it is conveyed. The first buyer's learning of the covenant two years after he acquired it is irrelevant, and does not incorporate Lot 1 into the common scheme of the subdivision; nor does the actual knowledge of any subsequent buyer of Lot 1 (even knowledge acquired before he took) have any effect. A common-scheme argument might prevail as to subsequent purchasers of other lots in the subdivision who took from the landowner after the landowner had already burdened other parcels with the restriction. As to Lot 1, however, the doctor may proceed with her plan to use part of the property as a medical office, because the restrictive covenant was not in the deed to the first buyer, nor was it in the deed to the doctor.

X. MODIFICATION AND TERMINATION OF COVENANTS AND SERVITUDES

A. **Modification and termination generally:**

4. **No expiration from passage of time:**

    Question: A grantor owned in fee simple two adjoining lots, Lots 1 and 2. He conveyed in fee simple Lot 1 to an investor. The deed was in usual form of a warranty deed with the following provision inserted in the appropriate place:

    "Grantor, for himself, his heirs and assigns, does covenant and agree that any reasonable expense incurred by grantee, his heirs and assigns, as the result of having to repair the retaining wall presently situated on Lot 1 at the common boundary with Lot 2, shall be reimbursed one-half the costs of repairs; and by this provision the parties intend a covenant running with the land."

    The investor conveyed Lot 1 in fee simple to a housewife by warranty deed in usual and regular form. The deed omitted any reference to the retaining wall or any covenant. Fifty years after the grantor's conveyance to the investor, the housewife conveyed Lot 1 in fee simple to a student by warranty deed in usual form; this deed omitted any reference to the retaining wall or the covenant.

    There is no statute that applies to any aspect of the problems presented except a recording act and a statute providing for acquisition of title after ten years of adverse possession.

    All conveyances by deeds were for a consideration equal to fair market value.

    The deed from the grantor to the investor was never recorded. All other deeds were promptly and properly recorded.

    Lot 2 is now owned by the grantor's son, who took by intestate succession from the grantor, now dead.

    The student expended $3,500 on the retaining wall. Then he obtained all of the original deeds in the chain from the grantor to him. Shortly thereafter, the student discovered the covenant in the grantor's deed to the investor. He demanded that the grantor's son pay $1,750, and when the son refused, the student instituted an appropriate action to recover that sum from the son. In such action, the son asserted all defenses available to him.

    If judgment is for the grantor's son, it will be because

    (A) the student is barred by adverse possession.

    (B) the investor's deed from the grantor was never recorded.

    (C) the student did not know about the covenant until after he had incurred the expenses and, hence, could not have relied on it.

(D) the student's expenditures were not proved to be reasonable and customary.
[Q2107]

Answer: Choice **(D)** is correct. When the grantor conveyed Lot 1 to the investor, the grantor burdened Lot 2 with the covenant to reimburse the owner of Lot 1 for wall-repair expenses. This covenant was enforceable, and ran with the land on both the burden and benefit side. Even though more than 50 years have passed, no event has occurred (e.g., change of circumstances rendering fulfillment of the covenant's purposes impossible) that would cause the covenant to be extinguished, and the mere passage of time does not suffice to end the covenant. The fact that the covenant ran with the land on the benefit side means that the student as present owner of the benefited lot gets to enforce the covenant; this running of the benefit side occurs even though the deed to conveying the benefited parcel to the student did not mention the covenant or the wall (since mention of the covenant in the deed to the benefited lot is simply not a requirement). The running of the covenant on the burden side means that the obligation of payment attached to the grantor's son's interest in Lot 2. Therefore, the only way the student can lose is if his expenditures were not reasonable and customary (in which case they would not be covered by the terms of the covenant, even though the covenant is still enforceable).

(A) is wrong because nothing occurred to cause the doctrine of adverse possession to affect title to the benefited lot (Lot 1) while that lot was held by either the investor, the housewife, or the student. For instance, no action by any owner of Lot 2 could even arguably have constituted the requisite hostile, notorious, open, and continuous possession of the wall so as to wipe out the covenant governing repairs.

(B) is wrong because the fact that the investor's deed from the grantor for Lot 1 was not recorded had no effect on anyone who ever had an interest in Lot 2. It's true that the grantor, by conveying Lot 1 to the investor, simultaneously created a covenant burdening Lot 2, which was an interest in Lot 2. But a grantee's failure to record under a recording act has no effect on the rights as between the original grantor and grantee; therefore, in a contest between the grantor and the investor, the investor's failure to record his covenant against Lot 2 would not prevent the investor from recovering reimbursement from the grantor while the grantor still owned Lot 2. The interesting question is whether the investor's failure to record can be taken advantage of by the grantor's son as the grantor's successor. In other words, is the grantor's son a "subsequent purchaser without notice" who can take advantage of the fact that the deed creating the covenant never appeared in his chain of title? The answer is that because recording acts invariably protect only "purchasers for value," and because the son took by intestate succession (and thus did not give value for his interest), the son is *not* a purchaser for value and thus *cannot* take advantage of the recording act. (If the son had purchased for value and without notice of the covenant, he *would* have been free of the covenant on account of the investor's failure to record.)

(C) is wrong because the owner of a parcel benefited by an affirmative covenant does not lose the benefit merely because he did not act in reliance on the covenant's existence.

Question: Oker owned in fee simple two adjoining lots, Lots 1 and 2. He conveyed in fee simple Lot 1 to Frank. The deed was in usual form of a warranty deed with the following provision inserted in the appropriate place:

> "Grantor, for himself, his heirs and assigns, does covenant and agree that any reasonable expense incurred by grantee, his heirs and assigns, as the result of having to repair the retaining wall presently situated on Lot 1 at the common boundary

with Lot 2, shall be reimbursed one-half the costs of repairs; and by this provision the parties intend a covenant running with the land."

Frank conveyed Lot 1 in fee simple to Sara by warranty deed in usual and regular form. The deed omitted any reference to the retaining wall or any covenant. Fifty years after Oker's conveyance to Frank, Sara conveyed Lot 1 in fee simple to Tim by warranty deed in usual form; this deed omitted any reference to the retaining wall or the covenant.

There is no statute that applies to any aspect of the problems presented except a recording act and a statute providing for acquisition of title after ten years of adverse possession.

All conveyances by deeds were for a consideration equal to fair market value.

The deed from Oker to Frank was never recorded. All other deeds were promptly and properly recorded.

Lot 2 is now owned by Henry, who took by intestate succession from Oker, now dead.

Tim expended $3,500 on the retaining wall. Then he obtained all of the original deeds in the chain from Oker to him. Shortly thereafter, Tim discovered the covenant in Oker's deed to Frank. He demanded that Henry pay $1,750, and when Henry refused, Tim instituted an appropriate action to recover that sum from Henry. In such action, Henry asserted all defenses available to him.

If judgment is for Henry, it will be because

(A) Tim is barred by adverse possession.

(B) Frank's deed from Oker was never recorded.

(C) Tim did not know about the covenant until after he had incurred the expenses and, hence, could not have relied on it.

(D) Tim's expenditures were not proved to be reasonable and customary.

[Q2107]

Answer: Choice **(D)** is correct. When Oker conveyed Lot 1 to Frank, Oker burdened Lot 2 with the covenant to reimburse the owner of Lot 1 for wall-repair expenses. This covenant was enforceable, and ran with the land on both the burden and benefit side. Even though more than 50 years have passed, no event has occurred (e.g., change of circumstances rendering fulfillment of the covenant's purposes impossible) that would cause the covenant to be extinguished, and the mere passage of time does not suffice to end the covenant. The fact that the covenant ran with the land on the benefit side means that Tim as present owner of the benefited lot gets to enforce the covenant; this running of the benefit side occurs even though the deed to conveying the benefited parcel to Tim did not mention the covenant or the wall (since mention of the covenant in the deed to the benefited lot is simply not a requirement). The running of the covenant on the burden side means that the obligation of payment attached to Henry's interest in Lot 2. Therefore, the only way Tim can lose is if his expenditures were not reasonable and customary (in which case they would not be covered by the terms of the covenant, even though the covenant is still enforceable).

(A) is wrong because nothing occurred to cause the doctrine of adverse possession to affect title to the benefitted lot (Lot 1) while that lot was held by either Frank, by Sara, or by Tim. For instance, no action by any owner of Lot 2 could even arguably have constituted the requisite hostile, notorious, open and continuous possession of the wall so as to wipe out the covenant governing repairs.

(B) is wrong because the fact that Frank's deed from Oker for Lot 1 was not recorded had no effect on anyone who ever had an interest in Lot 2. It's true that Oker, by conveying Lot 1 to

Frank, simultaneously created a covenant burdening Lot 2, which was an interest in Lot 2. But a grantee's failure to record under a recording act has no effect on the rights as between the original grantor and grantee; therefore in a contest between Oker and Frank, Frank's failure to record his covenant against Lot 2 would not prevent Frank from recovering reimbursement from Oker while Oker still owned Lot 2. The interesting question is whether Frank's failure to record can be taken advantage of by Henry as Oker's successor. In other words, is Henry a "subsequent purchaser without notice" who can take advantage of the fact that the deed creating the covenant never appeared in his chain of title? The answer is that because recording acts invariably protect only "purchasers for value," and because Henry took by intestate succession (and thus did not give value for his interest), Henry is *not* a purchaser for value and thus *cannot* take advantage of the recording act. (If Henry had purchased for value and without notice of the covenant, he *would* have been free of the covenant on account of Frank's failure to record.)

(C) is wrong because the owner of a parcel benefited by an affirmative covenant does not lose the benefit merely because he did not act in reliance on the covenant's existence.

CHAPTER 7

LAND SALE CONTRACTS, MORTGAGES, DEEDS AND WILLS

I. LAND SALE CONTRACTS

A. Statute of Frauds:

2. **Spot the issue:**

    Question: Ozzie owned and occupied Blackacre, which was a tract of land improved with a one-family house. His friend, Victor, orally offered Ozzie $50,000 for Blackacre, the fair market value, and Ozzie accepted. Because they were friends, they saw no need for attorneys or written contracts and shook hands on the deal. Victor paid Ozzie $5,000 down in cash and agreed to pay the balance of $45,000 at an agreed closing time and place.

    Before the closing, Victor inherited another home and asked Ozzie to return his $5,000. Ozzie refused, and, at the time set for the closing, Ozzie tendered a good deed to Victor and declared his intention to vacate Blackacre the next day. Ozzie demanded that Victor complete the purchase. Victor refused. The fair market value of Blackacre has remained $50,000.

    In an appropriate action brought by Ozzie against Victor for specific performance, if Ozzie loses, the most likely reason will be that

    (A) the agreement was oral.

    (B) keeping the $5,000 is Ozzie's exclusive remedy.

    (C) Victor had a valid reason for not closing.

    (D) Ozzie remained in possession on the day set for the closing.
    [Q1189]

    Answer: Choice **(A)** is correct. The Statute of Frauds applies to all contracts for the sale of land, or for the sale of an interest in land. Therefore, such a contract will not be enforced unless it is in writing. There are a few exceptions to this rule (e.g., where there has been part performance in reliance on an oral agreement), but none of those exceptions applies here.

(B) is wrong because it is not the case that the seller's exclusive remedy for breach is to keep the deposit; often, a court will order the buyer to specifically perform even where the seller has a deposit. (Furthermore, unless the parties have agreed that the deposit will be the exclusive measure, the seller will be entitled to recover her actual damages from the buyer's breach if these are greater than the deposit.)

(C) is wrong because the fact that Victor inherited a different home is not a valid reason for not closing; the doctrine of frustration of purpose occasionally applies to land-sale contracts, but would virtually never apply where the only event alleged to have frustrated the buyer's purpose is that he found or acquired other property he liked better.

(D) is wrong because Ozzie's anticipated one-day delay in vacating would not have been a material breach, unless the agreement or the circumstances indicated that time was of the essence. There's no indication that that happened here. Therefore, the one-day delay would not have deprived Ozzie of his otherwise-existing right to obtain specific performance.

C. Marketable title:

4. Time for measuring marketability:

a. Outstanding mortgage:

Question: A seller owned Greenacre, a tract of land, in fee simple. The seller entered into a valid written agreement with a purchaser under which the seller agreed to sell and the purchaser agreed to buy Greenacre by installment purchase. The contract stipulated that the seller would deliver to the purchaser, upon the payment of the last installment due, "a warranty deed sufficient to convey the fee simple." The contract contained no other provision that could be construed as referring to title.

The purchaser entered into possession of Greenacre. After making 10 of the 300 installment payments obligated under the contract, the purchaser discovered that there was outstanding a valid and enforceable mortgage on Greenacre, securing the payment of a debt in the amount of 25% of the purchase price the purchaser had agreed to pay. There was no evidence that the seller had ever been late in payments due under the mortgage and there was no evidence of any danger of insolvency of the seller. The value of Greenacre now is four times the amount due on the debt secured by the mortgage.

The purchaser quit possession of Greenacre and demanded that the seller repay the amounts the purchaser had paid under the contract. After the seller refused the demand, the purchaser brought an appropriate action against the seller to recover damages for the seller's alleged breach of the contract.

In such action, should damages be awarded to the purchaser?

(A) No, because the time for the seller to deliver marketable title has not arrived.

(B) No, because the purchaser assumed the risk by taking possession.

(C) Yes, because in the absence of a contrary express agreement, an obligation to convey marketable title is implied.

(D) Yes, because the risk of loss assumed by the purchaser in taking possession relates only to physical loss.

[Q3150]

Answer: Choice **(A)** is correct. Under an installment contract, marketable title need ordinarily not be delivered until *after the last payment*. There can be circumstances in which the buyer under an installment provision has reasonable grounds for worrying about whether the vendor will be able to convey marketable title when the time comes (e.g., the vendor simply doesn't seem to have record title at all). If the buyer has such grounds for insecurity, most courts say she can demand reasonable assurances that the defect will be cured, and if the assurances are not forthcoming, can rescind or sue for breach. But here, there are no grounds that would make a reasonable buyer insecure about whether marketable title will ultimately be forthcoming, given that the mortgage is small relative to the value of the property, that the seller is solvent and pays the mortgage on time each month, and that 97% of the purchase price remains to be paid (so that the purchaser will have ample time to see whether the mortgage is continuing to be paid). Consequently, the fact that a very curable encumbrance happens to exist at the moment will not constitute a breach by the seller.

(B) is wrong because a vendee who takes under an installment contract — and who (as is usually the case) takes possession before the installments are fully paid — does not "assume the risk" that the vendor won't be able to convey good title. If, for instance, the vendee has reasonable grounds for worrying about whether the vendor will have the ability to convey marketable title down the road, the vendee may be entitled to reasonable assurances that there won't be a problem (see the discussion of Choice (A) above).

(C) is wrong because, although an obligation to convey marketable title is implied in the absence of an express agreement to the contrary, the seller hasn't breached that obligation. The reference here to "a warranty deed sufficient to convey the fee simple" — although somewhat vague about just what type of deed has been promised — will not be found to constitute an express provision that marketable title is not required. So, since the promise is ambiguous, the usual presumption in favor of an obligation to convey marketable title will be applied. The fact that this is an installment contract does not change that presumption. However, for the reasons stated in Choice (A), the seller has not breached that obligation, making this choice wrong.

(D) is wrong because risk of loss relating to possession would not be grounds on which the purchaser could recover. It's true that any "risk of loss" assumed by the purchaser would relate only to physical events (e.g., destruction of a structure on the land). But the fact that "risk of loss" doesn't apply does not by itself mean that the purchaser can recover damages now. Indeed, because the time to deliver marketable title hasn't yet arrived, the purchaser will lose, not win, so Choice (D) can't be correct.

Question: A landowner mortgaged the land to a bank to secure his preexisting obligation to the bank. The mortgage was promptly and properly recorded. The landowner and a buyer then entered into a valid written contract for the purchase and sale of the land, which provided for the transfer of "a marketable title, free of encumbrances." The contract did not expressly refer to the mortgage.

Shortly after entering into the contract, the buyer found another property that much better suited her needs and decided to try to avoid her contract with the landowner. When the buyer discovered the existence of the mortgage, she asserted that the title was encumbered and that she would not close. The landowner responded by offering to provide for payment and discharge of the mortgage at the closing from the proceeds of the closing. The buyer refused to go forward, and the landowner brought an appropriate action against her for specific performance.

If the court holds for the landowner in this action, it will most likely be because

(A) the mortgage is not entitled to priority because it was granted for preexisting obligations.

(B) the doctrine of equitable conversion supports the result.

(C) the landowner's arrangements for the payment of the mortgage fully satisfied the landowner's obligation to deliver marketable title.

(D) the existence of the mortgage was not the buyer's real reason for refusing to close.
[Q2081]

Answer: Choice **(C)** is correct. Unless the sale contract specifies otherwise, the seller's title is not required to be marketable until the date set for the closing. The fact that there is an outstanding mortgage on the property, therefore, does not entitle the buyer to cancel the contract, as long as the seller has the right and probable ability to pay off the mortgage at the closing.

(A) is wrong because the fact that the mortgage was granted for pre-existing obligations (as opposed, say, to being a purchase money mortgage) is irrelevant to the issue of whether the seller's title is marketable. For instance, if the seller were not paying off the mortgage at the closing, the mortgage would indeed be an encumbrance rendering title unmarketable, even though it was granted to secure the seller's pre-existing obligation to the mortgagee.

(B) is wrong because the doctrine of equitable conversion is used to pass the risk of loss to the buyer under a purchase contract, and has nothing to do with whether the seller's title is marketable.

(D) is wrong because a purchaser's "real reason" (i.e., motive) for refusing to close is irrelevant to whether the purchaser has the right to so refuse. For example, if the seller's title had been unmarketable, the buyer would have been entitled to refuse to close even though her real reason for refusing was something entirely unrelated to the quality of the seller's title.

Question: Venner, the owner of Greenacre, a tract of land, entered into an enforceable written agreement with Brier providing that Venner would sell Greenacre to Brier for an agreed price. At the place and time designated for the closing. Venner tendered an appropriate deed, but Brier responded that he had discovered a mortgage on Greenacre and would not complete the transaction, because Venner's title was not free of encumbrances, as the contract required. Venner said that it was his intent to pay the mortgage from the proceeds of the sale, and he offered to put the proceeds in escrow for that purpose with any agreeable, responsible escrowee. The balance due on the mortgage was substantially less than the contract purchase price. Brier refused Venner's proposal. Venner began an appropriate legal action against Brier for specific performance. There is no applicable statute in the jurisdiction where Greenacre is located.

Venner's best legal argument in support of his claim for relief is that

(A) as the seller of real estate, he had an implied right to use the contract proceeds to clear the title being conveyed.

(B) the lien of the mortgage shifts from Greenacre to the contract proceeds.

(C) under the doctrine of equitable conversion, title has already passed to Brier and the only issue is how the purchase price is to be allocated.

(D) no provision of the contract has been breached by Venner.
[Q4109]

Answer: Choice **(A)** is correct. This choice correctly identifies that Venner can use the sale proceeds to pay off the mortgage, and thus force Brier to honor the contract. Where, as is usually the case, the seller in a land-sale contract covenants to deliver the property free and clear of encumbrances, the presence of a mortgage would be an encumbrance rendering the title unmarketable. But you're told here that the proceeds will cover the mortgage. When that's the case, the seller has an implied right to use the proceeds of the sale to pay off the mortgage.

When you think about it, this rule comports with what you'd expect to happen, since many homeowners, in real life, couldn't sell their home if this weren't the case.

(B) is wrong because it misstates the law. Although it's possible that the law of the jurisdiction may make the mortgage payable from the proceeds, and the mortgage agreement itself may insist on payoff if the property is conveyed, the "rule" stated in this choice wouldn't cause the mortgage to be removed from Greenacre — and that's the central problem here. Instead, the key is that the seller gets to use the sale proceeds to pay off the mortgage simultaneously with the closing of title.

(C) is wrong because the doctrine of equitable conversion would not apply to these facts. The doctrine of equitable conversion addresses the period between the signing of the land sale contract and the closing. Under the doctrine, the vendor has a personal property interest in the property, between the signing of the contract and the closing, in the form of the balance of the purchase price owed to him; the vendee is considered the beneficial owner of the property. The doctrine wouldn't help with the problem here, which is that Venner can't deliver marketable title unless he can remove the mortgage.

(D) is wrong because it states an insufficient ground on which Venner could prevail. Of course, his underlying argument must be that he hasn't breached the contract, because if he had, he wouldn't be entitled to specific performance. However, Choice (D), in and of itself, doesn't provide a rule allowing Venner to use the proceeds to pay off the mortgage, and enforce the contract. Only Choice (A) does this.

Question: A seller who owned land in fee simple entered into a valid written agreement to sell the land to a buyer by installment purchase. The contract stipulated that the seller would deliver to the buyer, upon the payment of the last installment due, "a warranty deed sufficient to convey a fee simple title." The contract contained no other provision that could be construed as referring to title.

The buyer entered into possession of the land. After making 10 of the 300 installment payments obligated under the contract, the buyer discovered that there was outstanding a valid and enforceable mortgage on the land, securing the payment of a debt in the amount of 25 percent of the purchase price that the buyer had agreed to pay. There was no evidence that the seller had ever been late in payments due under the mortgage and there was no evidence of any danger of insolvency of the seller. The value of the land was then four times the amount due on the debt secured by the mortgage.

The buyer quit possession of the land, stopped making payments on the contract, and demanded that the seller repay the amounts that the buyer had paid under the contract. After the seller refused the demand, the buyer sued the seller to recover damages for the seller's alleged breach of the contract.

In such action, should damages be awarded to the buyer?

(A) Yes, because in the absence of a contrary express agreement, an obligation to convey marketable title is implied.

(B) Yes, because an installment purchase contract is treated as a mortgage and the outstanding mortgage impairs the buyer's equity of redemption.

(C) No, because an installment purchase contract is treated as a security device.

(D) No, because the time for the seller to deliver marketable title has not arrived.

[QA044]

Chapter 7 - LAND SALE CONTRACTS, MORTGAGES, DEEDS AND WILLS

Answer: Choice **(D)** is correct. Under an installment contract, the seller need not deliver marketable title until *after the last payment* is made. There can be circumstances in which the buyer under an installment contract has reasonable grounds for worrying about whether the seller will be able to convey marketable title when the time comes. If the buyer has such grounds for insecurity, most courts say she can demand reasonable assurances that the defect will be cured, and if the assurances are not forthcoming, she can rescind or sue for breach. Here, though, there are no grounds that would make a reasonable buyer insecure about whether seller can ultimately convey marketable title. The mortgage is small relative to the value of the property (25% of the purchase price); the seller is solvent and paying the mortgage on time each month; and 97% of the installments have yet to be paid (so there is ample time for seller to pay off the mortgage, and for the buyer to suspend payments if the seller stops making mortgage payments). Consequently, the fact that a very curable encumbrance happens to exist at the moment does not constitute a breach by the seller. Therefore, the buyer is not entitled to damages.

(A) is wrong because, although an obligation to convey marketable title is implied in the absence of an express agreement to the contrary, the seller hasn't breached that obligation. The existence of a mortgage does not render title unmarketable, because the time to convey title has not yet arrived. Even if the buyer had reasonable grounds for worrying about whether the seller would be able to convey marketable title when the time comes, the buyer's remedy would not be to stop payments and demand rescission; instead, the remedy would be to demand reasonable assurances of performance from the seller. But here, the buyer doesn't even have reasonable grounds for worry, as is further explained in the discussion of Choice (D).

(B) is wrong because while an installment purchase contract is often treated as a mortgage, the seller must foreclose to impair buyer's equity of redemption. While the buyer here has stopped making payments, the seller has not yet sought to enforce the installment purchase contract. Rather, the buyer is seeking damages; thus, the buyer's equity of redemption is not at issue.

(C) is wrong because the characterization of an installment contract as a security device is irrelevant. When we say (accurately) that an installment contract is a "security device," we mean that such a contract is a way of giving the seller, in return for his "tying up" the property during the contract period, the assurance that the buyer will keep making payments or will lose those payments that she has already made. So the contract's status as a security device is irrelevant to the issue here, which is whether the existence of the mortgage entitled the buyer to cancel the contract.

5. ***Right to cancel for unmarketability belongs only to buyer:***

    Question: By a valid written contract, a seller agreed to sell land to a buyer. The contract stated, "The parties agree that closing will occur on next May 1 at 10 a.m." There was no other reference to closing. The contract was silent as to quality of title.

    On April 27, the seller notified the buyer that she had discovered that the land was subject to a longstanding easement in favor of a corporation for a towpath for a canal, should the corporation ever want to build a canal.

    The buyer thought it so unlikely that a canal would be built that the closing should occur notwithstanding this outstanding easement. Therefore, the buyer notified the seller on April 28 that he would expect to close on May 1.

    When the seller refused to close, the buyer sued for specific performance.

    Will the buyer prevail?

    (A) No, because the easement renders the seller's title unmarketable.

(B) No, because rights of third parties are unresolved.

(C) Yes, because the decision to terminate the contract for title not being marketable belongs only to the buyer.

(D) Yes, because the seller did not give notice of the easement a reasonable time before the closing date.

[QA053]

Answer: Choice **(C)** is correct. If a contract of sale is silent as to quality of title, the court will imply a marketable title, and an easement does affect the marketability of title. But while the seller has a duty to deliver a marketable title, the requirement of marketable title is for the *benefit of the buyer*, not the seller. Therefore, the buyer may always waive the right to have a marketable title, which is what the buyer did here.

(A) is wrong because, while the existence of the easement does often render seller's title unmarketable and courts will imply a requirement to convey marketable title if the contract is silent on the issue, that requirement is for the benefit of the buyer. Thus, the buyer may waive the right to receive marketable title, as she did here.

(B) is wrong because it misstates the facts. The corporation's rights are not unresolved: it has an easement that it may or may not choose to use. The existence of the corporation's easement may render title unmarketable (though a court might well hold that this particular easement is so unlikely to be asserted today that its existence does not in fact make title unmarketable). But in any event, the buyer always has the ability to waive the defect and complete the purchase, and that's what the buyer here has done.

(D) is wrong because the obligation to give reasonable notice and time to cure would be an obligation imposed on the buyer, not on the seller. Courts will imply an obligation to convey marketable title at closing. Where a buyer discovers a defect, she must notify the seller and give the seller a reasonable time to cure. But instead of doing this, the buyer can waive the right to marketable title (and enforce the contract). So the fact that the *seller* didn't give the *buyer* reasonable advance notice of the easement is irrelevant.

D. Remedies for failure to perform:

1. Damages:

b. Where no earnest money deposit:

i. Consideration argument:

Question: Able was the owner of Blackacre, an undeveloped city lot. Able and Baker executed a written document in which Able agreed to sell Blackacre to Baker and Baker agreed to buy Blackacre from Able for $200,000; the document did not provide for an earnest money down payment. Able recorded the document, as authorized by statute.

Able orally gave Baker permission to park his car on Blackacre without charge prior to the closing. Thereafter, Baker frequently parked his car on Blackacre.

Another property came on the market that Baker wanted more than Blackacre. Baker decided to try to escape any obligation to Able.

Baker had been told that contracts for the purchase and sale of real property require consideration and concluded that because he had made no earnest money down payment, he could refuse to close and not be liable. Baker notified Able of his intention not to close and, in fact, did refuse to close on the date set for the closing. Able brought an appropriate action to compel specific performance by Baker.

If Able wins, it will be because

(A) Baker's use of Blackacre for parking constitutes part performance.

(B) general contract rules regarding consideration apply to real estate contracts.

(C) the doctrine of equitable conversion applies.

(D) the document was recorded.

[Q2030]

Answer: Choice **(B)** is correct. It is likely, though not absolutely certain, that Abel will be able to obtain specific performance (the court will have to be satisfied that money damages would not give him an adequate remedy). But one thing that *is* certain is that Baker will fail with his lack-of-consideration argument, because the general contract principle that an exchange of promises meets the consideration requirement applies to real estate contracts. Able has made a promise (to convey in return for the purchase price), and Baker has made a return promise (to pay the purchase price in return for title), so standard consideration requirements are easily satisfied. The fact that there was no earnest money deposit is completely irrelevant to the consideration issue — an earnest money deposit is not required, and where present is merely a form of liquidated-damages clause.

(A) is wrong because the contract, since it is in writing and meets the consideration requirement, would be binding even if Baker had not parked on the property and therefore arguably partly performed. (If the contract had been oral, Baker's parking might supply him with an argument for application of the part-performance exception to the Statute of Frauds, but even here, he would probably lose because the parking was not really part "performance.")

(C) is wrong because equitable conversion, where applicable, vests "equitable title" in the vendee under a land sale contract (thus passing the risk of loss to the vendee), and neither equitable title nor risk of loss is at issue on these facts.

(D) is wrong because a vendor under a land sale contract can recover for breach (including specific performance if money damages would not be an adequate remedy) whether the contract was recorded or not — recording is merely relevant to the vendee's rights vis-à-vis later grantees from the vendor (by giving the world constructive notice of the pending transfer), not to the vendee's rights vis-à-vis the vendor.

2. **Specific performance:**

b. **Breaching buyer:**

Question: Adam entered into a valid written contract to sell Blackacre, a large tract of land, to Betsy. At that time, Blackacre was owned by Adam's father, Fred; Adam had no title to Blackacre and was not the agent of Fred.

After the contract was executed and before the scheduled closing date, Fred died intestate, leaving Adam as his sole heir. Shortly thereafter, Adam received an offer for Blackacre that was substantially higher than the purchase price in the contract with Betsy. Adam refused to close with Betsy although she was ready, willing, and able to close pursuant to the contract.

Betsy brought an appropriate action for specific performance against Adam.

In that action, Betsy should be awarded

(A) nothing, because Adam had no authority to enter into the contract with Betsy.

(B) nothing, because the doctrine of after-acquired title does not apply to executory contracts.

(C) judgment for specific performance, because Adam acquired title prior to the scheduled closing.

(D) judgment for specific performance, to prevent unjust enrichment of Adam.

[Q1071]

Answer: Choice **(C)** is correct. The purchaser under a land-sale contract will normally be entitled to a decree of specific performance if the seller is able but unwilling to perform. Here, the fact that Adam did not have title at the time he signed the contract is irrelevant; the contract called for him to make a conveyance at the scheduled closing date, and he is able to do that. The case therefore falls within the familiar principle that the time for measuring whether a seller has marketable title is the time for closing, not some earlier date.

(A) is wrong because the fact that Adam did not have authority to sell the land at the moment of signing is irrelevant; he has title by now (prior to the scheduled closing date), and that's all that matters for purposes of specific performance.

(B) is wrong because the doctrine of after-acquired title is not necessary for a decree of specific performance here; all that matters is that Adam has title by the time scheduled for performance.

(D) is wrong because specific performance is used for breach of contract where (as here) damages would be an inadequate remedy, and the concept of unjust enrichment is not needed or relevant to whether specific performance should be decreed.

3. **Deposit:**

   a. **Reasonable estimate:**

   Question: Three months ago, Bert agreed in writing to buy Sam's single-family residence, Liveacre, for $110,000. Bert paid Sam a $5,000 deposit to be applied to the purchase price. The contract stated that Sam had the right at his option to retain the deposit as liquidated damages in the event of Ben's default. The closing was to have taken place last week. Six weeks ago, Bert was notified by his employer that he was to be transferred to another job 1,000 miles away. Bert immediately notified Sam that he could not close, and therefore he demanded the return of his $5,000. Sam refused, waited until after the contract closing date, listed with a broker, and then conveyed Liveacre for $108,000 to Conner, a purchaser found by the real estate broker. Conner paid the full purchase price and immediately recorded his deed. Conner knew of the prior contract with Bert. In an appropriate action, Bert seeks to recover the $5,000 deposit from Sam.

   The most probable result will be that Sam

   (A) must return the $5,000 to Bert, because Sam can no longer carry out his contract with Bert.

   (B) must return the $5,000 to Bert, because was legally justified in not completing the contract.

   (C) must return $3,000 to Bert, because Sam's damages were only $2,000.

   (D) may keep the $5,000 deposit, because Bert breached the contract.

   [Q2023]

   Answer: Choice **(D)** is correct. The contract provision concerning the deposit was a liquidated damages clause. In most courts, a liquidated damages clause is enforceable if it was a reasonable estimate (viewed *either* as of the time the contract was made or at the time of suit) of the damages that the seller would likely incur if the buyer breached. Here, an estimate, as of the time the contract was signed, that the seller would sustain $5,000 in damages if there was a breach on a $110,000 contract, seems reasonable. The fact that the seller ended up with a slightly smaller-than-predicted loss of $2,000 (not counting any incidental expenses to the seller from having to re-list the property or wait for a later sale) does not change the reasonableness of the time-of-contract estimate; in fact, the $5,000 estimate is probably also reasonable viewed as of the time of suit.

(A) is wrong because Sam's present ability to carry out his contract with Bert was caused by Bert's breach, and therefore does not nullify Sam's ability to rely on the liquidated damages clause.

(B) is wrong because Bert's need to transfer is not the sort of extraordinary event that would excuse Bert's nonperformance.

(C) is wrong because, as explained in (D), the liquidated damages clause will be enforced here, even though it differs from the seller's actual damages.

b. **Unreasonable estimate:**

Question: A vendor owned a tract of land in fee simple. The vendor and a vendee entered into a written agreement under which the vendee agreed to buy the property for $100,000, its fair market value. The agreement contained all the essential terms of a real estate contract to sell and buy, including a date for closing. The required $50,000 down payment was made. The contract provided that in the event of the vendee's breach, the vendor could retain the $50,000 deposit as liquidated damages.

Before the date set for the closing in the contract, the vendee died. On the day that a woman was duly qualified as administratrix of the estate of the vendee, which was after the closing date, the administratrix made demand for return of the $50,000 deposit. The vendor responded by stating that he took such demand to be a declaration that the administratrix did not intend to complete the contract and that the vendor considered the contract at an end. The vendor further asserted that he was entitled to retain, as liquidated damages, the $50,000. The reasonable market value of the property had increased to $110,000 at that time.

The administratrix brought an appropriate action against the vendor to recover the $50,000. In answer, the vendor made no affirmative claim but asserted that he was entitled to retain the $50,000 as liquidated damages as provided in the contract.

In such lawsuit, judgment should be for

(A) the administratrix, because the provision relied upon by the vendor is unenforceable.

(B) the administratrix, because the death of the vendee terminated the contract as a matter of law.

(C) the vendor, because the court should enforce the express agreement of the contracting parties.

(D) the vendor, because the doctrine of equitable conversion prevents termination of the contract upon the death of a party.

[Q3119]

Answer: Choice **(A)** is correct. In order for a deposit / liquidated damages clause in a land sale contract to be enforceable, even in an easy-to-satisfy court the amount fixed must be reasonable relative to *either* the *anticipated* loss (viewed as of the time the contract was signed) or to the *actual* loss (as determined by the passage of time). The clause here does not meet this standard. It was not a reasonable forecast viewed as of the time the contract was made, because a loss of $50,000 in value during the contract-closing gap is highly unlikely given that the market value at the outset was $100,000 (i.e., a 50% loss of value during a relatively short 2- or 3-month period). Nor was the amount set in the clause reasonable compared with the actual damages, since we're told that the value of the property had actually increased between the signing and the time for closing. So the clause was not reasonable relative to either the anticipated or actual loss, making it an unenforceable penalty.

(B) is wrong as a matter of law — the death of the purchaser under a land-sale contract does not terminate the contract. Instead, both sides remain liable, with the purchaser's estate legally obligated to pay the purchase price assuming that all conditions to closing are satisfied.

(C) is wrong, because the court would not enforce an unenforceable term of a contract.

(D) is wrong because it reaches the wrong outcome, and because equitable conversion has nothing to do with this fact pattern. Equitable conversion, if a court decides to apply it, causes the risk of loss to pass from seller to buyer at the signing of a land-sale contract. Here, it was not equitable conversion that prevented the purchaser's death from terminating the contract. And in any event, the purchaser is entitled to a return of the deposit less any actual damages (which will be zero or negligible in light of the run-up in value).

E. Equitable conversion:

1. Risk of loss:

Question: A seller owned a single family house. A buyer gave the seller a signed handwritten offer to purchase the house. The offer was unconditional and sufficient to satisfy the statute of frauds, and when the seller signed an acceptance an enforceable contract resulted.

The house on the land had been the seller's home, but he had moved to an apartment, so the house was vacant at all times relevant to the proposed transaction. Two weeks after the parties had entered into their contract, one week after the buyer had obtained a written mortgage lending commitment from a lender, and one week before the agreed-upon closing date, the house was struck by lightning and burned to the ground. The loss was not insured, because three years earlier, the seller had let his homeowner's insurance policy lapse after he had paid his mortgage debt in full.

The handwritten contract was wholly silent as to matters of financing, risk of loss, and insurance. The buyer declared the contract voided by the fire, but the seller asserted a right to enforce the contract despite the loss.

There is no applicable statute.

If a court finds for the seller, what is the likely reason?

(A) The contract was construed against the buyer, who drafted it.

(B) The lender's written commitment to make a mortgage loan to the buyer made the contract of sale fully binding on the buyer.

(C) The risk of loss falls on the party in possession, and constructive possession passed to the buyer on the contract date.

(D) The risk of loss passed to the buyer on the contract date under the doctrine of equitable conversion.

[QA022]

Answer: Choice **(D)** is correct. If the court finds for the seller, it will be because it applied the doctrine of equitable conversion. Under the equitable conversion doctrine, courts treat the signing of the contract as vesting in the purchaser equitable ownership of the land. (Conversely, the seller is treated as becoming the equitable owner of the purchase price.) Not all courts apply the doctrine of equitable conversion (though most do). When a court *does* apply the doctrine, the main result is that the risk of loss is deemed to belong to the equitable owner of the land, *i.e.*, the buyer. So where, as here, the contract is unconditional and silent as to the risk of loss, the buyer will be deemed to bear the risk of loss and cannot cancel the contract.

(A) is wrong because it relies on an irrelevant fact. It does not matter who drafted the contract if it is silent as to risk of loss and there is no applicable statute. By contrast (and as further described in the analysis of Choice (D) above), it *does* matter whether the court applies the doctrine of equitable conversion. If the doctrine applies (as it does in the majority of courts), the risk of loss is deemed to pass to the buyer as soon as the contract is signed, assuming that the contract is silent on the risk-of-loss issue. If equitable conversion does not apply, the court will apply the minority common law rule, under which the risk of loss remains with the seller until the closing.

(B) is wrong because it relies on an irrelevant fact. The contract became binding when seller accepted buyer's offer. The facts state that the offer to purchase was unconditional, so the buyer was obligated to purchase the house whether or not he got a loan commitment. In a jurisdiction applying equitable conversion, the buyer was thus the equitable owner as of the time seller signed an acceptance and, as of that moment, the buyer bore the risk of loss.

(C) is wrong because possession does not pass to the buyer until closing, absent a contrary provision in the contract of sale. On the other hand, equitable ownership passes on the signing of the contract, and that is enough to transfer the risk of loss to buyer if the jurisdiction applies the doctrine of equitable conversion (as described above in the analysis of Choice (D)).

Question: Landover, the owner in fee simple of Highacre, an apartment house property, entered into an enforceable written agreement with VanMeer to sell Highacre to VanMeer. The agreement provided that a good and marketable title was to be conveyed free and clear of all encumbrances. However, the agreement was silent as to the risk of fire prior to the closing, and there is no applicable statute in the state where the land is located. The premises were not insured. The day before the scheduled closing date, Highacre was wholly destroyed by fire. When VanMeer refused to close, Landover brought an action in specific performance. If Landover prevails, the most likely reason will be that

(A) the failure of VanMeer to insure his interest as the purchaser of Highacre precludes any relief for him.

(B) the remedy at law is inadequate in actions concerning real estate contracts and either party is entitled to specific performance.

(C) equity does not permit consideration of surrounding circumstances in actions concerning real estate contracts.

(D) the doctrine of equitable conversion applies.
[Q4152]

Answer: Choice **(D)** is correct. Under the doctrine of equitable conversion, the vendee is considered the beneficial owner of the property after the sales contract takes effect, leaving the vendor with a personal property interest in the property, in the form of the balance of the purchase price the vendee owes him. This common law doctrine is followed by most states. In a state following equitable conversion, the vendee is required to close, even though the structures on the property have been destroyed. (But the vendee gets the benefit of any insurance policy the vendor may have had on the structure.)

(A) is wrong because it relies on a fact which is irrelevant: VanMeer's failure to insure the property is not dispositive of Landover's ability to recover the purchase price. Whether VanMeer did or did not buy insurance (which he could have — he had an insurable interest as soon as he signed the contract), Landover would still be able to force a closing, if and only if the jurisdiction applies equitable conversion (see Choice (D) above).

(B) is wrong because although it is a correct statement of the law, it would be insufficient, under these facts, to result in a decision for Landover. (B) is correct in that, in general, remedies at law (e.g., damages) are inadequate in actions where real estate is involved, since real estate is "unique." In such situations, specific performance is an appropriate remedy. However, specific performance is an *equitable* remedy, meaning that equitable considerations will be taken into account to determine if it's appropriate. Choice (D) is just such a consideration – the doctrine of equitable conversion. Conversely, if the jurisdiction does not apply equitable conversion, Landover won't be able to force a closing even though his remedy at law is inadequate.

(C) is wrong because it misstates the law. Specific performance is an equitable remedy. Equitable remedies are granted by determining whether the remedy will be just in the circumstances. As a result, the circumstances surrounding the contract *are* considered.

II. MORTGAGES AND INSTALLMENT CONTRACTS

A. **Nature of mortgage:**

    4. **Sale of mortgaged property:**

        a. **Sale "subject to" mortgage:**

            i. **Payments in "subject to" scenario:**

Question: Several years ago, a man purchased property, financing a large part of the purchase price by a loan from a bank that was secured by a mortgage. The man made the installment payments on the mortgage regularly until last year. Then the man persuaded a woman to buy the property from him, subject to the mortgage to the bank. They expressly agreed that the woman would not assume and agree to pay the man's debt to the bank. The man's mortgage to the bank contained a due-on-sale clause stating, "If Mortgagor transfers his/her interest without the written consent of Mortgagee first obtained, then at Mortgagee's option the entire principal balance of the debt secured by this Mortgage shall become immediately due and payable." However, without seeking the bank's consent, the man conveyed the property to the woman, the deed stating in pertinent part ". . . subject to a mortgage to [the bank] [giving details and recording data]."

The woman took possession of the property and made several mortgage payments, which the bank accepted. Now, however, neither the woman nor the man has made the last three mortgage payments. The bank has brought an appropriate action against the woman for the amount of the delinquent payments.

In this action, judgment should be for

(A) the woman, because she did not assume and agree to pay the man's mortgage debt.

(B) the woman, because she is not in privity of estate with the bank.

(C) the bank, because the man's deed to the woman violated the due-on-sale clause.

(D) the bank, because the woman is in privity of estate with the bank.
[Q1033]

Answer: Choice **(A)** is correct. The woman would have to assume the man's mortgage to be liable under it. When a person buys a mortgaged property without assuming the mortgage, the buyer has no liability on the mortgage. That's true even if the mortgage contains a due-on-sale clause — the clause will be enforced (and will entitle the mortgagee to accelerate the mortgage), but the clause won't cause the buyer to be deemed to have assumed the mortgage. Nor will the fact that the buyer actually makes several mortgage payments cause her to be deemed to have assumed the mortgage and thus be personally liable.

(B) is wrong because privity of estate is not an issue in mortgage cases. Privity of estate makes a difference in cases involving covenants at law — absence of privity of estate means that a successor to the covenantor won't be bound. But a mortgage is not a covenant running with the land, so privity of estate doesn't matter.

(C) is wrong because a due-on-sale clause wouldn't create liability on the part of the buyer. A due-on-sale clause allows a lender to demand full payment of the remainder of an existing loan if the mortgagor transfers any interest in the property securing the loan without the lender's consent. The violation of the due-on-sale clause would give the bank grounds for a case against the man, and grounds to accelerate the mortgage, but not grounds to obtain a personal judgment against the woman.

(D) is wrong for the same reason as (B): a mortgage is not a covenant running with the land, making privity of estate irrelevant.

[Q1033]

b. **Assumption:**

i. **Receipt of deed with assumption clause:**

Question: A man borrowed money from a bank and executed a promissory note for the amount secured by a mortgage on his residence. Several years later, the man sold his residence. As provided by the contract of sale, the deed to the buyer provided that the buyer agreed "to assume the existing mortgage debt" on the residence.

Subsequently, the buyer defaulted on the mortgage loan to the bank, and appropriate foreclosure proceedings were initiated. The foreclosure sale resulted in a deficiency.

There is no applicable statute.

Is the buyer liable for the deficiency?

(A) No, because even if the buyer assumed the mortgage, the seller is solely responsible for any deficiency.

(B) No, because the buyer did not sign a promissory note to the bank and therefore has no personal liability.

(C) Yes, because the buyer assumed the mortgage and therefore became personally liable for the mortgage loan and any deficiency.

(D) Yes, because the transfer of the mortgage debt to the buyer resulted in a novation of the original mortgage and loan and rendered the buyer solely responsible for any deficiency.

[QA016]

Answer: Choice **(C)** is correct. When a buyer assumes the seller's mortgage, the buyer becomes primarily liable for the mortgage debt. (The seller is secondarily liable, assuming there is no release.) The lender may therefore sue buyer for the deficiency when foreclosure sale is not sufficient to discharge the debt. (Contrast this to the situation where the buyer takes "subject to the mortgage." In that situation, the buyer would not be personally liable for the mortgage debt or for a deficiency judgment after foreclosure.) When a buyer knowingly receives a deed that recites that the buyer is assuming the mortgage and intends to be bound, assumption occurs even though the buyer has not signed the deed. (Here, where the buyer previously signed the contract, which called for assumption, it's even more clear that the buyer will be deemed to have assumed even though he never signed the deed.)

(A) is wrong because it misstates the law. When a buyer agrees to "assume" a mortgage, this language is always interpreted to mean that if the lender forecloses and is left with a deficiency judgment, the lender can recover that deficiency from the assuming buyer without first trying to recover it from the original borrower. In other words, the assuming buyer becomes "primarily liable" for the mortgage debt and for any deficiency after foreclosure sale.

(B) is wrong because it was not necessary for the buyer to sign a promissory note to be liable. Once the buyer assumed the mortgage, he became primarily liable on the mortgage and thus is liable for the deficiency. (And the fact that the buyer didn't sign the deed doesn't prevent him from being deemed to have assumed, as long as the buyer knew the deed contained an assumption provision; see Choice (C) for more about this.)

(D) gives the right result but the wrong rationale. The buyer's assumption of the mortgage is not the same as a novation. With a novation, the bank agrees to *substitute* the personal liability of the buyer for that of the original debtor and *releases* the original debtor. Nothing in the facts suggests the bank's involvement in the transaction at all, let alone its willingness to release the original borrower.

Question: Ashton owned Woodsedge, a tract used for commercial purposes, in fee simple and thereafter mortgaged it to First Bank. She signed a promissory note secured by a duly executed and recorded mortgage. There was no "due on sale" clause, that is, no provision that, upon sale, the whole balance then owing would become due and owing. Ashton conveyed Woodsedge to Beam "subject to a mortgage to First Bank, which the grantee assumes and agrees to pay." Beam conveyed Woodsedge to Carter "subject to an existing mortgage to First Bank." A copy of the note and the mortgage that secured it had been exhibited to each grantee.

After Carter made three timely payments, no further payments were made by any party. In fact, the real estate had depreciated to a point where it was worth less than the debt.

There is no applicable statute or regulation.

In an appropriate foreclosure action, First Bank joined Ashton, Beam, and Carter as defendants. At the foreclosure sale, although the fair market value for Woodsedge in its depreciated state was obtained, a deficiency resulted.

First Bank is entitled to collect a deficiency judgment against

(A) Ashton only.

(B) Ashton and Beam only.

(C) Beam and Carter only.

(D) Ashton, Beam, and Carter.

[Q2147]

Answer: Choice **(B)** is correct. Ashton is personally liable because she signed the original promissory note. Beam is personally liable because he assumed the mortgage by means of the document that conveyed to him (and the fact that Beam may not have signed the deed won't matter, as long as he was aware of the assumption language in the deed and intended to be bound by it.) First Bank can recover even though it was not a party to the Beam-to-Ashton promise, because First Bank would be found to be an intended beneficiary (and thus a third party beneficiary who may recover) of that promise. Carter is not personally liable, because a person who receives a conveyance stating that the transfer is "subject to" an outstanding mortgage does not, without more, assume (i.e., become personally liable for) the mortgage. Carter's lack of liability did not change by virtue of the fact that he made several timely payments; only an express promise of assumption by Carter (made either to Ashton, Beam or First Bank) could have rendered him personally liable.

(A), (C), and (D) are wrong to the extent that they are inconsistent with the above analysis.

5. **Redemption of mortgage:**

   a. **Who has right:**

      i. **No redemption until entire mortgage paid off:**

   Question: A brother and sister owned a property in fee simple as tenants in common, each owning an undivided one-half interest. The two joined in mortgaging the property to an investor by a properly recorded mortgage that contained a general warranty clause. The brother became disenchanted with land-owning and notified his sister that he would no longer contribute to the payment of installments due to the investor. After the mortgage was in default and the investor made demand for payment of the entire amount of principal and interest due, the sister tendered to the investor, and the investor deposited, a check for one-half of the amount due the investor. The sister then demanded a release of her undivided one-half interest. The investor refused to release any interest in the property. The sister promptly brought an action against the investor to quiet title to an undivided one-half interest in the property.

   In such action, the sister should

   (A) lose, because the investor's title had been warranted by an express provision of the mortgage.

   (B) lose, because there was no redemption from the mortgage.

   (C) win, because the sister is entitled to marshalling.

   (D) win, because the cotenancy of the mortgagors was in common and not joint.
   [Q3065]

   Answer: Choice **(B)** is correct. The mortgage attached to the entire property, and payment of 1/2 the total amount therefore did not "free up" a 1/2 undivided interest. The investor as mortgagee has a lien on the *entire property*. That is, the investor received a security interest on the full property — and the concomitant right upon default to conduct a judicial sale of the full property to get her debt repaid — regardless of whether one party paid that party's full share. A.L.P. § 16.172. In other words, the investor is entitled to say, "Who paid what is between the two of you — I've got the right to have the whole property sold at foreclosure if any part of my loan is in default and the default is not wholly cured." That's what happened here. (The sister's remedy is a suit in contribution against the brother for 1/2 the amount she paid to the investor.)

   (A) is wrong, because the investor did not have title to the property. A mortgage is a security interest in a property securing a loan. The fact that the mortgage instrument contained a clause in which the brother and sister warranted that they owned the property free of encumbrances (which is what the general warranty clause did) is irrelevant to the issue of whether the sister is entitled to quiet title.

   (C) is wrong, because the equitable doctrine of marshalling does not apply to these facts. Marshalling is the ranking of assets in a certain order toward the payment of debts. The concept arises in equity, and means that where there are two creditors, with the senior one having two funds to satisfy his debt, that senior creditor must resort first to the fund which is not subject to demand of the junior creditor. The concept is misapplied to this fact pattern, because the doctrine would be one a second mortgagee invoked to protect his interest from the first mortgagee's foreclosure. Under these facts there is only one mortgage on the property, and as a party who joined with the brother in making the mortgage on the property, the sister would not be able to have her interest released.

(D) is wrong, because the sister would lose even if the cotenancy was joint. Joint tenancy differs from tenancy in common only with respect to the right of survivorship, which exists as to the former but not the latter. There is no difference in the legal analysis here between the joint-tenancy and tenancy-in-common scenarios.

b. *Statutory redemption right after foreclosure:*

Question: A man owned property that he used as his residence. The man received a loan, secured by a mortgage on the property, from a bank. Later, the man defaulted on the loan. The bank then brought an appropriate action to foreclose the mortgage, was the sole bidder at the judicial sale, and received title to the property as a result of the foreclosure sale.

Shortly after the foreclosure sale, the man received a substantial inheritance. He approached the bank to repurchase the property, but the bank decided to build a branch office on the property and declined to sell.

If the man prevails in an appropriate action to recover title to the property, what is the most likely reason?

(A) He had used the property as his residence.

(B) He timely exercised an equitable right of redemption.

(C) The court applied the doctrine of exoneration.

(D) The jurisdiction provides for a statutory right of redemption.

[QA032]

Answer: Choice **(D)** is correct. When a mortgage is paid off, the property is said to have been "redeemed" from the mortgage. There are two types of redemption rights: equitable and statutory. After default but before foreclosure, any borrower has the right to redeem (i.e., pay off the mortgage and free up the property), even if there is no statute conferring this right; the redemption right is said to be "equitable." However, that equitable right is extinguished at the moment the foreclosure sale occurs. But some states also give the borrower a statutory right of redemption — the legislature decrees that the borrower/mortgagor has a certain period of time *after* the foreclosure sale during which he may regain title by paying a set amount (usually the foreclosure-sale price plus expenses) to the successful bidder. Where such a statutory right exists, the mortgagor retains possession of the property during the statutory redemption period. Here, the man approached the bank after the foreclosure sale, so his equitable right of redemption is gone, and the only way he can prevail is if the jurisdiction provides a statutory right of redemption.

(A) is wrong because man's use of the property as his residence is irrelevant. The only way he can recover title after foreclosure is if the jurisdiction provides a statutory right of redemption. The residential nature of the property would matter only if the statutory right were so limited, and there is nothing in these facts to suggest any such limitation.

(B) is wrong because it confuses the equitable right of redemption with a statutory right of redemption. When the bank foreclosed, it extinguished the man's equitable right of redemption – i.e., the right to pay off the mortgage after default and gain title. The only way the man can prevail is if he has a statutory right of redemption giving him additional time to pay off the obligation after foreclosure (as described more fully in Choice (D)).

(C) is wrong because the common law doctrine of exoneration does not apply to these facts. Under that doctrine, a person who receives a bequest of property that is subject to a lien or mortgage is entitled to take the property "free and clear" of the lien or mortgage if there is no evidence that the testator intended a contrary result. When exoneration applies, the estate's personal property – i.e., its cash – is used to pay off the lien or mortgage. Since the man did not receive a bequest of encumbered real estate, the doctrine could not have applied.

7. **Foreclosure:**

   c. *Wipes out all junior interests:*

   Question: A farmer borrowed $100,000 from a bank and gave the bank a promissory note secured by a mortgage on the farm that she owned. The bank promptly and properly recorded the mortgage, which contained a due-on-sale provision.

   A few years later, the farmer borrowed $5,000 from a second bank and gave it a promissory note secured by a mortgage on her farm. The bank promptly and properly recorded the mortgage.

   Subsequently, the farmer defaulted on her obligation to the first bank, which then validly accelerated the debt and instituted nonjudicial foreclosure proceedings as permitted by the jurisdiction. The second bank received notice of the foreclosure sale but did not send a representative to the sale. At the foreclosure sale, a buyer who was not acting in collusion with the farmer outbid all other bidders and received a deed to the farm.

   Several months later, the original farmer repurchased her farm from the buyer, who executed a warranty deed transferring the farm to her. After the farmer promptly and properly recorded that deed, the second bank commenced foreclosure proceedings on the farm. The farmer denied the validity of the second bank's mortgage.

   Does the second bank continue to have a valid mortgage on the farm?

   (A) Yes, because of the doctrine of estoppel by deed.

   (B) Yes, because the original owner reacquired title to the farm.

   (C) No, because the purchase at the foreclosure sale by the buyer under these facts eliminated the second bank's junior mortgage lien.

   (D) No, because of the due-on-sale provision in the farmer's mortgage to the first bank.
   [QA033]

   Answer: Choice **(C)** is correct. The first bank had priority over the second bank. When a mortgage is properly foreclosed on, the foreclosure sale acts to wipe out all interests in the property junior to the mortgage being foreclosed on, so that the buyer at the foreclosure sale gets a title that is "clean" of all such junior interests. For a mortgage foreclosure sale to have this effect of wiping out all junior interests, all holders of the junior interests must be notified of the foreclosure proceedings, and made a party to those proceedings. That's what happened here: the second (junior) bank was a necessary party to the foreclosure proceeding and was given notice of the sale. When the second bank failed to appear at the foreclosure proceeding, or to take any other action, the buyer at the sale received the title the farmer had at the time the mortgage was given to the first bank, i.e., a title free of any lien to the second bank. And when the farmer bought back the winning bidder's title, the farmer got the very same free-and-clear title that the bidder had received as the result of the auction. (The fact that the buyer and the farmer did not act in collusion means that the second bank cannot now try to circumvent this result by claiming fraud.)

   (A) is wrong because the doctrine of estoppel by deed does not apply to these facts. The doctrine of estoppel by deed applies when a person purports to convey land to which she does not in fact have title (or to which she has a lesser interest than she purports to convey); if such a grantor subsequently acquires title to the land, most courts apply the estoppel doctrine, which causes the title to the land to be deemed to pass immediately to the grantee. That is not the situation here, because mortgages are liens, not conveyances (so the farmer is not deemed to have ever conveyed the property to the second bank).

(B) is wrong because the winning buyer at the foreclosure sale could have re-sold the farm to anyone. The fact that it was the farmer who repurchased it is irrelevant, because the facts state that the buyer and the farmer were not acting in collusion. When the second bank failed to participate in the foreclosure, the buyer took title to the property free and clear of any liens and was able to convey that clean title to whomever he wanted.

(D) is wrong because it arrives at the right conclusion but does so for the wrong reason. The existence of the due-on-sale clause is irrelevant because the farmer never sold the property. A due-on-sale clause allows the mortgagee to accelerate the debt in the event of a sale by the mortgagor (i.e., the clause prevents the buyer from either assuming or taking subject to the mortgage). Here, the farmer went into default, so the first bank commenced and completed foreclosure proceedings without there ever being a conveyance to trigger the due-on-sale clause.

8. **Priorities (allocation of foreclosure proceeds):**

   a. **Judgment lien creditor's status:**

      i. **Two-property scenario:**

      Question: A businessman owned a hotel, subject to a mortgage securing a debt he owed to a bank. The businessman later acquired a nearby parking garage, financing a part of the purchase price by a loan from a financing company, secured by a mortgage on the parking garage. Two years thereafter, the businessman defaulted on the loan owed to the bank, which caused the full amount of that loan to become immediately due and payable. The bank decided not to foreclose the mortgage on the hotel at that time, but instead properly sued for the full amount of the defaulted loan. The bank obtained and properly filed a judgment for that amount. A statute of the jurisdiction provides: "Any judgment properly filed shall, for ten years from filing, be a lien on the real property then owned or subsequently acquired by any person against whom the judgment is rendered." There is no other applicable statute, except the statute providing for judicial foreclosure of mortgages, which places no restriction on deficiency judgments. Shortly thereafter, the bank brought an appropriate action for judicial foreclosure of its first mortgage on the hotel and of its judgment lien on the parking garage. The financing company was joined as a party defendant, and appropriately counterclaimed for foreclosure of its mortgage on the parking garage, which was also in default. All procedures were properly followed and the confirmed foreclosure sales resulted in the following: The net proceeds of the sale of the hotel to a third party were $200,000 less than the bank's mortgage balance. The net proceeds of the sale of the parking garage to a fourth party were $200,000 more than the financing company's mortgage balance.

      How should the $200,000 surplus arising from the bid on the parking garage be distributed?

      (A) It should be paid to the bank.

      (B) It should be paid to the businessman.

      (C) It should be paid to the financing company.

      (D) It should be split equally between the bank and the financing company.
      [Q7057]

      Answer: Choice **(A)** is correct. The foreclosure sale of the bank's mortgage on the hotel was insufficient to pay the businessman's debt to the bank. The bank had received a judgment against the businessman for the entire amount of the defaulted loan. This lien was properly recorded and applied to all property owned by the businessman during the following ten-year time period, including the parking garage. After the financing company was paid in full from the funds generated by the foreclosure sale of its mortgage on the parking garage, the additional funds generated by that sale would be paid to the bank not as a deficiency judgment, but because of the unsatisfied amount of the prior money judgment.

(B) is incorrect. The judgment lien was properly filed against the businessman. Therefore, the garage was subject not only to the loan of the financing company, but also to the judgment lien as a second priority. The businessman would be entitled to surplus proceeds only if both liens had been fully paid.

(C) is incorrect. The foreclosure sale of the financing company's mortgage on the parking garage was sufficient to pay the businessman's debt to the financing company in full. The fact that the garage was sold for more money than was owed under the garage mortgage is irrelevant to the amount owed to the financing company — a mortgagee doesn't receive any part of the "surplus" after its mortgage has been paid in full.

(D) is incorrect for the same reason that (C) is incorrect.

c. **Mortgagee can't get excess:**

Question: Owner owned a hotel, subject to a mortgage securing a debt Owner owed to Lender One. Owner later acquired a nearby parking garage, financing a part of the purchase price by a loan from Lender Two, secured by a mortgage on the parking garage. Two years thereafter, Owner defaulted on the loan owed to Lender One, which caused the full amount of that loan to become immediately due and payable. Lender One decided not to foreclose the mortgage on Owner's hotel at that time, but instead brought an action, appropriate under the laws of the jurisdiction and authorized by the mortgage loan documents, for the full amount of the defaulted loan. Lender One obtained and properly filed a judgment for that amount.

A statute of the jurisdiction provides: "Any judgment properly filed shall, for ten years from filing, be a lien on the real property then owned or subsequently acquired by any person against whom the judgment is rendered."

There is no other applicable statute, except the statute providing for judicial foreclosure of mortgages, which places no restriction on deficiency judgments.

Lender One later brought an appropriate action for judicial foreclosure of its first mortgage on the hotel and of its judgment lien on the parking garage. Lender Two was joined as a party defendant, and appropriately counterclaimed for foreclosure of its mortgage on the parking garage, which was also in default. All procedures were properly followed and the confirmed foreclosure sales resulted as follows:

Lender One purchased the hotel for $100,000 less than its mortgage balance.

Lender One purchased the parking garage for an amount that is $200,000 in excess of Lender Two's mortgage balance.

The $200,000 surplus arising from the bid paid by Lender One for the parking garage should be paid

(A) $100,000 to Lender One and $100,000 to Owner.

(B) $100,000 to Lender Two and $100,000 to Owner.

(C) $100,000 to Lender One and $100,000 to Lender Two.

(D) $200,000 to Owner.

[Q3144]

Answer: Choice **(A)** is correct, because Lender One's judgment lien on the garage came ahead of Owner's equity. When Lender One filed its judgment for the amount owed on the hotel, that lender got a lien against the garage (as well as against the hotel) for the full amount owed on the hotel. So at that moment, Lender One was in the position of a second mortgagee on the garage, behind Lender Two. Then, when Lender One purchased the hotel for $100,000 less than the mortgage balance, Lender One obtained a deficiency judgment for that $100,000 amount. This became the amount covered by the earlier-filed judgment lien, and was secured by a second position on the garage. (It's irrelevant that the hotel was bought by Lender One: the same result, a $100,000 second-position lien for Lender One on the garage, would have come into existence regardless of who bought the hotel at foreclosure, if the price paid was $100,000 less than the balance due.) When Lender One paid $200,000 more than the outstanding Lender Two mortgage balance for the garage, this $200,000 amount was "excess," and was required to be handled the same way as if Lender Two had had no mortgage and the total purchase price was $200,000. That is, Lender One's lien now moved to first position, and was entitled to be paid in full before anything went to the equity owner (Owner). So Lender One got the first $100,000 of the excess. The balance, $100,000, went to the equity owner (Owner).

(B), (C), and (D) are wrong, since they involve computations that are inconsistent with this analysis. In particular, you should have been able to immediately eliminate choices (B) and (C), since these involved payments to Lender Two. Like any mortgagee, Lender Two was not entitled to any money brought in by a foreclosure that was in excess of the money then owed to it on the mortgage.

d. Equitable subrogation:

i. Where relevant:

Question: Stoven, who owned Craigmont in fee simple, mortgaged Craigmont to Ulrich to secure a loan of $100,000. The mortgage was promptly and properly recorded. Stoven later mortgaged Craigmont to Martin to secure a loan of $50,000. The mortgage was promptly and properly recorded. Subsequently, Stoven conveyed Craigmont to Fritsch. About a year later, Fritsch borrowed $100,000 from Zorn, an elderly widow, and gave her a mortgage on Craigmont to secure repayment of the loan. Zorn did not know about the mortgage held by Martin. The understanding between Fritsch and Zorn was that Fritsch would use the $100,000 to pay off the mortgage held by Ulrich and that Zorn would, therefore, have a first mortgage on Craigmont. Zorn's mortgage was promptly and properly recorded. Fritsch paid the $100,000 received from Zorn to Ulrich and obtained and recorded a release of the Ulrich mortgage.

The $50,000 debt secured by the Martin mortgage was not paid when it was due, and Martin brought an appropriate action to foreclose, joining Stoven, Fritsch, and Zorn as defendants and alleging that Martin's mortgage was senior to Zorn's mortgage on Craigmont.

If the court rules that Zorn's mortgage is entitled to priority over Martin's mortgage, which of the following determinations are necessary to support that ruling?

I. Ulrich's mortgage was originally senior to Martin's mortgage.

II. Zorn is entitled to have Ulrich's mortgage revived for her benefit, and Zorn is entitled to be subrogated to Ulrich's original position as senior mortgagee.

III. There are no countervailing equities in favor of Martin.

(A) I and II only.

(B) I and III only.

(C) II and III only.

(D) I, II, and III.

[Q1125]

Answer: Choice **(D)** is correct. Under the doctrine of equitable subrogation, a junior claimant who pays off a senior mortgage becomes by subrogation the owner of the senior mortgage to the extent necessary to prevent unjust enrichment; the senior mortgage is preserved, and retains its priority in the hands of the subrogee (the person who paid it off). Zorn has a good chance of having the doctrine applied to his benefit here, but to do so he will have to establish the following: (I) that Ulrich's mortgage was senior to Martin's (since otherwise, Zorn's succeeding to Ulrich's priority won't help Zorn taken ahead of Martin); (II) that under the doctrine, the Ulrich mortgage should be revived for Zorn's benefit instead of being treated as discharged; and (III) that there are no countervailing equities in favor of Martin (since equitable subordination is, as the name implies, an equitable doctrine and thus requires consideration of the equities on both sides). Therefore, (I), (II) and (III) must all be satisfied for the equitable subrogation doctrine to apply here.

III. DEEDS

B. Formalities:

3. Identification of parties:

a. Void if not satisfied:

i. Imprecise identification:

Question: A landowner owned a valuable parcel of land located in York County. The landowner executed a document in the form of a warranty deed of the parcel, which was regular in all respects except that the only language designating the grantees in each of the granting and *habendum* clauses was: "The leaders of all the Protestant Churches in York County." The instrument was acknowledged as required by statute and promptly and properly recorded. The landowner told his lawyer, but no one else, that he had made the conveyance as he did because he abhorred sectarianism in the Protestant movement and because he thought that the leaders would devote the asset to lessening sectarianism.

The landowner died suddenly and unexpectedly a week later, leaving a will that bequeathed and devised his entire estate to his cousin. After probate of the will became final and the administration on the landowner's estate was closed, the cousin instituted an appropriate action to quiet title to the parcel and properly served as defendant each Protestant church situated in the county.

The only evidence introduced consisted of the chain of title under which the landowner held, the probated will, the recorded deed, the fact that no person knew about the deed except the landowner and his lawyer, and the conversation the landowner had with his lawyer described above.

In such action, judgment should be for

(A) the cousin, because there is inadequate identification of grantees in the deed.

(B) the cousin, because the state of the evidence would not support a finding of delivery of the deed.

(C) the defendants, because a deed is *prima facie* valid until rebutted.

(D) the defendants, because recording established delivery *prima facie* until rebutted.

[Q1132]

Answer: Choice **(A)** is correct. In order to be valid, a deed must identify the grantee(s) with reasonable precision. Here, the grantees are "the leaders of all the Protestant churches in York County." It may be possible to identify with acceptable confidence all Protestant churches in the county, but it is unlikely that the "leader" of each church can be identified, given the imprecision of the term "leader" in the context of a church (is it the minister, or is it the president of the congregation, or is it the entire board of directors of the organization?). Where a deed does not identify the grantee with acceptable precision, the deed will be treated as if it had never been made. That would mean that the landowner died still holding title, which passed to the cousin.

(B) is wrong because the fact that the deed was recorded furnishes a strong presumption that delivery occurred (i.e., that the grantor intended the deed to take effect immediately, which is all that "delivery" means).

(C) is wrong because, while it may be true that a deed is presumed valid, the lack of an acceptably-precise designation of grantees here would be sufficient to rebut the presumption of validity.

(D) is wrong because, while recording will indeed create a *prima facie* (but rebuttable) case that delivery occurred, the problem here is not delivery but imprecision in the designation of the grantees.

b. **Deceased grantee:**

Question: A vendee entered into a valid written contract to purchase a large tract of land from a vendor for its fair market value of $50,000. The contract was assignable by the vendee. The vendee duly notified the vendor to convey title jointly to the vendee and "Charles," Charles being the vendee's friend whom the vendee had not seen for many years.

When the vendee learned that Charles would have to sign certain documents in connection with the closing, she prevailed upon her brother to attend the closing and pretend to be Charles. The vendee and her brother attended the closing, and the vendor executed an instrument in the proper form of a deed, purporting to convey the property to "[the vendee] and Charles, as tenants in common." The brother pretended that he was Charles, and he signed Charles's name to all the required documents. The vendee provided the entire $50,000 consideration for the transaction. The deed was promptly and properly recorded.

Unknown to the vendee or her brother, Charles had died several months before the closing. Charles's will, which was duly probated, devised "all my real estate to my nephew" and the residue of his estate to the vendee.

The vendee and the nephew have been unable to agree as to the status or disposition of the property. The nephew brought an appropriate action against the vendor and the vendee to quiet legal title to an undivided one-half interest in the property.

The court should hold that legal title to the property is vested

(A) all in the vendor.

(B) all in the vendee.

(C) one-half in the vendee and one-half in the vendor.

(D) one-half in the vendee and one-half in the nephew.

[Q2114]

Answer: Choice **(C)** is correct. Because Charles was dead at the time of the purported conveyance to the vendee and Charles as tenants in common, the deed's attempt to pass an interest to him was not effective (i.e., the deed was "void" as to him). Therefore, no interest passed through to his estate or via his estate to his nephew. The "Charles" portion of the tenancy in common therefore remained in the vendor. The deed was effective as to the vendee's interest, however, since she was correctly named and the deed was delivered to and accepted by her; therefore, she has the tenancy in common interest that the vendor intended to convey to her.

Choices (A), (B), and (D) are wrong because they are inconsistent with the above analysis.

5. **Consideration not required:**

   Question: Owner owned Greenacre, a tract of land, in fee simple. Owner executed an instrument in the proper form of a deed, purporting to convey Greenacre to Purchaser in fee simple. The instrument recited that the conveyance was in consideration of "$5 cash in hand paid and for other good and valuable consideration." Owner handed the instrument to Purchaser and Purchaser promptly and properly recorded it.

   Two months later, Owner brought an appropriate action against Purchaser to cancel the instrument and to quiet title. In support, Owner proved that no money in fact had been paid by Purchaser, notwithstanding the recitation, and that no other consideration of any kind had been supplied by Purchaser.

   In such action, Owner should

   (A) lose, because any remedy Owner might have had was lost when the instrument was recorded.

   (B) lose, because the validity of conveyance of land does not depend upon consideration being paid, whether recited or not.

   (C) prevail, because the recitation of consideration paid may be contradicted by parol evidence.

   (D) prevail, because recordation does not make a void instrument effective.
   [Q3111]

   Answer: Choice **(B)** is correct, because consideration is not required to make a deed valid. Therefore, even if Owner was able to prove that no money had in fact been paid by Purchaser, notwithstanding the recitation, and that no other consideration of any kind had been supplied by Purchaser, Owner would still lose.

   (A) is wrong because Purchaser's recording did not end Owner's right to bring suit. Recorded deeds are presumed valid. But notwithstanding the deed's recordation, Owner could still challenge its validity if he had substantive grounds to do so (e.g., because it was forged or never delivered). However, under these facts, the deed was authentic and validly delivered, notwithstanding the lack of consideration and the false recital about it; therefore, Owner's attempt to rebut the presumption of validity from recording would fail.

   (C) is wrong because whether consideration was paid (and therefore how the existence of consideration can be proved) is irrelevant, as described in (B) above.

   (D) is wrong because the deed was valid, not a void instrument. It's true that recordation does not validate an invalid conveyance, such as a forged or undelivered deed; however, that rule does not apply to these facts.

C. **Delivery of deed:**

3. **Delivery to agent of grantee:**

Question: When a homeowner became ill, he properly executed a deed sufficient to convey his home to his nephew, who was then serving overseas in the military. Two persons signed as witnesses to qualify the deed for recordation under an applicable statute. The homeowner handed the deed to his nephew's friend and said, "I want [the nephew] to have my home. Please take this deed for him." Shortly thereafter, the nephew's friend learned that the homeowner's death was imminent. One day before the homeowner's death, the nephew's friend recorded the deed. The nephew returned home shortly after the homeowner's death. The nephew's friend brought him up to date, and he took possession of the home. The homeowner died intestate, leaving a daughter as his sole heir. She asserted ownership of his home. The nephew brought an appropriate action against her to determine title to the home. The law of the jurisdiction requires only two witnesses for a will to be properly executed.

If the court rules for the nephew and against the daughter, what is the most likely explanation?

(A) The deed was delivered when the homeowner handed it to the nephew's friend.

(B) The delivery of the deed was accomplished by the recording of the deed.

(C) The homeowner's death consummated a valid gift causa mortis to the nephew.

(D) The homeowner's properly executed deed was effective as a testamentary document.
[Q7070]

Answer: Choice **(A)** is correct. An inter vivos gift (i.e., one made during the giver's lifetime) may be made of real estate. The gift is deemed made when "delivery" occurs, accompanied by the requisite donative intent. Here, the homeowner had the requisite donative intent as shown by his words. Delivery occurred when the homeowner physically handed the deed to the nephew's friend as the agent of the nephew; this was delivery because it is clear from the homeowner's words that he intended the gift to take place immediately rather than at some future time. Acceptance is presumed if the gift is beneficial. Once delivery occurred, the homeowner could not recall the gift.

(B) is incorrect, because although the recording of a deed may create a presumption of delivery, here the delivery occurred prior to the recordation of the deed (at the moment the homeowner physically handed the deed to the nephew's friend as the agent of the nephew, with the intent to pass the title).

(C) is incorrect, because a gift causa mortis may only be made of personal property. In addition, the gift was not made in view of pending death from a stated peril (the facts only note that the homeowner was ill).

(D) is incorrect, because a testamentary document takes effect at the death of the testator and must have been executed with the requisite testamentary intent. Here, the homeowner wanted the nephew to have title immediately and thus delivered the deed to the nephew's friend; the homeowner did not want to postpone delivery until his death.

4. **Promise of later delivery:**

Question: Olivia, owner in fee simple of Richacre, a large parcel of vacant land, executed a deed purporting to convey Richacre to her nephew, Grant. She told Grant, who was then 19, about the deed and said that she would give it to him when he reached 21 and had received his undergraduate college degree. Shortly afterward, Grant searched Olivia's desk, found and removed the deed, and recorded it.

A month later, Grant executed an instrument in the proper form of a warranty deed purporting to convey Richacre to his fiancée, Bonnie. He delivered the deed to Bonnie, pointing out that the deed recited that it was given in exchange for "$1 and other good and valuable consideration," and that to make it valid Bonnie must pay him $1. Bonnie, impressed and grateful, did so. Together, they went to the recording office and recorded the deed. Bonnie assumed Grant had owned Richacre, and knew nothing about Grant's dealing with Olivia. Neither Olivia's deed to Grant nor Grant's deed to Bonnie said anything about any conditions.

The recording act of the jurisdiction provides: "No conveyance or mortgage of real property shall be good against subsequent purchasers for value and without notice unless the same be recorded according to law."

Two years passed. Grant turned 21, then graduated from college. At the graduation party, Olivia was chatting with Bonnie and for the first time learned the foregoing facts.

The age of majority in the jurisdiction is 18 years.

Olivia brought an appropriate action against Bonnie to quiet title to Richacre.

The court will decide for

(A) Olivia, because Grant's deed to Bonnie before Grant satisfied Olivia's conditions was void, as Bonnie had paid only nominal consideration.

(B) Olivia, because her deed to Grant was not delivered.

(C) Bonnie, because Grant has satisfied Olivia's oral conditions.

(D) Bonnie, because the deed to her was recorded.

[Q3016]

Answer: Choice **(B)** is correct, because the lack of delivery by Olivia caused the deed to Grant to be void, and there was therefore no title for Bonnie to take, regardless of whether she was a BFP and regardless of whether she paid value. For a deed to be valid, it must not only be executed but also "delivered." The delivery requirement is satisfied by words or conduct of the grantor which evidence his intention to make his deed *presently operative*, so as to vest title in the grantee and to surrender his own control over title. Here, there was no actual delivery of Olivia's deed for Richacre to Grant. In fact, Olivia's words and deeds made clear that she did *not* intend for the deed to be presently operative. Without delivery by Olivia, title to Richacre never vested in Grant. Since title never vested in Grant, he had nothing to convey to Bonnie. Therefore, whether she knew or didn't know of Grant's deceit, and whether she did or didn't give value, never even become issues. And the recording act's provisions never govern the case at all. (Nor does it matter that Grant eventually turned 21 and graduated from college — there had to be a moment at which Olivia had the present intent to make an immediately-effective conveyance, and that moment never occurred; this is further discussed as to Choice (C) below.)

(A) is wrong because it is an incorrect legal explanation for the correct result. As described above, title never vested in Grant because the deed to him was never delivered. Consequently, Grant had nothing to convey to Bonnie. Therefore, the fact that Bonnie paid only nominal consideration is irrelevant — even if she had paid full consideration, she still would have received nothing. (Conversely, if there had been a valid delivery to Grant, such that he received title, the absence of real consideration for the Grant-to-Bonnie deed would not have prevented Bonnie from getting title.)

(C) is wrong because Grant never received title, regardless of the fact that he eventually satisfied the conditions that Olivia had announced. As described in the analysis of Choice (B), nothing passed to Grant, because there was no delivery. The fact that Grant later satisfied Olivia's oral conditions is irrelevant — the statement of conditions was at most a promise to make a conveyance in the future, and satisfaction of those conditions would not cause delivery to automatically occur. So even assuming that Grant met the previously-announced conditions eventually, Olivia would still be treated as never having made delivery. Since Olivia never made delivery, there never was anything for Grant to convey to Bonnie.

(D) is wrong, because Bonnie had no interest to record. The deed Grant conveyed to Bonnie was void, because Grant had no interest to convey to Bonnie (for the delivery-related reasons described in the analysis of (C)). Since Bonnie had no interest in Richacre to record, the fact that she recorded was meaningless.

7. **Not revocable:**

   a. **Testable:**

   Question: A landowner executed an instrument in the proper form of a deed, purporting to convey his land to a friend. The landowner handed the instrument to the friend, saying, "This is yours, but please do not record it until after I am dead. Otherwise, it will cause me no end of trouble with my relatives." Two days later, the landowner asked the friend to return the deed to him because he had decided that he should devise the land to the friend by will rather than by deed. The friend said that he would destroy the deed and a day or so later falsely told the landowner that the deed had been destroyed. Six months ago, the landowner, who had never executed a will, died intestate, survived by a daughter as his sole heir at law. The day after the landowner's death, the friend recorded the deed from him. As soon as the daughter discovered this recording and the friend's claim to the land, she brought an appropriate action against the friend to quiet title to the land.

   For whom should the court hold?

   (A) The daughter, because the death of the landowner deprived the subsequent recordation of any effect.

   (B) The daughter, because the friend was dishonest in reporting that he had destroyed the deed.

   (C) The friend, because the deed was delivered to him.

   (D) The friend, because the deed was recorded by him.
   [Q7009]

   Answer: Choice **(C)** is correct. A deed must be delivered to be valid. Delivery is a question of intent. The words of the landowner included "this is yours," showing the necessary intent to strip himself of dominion and control over the deed and to immediately transfer the title. In addition, handing the deed to the grantee raises a rebuttable presumption of delivery. Recording the deed is not required and thus the request not to record the document until later was irrelevant so long as delivery was present. Once the deed was delivered in the initial encounter, the friend's false statement that he had destroyed the deed did not reverse the deed's effect, since that lie did not meet the requirements for a valid reconveyance. (Indeed, even if the friend had in fact destroyed the deed, this wouldn't have changed the fact that the friend was the owner, since a grantee's destruction of a deed does not constitute a conveyance back to the original grantor.)

   (A) is incorrect, because the deed to the friend was delivered to him when the landowner handed over the deed; neither the death of the landowner nor the friend's subsequent recording of the deed had any effect on the deed's validity.

   (B) is incorrect, because delivery occurred at the time the deed was handed to the friend with the words "this is yours," and the subsequent misrepresentation that the friend made that he had destroyed the deed has no effect on the prior valid delivery.

(D) is incorrect, because recording a document has no effect on its validity. The deed to the friend was valid because it was in the proper form and was delivered to him, and his subsequent recording of the deed had no effect on his claim of ownership (though it would provide constructive notice to other later claimants).

Question: Ogle owned Greenacre, a tract of land, in fee simple. Five years ago, he executed and delivered to Lilly an instrument in the proper form of a warranty deed that conveyed Greenacre to Lilly "for and during the term of her natural life." No other estate or interest or person taking an interest was mentioned. Lilly took possession of Greenacre and has remained in possession.

Fifteen months ago, Ogle died, leaving a will that has been duly admitted to probate. The will, *inter alia,* had the following provision:

"I devise Greenacre to Mina for her natural life and from and after Mina's death to Rex, his heirs and assigns, forever."

Administration of Ogle's estate has been completed. Mina claims the immediate right to possession of Greenacre. Rex also asserts a right to immediate possession.

In an appropriate lawsuit to which Lilly, Mina, and Rex are parties, who should be adjudged to have the right to immediate possession?

(A) Lilly, because no subsequent act of Ogle would affect her life estate.

(B) Mina, because Ogle's will was the final and definitive expression of his intent.

(C) Mina, because Lilly's estate terminated with the death of Ogle.

(D) Rex, because Lilly's estate terminated with Ogle's death and all that Ogle had was the right to transfer his reversion in fee simple.

[Q2092]

Answer: Choice **(A)** is correct. When Ogle delivered the deed to Lilly, she received a life estate, and nothing Ogle did thereafter could undo or modify that life estate. Therefore, the clause in Ogle's will leaving a life estate to Mina did not affect Lilly's life estate. (Instead, Mina got an executory life estate that would not start until Lilly's death.)

(B) is wrong because of the principle stated in Choice (A) above. (C) and (D) are wrong because of this same principle; notice that a grantor (here, Ogle) can create a life estate in the grantee, and the grantor's death does not act to terminate that life estate, as Choices (C) and (D) suggest that it would.

E. **Covenants for title in warranty deed:**

2. **Present vs. future covenants:**

   b. **Future covenants:**

      i. **List of future covenants:**

Question: Seller owned Blackacre, improved with an aging four-story warehouse. The warehouse was built to the lot lines on all four sides. On the street side, recessed loading docks permitted semi-trailers to be backed in. After the tractors were unhooked, the trailers extended into the street and occupied most of one lane of the street. Over the years, as trailers became larger, the blocking of the street became more severe. The municipality advised Seller that the loading docks could not continue to be used because the trailers blocked the street; it gave Seller 90 days to cease and desist.

During the 90 days, Seller sold and conveyed Blackacre by warranty deed for a substantial consideration to Buyer. The problem of the loading docks was not discussed in the negotiations.

Upon expiration of the 90 days, the municipality required Buyer to stop using the loading docks. This action substantially reduced the value of Blackacre.

Buyer brought an appropriate action against Seller seeking cancellation of the deed and return of all monies paid.

Such action should be based upon a claim of

(A) misrepresentation.

(B) breach of the covenant of warranty.

(C) failure of consideration.

(D) mutual mistake.

[Q2135]

Answer: Choice (B) is **incorrect**. The covenant of warranty protects the grantee only against an eviction or disturbance, due to absence of title or to an encumbrance. So the facts here fail to support a claim for breach of the warranty covenant in two respects: (1) the problem with using the loading docks was not a problem with title or an encumbrance (merely a problem that the existing use violated city rules), and (2) more fundamentally, Buyer has not been evicted or even threatened with eviction (he can stay on the property forever as long as he doesn't unload trailers in a way that blocks the street).

(The correct choice is (A). By concealing the fact that the present use is the subject of current enforcement proceedings, Seller is liable on a fraudulent misrepresentation theory.)

3. **No protection against having to defend invalid claim:**

   Question: A grantor, who owned a farm in fee simple, conveyed the farm to a grantee by warranty deed. A neighbor, who owned the adjoining property, asserted title to the farm and brought an appropriate action against the grantee to quiet title to the farm. The grantee demanded that the grantor defend the grantee's title under the deed's covenant of warranty, but the grantor refused. The grantee then successfully defended at her own expense.

   The grantee brought an appropriate action against the grantor to recover the grantee's expenses incurred in defending against the neighbor's action to quiet title to the farm.

   In this action, the court should decide for

   (A) the grantee, because in effect it was the grantor's title that was challenged.

   (B) the grantee, because the grantor's deed to her included the covenant of warranty.

   (C) the grantor, because the title he conveyed was not defective.

   (D) the grantor, because the neighbor may elect which of the grantor or the grantee to sue.
   [Q3159]

   Answer: Choice **(C)** is correct. The covenant of warranty requires defense only against suits that turn out to be meritorious. The covenant of warranty includes a promise by the covenantor to defend on behalf of the covenantee any lawful or reasonable claims of title by a third party. So if the grantee had lost the suit, she could have recovered her legal costs (and the value of the property) from the grantor. But ironically, by winning against the neighbor, the grantee lost her right to recover from the grantor. When the grantee won versus the neighbor, she established that the neighbor's claim was without merit. At that point, the grantor had no obligation to reimburse her for defending this now-known-to-be-valueless claim.

(A), (B), and (D) are wrong because each is, in some way, inconsistent with the above analysis. ((D) is also incorrect as a matter of law, because the neighbor cannot elect to sue either the grantor or the grantee — the grantee presently claims to have title to the property, so she, not the grantor, is the proper target for the neighbor's suit.)

[Q3159]

Question: Art, who owned Blackacre in fee simple, conveyed Blackacre to Bea by warranty deed. Celia, an adjoining owner, asserted title to Blackacre and brought an appropriate action against Bea to quiet title to Blackacre. Bea demanded that Art defend Bea's title under the deed's covenant of warranty, but Art refused. Bea then successfully defended at her own expense.

Bea brought an appropriate action against Art to recover Bea's expenses incurred in defending against Celia's action to quiet title to Blackacre.

In this action, the court should decide for

(A) Bea, because in effect it was Art's title that was challenged.

(B) Bea, because Art's deed to her included the covenant of warranty.

(C) Art, because the title Art conveyed was not defective.

(D) Art, because Celia may elect which of Art or Bea to sue.

[Q3159]

Answer: Choice **(C)** is correct, because the covenant of warranty requires defense only against suits that turn out to be meritorious. The covenant of warranty includes a promise by the covenantor to defend on behalf of the covenantee any lawful or reasonable claims of title by a third party. So if Bea had lost the suit, she could have recovered her legal costs (and the value of the property) from Art. But ironically, by winning against Celia, Bea lost her right to recover from Art. When Bea won against Celia, she established that Celia's claim was without merit. At that point, Art had no obligation to reimburse her for defending this now-known-to-be-valueless claim.

(A), (B), and (D) are wrong because each is, in some way, inconsistent with the above analysis. ((D) is incorrect as a matter of law, because Celia cannot elect to sue either Art or Bea — Bea presently claims to have title to Blackacre, so she, not Art, is the proper target for Celia's suit.)

F. **Estoppel by deed:**

Question: An uncle was the record title holder of a vacant tract of land. He often told friends that he would leave the land to his nephew in his will. The nephew knew of these conversations. Prior to the uncle's death, the nephew conveyed the land by warranty deed to a woman for $10,000. She did not conduct a title search of the land before she accepted the deed from the nephew. She promptly and properly recorded her deed. Last month, the uncle died, leaving the land to the nephew in his duly probated will. Both the nephew and the woman now claim ownership of the land. The nephew has offered to return the $10,000 to the woman.

Who has title to the land?

(A) The nephew, because at the time of the deed to the woman, the uncle was the owner of record.

(B) The nephew, because the woman did not conduct a title search.

(C) The woman, because of the doctrine of estoppel by deed.

(D) The woman, because she recorded her deed prior to the uncle's death.

[Q7082]

Answer: Choice **(C)** is correct. Estoppel by deed applies to validate a deed, and in particular a warranty deed, that was executed and delivered by a grantor who had no title (or less-than-perfect title) to the land at that time, but who represented that he had such title and who thereafter acquired such title. (The doctrine is sometimes called "after-acquired title.") In this case, estoppel by deed would apply in the woman's favor to estop the nephew from claiming ownership of the land upon the death of his uncle.

(A) is incorrect because the fact that the uncle was the owner of record on the date of transfer to the woman would be relevant in a dispute between the uncle and the woman, but is not relevant in a dispute between the nephew and the woman.

(B) is incorrect because while it is true that a title search would have revealed that the uncle was the owner of record on the date of transfer, the uncle's ownership is only relevant to a dispute between the woman and the uncle, not to a dispute between the nephew and the woman. In fact, the woman owns the land because of the operation of estoppel by deed, as described in Choice (C).

(D) is incorrect because although this option correctly states that the woman owns the land, it misstates the reason why this is so. The woman's recording of the deed provided notice to the world of her interest from the time of recording, but had no bearing on the validity of her claim vis-a-vis the nephew.

Question: A farmer borrowed $100,000 from a bank and gave the bank a promissory note secured by a mortgage on the farm that she owned. The bank promptly and properly recorded the mortgage, which contained a due-on-sale provision.

A few years later, the farmer borrowed $5,000 from a second bank and gave it a promissory note secured by a mortgage on her farm. The bank promptly and properly recorded the mortgage.

Subsequently, the farmer defaulted on her obligation to the first bank, which then validly accelerated the debt and instituted nonjudicial foreclosure proceedings as permitted by the jurisdiction. The second bank received notice of the foreclosure sale but did not send a representative to the sale. At the foreclosure sale, a buyer who was not acting in collusion with the farmer outbid all other bidders and received a deed to the farm.

Several months later, the original farmer repurchased her farm from the buyer, who executed a warranty deed transferring the farm to her. After the farmer promptly and properly recorded that deed, the second bank commenced foreclosure proceedings on the farm. The farmer denied the validity of the second bank's mortgage.

Does the second bank continue to have a valid mortgage on the farm?

(A) Yes, because of the doctrine of estoppel by deed.

(B) Yes, because the original owner reacquired title to the farm.

(C) No, because the purchase at the foreclosure sale by the buyer under these facts eliminated the second bank's junior mortgage lien.

(D) No, because of the due-on-sale provision in the farmer's mortgage to the first bank.

[QA033]

Answer: Choice **(A)** is **incorrect**, because the doctrine of estoppel by deed does not apply to these facts. The doctrine of estoppel by deed applies when a person purports to convey land to which she does not in fact have title (or to which she has a lesser interest than she purports to convey); if such a grantor subsequently acquires title to the land, most courts apply the estoppel doctrine, which causes the title to the land to be deemed to pass immediately to the grantee. That is not the situation here, because mortgages are liens, not conveyances (so the farmer is not deemed to have ever conveyed the property to the second bank). (The correct answer is (C); see p. 184 for details.)

G. Undisclosed condition in house:

2. Emerging trend of liability for failure to disclose material defect:

Question: Able, who owned Blackacre, a residential lot improved with a dwelling, conveyed it for a valuable consideration to Baker. The dwelling had been constructed by a prior owner. Baker had inspected Blackacre prior to the purchase and discovered no defects. After moving in, Baker became aware that sewage seeped into the basement when the toilets were flushed. Able said that this defect had been present for years and that he had taken no steps to hide the facts from Baker. Baker paid for the necessary repairs and brought an appropriate action against Able to recover his cost of repair.

If Baker wins, it will be because

(A) Able failed to disclose a latent defect.

(B) Baker made a proper inspection.

(C) the situation constitutes a health hazard.

(D) Able breached the implied warranty of habitability and fitness for purpose.

[Q2120]

Answer: Choice **(A)** is correct. An increasing number of courts now impose liability on a home seller who is aware of a material defect and who fails to disclose it to a buyer, where the defect is a latent one that cannot easily be found by an inspection. It is by no means certain that a court would find for Baker on this ground, but of the four possibilities this is the only one that offers Baker even a plausible chance of success.

(B) is wrong because Baker's having made a proper inspection, by itself, would not be enough to ensure him a victory. For instance, if the defect had been a "patent" one (one that ought to have been discovered by a reasonable inspection), virtually no courts would impose liability.

(C) is wrong because, while the fact that the condition constitutes a health hazard is a factor making liability slightly more likely, the key factor leading to liability is that the defect was latent (not readily discoverable), a factor that this choice does not refer to at all.

(D) is wrong because courts virtually never hold that the seller of a "used" house built by someone else makes an implied warranty of habitability or fitness for particular purpose; since the facts tell us that a prior owner built the house, this rule precludes liability on warranty-of-habitability grounds.

IV. CONVEYANCING BY WILL: ADEMPTION, EXONERATION AND LAPSE

C. Exoneration:

Question: A man owned property that he used as his residence. The man received a loan, secured by a mortgage on the property, from a bank. Later, the man defaulted on the loan. The bank then brought an appropriate action to foreclose the mortgage, was the sole bidder at the judicial sale, and received title to the property as a result of the foreclosure sale.

Shortly after the foreclosure sale, the man received a substantial inheritance. He approached the bank to repurchase the property, but the bank decided to build a branch office on the property and declined to sell.

If the man prevails in an appropriate action to recover title to the property, what is the most likely reason?

(A) He had used the property as his residence.

(B) He timely exercised an equitable right of redemption.

(C) The court applied the doctrine of exoneration.

(D) The jurisdiction provides for a statutory right of redemption.

[QA032]

Answer: (C) is **incorrect**, because the common law doctrine of exoneration does not apply to these facts. Under that doctrine, a person who receives a bequest of property that is subject to a lien or mortgage is entitled to take the property "free and clear" of the lien or mortgage if there is no evidence that the testator intended a contrary result. When exoneration applies, the estate's personal property – *i.e.*, its cash – is used to pay off the lien or mortgage. Since the man did not receive a bequest of encumbered real estate, the doctrine could not have applied. (The correct answer is (D), because a statutory right of redemption would let the man get post-foreclosure-sale relief; see *supra*, p. 183.)

Chapter 8
RECORDING ACTS

IV. WHAT INSTRUMENTS MUST BE RECORDED

A. **What instruments must be recorded:**

  1. **Contract of sale:**

      a. **Testable:**

      Question: Able was the owner of Greenacre, a large tract of land. Able entered into a binding written contract with Baker for the sale and purchase of Greenacre for $125,000. The contract required Able to convey marketable record title.

      Baker decided to protect his interest and promptly and properly recorded the contract.

      Thereafter, but before the date scheduled for the closing, Charlie obtained and properly filed a final judgment against Able in the amount of $1 million in a personal injury suit. A statute in the jurisdiction provides: "Any judgment properly filed shall, for ten years from filing, be a lien on the real property then owned or subsequently acquired by any person against whom the judgment is rendered."

      The recording act of the jurisdiction authorizes recording of contracts and also provides: "No conveyance or mortgage of real property shall be good against subsequent purchasers for value and without notice unless the same be recorded according to law."

      There are no other relevant statutory provisions.

      At the closing, Baker declined to accept the title of Able on the ground that Charlie's judgment lien encumbered the title he would receive and rendered it unmarketable. Able brought an appropriate action against Baker for specific performance of the contract and joined Charlie as a party.

In this action, the judgment should be for

(A) Able, because in equity a purchaser takes free of judgment liens.

(B) Able, because the contract had been recorded.

(C) Baker, because Able cannot benefit from Baker's action in recording the contract.

(D) Baker, because the statute creating judgment liens takes precedence over the recording act.
[Q2104]

Answer: Choice **(B)** is correct. In most states, a land-sale contract is recordable, and the facts here tell us that this is so for the state in question (by telling us that Baker "properly recorded the contract"). Once the contract was recorded, it created an interest in land on the part of the vendee (namely, the right to buy on the stated terms) that was superior to any later-created interest in the property. Therefore, Baker's right to purchase was superior to the later-filed judgment lien obtained by Charlie. Consequently, Able would be deemed to have marketable title, because notwithstanding the judgment lien he was capable of conveying the property free and clear to Baker.

(A) is wrong because it states the right result, but for the wrong reason. A purchaser would not always take free of a judgment lien; for instance, a purchaser would not take free of a judgment lien that was filed before the purchase contract. It is only the fact that the sale contract was recorded before the judgment lien was filed that lets the purchaser here take free of the lien.

(C) is wrong because Able can indeed benefit from Baker's action in recording. The issue is whether Able can convey marketable title to Baker, and the fact that Baker recorded means that Able can do this; there is no rule that one party cannot benefit from the other's action in recording.

(D) is wrong because it is a misstatement of law. The statute creating judgment liens merely describes that a judgment lien is an interest in property; the statute does not say anything about priorities, a subject that is left to the recording act. Under the recording act, an early-filed interest in land (here, the vendee's rights under the sale contract) takes priority over a later-filed interest (here, the judgment lien).

V. WHO IS PROTECTED BY THE RECORDING ACT

B. Who is a bona fide purchaser (BFP):

Question: A grantor owned a tract of land in fee simple. By warranty deed, she conveyed the land in fee simple to her lawyer for a recited consideration of "$10 and other valuable consideration." The deed was promptly and properly recorded. One week later, the grantor and the lawyer executed a written document that stated that the conveyance of the property was for the purpose of establishing a trust for the benefit of the grantor's child. The lawyer expressly accepted the trust and signed the document with the grantor. This written agreement was not authenticated to be eligible for recordation and there never was an attempt to record it.

The lawyer entered into possession of the land and distributed the net income from it to the child at appropriate intervals.

Five years later, the lawyer conveyed the property in fee simple to a buyer by warranty deed. The buyer paid the fair market value of the property, had no knowledge of the written agreement between the grantor and the lawyer, and entered into possession of the property.

The grantor's child made demand upon the buyer for distribution of income at the next usual time the lawyer would have distributed. The buyer refused. The child brought an appropriate action against the buyer for a decree requiring her to perform the trust the lawyer had theretofore recognized.

In such action, judgment should be for

(A) the child, because a successor in title to the trustee takes title subject to the grantor's trust.

(B) the child, because equitable interests are not subject to the recording act.

(C) the buyer, because, as a bona fide purchaser, she took free of the trust encumbering the lawyer's title.

(D) the buyer, because no trust was ever created since the grantor had no title at the time of the purported creation.

[Q3005]

Answer: Choice **(C)** is correct. The buyer's status as a bona fide purchaser (BFP) entitled her to priority over the lawyer. One who purchases from the record owner of property is eligible for the protection of the recording act, as against someone else who previously took from that same record owner and did not properly record. Here, at the time the buyer took, the lawyer was the record owner (in fee simple), and the child was a "prior transferee" from the lawyer. (That is, the lawyer created an interest in the child by the trust document, and this interest was created prior to the conveyance to the buyer.) So the buyer is in a position to use the recording act to gain protection against the child as prior transferee from the same grantor (the lawyer). To get the benefit of the recording act, the buyer had to be a BFP; that is, she had to have (1) taken her position for value, and (2) been without notice (actual, constructive, or inquiry) of the prior instrument at the time she took. The buyer meets requirement (1) because the facts tell us that she "paid the fair market value"; and she meets requirement (2) because the facts tell us that she "had no knowledge of the written agreement between the grantor and the lawyer" (and that written agreement *is* the prior grant).

(A) is wrong because it ignores the effect of the recording act. It may be true as a general principle that "a successor in title to the trustee takes title subject to the grantor's trust." But this is subject to the rule that a bona fide purchaser (BFP) from the trustee will take free of the unrecorded instrument by which the BFP's grantor created the trust. (If this were not true, no one could ever safely buy property — there would always be the risk that the grantor had secretly created a trust encumbering the property.)

(B) is wrong because trusts creating equitable interests *are* subject to the recording act. A beneficiary's interest in a trust is indeed, as this choice suggests, an equitable interest. (The trustee has legal title.) But this choice is false in stating that equitable interests are not subject to recording acts. Because the instrument creating the trust was never recorded, the trust was not in the chain of title and the buyer did not have inquiry notice of the trust (letting her take the property as a BFP). The fact that the trust was not "authenticated to be eligible for recordation" (i.e., not witnessed or notarized) doesn't help the child as grantee — it was up to him to make sure that the document was authenticated and then to record it, if he wanted not to take the risk of being undone by a later transfer by his grantor.

(D) is wrong because a trust *was* created. It's true that the lawyer may initially have had a fee simple. But once he signed the written trust document with the grantor, he was in effect creating a new interest in the property, a trust for the benefit of the child. The fact that the grantor had no title at the time this trust was executed is irrelevant (the lawyer could simply have decided on his own to create a trust for the child).

Question: Devlin was the owner of a large subdivision. Parnell became interested in purchasing a lot but could not decide between Lot 40 and Lot 41. The price and fair market value of each of those two lots was $50,000. Parnell paid Devlin $50,000, which Devlin accepted, and Devlin delivered to Parnell a deed which was properly executed, complete, and ready for recording in every detail except that the space in the deed for the lot number was left blank. Devlin told Parnell to fill in either Lot 40 or Lot 41 according to his decision and then record the deed. Parnell visited the development the next day and completely changed his mind, selecting Lot 25. He filled in Lot 25 and duly recorded the deed. The price of Lot 25 and its fair market value was $75,000.

Before Devlin had time to learn of Parnell's actions, Parnell sold Lot 25 to Caruso for $60,000 by a duly and properly executed, delivered, and recorded warranty deed. Caruso knew that Devlin had put a price of $75,000 on Lot 25, but he knew no other facts regarding the Devlin-Parnell transaction. Caruso's attorney accurately reported Parnell's record title to be good, marketable, and free of encumbrances. Neither Caruso nor his attorney made any further investigation outside the record. Devlin brought an appropriate action against Caruso to recover title to Lot 25. If Devlin loses, the most likely basis for the judgment is that

(A) the Statute of Frauds prevents the introduction of any evidence of Devlin's and Parnell's agreement.

(B) recording of the deed from Devlin to Parnell precludes any question of its genuineness.

(C) as between Devlin and a bona fide purchaser, Devlin is estopped.

(D) the clean hands doctrine bars Devlin from relief.

[Q4062]

Answer: Choice **(C)** is correct. The goal of recording statutes is to protect subsequent bona fide purchasers and incumbrancers — those who pay value and take without notice of prior conveyances, in good faith. Here, Caruso is a bona fide purchaser, because he has no notice of any defects in the chain of title. The price he paid, $60,000, was a bargain compared to what Devlin asked previously, but this would not in and of itself negate his bona fide purchaser status, since it would still constitute "value" and would not, barring other facts, indicate something untoward was involved. Since the chain of title indicates that Parnell was conveying marketable title, Caruso was not obligated to look further. Choice (C) goes on to suggest that Devlin is "estopped" from denying the validity of the deed. An estoppel occurs, in facts like these, when one has done or omitted to do something, and is as a result forbidden from pleading or proving an otherwise-important fact. Here, Devlin's carelessness in allowing Parnell to fill in the deed will lead to his being bound by the resultant deed — he'll be "estopped" from denying its validity.

(A) is wrong because the Statute of Frauds would *not* prevent proof of Devlin's and Parnell's oral agreement. Devlin is trying to show that the deed he signed has the wrong lot number on it, due to Parnell's wrongdoing. That's not a contracts problem, and the Statute of Frauds applies only to contracts. Except for the estoppel problem (discussed in (C)), Devlin would be able to show that the deed as filed was not genuine (i.e., was a forgery as to the lot number). And that would be true even though Devlin's proof would consist of proof of an oral agreement. So the Statute of Frauds wouldn't be relevant.

(B) is wrong because it states an incorrect rule of law: Recording a deed does not preclude any question as to its genuineness. The mere act of recording would not, for instance, make a fraudulent deed genuine. The upshot, nonetheless, might be that, *despite* the fact a deed is incorrect, *the bona fide purchaser may still prevail,* on grounds of estoppel. But (B) states as a concrete rule that recording a deed means its genuineness cannot be questioned, and this is incorrect.

(D) is wrong because it misstates the facts: Devlin's hands are not "unclean." Under the equitable doctrine of "unclean hands," one who has acted "unconscionably," or in a morally reprehensible manner, cannot recover. Here, at most Devlin has behaved negligently; there is no basis on which to attach any bad faith to his behavior. If anything, he was gullible in trusting Parnell to fill in the blank in the deed as instructed; but the creation of the agency did not involve wrongdoing. If anyone, it's Parnell who's the wrongdoer.

C. The "gave value" requirement:

5. Judgment creditors:

a. Lien creditor loses:

Question: A seller owned a piece of land in fee simple, as the land records showed, when he contracted to sell the land to a buyer. Two weeks later, the buyer paid the agreed price and received a warranty deed. A week thereafter, when neither the contract nor the deed had been recorded and while the seller remained in possession of the property, a creditor of the seller properly filed a money judgment against the seller. The creditor knew nothing of the buyer's interest.

A statute in the jurisdiction provides: "Any judgment properly filed shall, for ten years from filing, be a lien on the real property then owned or subsequently acquired by any person against whom the judgment is rendered."

The recording act of the jurisdiction provides: "No conveyance or mortgage of real property shall be good against subsequent purchasers for value and without notice unless the same be recorded according to law."

The creditor brought an appropriate action to enforce her lien against the property in the buyer's hands.

If the court decides for the buyer, it will most probably be because

(A) the doctrine of equitable conversion applies.

(B) the jurisdiction's recording act does not protect creditors.

(C) the seller's possession gave the creditor constructive notice of the buyer's interest.

(D) the buyer was a purchaser without notice.

[Q3123]

Answer: Choice **(B)** is correct. Where the language of the recording act is ambiguous about whether judgment creditors are covered (e.g., where, as here, "purchasers for value" are what are covered), most courts have interpreted the statute so as not to cover the judgment creditor. There is no guarantee that a court would interpret the statute in this anti-creditor way, but that's at least a possibility, and of the four choices this is the most likely explanation for an anti-creditor result. (Remember, you're not asked to say how the case will come out — you're merely asked to say what the most likely rationale will be *if* the case is decided for the buyer.)

Choice (A) is wrong because the doctrine of equitable conversion has nothing to do with any issue presented by this question. Equitable conversion, where the court chooses to apply it, makes a vendor under a land-sale agreement the "equitable seller," and the vendee the "equitable buyer." The main consequence of the doctrine's application is that risk of loss passes to the buyer upon the signing of the contract, even though the seller still holds the legal title.

Choice (C) is wrong, because the seller's possession would not suggest the seller had sold the property to the buyer. Under a recording statute like the one here, a subsequent bona fide purchaser (i.e., a person who gives valuable consideration and has no actual or constructive notice of the prior instrument) prevails over a prior grantee who failed to record. If the creditor was trying to become covered by the recording act, and *the buyer* had been in possession at the time the creditor filed her lien, the fact that the buyer (not the seller, who was the record owner) was in possession at the date of lien filing might have been enough to cause the buyer to lose, since this possession might have put her on inquiry notice that the seller was perhaps no longer the owner. But the fact that *the seller* was still in possession didn't put the buyer on notice of anything, so it's irrelevant on these facts.

Choice (D) is wrong, because recording acts protect the second, not the first, purchaser in certain circumstances. Here, it would be the creditor (who can argue that she "purchased" by filing her lien), not the buyer, who is trying to get the protection of the recording act. It is the person seeking the protection of the recording act (the second purchaser), not the person resisting application of the act (the first purchaser) who needs to be "without notice." So here, the notice status of the creditor might well matter (if the recording act otherwise applied to judgment lien creditors). But the notice status of the buyer, the first "purchaser," does not matter at all.

Question: Owen owned Blackacre in fee simple, as the land records showed, when he contracted to sell Blackacre to Bryer. Two weeks later, Bryer paid the agreed price and received a warranty deed. A week thereafter, when neither the contract nor the deed had been recorded and while Owen remained in possession of Blackacre, Cred properly filed her money judgment against Owen. She knew nothing of Bryer's interest.

A statute in the jurisdiction provides: "Any judgment properly filed shall, for ten years from filing, be a lien on the real property then owned or subsequently acquired by any person against whom the judgment is rendered."

The recording act of the jurisdiction provides: "No conveyance or mortgage of real property shall be good against subsequent purchasers for value and without notice unless the same be recorded according to law."

Cred brought an appropriate action to enforce her lien against Blackacre in Bryer's hands.

If the court decides for Bryer, it will most probably be because

(A) the doctrine of equitable conversion applies.

(B) the jurisdiction's recording act does not protect creditors.

(C) Owen's possession gave Cred constructive notice of Bryer's interest.

(D) Bryer was a purchaser without notice.

[Q3123]

Answer: Choice **(B)** is correct because creditors are probably not "purchasers for value" as required for protection under the recording act. Where the language of the recording act is ambiguous about whether judgment creditors are covered (e.g., where, as here, "purchasers for value" are what are covered), most courts have interpreted the statute so as not to cover the judgment creditor. There is no guarantee that a court would interpret the statute in this anti-creditor way, but that's at least a possibility, and of the four choices this is the most likely explanation for an anti-creditor result. (Remember, you're not asked to say how the case will come out — you're merely asked to say what the most likely rationale will be *if* the case is decided for Bryer.)

(A) is wrong because the doctrine of equitable conversion is used to pass the risk of loss to the buyer under a purchase contract, and has nothing to do with whether a creditor's lien has priority over a prior unrecorded interest.

(C) is wrong because Owen's possession would not suggest Owen had sold Blackacre to Bryer. Under a recording statute like the one here, a subsequent bona fide purchaser (i.e., a person who gives valuable consideration and has no actual or constructive notice of the prior instrument) prevails over a prior grantee who failed to record. If Cred was trying to become covered by the recording act, and *Bryer* had been in possession at the time Cred filed her lien, the fact that Bryer (not Owen, the record owner) was in possession at the date of lien filing might have been enough to cause Bryer to lose, since this possession might have put her on inquiry notice that Owen was perhaps no longer the owner. But the fact that *Owen* was still in possession didn't put Bryer on notice of anything, so it's irrelevant on these facts.

(D) is wrong because recording acts protect the second, not the first, purchaser in certain circumstances. Here, it would be Cred (who can argue that she "purchased" by filing her lien), not Bryer, who is trying to get the protection of the recording act. It is the person seeking the protection of the recording act (the second purchaser), not the person resisting application of the act (the first purchaser) who needs to be "without notice." So here, the notice status of Cred might well matter (if the recording act otherwise applied to judgment lien creditors). But the notice status of Bryer, the first "purchaser," does not matter at all.

Question: Able conveyed Blackacre to Baker by a warranty deed. Baker recorded the deed four days later. After the conveyance but prior to Baker's recording of the deed, Smollett properly filed a judgment against Able.

The two pertinent statutes in the jurisdiction provide the following: (1) any judgment properly filed shall, for ten years from filing, be a lien on the real property then owned or subsequently acquired by any person against whom the judgment is rendered, and (2) no conveyance or mortgage of real property shall be good against subsequent purchasers for value and without notice unless the same be recorded according to law.

The recording act has no provision for a grace period.

Smollett joined both Able and Baker in an appropriate action to foreclose the judgment lien against Blackacre.

If Smollett is unsuccessful, it will be because

(A) Able's warranty of title to Baker defeats Smollett's claim.

(B) Smollett is not a purchaser for value.

(C) any deed is superior to a judgment lien.

(D) four days is not an unreasonable delay in recording a deed.

[Q2048]

Answer: Choice **(B)** is correct. Smollett could win only if he were protected by the recording act. This is so because without the recording act's protection, Smollett would have to lose since Baker received his conveyance before Smollett filed his lien (meaning that Able no longer had any interest in the property at the moment Smollett's judgment became a lien on Able's "property" by means of Smollett's filing). In most jurisdictions, if the recording act protects only "purchasers for value," a judgment creditor will not be deemed to be a "purchaser." So if Smollett were found not to be a purchaser, and therefore not to receive any protection from the recording act, he would lose. It is not certain that the recording act here would be interpreted so as to not protect lien creditors, but of the four choices, this is the only one that could plausibly yield a defeat for Smollett.

(A) is wrong because Able's warranty of title to Baker might help Baker in a suit against Able, but would not help Baker in a suit against Smollett. Where a party (here, Baker) doesn't record immediately (or within the applicable grace period if any), nothing in that party's deed can save her from losing to a subsequent purchaser for value who is protected by the recording act. (That's the purpose of recording acts — to protect subsequent purchasers for value, and to allow them to rely on the record as of the time of the subsequent purchase.)

(C) is wrong because it is a gross misstatement of law, especially the law of the jurisdiction in question here. The first statute cited in the question gives a filed judgment a lien against all real property then owned by the judgment debtor; so if the judgment had been filed before the conveyance to Baker, the judgment lien would indeed be superior to Baker's deed (which this choice says could never happen).

(D) is wrong because, when a recording act does not have a grace period, the purchaser takes the risk of a subsequent purchaser's gaining rights in the gap between the first conveyance and a recording of that conveyance, no matter how small this gap is. (If there *had* been a grace period of more than four days, this choice would have been a good explanation of why Smollett would lose.)

b. *Hasn't recorded yet:*

Question: Corp, a corporation, owned Blackacre in fee simple, as the real estate records showed. Corp entered into a valid written contract to convey Blackacre to Barbara, an individual. At closing, Barbara paid the price in full and received an instrument in the proper form of a deed, signed by duly authorized corporate officers on behalf of Corp, purporting to convey Blackacre to Barbara. Barbara did not then record the deed or take possession of Blackacre.

Next, George (who had no knowledge of the contract or the deed) obtained a substantial money judgment against Corp. Then, Barbara recorded the deed from Corp. Thereafter, George properly filed the judgment against Corp.

A statute of the jurisdiction provides: "Any judgment properly filed shall, for ten years from filing, be a lien on the real property then owned or subsequently acquired by any person against whom the judgment is rendered."

Afterward, Barbara entered into a valid written contract to convey Blackacre to Polly. Polly objected to Barbara's title and refused to close.

The recording act of the jurisdiction provides: "Unless the same be recorded according to law, no conveyance or mortgage of real property shall be good against subsequent purchasers for value and without notice."

Barbara brought an appropriate action to require Polly to complete the purchase contract.

The court should decide for

(A) Polly, because George's judgment was obtained before Barbara recorded the deed from Corp.

(B) Polly, because even though Corp's deed to Barbara prevented George's judgment from being a lien on Blackacre, George's filed judgment poses a threat of litigation.

(C) Barbara, because Barbara recorded her deed before George filed his judgment.

(D) Barbara, because Barbara received the deed from Corp before George filed his judgment.

[Q3042]

Answer: Choice **(D)** is correct, because by the time George purported to get his lien Barbara, not Corp, was the owner of Blackacre. The statute here says that George could get a lien on property "then owned or subsequently acquired" by his judgment debtor. A court would almost certainly conclude that by the time George filed, the property was not "then owned" by Corp. That's because this type of statute is generally interpreted to exclude any property that has been properly conveyed by the judgment debtor, even if the conveyance has not been recorded. (By the way, in most courts George would also lose for a second reason: as a judgment lien creditor, he would probably be held not to be a "purchaser for value.")

Choice (A) is wrong, because George's mere receipt of the judgment did not affect Barbara's title. It's only the *filing* of a judgment lien, not the mere obtaining of a judgment, that causes an encumbrance on the judgment debtor's real estate. So the fact that George got his judgment before Barbara recorded is irrelevant.

Choice (B) is wrong, because any suit by George would almost certainly fail (for the reasons described in Choice (D) above), so that the threat of meritless litigation would not be enough to cloud Barbara's title. The obligation to convey marketable title does not mean an obligation to convey "perfect title," or title that could not possibly be attacked by anyone — so long as it is quite clear (not merely "barely probable") that the vendor would be found in litigation to have valid unencumbered title, the title is not unmarketable.

Choice (C) is wrong, because it wasn't the fact that Barbara won the race to record that caused her to prevail. As explained in Choice (D) above, as soon as the unrecorded conveyance to Barbara occurred, Corp no longer owned the property, and any filing by George of his judgment that occurred after that would have had no effect. So this choice explains the correct outcome by incorrect reasoning — even if Barbara had not recorded until after George filed, Barbara would still have won because George's filing was of no effect.

E. Recording first in a race or race-notice state:

Question: A landowner owned a piece of land in fee simple of record on January 10. On that day, a bank loaned the landowner $50,000 and the landowner mortgaged the property to the bank as security for the loan. The mortgage was recorded on January 18.

The landowner conveyed the property to an investor for a valuable consideration on January 11. The bank did not know of this, nor did the investor know of the mortgage to the bank, until both discovered the facts on January 23, the day on which the investor recorded his deed from the landowner.

The recording act of the jurisdiction provides: "No unrecorded conveyance or mortgage of real property shall be good against subsequent purchasers for value without notice, who shall first record." There is no provision for a period of grace and there is no other relevant statutory provision.

The bank sued the investor to establish that its mortgage was good against the property.

The court should decide for

(A) the investor, because he paid valuable consideration without notice before the bank recorded her mortgage.

(B) the investor, because the bank's delay in recording means that she is estopped from asserting her priority in time.

(C) the bank, because the investor did not record his deed before the mortgage was recorded.

(D) the bank, because after the mortgage to it, the landowner's deed to the investor was necessarily subject to the mortgage.

[Q1054]

Answer: Choice **(C)** is correct. This is a race notice statute, since it says that it protects only "subsequent purchasers for value without notice, *who shall first record*." Therefore, the investor could only obtain the protection of the recording statute if he recorded before the prior interest (the bank's mortgage) was recorded. Since the bank recorded on Jan. 18 and the investor on Jan. 23, the investor did not satisfy the record-first requirement. Therefore, the recording act does not apply, and the bank wins under the common-law principle that the first-in-time conveyance takes priority over the second conveyance.

(A) is wrong because, while the investor's paying valuable consideration and taking without notice prior to the bank's recording were *necessary* elements for him to be covered by the recording act, they were not *sufficient* elements — he was also required to record first.

(B) is wrong because there is no principle of estoppel by which a party who delays in recording loses the right to rely on the recording act; the only risk taken by the delaying party is that during the delay, a subsequent purchaser may meet the requirements for protection under the recording act.

(D) is wrong because it gives an incorrect explanation for the correct result: after the bank received its mortgage, it would still lose to a subsequent purchaser for value without notice who beat it to the recording office.

VI. PURCHASER MUST TAKE "WITHOUT NOTICE"

A. **Notice to subsequent claimants:**

2. **Record notice:**

b. **Imputed knowledge:**

i. *Mortgage and note:*

Question: A landowner executed and delivered a promissory note and a mortgage securing the note to a mortgage company, which was named as payee in the note and as mortgagee in the mortgage. The note included a statement that the indebtedness evidenced by the note was "subject to the terms of a contract between the maker and the payee of the note executed on the same day" and that the note was "secured by a mortgage of even date." The mortgage was promptly and properly recorded. Subsequently, the mortgage company sold the landowner's note and mortgage to a bank and delivered to the bank a written assignment of the note and mortgage. The assignment was promptly and properly recorded. The mortgage company retained possession of both the note and the mortgage in order to act as collecting agent. Later, being short of funds, the mortgage company sold the note and mortgage to an investor at a substantial discount. The mortgage company executed a written assignment of the note and mortgage to the investor and delivered to him the note, the mortgage, and the assignment. The investor paid value for the assignment without actual knowledge of the prior assignment to the bank and promptly and properly recorded his assignment. The principal of the note was not then due, and there had been no default in payment of either interest or principal.

If the issue of ownership of the landowner's note and mortgage is subsequently raised in an appropriate action by the bank to foreclose, the court should hold that

(A) the investor owns both the note and the mortgage.

(B) the bank owns both the note and the mortgage.

(C) the investor owns the note and the bank owns the mortgage.

(D) the bank owns the note and the investor owns the mortgage.
[Q1123]

Answer: Choice **(B)** is correct. The bank was the first grantee of both the note and the mortgage, so the bank is the owner unless the recording act somehow gave the investor superior title. When the bank promptly recorded the assignment to it of the note and mortgage, the bank complied with all requirements of the recording act. Therefore, no later assignment by the mortgage company to the investor (or anyone else) could take priority, under the recording act, over the assignment to the bank. The fact that the investor paid value for his assignment, and without actual notice of the prior assignment to the bank, doesn't change any of this — the investor is deemed to be on notice of what a proper record search would have indicated, and here a search on the mortgage company in the records would have disclosed the prior assignment to the bank. Similarly, the fact that the mortgage company kept possession of the note and mortgage after assigning these to the bank makes no difference; the investor as second grantee cannot take priority over a prior conveyance that was properly recorded.

(A), (C), and (D) are wrong because they are inconsistent with the above analysis.

3. **Inquiry notice:**

   a. **Possession:**

      i. **Easements:**

Question: A landowner owned Blackacre, which was improved with a dwelling. A neighbor owned an adjoining unimproved lot suitable for constructing a dwelling. The neighbor executed and delivered a deed granting to the landowner an easement over the westerly 15 feet of the lot for convenient ingress and egress to a public street, although Blackacre did abut another public street. The landowner did not then record the neighbor's deed. After the landowner constructed and started using a driveway within the described 15-foot strip in a clearly visible manner, the neighbor borrowed $10,000 cash from a bank and gave the bank a mortgage on the neighbor's property. The mortgage was promptly and properly recorded. The landowner then recorded the neighbor's deed granting the easement. The neighbor subsequently defaulted on her loan payments to the bank.

The recording act of the jurisdiction provides: "No conveyance or mortgage of real property shall be good against subsequent purchasers for value and without notice unless the same be recorded according to law."

In an appropriate foreclosure action as to the neighbor's land, brought against the neighbor and the landowner, the bank seeks, among other things, to have the landowner's easement declared subordinate to the bank's mortgage, so that the easement will be terminated by completion of the foreclosure.

If the landowner's easement is NOT terminated, it will be because

(A) the recording of the deed granting the easement prior to the foreclosure action protects the landowner's rights.

(B) the easement provides access from Blackacre to a public street.

(C) the landowner's easement is appurtenant to Blackacre and thus cannot be separated from Blackacre.

(D) visible use of the easement by the landowner put the bank on notice of the easement.

[Q3010]

Answer: Choice **(D)** is correct. The landowner's use of the easement put the bank on notice of her interest, preventing the bank from being a purchaser "without notice" who is entitled to the protection of the recording act. Under a recording statute like the one here, a subsequent BFP prevails over a prior grantee who failed to record by the time of the subsequent grant. But the statute gives subsequent purchaser protection only if she had *no actual or constructive notice* at the time of the conveyance. One type of constructive notice is "inquiry notice": notice of any matter as to which the grantee is (or should be) in possession of facts which would lead the grantee to make an investigation. One source of inquiry notice is that where the property is in possession of one other than the record owner, the prospective grantee is under a duty to inquire about the facts that put that person into possession (since the reason may be that the possessor has an unrecorded interest). Here, the bank should have noticed that even though the strip was shown as belonging to the neighbor's parcel, it was "possessed" by the landowner in the form of the driveway. Had the bank made inquiry of the landowner, she would presumably have told the bank about her easement. Consequently, the bank is deemed to have been on notice of the landowner's easement, preventing the bank from being the "subsequent purchaser for value and without notice" required for protection under the recording statute. Since the landowner's interest precedes the bank's, the bank could win only with the protection of the recording act, so it loses.

Choice (A) is wrong, because the landowner's recording of the deed prior to the foreclosure action would not protect the landowner's rights. If the bank had been a BFP without notice of the landowner's interest at the time the bank made the mortgage, the landowner's interest would be subordinate to the bank's recorded mortgage, and the fact that the landowner later (after the mortgage) recorded would not change this. In other words, under this statute, the time for testing whether the first conveyance (here, the easement) was "recorded according to law" would be at the time that the "subsequent purchaser" took its interest, not the time when that subsequent purchaser tried, say, to gain title by foreclosure. (You can see how this would have to work this way if lenders are to be able to lend in reliance on the records — once the loan is made, the lender needs to be able to be confident that no later-filed interest can take priority over its own interest.)

Choice (B) is wrong, because the mere fact that the easement provided access to a public street from Blackacre would not prevent the recording act from causing the landowner to lose. The examiners were probably trying to trick you into thinking that because the easement provides access from Blackacre to a public street, the easement would be one of "necessity," and remain valid even though unrecorded. But even in courts recognizing easements by necessity, the easement here would not qualify, because the facts tell us that Blackacre also has direct access to a different public street. The easement here was an express easement, and if it is not recorded, the grantee risks losing it to a subsequent grantee from the original grantor.

Choice (C) is wrong because it misstates how the assignment of appurtenant easements works, and also ignores the significance of the recording act. The easement here is, indeed, "appurtenant" rather than "in gross." (That is, it pertains to a particular benefited parcel, Blackacre.) It's true that an easement appurtenant generally passes with the property — so if the landowner sold Blackacre, the easement would pass with Blackacre, rather than being extinguished. But here, these mechanics are irrelevant; for one thing, the landowner isn't transferring her interest in Blackacre. The recording act operates completely separately from the assignment of appurtenant easements — the easement is an interest in the neighbor's parcel, and needed to be recorded if it was not to be subordinated to a BFP of the neighbor's parcel. (In other words, it was only the bank's inquiry notice that prevented the bank from getting protection of the recording statute vis-a-vis the landowner's easement.)

C. Purchaser from one without notice:

1. Donee from person protected by act:

Question: A grantor who owned a parcel conveyed it by quitclaim deed as a gift to a woman, who did not then record her deed. Later, the grantor conveyed the parcel by warranty deed to a man, who paid valuable consideration, knew nothing of the woman's claim, and promptly and properly recorded. Next, the woman recorded her deed. Then the man conveyed the parcel by quitclaim deed to his nephew as a gift. When the possible conflict with the woman was discovered, the nephew recorded his deed.

The parcel at all relevant times has been vacant unoccupied land.

The recording act of the jurisdiction provides:

"No unrecorded conveyance or mortgage of real property shall be good against subsequent purchasers for value without notice, who shall first record." No other statute is applicable.

The nephew has sued the woman to establish who owns the parcel.

The court will hold for

(A) the nephew, because the woman was a donee.

(B) the nephew, because the man's purchase cut off the woman's rights.

(C) the woman, because she recorded before the nephew.

(D) the woman, because the nephew was a subsequent donee.
[Q2163]

Answer: Choice **(B)** is correct. The man met all the requirements of the recording statute: he took for value, he took without notice of the prior conveyance, and he recorded before the prior conveyance was recorded. Once the man met those requirements, his interest cut off all rights of the prior grantee (the woman) who didn't record first. The man therefore had the ability to pass a valid title to his nephew, even though the nephew did not take for value, and even though the nephew was on record notice of the woman's claim at the time he took (since by then the woman had recorded).

(A) is wrong because it is not the woman's status as a donee that causes her to lose, it is the fact that she did not record before a subsequent BFP (the man) recorded. Remember that under recording acts, it is never significant whether the *first* grantee took for value; it only matters whether the *subsequent* grantee, who is trying to take advantage of the recording act, took for value.

(C) is wrong because the fact that the woman recorded before the nephew cannot save her; once a subsequent grantee (the man) took for value and without notice and then recorded first, a person downstream from that subsequent grantee (the nephew) wins against the original late-filing grantee regardless of whether the downstreamer took for value, took without notice, or recorded first.

(D) is wrong because the fact that the nephew did not give value doesn't matter; as with Choice (C), once the subsequent grantee (the man) got the protection of the recording act, it doesn't matter whether a person downstream from him gave value, recorded first, or took without notice.

2. Lender to person protected by act:

Question: Five years ago, an investor who owned a vacant lot in a residential area borrowed $25,000 from a friend and gave the friend a note for $25,000 due in five years, secured by a mortgage on the lot. The friend neglected to record the mortgage. The fair market value of the lot was then $25,000.

Three years ago, the investor discovered that the friend had not recorded his mortgage and in consideration of $50,000 conveyed the lot to a buyer. The fair market value of the lot was then $50,000. The buyer knew nothing of the friend's mortgage. One month thereafter, the friend discovered the sale to the buyer, recorded his $25,000 mortgage, and notified the buyer that he held a $25,000 mortgage on the lot.

Two years ago, the buyer needed funds. Although she told her bank of the mortgage claimed by the investor's friend, the bank loaned her $15,000, and she gave the bank a note for $15,000 due in two years secured by a mortgage on the lot. The bank promptly and properly recorded the mortgage. At that time, the fair market value of the lot was $75,000.

The recording act of the jurisdiction provides: "No conveyance or mortgage of real property shall be good against subsequent purchasers for value and without notice unless the same be recorded according to law."

Both notes are now due and both the investor and the buyer have refused to pay. The lot is now worth only $50,000.

What are the rights of the investor's friend and the bank in the lot?

(A) Both mortgages are enforceable liens and the friend's has priority because it was first recorded.

(B) Both mortgages are enforceable liens, but the bank's has priority because the buyer was an innocent purchaser for value.

(C) Only the friend's mortgage is an enforceable lien, because the bank had actual and constructive notice of the investor's fraud.

(D) Only the bank's mortgage is an enforceable lien, because the buyer was an innocent purchaser for value.

[QA089]

Answer: Choice **(D)** is correct. This is a complicated fact pattern, but the essential information is that the buyer purchased the lot from the investor before the friend recorded his mortgage. Thus, (1) the buyer was a bona fide purchaser (BFP) for value and is protected by the recording statute; and (2) the bank who lent to the buyer is also protected despite the fact that the buyer knew of the prior mortgage when it lent.

The jurisdiction's recording act is a "notice" statute because it provides, "No conveyance or mortgage of real property shall be good against subsequent purchasers for value and without notice *unless same be recorded according to law.*" A notice statute protects only a subsequent taker who takes for value and without notice of the prior conveyance or mortgage. (Because this is a pure notice rather than race-notice statute, the subsequent taker doesn't have to have recorded before the prior grantee or mortgagee records.) Notice can be actual, record, or inquiry. The facts do not indicate that the buyer had actual notice of the friend's mortgage. Since the friend had not recorded the mortgage at the time buyer purchased the lot, the buyer did not have record notice. Finally, the property is a vacant lot; so even if the buyer had inspected the property, he would not have been put on inquiry notice of the friend's mortgage. Thus, the buyer is a BFP (i.e., he took without any kind of notice) and receives the protection of the recording act. Therefore, the friend's lien is unenforceable against the buyer (or against anyone who deals with him, as we'll see in a minute).

The bank's mortgage, on the other hand, *is* an enforceable lien against the property, because the buyer is a party to the mortgage and the bank promptly and properly recorded the mortgage. (Even if you did not know this, you would be able to pick the correct answer by eliminating the other three choices, which all rely on the friend's having an enforceable lien.) And the fact that the bank made its loan while having notice (both actual and record) of the prior mortgage to the friend does not prevent the bank's mortgage from being a valid first lien — that's because the buyer took free of the friend's mortgage for the reasons described above, and once the buyer had this free-and-clear title he was entitled to place a first mortgage on it (or re-sell it) regardless of the state of knowledge possessed by the new mortgagee (or new buyer). If the rule were otherwise, an innocent buyer would never be able to take out a first mortgage or re-sell, if the holder of a prior interest who didn't record promptly eventually recorded, as happened here.

(A) is wrong because, for the reasons explained in the analysis of Choice (D), the friend did not have an enforceable lien against the property. Thus, the fact that the friend recorded before the bank is irrelevant.

(B) is wrong because, for the reasons explained in the analysis of Choice (D), the friend did not have an enforceable lien against the property. This answer choice misstates the significance of the buyer's being an innocent purchaser for value. The buyer's BFP status protects him from the enforcement of the friend's lien; it does not affect the "priority" of the liens (since there is only one valid lien, the bank's).

(C) is wrong because, for the reasons explained in the analysis of Choice (D), the friend did not have an enforceable lien against the property. The friend recorded too late to prevent the buyer from being a BFP; so, the fact that the buyer later learned of the friend's mortgage is of no consequence — the buyer took free of the friend's mortgage. Once the buyer had this free-and-clear title, he was entitled to place a first mortgage on it (or sell it) regardless of the state of knowledge possessed by the new mortgagee (or new buyer). Such a rule is necessary to protect the innocent buyer's financing and resale market. See the analysis of Choice (D) for more about this.

CHAPTER 9

RIGHTS INCIDENT TO LAND

I. NUISANCE

C. **Private nuisance:**

1. **Private nuisance more likely than public nuisance:**

   a. **Distinguishing the two types of nuisance:**

   Question: On a parcel of land immediately adjacent to a woman's 50-acre farm, a public school district built a large consolidated high school that included a 5,000-seat lighted athletic stadium. The woman had objected to the district's plans for the stadium and was particularly upset about nighttime athletic events that attracted large crowds and that, at times, resulted in significant noise and light intensity levels. On nights of athletic events, the woman and her family members wore earplugs and could not sleep or enjoy a quiet evening until after 10 p.m. In addition, light from the stadium on those nights was bright enough to allow reading a newspaper in the woman's yard.

   Which of the following doctrines would best support the woman's claim for damages?

   (A) Constructive eviction.

   (B) Private nuisance.

(C) Public nuisance.

(D) Waste.

[Q7090]

Answer: Choice **(B)** is correct. Damages may be awarded if a private nuisance is proven. A private nuisance is a substantial and unreasonable non-trespassory interference with the use or enjoyment of one's land. The woman's use and enjoyment of her land are being interfered with here, so private nuisance is by far her best claim.

(A) is wrong because constructive eviction applies to landlords and tenants, and there is no indication that the woman in question is a tenant. Constructive eviction occurs when a leased property is rendered uninhabitable by some action or inaction of the landlord, and the tenant is permitted to treat the situation the same way as if the tenant had been physically evicted. Where plaintiff alleges that someone who has no interest in the property has made it uninhabitable for her, courts use a private-nuisance rather than constructive-eviction analysis.

(C) is wrong because a public nuisance is a violation of a legal right that is common to the public as a group. The activities at the school, although a public school, are disturbing only one landowner. Therefore, the facts demonstrate a private, not public, nuisance.

(D) is wrong because there has been no waste. A lawsuit for waste can be brought against a life tenant or lessee of a leasehold estate, either by a current landlord or by the owner of a vested future interest, when the tenant is doing something to substantially impair the value of the property. Here, the defendant does not have a leasehold estate or life estate in the plaintiff's farm, so the waste doctrine does not apply.

6. **Failure to abate natural condition:**

   b. **Physical danger:**

   Question: A man owns a small lot in fee simple, and a woman owns the adjoining large lot in fee simple. The man has kept the lawns and trees on the small lot trimmed and neat. The woman "lets nature take its course" at the large lot. The result on the large lot is a tangle of underbrush, fallen trees, and standing trees that are in danger of losing limbs. Many of the trees on the large lot are near the small lot. In the past, debris and large limbs have been blown from the large lot onto the small lot. By local standards the large lot is an eyesore that depresses market values of real property in the vicinity, but the condition of the large lot violates no applicable laws or ordinances.

   The man demanded that the woman keep the trees near the small lot trimmed. The woman refused.

   The man brought an appropriate action against the woman to require her to abate what the man alleges to be a nuisance. In the lawsuit, the only issue is whether the condition of the large lot constitutes a nuisance.

   The strongest argument that the man can present is that the condition of the large lot

   (A) has an adverse impact on real estate values.

   (B) poses a danger to the occupants of the small lot.

   (C) violates community aesthetic standards.

   (D) cannot otherwise be challenged under any law or ordinance.

   [Q3175]

   Answer: Choice **(B)** is correct. Normally, an owner's refusal to abate a naturally-occurring condition on his land will not be deemed to be a nuisance. But nearly all courts have long recognized an exception for trees that pose the risk of falling on the public highway, and some courts have extended this exception to trees that pose a risk of physical danger to those on adjacent non-highway property. A court would not necessarily find that the risk of danger from the fallen trees makes the condition a nuisance, but of the four choices this is the only one that could plausibly lead to a finding of nuisance.

(A) and (C) are wrong because, while these might be reasons for holding that a man-made feature poses a nuisance, they would not be grounds for overruling the usual rule that failure to abate a naturally-occurring condition is a nuisance.

(D) is wrong because the fact that a condition cannot be challenged by any other law or ordinance does not mean that the court will find it to constitute a nuisance — the man will have to show that the conditions here cause him a substantial interference with his use and enjoyment of his property, and the fact that the condition doesn't violate a law or ordinance doesn't say anything about whether the man can meet this standard.

II. LATERAL AND SUBJACENT SUPPORT

B. Lateral support:

1. Building:

Question: A businessman owned in fee simple Lot 1 in a properly approved subdivision, designed and zoned for industrial use. An investor owned the adjoining Lot 2 in the same subdivision. The plat of the subdivision was recorded as authorized by statute.

Twelve years ago, the businessman erected an industrial building wholly situated on Lot 1 but with one wall along the boundary common with Lot 2. The construction was done as authorized by a building permit, validly obtained under applicable statutes, ordinances, and regulations. Further, the construction was regularly inspected and passed as being in compliance with all building code requirements.

Lot 2 remained vacant until six months ago, when the investor began excavation pursuant to a building permit authorizing the erection of an industrial building situated on Lot 2 but with one wall along the boundary common with Lot 1. The excavation caused subsidence of a portion of Lot 1 that resulted in injury to the business owner's building. The excavation was not done negligently or with any malicious intent to injure. In the jurisdiction, the time to acquire title by adverse possession or rights by prescription is 10 years.

The businessman brought an appropriate action against the investor to recover damages resulting from the injuries to the building on Lot 1.

In such lawsuit, judgment should be for

(A) the businessman if, but only if, the subsidence would have occurred without the weight of the building on Lot 1.

(B) the businessman, because a right for support, appurtenant to Lot 1, had been acquired by adverse possession or prescription.

(C) the investor, because Lots 1 and 2 are urban land, as distinguished from rural land and, therefore, under the circumstances the businessman had the duty to protect any improvements on Lot 1.

(D) the investor, because the construction and the use to be made of the building were both authorized by the applicable law.

[Q3087]

Answer: Choice **(A)** is correct. The investor is strictly liable if the businessman's building did not contribute to the subsidence, but not liable otherwise. Every landowner is entitled to have his land receive the necessary physical support from adjacent and underlying soil. This right to lateral support is absolute — that is, once support has been withdrawn and injury occurs, the responsible person is liable even if he used utmost care (as the facts tell us the investor used). However, the absolute right to later support exists *only with respect to land in its natural state* — if D's excavation causes a cave-in on an adjacent parcel owned by P, P cannot win if the subsidence would not have occurred but for the weight of a structure on P's land. Choice (A) accurately states this rule.

(B) is wrong because the businessman's right to lateral support was a basic right incident to his ownership of his own land, and did not need to be gained by adverse possession or prescription.

(C) is wrong because an owner's inherent right to lateral support applies whether the land is "urban" or "rural."

(D) is wrong because the investor's following the laws as to construction and use would not give her an excuse or a defense to her strict duty to provide lateral support.

III. WATER RIGHTS

A. **Drainage of surface waters:**

2. **When party wants to get rid of the water:**

    Question: A rancher and a farmer own adjacent tracts of rural land. For the past nine years, the rancher has impounded on her land the water that resulted from rain and melting snow, much of which flowed from the farmer's land. The rancher uses the water in her livestock operation. Recently, the farmer increased the size of his farming operation and built a dam on his land near the boundary between the two tracts. Because of the dam, these waters no longer drain from the farmer's land onto the rancher's land. There is no applicable statute. The rancher sued the farmer to restrain him from interfering with the natural flow of the water onto her land.

    Who is likely to prevail?

    (A) The farmer, because he has the right to use all of the water impounded on his land.

    (B) The farmer, because the rancher's past impoundment of water estops her from asserting the illegality of the farmer's dam.

    (C) The rancher, because she has acquired riparian rights to use the water.

    (D) The rancher, because the farmer is estopped to claim all of the surface water on his land.
    [Q7052]

    Answer: Choice **(A)** is correct. This water is diffuse surface water. Although there are three different views regarding the way an owner may *expel* such water if he doesn't want it, there is only one view about whether the owner may impound it if he does want it: the rule is that an owner such as the farmer may impound all such water, at least in the absence of any malice (and there is none here).

    (B) is wrong because although this option correctly concludes that the farmer will prevail, it misstates the reason why this is so. At least in the absence of malice, either landowner may impound diffuse surface waters, and that would be true even if the other party hadn't also previously impounded (so that the doctrine of estoppel doesn't apply).

(C) is wrong because water from melting snows and rain is diffuse surface water. Riparian waters are waters with defined beds and banks, such as streams, rivers, and lakes, and a riparian owner is one whose land borders such waters. Here, the only water at issue is diffuse surface water, and the rule for such waters is as stated in the discussion of Choice (A).

(D) is wrong because as described above, either party may impound surface waters that are on his own land, and the doctrine of estoppel would not apply to change this general rule.

IV. AIR RIGHTS

B. Other air-rights issues:

2. Right to sunlight:

Question: Pauline and Doris own adjacent parcels of land. On each of their parcels was a low-rise office building. The two office buildings were of the same height.

Last year Doris decided to demolish the low-rise office building on her parcel and to erect a new high-rise office building of substantially greater height on the parcel as permitted by the zoning and building ordinances. She secured all the governmental approvals necessary to pursue her project.

As Doris's new building was in the course of construction, Pauline realized that the shadows it would create would place her (Pauline's) building in such deep shade that the rent she could charge for space in her building would be substantially reduced.

Pauline brought an appropriate action against Doris to enjoin the construction in order to eliminate the shadow problem and for damages. Pauline presented uncontroverted evidence that her evaluation as to the impact of the shadow on the fair rental value of her building was correct. There is no statute or ordinance (other than the building and zoning ordinances) that is applicable to the issues before the court.

The court should

(A) grant to Pauline the requested injunction.

(B) award Pauline damages measured by the loss of rental value, but not an injunction.

(C) grant judgment for Doris, because she had secured all the necessary governmental approvals for the new building.

(D) grant judgment for Doris, because Pauline has no legal right to have sunshine continue to reach the windows of her building.

[Q2124]

Answer: Choice **(D)** is correct. A landowner has no legal right to have sunlight continue to reach her building. For example, it is not a nuisance for a one owner to block another owner's access to sunlight, even if the consequence of the blockage is to reduce the latter building's rental or market value.

Since Doris has done nothing wrong, both (A) and (B) are incorrect.

Although (C) states the right result, the fact that Doris secured all necessary government approvals is not dispositive; for instance, if the government-approved building built by Doris had released noxious odors that substantially impaired the value of Pauline's building, the fact that Doris had obtained all necessary permits would not be a defense to Pauline's nuisance suit.

Question: The plaintiff and the defendant own adjoining lots in the central portion of a city. Each of their lots had an office building. The defendant decided to raze the existing building on her lot and to erect a building of greater height. The defendant received all governmental approvals required to pursue her project. There is no applicable statute or ordinance (other than those dealing with various approvals for zoning, building, etc.).

The defendant constructed her new building without incident. However, when it was completed, the plaintiff discovered that the shadow created by the new higher building placed the plaintiff's building in such deep shade that her ability to lease space was diminished and that the rent she could charge and the occupancy rate were substantially lower. Assume that these facts are proved in an appropriate action the plaintiff instituted against the defendant for all and any relief available.

Which of the following is the most appropriate comment concerning this lawsuit?

(A) The plaintiff is entitled to a mandatory injunction requiring the defendant to restore conditions to those existing with the prior building insofar as the shadow is concerned.

(B) The court should award permanent damages, in lieu of an injunction, equal to the present value of all rents lost and loss on rents for the reasonable life of the building.

(C) The court should award damages for losses suffered to the date of trial and leave open recovery of future damages.

(D) Judgment should be for the defendant, because the plaintiff has no cause of action.

[Q1157]

Answer: Choice **(D)** is correct. A landowner has no legal right to have sunlight continue to reach her building. Therefore, it is not a nuisance or other violation for one owner to block another owner's access to sunlight, even if the consequence of the blockage is to reduce the latter building's rental or market value.

Since the defendant has done nothing wrong, (A), (B), and (C) are all incorrect.

CONSTITUTIONAL LAW

CONSTITUTIONAL LAW Q&A BY TOPIC

Headings in this Q&A material are the same as in the *Steve Emanuel's Bootcamp for the MBE: Constitutional Law* subject-matter outline, and are presented in the same order as in that outline. Therefore, to locate questions on any topic, check the topic in the subject-matter outline, then look under the same heading in this book. Some questions are reprinted multiple times; when that occurs, one version of the question usually includes a discussion of all four choices, whereas the other version(s) typically discuss just one particular wrong choice. Occasionally, in the interests of clarity we have chosen to use a heading here that was not present in the subject-matter outline; when that happens, we indicate this by putting the header in italics.

Questions from the Self-Assessment Test that is part of your materials are reprinted here in full, as are many questions that were not part of the Self-Assessment Test. Questions from the 200-Question Simulated MBE are not reprinted or referred to here (a book with the questions and answers to the Simulated MBE is also part of your materials).

All cases cited are U.S. Supreme Court cases unless otherwise noted.

CHAPTER 1

THE SUPREME COURT'S AUTHORITY AND THE FEDERAL JUDICIAL POWER

I. THE SUPREME COURT'S AUTHORITY AND THE FEDERAL JUDICIAL POWER

B. **Supreme Court review of state court decision:**

1. **"Independent and adequate state grounds":**

   a. **Violations of state and federal constitutions:**

   i. **How to tell:**

   Question: A state constitution provides that in every criminal trial "the accused shall have the right to confront all witnesses against him face to face." A defendant was convicted in state court of child abuse based on testimony from a six-year-old child. The child testified while she was seated behind one-way glass, which allowed the defendant to see the child but did not allow the child to see the defendant. The defendant appealed to the state supreme court claiming that the inability of the witness to see the defendant while she testified violated both the United States Constitution and the state constitution. Without addressing the federal constitutional issue, the state supreme court reversed the defendant's conviction and ordered a new trial. The state supreme court held that "the constitution of this state is clear, and it requires that while testifying in a criminal trial, a witness must be able to see the defendant." The state petitioned the United States Supreme Court for a writ of certiorari.

   On which ground should the United States Supreme Court DENY the state's petition?

(A) A state may not seek appellate review in the United States Supreme Court of the reversal of a criminal conviction by its own supreme court.

(B) The decision of the state supreme court was based on an adequate and independent state ground.

(C) The Sixth Amendment to the United States Constitution does not require that a witness against a criminal defendant be able to see the defendant while the witness testifies.

(D) The state supreme court's decision requires a new trial, and therefore it is not a final judgment.

[Q7025]

Answer: Choice **(B)** is correct. The Supreme Court may not review a judgment by the highest court of a state if that judgment is supported entirely by state law and is wholly independent of the interpretation and application of federal law. In this case, although the defendant claimed a violation of the Sixth Amendment of the U.S. Constitution, the state supreme court based its decision entirely on the state constitution without addressing the federal constitutional issue.

(A) is wrong because the Supreme Court *may* review a judgment of the highest court of a state reversing a criminal conviction, if the state high court's decision turns on a question arising under federal law. (But what happened here was that the state court decision was based entirely on state, not federal, law.)

(C) is wrong for two reasons. First, the Sixth Amendment right of a criminal defendant (even in a state-court rather than federal-court proceeding) to confront the witnesses against him *does* usually include the right to view the witness, so this choice is wrong as a matter of law. Second, the Supreme Court would not reach even the merits of the defendant's Sixth Amendment claim, for the reason stated in (B) above.

(D) is wrong because although the Supreme Court may only review final judgments and decrees from the highest state courts, this judgment qualifies because it finally settled the confrontation issue (i.e., that issue would not arise again on re-trial, so the present petition provided the U.S. Supreme Court its only opportunity to review the confrontation issue).

Question: Plaintiff challenged the constitutionality of a state tax law, alleging that it violated the equal protection clauses of both the United States Constitution and the state constitution. The state supreme court agreed and held the tax law to be invalid. It said: "We hold that this state tax law violates the equal protection clause of the United States Constitution and also the equal protection clause of the state constitution because we interpret that provision of the state constitution to contain exactly the same prohibition against discriminatory legislation as is contained in the equal protection clause of the Fourteenth Amendment to the United States Constitution."

The state sought review of this decision in the United States Supreme Court, alleging that the state supreme court's determination of the federal constitutional issue was incorrect.

How should the United States Supreme Court dispose of the case if it believes that this interpretation of the federal Constitution by the state supreme court raises an important federal question and is incorrect on the merits?

(A) Reverse the state supreme court decision, because the equal protection clause of a state constitution must be construed by the state supreme court in a manner that is congruent with the meaning of the equal protection clause of the federal Constitution.

(B) Reverse the state supreme court decision with respect to the equal protection clause of the federal Constitution and remand the case to the state supreme court for further proceedings, because the state and federal constitutional issues are so intertwined that the federal issue must be decided so that this case may be disposed of properly.

(C) Refuse to review the decision of the state supreme court, because it is based on an adequate and independent ground of state law.

(D) Refuse to review the decision of the state supreme court, because a state government may not seek review of decisions of its own courts in the United States Supreme Court.

[Q1010]

Answer: Choice **(B)** is correct. Although the state supreme court made a finding about what the state constitution required, this decision was not truly "independent" of federal constitutional law, because the facts make it clear that the state court was first determining what the federal constitution required, and only then concluding that the state constitution required the same thing. Therefore, the Supreme Court can and should correct the state court's error in federal constitutional law. Once the Supreme Court has done this, it should then remand in order to give the state court the opportunity to conclude, after further reflection, that the state constitution's ban on discriminatory legislation goes further than the federal ban.

Choice (A) is wrong as a pure matter of law: even where provisions of a state and the federal constitution contain identical language, the state court is always free to interpret the state constitution as imposing different requirements than the apparently-identical federal provision.

Choice (C) is wrong because, for the reasons described above, the state court's decision was not in fact based on an adequate and independent state ground.

Choice (D) is wrong as a pure matter of law: nothing prevents a state government from seeking review of the decisions of its own courts in the U.S. Supreme Court, as long as the decision poses some serious question of federal law.

C. Federal judicial power:

Question: With the advice and consent of the Senate, the President entered into a self-executing treaty with a foreign country. The treaty provided that citizens of both nations were required to pay whatever torts damages were awarded against them by a court of either nation.

A man and a woman who were U.S. citizens and residents of the same state were traveling separately in the foreign country when their cars collided. The foreign court awarded the woman a judgment for $500,000 in damages for her injuries from the accident.

In federal district court in their home state, the woman filed suit against the man to enforce the judgment. The man filed a motion to dismiss for lack of jurisdiction.

Should the court grant the motion to dismiss?

(A) Yes, because the citizenship of the parties is not diverse.

(B) Yes, because the traffic accident was a noncommercial transaction outside interstate commerce.

(C) No, because the case falls within the federal question jurisdiction of the court.

(D) No, because the treaty power is plenary and not subject to judicial review.

[QA008]

Answer: Choice **(C)** is correct. Article III's grant of federal jurisdiction applies to a number of categories, one of which is cases arising under U.S. treaties. These categories together are lumped under the broader category of "federal question" cases. (This broad category also includes cases arising under "the Laws of the United States," i.e., federal statutes.) Since the issue of whether this damage award is enforceable by federal courts involves the interpretation of a U.S. treaty, the court has federal-question jurisdiction over the case.

(A) is wrong because it ignores the significance of the fact that the case involves interpretation of a treaty. It's true that the district court lacks diversity jurisdiction because the parties are citizens of the same state. But the court nevertheless has federal question jurisdiction over the case, because the case "arises under" a treaty of the United States, as provided for by Article III of the Constitution.

(B) is wrong because it cites an irrelevant fact. The relationship of a matter to interstate commerce is relevant to the *legislative* power of Congress pursuant to Article I, but not to the jurisdiction of federal courts pursuant to Article III. The court has federal question jurisdiction over the case because it "arises under" a treaty of the United States, as provided for by Article III of the Constitution.

(D) is wrong because it misstates the law. The scope of the President's power to enter into treaties with the advice and consent of the Senate is quite broad, but that scope is irrelevant to this question, which concerns the power of a federal court to hear a case. The court has federal question jurisdiction over the case because it "arises under" a treaty of the United States, as provided for by Article III.

1. **Supreme Court's jurisdiction:**

    a. **Two types:**

    Question: A federal statute provides that the United States Supreme Court has authority to review any case filed in a United States Court of Appeals, even though that case has not yet been decided by the court of appeals.

    The Environmental Protection Agency (EPA), an agency in the executive branch of the federal government, issued an important environmental rule. Although the rule had not yet been enforced against them, companies that would be adversely affected by the rule filed a petition for review of the rule in a court of appeals, seeking a declaration that the rule was invalid solely because it was beyond the statutory authority of the EPA. The companies made no constitutional claim. A statute specifically provides for direct review of EPA rules by a court of appeals without any initial action in a district court.

    The companies have filed a petition for a writ of certiorari in the Supreme Court requesting immediate review of this case by the Supreme Court before the court of appeals has actually decided the case. The EPA acknowledges that the case is important enough to warrant Supreme Court review and that it should be decided promptly, but it asks the Supreme Court to dismiss the petition on jurisdictional grounds.

    The best constitutional argument in support of the EPA's request is that

    (A) the case is not within the original jurisdiction of the Supreme Court as defined by Article III, and it is not a proper subject of that court's appellate jurisdiction because it has not yet been decided by any lower court.

    (B) the case is appellate in nature, but it is beyond the appellate jurisdiction of the Supreme Court, because Article III states that its jurisdiction extends only to cases arising under the Constitution.

(C) Article III precludes federal courts from reviewing the validity of any federal agency rule in any proceeding other than an action to enforce the rule.

(D) Article III provides that all federal cases, except those within the original jurisdiction of the Supreme Court, must be initiated by an action in a federal district court.

[Q3089]

Answer: (A) is the best response, because the case is within neither the Court's original or appellate jurisdiction.

As to original jurisdiction: Under Article III, §2, Clause 1, the Supreme Court has original jurisdiction in (and only in) all cases affecting Ambassadors, other public Ministers and Counsels, and those in which a State is a party. The case here does not involve any of those categories, so original jurisdiction does not exist.

As to appellate jurisdiction: Article III, §2, Clause 2, says that in those cases arising under the Constitution, by an Act of Congress, or by treaty, the Supreme Court shall have appellate jurisdiction subject to limitations imposed by Congress. But "appellate" jurisdiction presupposes that there is an appeal from a lower-court decision. Here, there isn't one. It's true that, as the facts tell us, a federal statute gives the Supreme Court the authority to review any case filed in a United States Court of Appeals, even though that case has not yet been decided by the court of appeals; that statute is constitutional as long as there has been some decision (i.e., by a district court). But here, where neither a district court nor a court of appeals has heard the case, there is no appeal, and thus no "appellate jurisdiction."

(B) is wrong because the case here is not really "appellate" in nature, for the reason described above.

(C) is wrong because the answer is an inaccurate statement of the law. Article III, §2 limits federal court jurisdiction to "cases" and "controversies," so the federal courts may not issue "advisory opinions" (i.e., opinions giving advice about particular legislative or executive action, when no party is before the court who has suffered or imminently faces specific injury). Federal courts can, however, issue *declaratory judgments*, where the court is not requested to award damages or an injunction, but rather is requested to state what the legal effect would be of proposed conduct by one of the parties. Because an action for declaratory judgment would be within federal courts' Article III power, yet such an action would not be an "action to enforce the rule," (C) is wrong.

(D) is wrong because it misstates Article III — Article III does not prevent federal cases from being initiated by an action filed in a court of appeals. For instance, Congress's constitutional power to control the jurisdiction of the lower federal courts means that Congress may by statute say that a certain category of case may (or even must) be filed in a federal court of appeals rather than in a federal district court.

II. CONGRESS'S CONTROL OF FEDERAL JUDICIAL POWER

B. Congress's power to decide:

1. Limits by Congress:

Question: Assume that Congress passed and the President signed the following statute:

"The appellate jurisdiction of the United States Supreme Court shall not extend to any case involving the constitutionality of any state statute limiting the circumstances in which a woman may obtain an abortion, or involving the constitutionality of this statute."

The strongest argument against the constitutionality of this statute is that

(A) Congress may not exercise its authority over the appellate jurisdiction of the Supreme Court in a way that seriously interferes with the establishment of a supreme and uniform body of federal constitutional law.

(B) Congress may only regulate the appellate jurisdiction of the Supreme Court over cases initially arising in federal courts.

(C) the appellate jurisdiction of the Supreme Court may only be altered by constitutional amendment.

(D) the statute violates the equal protection clause of the Fourteenth Amendment.
[Q2097]

Answer: The correct choice is **(A)**. In cases not falling within the Supreme Court's original jurisdiction (e.g., cases in which a state is a party), the Supreme Court has "appellate Jurisdiction, both as to Law and Fact, with such Exceptions, and under such Regulations as the Congress shall make." (Article III, Sec. 2, Cl. 2.) So Congress, acting under this clause, has the power to regulate (including limit) the appellate jurisdiction of the Supreme Court. However, the Court held in *U.S. v. Klein* that Congress cannot use this power to specify jurisdiction as a "mean to an end" to make a particular substantive question come out a certain way. Choice (A) best captures this limitation, by suggesting that Congress was attempting to freeze then-current abortion law and to prevent a future Supreme Court from developing constitutional law in this area as the Court sees fit. This argument might not succeed, but it is the only choice that could even theoretically work.

(B) is simply wrong — Congress can under Article III, Sec. 2, Cl. 2 regulate the appellate jurisdiction of the Supreme Court whether the case originally arose in federal court or state court (and the only significance of where the case arose is that in those rare cases falling within the original jurisdiction of the Supreme Court itself, no "appellate jurisdiction" is necessary, so that there is no appellate jurisdiction which Congress might limit.)

(C) is also simply wrong — as discussed in (A) above, Article III, Sec. 2, Cl. 2 lets Congress, acting without a constitutional amendment, change the appellate jurisdiction of the Supreme Court.

(D) is wrong because the Fourteenth Amendment's Equal Protection Clause protects only against classifications made by state governments, and if there is any classification being made here (doubtful), it is being made by Congress, not a state.

Question: Which of the following acts by the United States Senate would be constitutionally IMPROPER?

(A) The Senate decides, with the House of Representatives, that a disputed state ratification of a proposed constitutional amendment is valid.

(B) The Senate determines the eligibility of a person to serve as a senator.

(C) The Senate appoints a commission to adjudicate finally a boundary dispute between two states.

(D) The Senate passes a resolution calling on the President to pursue a certain foreign policy.
[Q1087]

Answer: Choice **(C)** is correct. Art. III, Sec. 2, says that the federal judicial power extends "to controversies between two or more States." Art. III, Sec. 3 then says that "in all cases ... in which a State shall be a Party, the supreme Court shall have original jurisdiction." That same article says that the Supreme Court's "appellate jurisdiction" shall be "with such exceptions, and under such regulations as the Congress shall make." There is no similar provision allowing Congress to make exceptions to (i.e., restrictions on) the Supreme Court's original jurisdiction, so Congress can't restrict the Supreme Court's original jurisdiction. Since a boundary dispute between two states is a dispute in which "a State shall be a party," since the Supreme Court has original jurisdiction over cases involving a party, and since Congress is not authorized to limit the Supreme Court's original jurisdiction, it follows that Congress cannot "adjudicate finally" (i.e., remove the Supreme Court's right to adjudicate) the boundary dispute.

Choice (A) is wrong because, under *Coleman v. Miller* (1939), the House and Senate together *do* have the right (indeed, the exclusive right) to determine whether a disputed state ratification of an amendment is valid.

Choice (B) is incorrect because the Senate *does* have the power to determine the eligibility of its members — Art. I, Sec. 5, Cl. 1 says that "each House shall be the judge of the Elections, Returns, and *Qualifications* of its own Members."

Choice (D) is wrong because Art. I, Sec. 7, Cl. 3 says that "Every Order, *Resolution*, or Vote to which the Concurrence of the Senate and House of Representatives may be necessary ... shall be presented to the President of the United States[.]" This clause implicitly gives each house the power to adopt resolutions; a resolution will not become law unless signed by the President, but the clause means that either house's adoption of a resolution is proper.

CHAPTER 2

FEDERALISM AND FEDERAL POWER GENERALLY

I. THE CONCEPT OF FEDERALISM

B. **Federal government has limited powers:**

1. **No general police power:**

    a. **Tax and spend for general welfare:**

    Question: National statistics revealed a dramatic increase in the number of elementary and secondary school students bringing controlled substances to school for sale. In response, Congress enacted a statute requiring each state legislature to enact a state law making it a crime for any person to sell, within 1,000 feet of any elementary or secondary school, any controlled substance that had previously been transported in interstate commerce.

    Is the federal statute constitutional?

    (A) No, because Congress has no authority to require a state legislature to enact any specified legislation.

    (B) No, because the sale of a controlled substance in close proximity to a school does not have a sufficiently close nexus to interstate commerce to justify its regulation by Congress.

    (C) Yes, because it contains a jurisdictional provision that will ensure, on a case-by-case basis, that any particular controlled substance subject to the terms of this statute will, in fact, affect interstate commerce.

    (D) Yes, because Congress possesses broad authority under both the general welfare clause and the commerce clause to regulate any activities affecting education that also have, in inseverable aggregates, a substantial effect on interstate commerce.

[QA084]

Answer: Choice **(D)** is **incorrect**, because it both ignores the Tenth Amendment problem and relies on a non-existent power. First, the Tenth Amendment has been interpreted to bar Congress from ordering a state to enact any particular legislation. Second, there is no clause of the Constitution that gives Congress power generally to regulate for the general welfare. (Article I gives Congress the power to *tax and spend* for the general welfare, but there's no taxing or spending that is part of the regulatory scheme here.) The correct choice is (A); see *infra*, p. 236.)

Question: Congress wishes to enact legislation prohibiting discrimination in the sale or rental of housing on the basis of the affectional preference or sexual orientation of the potential purchaser or renter. Congress wishes this statute to apply to all public and private vendors and lessors of residential property in this country, with a few narrowly drawn exceptions.

The most credible argument for congressional authority to enact such a statute would be based upon the

(A) general welfare clause of Article I, § 8, because the conduct the statute prohibits could reasonably be deemed to be harmful to the national interest.

(B) commerce clause of Article I, Sec. 8, because, in inseverable aggregates, the sale or rental of almost all housing in this country could reasonably be deemed to have a substantial effect on interstate commerce.

(C) enforcement clause of the Thirteenth Amendment, because that amendment clearly prohibits discrimination against the class of persons protected by this statute.

(D) enforcement clause of the Fourteenth Amendment, because that amendment prohibits all public and private actors from engaging in irrational discrimination.

[Q3170]

Answer: Choice **(A)** is **incorrect,** because Congress has no power to regulate for the general welfare. Article I, Sec. 8 gives Congress the power to *"tax and spend"* for the general welfare, but that's not what's happening here — what's happening here is pure regulation. (Choice (B) is correct; see *infra*, p. 232.)

CHAPTER 3

POWERS OF THE FEDERAL GOVERNMENT; THE SEPARATION OF POWERS

I. POWERS OF THE THREE FEDERAL BRANCHES

A. **Powers of the three branches:**

1. **Congress:**

d. **Federal property:**

Question: The National Ecological Balance Act prohibits the destruction or removal of any wild animals located on lands owned by the United States without express permission from the Federal Bureau of Land Management. Violators are subject to fines of up to $1,000 per offense.

After substantial property damage was inflicted on residents of a state by hungry coyotes, the state legislature passed the Coyote Bounty Bill, which offers $25 for each coyote killed or captured within the state. A National Forest, owned by the federal government, is located entirely within that state. Many coyotes live in the National Forest.

Without seeking permission from the Bureau of Land Management, a hunter shot several coyotes in the National Forest and collected the bounty from the state. As a result, he was subsequently tried in federal district court, convicted, and fined $1,000 for violating the National Ecological Balance Act. The hunter appealed his conviction to the United States Court of Appeals.

On appeal, the Court of Appeals should hold the National Ecological Balance Act, as applied to the hunter, to be

(A) constitutional, because the property clause of Article IV, Section 3, of the Constitution authorizes such federal statutory controls and sanctions.

(B) constitutional, because Article I, Section 8, of the Constitution authorizes Congress to enact all laws necessary and proper to advance the general welfare.

(C) unconstitutional, because Congress may not use its delegated powers to override the Tenth Amendment right of the state to legislate in areas of traditional state governmental functions, such as the protection of the property of its residents.

(D) unconstitutional, because Congress violates the full faith and credit clause of Article IV when it punishes conduct that has been authorized by state action.

[Q2079]

Answer: Choice **(A)** is correct. Art. IV, Sec. 3, Cl. 2 gives Congress the power to "make all needful Rules and Regulations respecting the Territory or other Property belonging to the United States[.]" Since the National Forest is federally-owned property, this clause gives Congress the power to pass regulations governing it. Under the supremacy clause, those regulations would take precedence over any conflicting state regulations, such as the right to kill coyotes implied by the state bounty bill.

(B) is wrong because it suggests that there is an independent congressional power to act to advance "the general welfare." This is not so — there's a power to "*tax and spend* ... for the general welfare," but that's not what's at issue here (because Congress is doing pure regulating, not taxing or spending).

(C) is wrong because if Congress has been given an explicit power in a certain area (here, the power to regulate on federal lands), Congress can indeed override whatever right the state might otherwise have to legislate in areas of traditional state governmental functions.

(D) is wrong because the Full Faith and Credit clause does not block Congress from punishing conduct that has been authorized by a state; the clause merely requires one state to enforce every other state's judgments.

2. **President:**

   b. **CEO of the U.S., and "Executive Orders":**

      ii. **Direction to private party:**

Question: The president issued an executive order in an effort to encourage citizens to use the metric (Celsius) system of temperatures. Sec. 1 of the executive order requires the United States Weather Bureau, a federal executive agency, to state temperatures only in Celsius in all weather reports. Sec. 2 of the executive order requires all privately owned federally licensed radio and television stations giving weather reports to report temperatures only in Celsius. No federal statute is applicable.

Is the president's executive order constitutional?

(A) Sec. 1 is constitutional, but Sec. 2 is not.

(B) Sec. 2 is constitutional, but Sec. 1 is not.

(C) Sections 1 and 2 are constitutional.

(D) Sections 1 and 2 are unconstitutional.

[Q7064]

Answer: Choice **(A)** is correct. Sec. 1 of the executive order is constitutional, because the President, as the chief executive officer of the U.S. government, has authority to direct the actions of federal executive agencies, so long as the President's directives are not inconsistent with an act of Congress. (The facts state that there is no applicable statute here.) Sec. 2 of the executive order is unconstitutional. At least as a general rule, the President does not have authority to direct the actions of persons outside the executive branch unless the President's direction is authorized by an act of Congress. There are no circumstances presented in the facts (such as a sudden attack on the U.S.) that might justify an exception to this general rule.

(B), (C) and (D) are wrong because each is inconsistent with the above analysis.

f. Pardons:

Question: Congress passed a bill prohibiting the President from granting a pardon to any person who had not served at least one-third of the sentence imposed by the court which convicted that person. The President vetoed the bill, claiming that it was unconstitutional. Nevertheless, Congress passed it over his veto by a two-thirds vote of each house.

This act of Congress is

(A) constitutional, because it was enacted over the President's veto by a two-thirds vote of each house.

(B) constitutional, because it is a necessary and proper means of carrying out the powers of Congress.

(C) unconstitutional, because it interferes with the plenary power of the President to grant pardons.

(D) unconstitutional, because a Presidential veto based upon constitutional grounds may be overridden only with the concurrence of three-fourths of the state legislatures.

[Q1179]

Answer: The correct choice is **(C)**. The President's pardon power is indeed plenary. Therefore, when Congress purported to place conditions on that power, those conditions were ineffective. For the same reason, Choices (A), (B), and (D) are wrong. (By the way, Choice (D) is also grossly incorrect as a statement of the law of vetoes: where the President vetoes a bill passed by Congress, Article I, Sec. 7, Cl. 2 says that the veto can be overridden by a two-thirds vote of both houses. There is no procedure by which the concurrence of three-fourths of state legislatures can act as an overriding method.)

g. Veto:

Question: [Same Question as prior one.] Congress passed a bill prohibiting the President from granting a pardon to any person who had not served at least one-third of the sentence imposed by the court which convicted that person. The President vetoed the bill, claiming that it was unconstitutional. Nevertheless, Congress passed it over his veto by a two-thirds vote of each house,

This act of Congress is

(A) constitutional, because it was enacted over the President's veto by a two-thirds vote of each house.

(B) constitutional, because it is a necessary and proper means of carrying out the powers of Congress.

(C) unconstitutional, because it interferes with the plenary power of the President to grant pardons.

(D) unconstitutional, because a Presidential veto based upon constitutional grounds may be overridden only with the concurrence of three-fourths of the state legislatures.

[Q1179]

Answer: Choice **(D)** is **incorrect** as a statement of the law of vetoes: where the President vetoes a bill passed by Congress, Article I, Sec. 7, Cl. 2 says that the veto can be overridden by a two-thirds vote of both houses. There is no procedure by which the concurrence of three-fourths of state legislatures can act as an overriding method. (The correct answer is (C); see *supra*, p. 230.)

II. THE FEDERAL COMMERCE POWER

B. **Summary of modern view:**

4. **"Substantially affecting" commerce:**

a. **Activity is commercial:**

Question: A federal statute prohibits the sale or resale, in any place in this country, of any product intended for human consumption or ingestion into the human body that contains designated chemicals known to cause cancer, unless the product is clearly labeled as dangerous.

The constitutionality of this federal statute may most easily be justified on the basis of the power of Congress to

(A) regulate commerce among the states.

(B) enforce the Fourteenth Amendment.

(C) provide for the general welfare.

(D) promote science and the useful arts.

[Q1026]

Answer: Choice **(A)** is correct. The key point is that Congress can use its commerce powers to regulate even entirely *intrastate* transactions, on the theory that such transactions are being regulated as part of a broader regulation of interstate transactions, and excluding purely intrastate transactions from the overall scheme would be unwieldy. So, for instance, Congress here can forbid a farmer's sale, at a roadside stand adjacent to his farm, of a tomato that he had raised, where the farmer sprayed a cancer-causing substance produced inside that same state onto the tomato — even though this is an entirely intrastate transaction, it is still a "commercial" transaction, and can be regulated pursuant to Congress's broader interstate-commerce regulatory scheme.

(B) is wrong for several reasons; most importantly, the Fourteenth Amendment protects only against various conduct (e.g., denials of equal protection and due process) involving "state action," and while Congress has the power to enforce that Amendment by appropriate legislation, Congress here is not focused on attempting to prohibit any state from violating the Amendment.

(C) is wrong because there is no general congressional power to "provide for the general welfare"; there is only a power to *tax and spend* for the general welfare.

(D) is similarly incorrect because there is no general congressional power to "promote science and the useful arts"; there is only the limited power in Art. I, Sec. 8, Cl. 8 to "promote the progress of science and useful arts" by "securing for limited times to authors and inventors the exclusive right to their respective writings and discoveries" (i.e., the power to issue *patents* and *copyrights*).

Question: Congress wishes to enact legislation prohibiting discrimination in the sale or rental of housing on the basis of the affectional preference or sexual orientation of the potential purchaser or renter. Congress wishes this statute to apply to all public and private vendors and lessors of residential property in this country, with a few narrowly drawn exceptions.

The most credible argument for congressional authority to enact such a statute would be based upon the

(A) general welfare clause of Article I, Sec. 8, because the conduct the statute prohibits could reasonably be deemed to be harmful to the national interest.

(B) commerce clause of Article I, Sec. 8, because, in inseverable aggregates, the sale or rental of almost all housing in this country could reasonably be deemed to have a substantial effect on interstate commerce.

(C) enforcement clause of the Thirteenth Amendment, because that amendment clearly prohibits discrimination against the class of persons protected by this statute.

(D) enforcement clause of the Fourteenth Amendment, because that amendment prohibits all public and private actors from engaging in irrational discrimination.

[Q3170]

Answer: (B) is correct, because the "substantial effect on commerce" rationale has been accepted by the Supreme Court. For instance, in *Wickard v. Filburn* (1942), the Court held that Congress could regulate even the consumption of wheat on the farm where it was produced, because such intrastate uses had a substantial effect on interstate commerce. The same principle would apply here: (1) the rental or sale of property is clearly "commercial"; and (2) even a local ("intrastate") sale or rental of property would indirectly affect interstate commerce (e.g., by substantially affecting the demand for housing-construction materials from out of state).

Question: "Look-alike drugs" is the term used to describe nonprescription drugs that look like narcotic drugs and are sold on the streets as narcotic drugs. After extensive hearings, Congress concluded that the sale of look-alike drugs was widespread in this country and was creating severe health and law enforcement problems. To combat these problems, Congress enacted a comprehensive statute that regulates the manufacture, distribution, and sale of all nonprescription drugs in the United States.

Which of the following sources of constitutional authority can most easily be used to justify the authority of Congress to enact this statute?

(A) The spending power.

(B) The commerce clause.

(C) The general welfare clause.

(D) The enforcement powers of the Fourteenth Amendment.

[Q1029]

Answer: Choice **(B)** is correct. All of the activities being regulated by Congress here — manufacturing, distribution and sale of drugs — pertain to commerce. Therefore, Congress's power to regulate commerce is an ample source of authority for the regulatory scheme here. That is true even though the overall objectives being sought by Congress — the protection of health and the enforcement of law at the local level — are arguably "local" concerns traditionally left to the states.

(A) is wrong because the congressional statute here is essentially regulatory, and does not involve significant spending of federal funds.

(C) is wrong because there *is* no "general welfare" clause in the sense of a freestanding congressional power to legislate for the general welfare; there is, instead, only the power to tax and spend to achieve the general welfare, and Congress is not doing meaningful taxing or spending in the regulation at issue here.

(D) is wrong because the Fourteenth Amendment protects only against various conduct (e.g., denials of equal protection and due process) involving "state action," and while Congress has the power to enforce that Amendment by appropriate legislation, Congress here is not focused on attempting to prohibit states from violating the Amendment; for instance, there is no indication that Congress is trying to prevent the states from discriminating in the sale of nonprescription drugs or from denying anyone due process as to such drugs.

b. **Activity is not commercial:**

   i. **Jurisdictional hook:**

Question: National statistics revealed a dramatic increase in the number of elementary and secondary school students bringing controlled substances to school for sale. In response, Congress enacted a statute requiring each state legislature to enact a state law making it a crime for any person to sell, within 1,000 feet of any elementary or secondary school, any controlled substance that had previously been transported in interstate commerce.

Is the federal statute constitutional?

(A) No, because Congress has no authority to require a state legislature to enact any specified legislation.

(B) No, because the sale of a controlled substance in close proximity to a school does not have a sufficiently close nexus to interstate commerce to justify its regulation by Congress.

(C) Yes, because it contains a jurisdictional provision that will ensure, on a case-by-case basis, that any particular controlled substance subject to the terms of this statute will, in fact, affect interstate commerce.

(D) Yes, because Congress possesses broad authority under both the general welfare clause and the commerce clause to regulate any activities affecting education that also have, in inseverable aggregates, a substantial effect on interstate commerce.

[QA084]

Answer: Choice **(B)** is **incorrect**, because it reaches the correct outcome by incorrect reasoning. The commerce clause of Article I empowers Congress to regulate economic or commercial activity that, in the aggregate, has a substantial effect on interstate commerce. The sale of controlled substances is a commercial activity, even if the particular sale being forbidden occurs entirely within a state. The facts here disclose "a dramatic increase in the number of elementary and secondary school students bringing controlled substances to school for sale," suggesting that, in the aggregate, this activity has a sufficient effect on interstate commerce to bring the regulation within Congress's commerce power. The examiners seem to be trying to trick you into thinking that the case is like *U.S. v. Lopez* (1995), where the Court held that Congress did not have power under the commerce clause to bar the possession of guns near schools. But in *Lopez*, the activity being regulated (possession of guns) was not inherently "commercial," whereas the activity being regulated here (sale of a substance) *is* inherently commercial.

There is a second distinction between the regulation at issue here and the one struck down in *Lopez*. Here, the statute applies only to those controlled substances that have been previously *transported in interstate commerce*. In *Lopez*, by contrast, possession of *any* gun, even one that had not moved in interstate commerce, was prohibited. It's likely that the "jurisdictional hook" here would suffice to make the statute a proper exercise of the commerce power even if no commercial transaction were present. (For instance, if Congress made it a crime to *possess* any controlled substance near a school if the substance had moved in interstate commerce, the statute would likely be a valid exercise of commerce power even though mere possession of such a substance is not itself a commercial activity.) Certainly the *combination* of the requirement that the item have previously moved in commerce, and the requirement that the item be sold rather than just possessed, is easily enough to bring the statute within Congress's commerce power.

(C) is **incorrect**, because it ignores the Tenth Amendment problem. It's true that the statutory limitation requiring that any controlled substance must have been previously transported in interstate commerce likely provides a sufficient jurisdictional nexus with interstate commerce to bring Congress's statute within the commerce power. But the statute here is nevertheless unconstitutional because the U.S. Supreme Court held, in *New York v. United States* (1992), that the concept of federalism embedded in the Tenth Amendment disables Congress from requiring states to enact laws or to administer federal law. So although Congress could make it a *federal* crime to sell (or even possess) near a school a controlled substance that had moved in interstate commerce, Congress cannot force a state to use the state's lawmaking mechanism to enact this (or any) criminal prohibition.

(The correct answer is (A), based on the Tenth Amendment; see *infra*, p. 236.)

C. The Tenth Amendment as a limit on Congress's power:

Question: A federal law provides that all motor vehicle tires discarded in this country must be disposed of in facilities licensed by the federal Environmental Protection Agency. Pursuant to this federal law and all proper federal procedural requirements, that agency has adopted very strict standards for the licensing of such facilities. As a result, the cost of disposing of tires in licensed facilities is substantial. The state of East Dakota has a very large fleet of motor vehicles, including trucks used to support state-owned commercial activities and police cars. East Dakota disposes of used tires from both kinds of state motor vehicles in a state-owned and operated facility. This state facility is unlicensed, but its operation in actual practice meets most of the standards imposed by the federal Environmental Protection Agency on facilities it licenses to dispose of tires.

Consistent with United States Supreme Court precedent, may the state of East Dakota continue to dispose of its used tires in this manner?

(A) No, because a state must comply with valid federal laws that regulate matters affecting interstate commerce.

(B) No, because some of the tires come from vehicles that are used by the state solely in its commercial activities.

(C) Yes, because some of the tires come from vehicles that are used by the state in the performance of core state governmental functions such as law enforcement.

(D) Yes, because the legitimate needs of the federal government are satisfied by the fact that the unlicensed state disposal scheme meets, in actual practice, most of the federal standards for the licensing of such facilities.

[Q1046]

Answer: The correct choice is **(A)**. The federal law on tire disposal was a proper exercise of Congress's power to regulate interstate commerce, so the law was validly enacted. The fact that Congress has chosen to regulate the actions of state governments does not prevent an otherwise-valid statute from being constitutional. There is one major exception — the Tenth Amendment prevents Congress from "commandeer[ing] the legislative processes of the states" by directly compelling states to enact or enforce a federal regulatory program [*New York v. U.S.*] But here, although Congress is regulating the states, it is not forcing the states to enact or enforce any federal regulatory program (merely forcing the states to obey the federal program in the state's own internal operations), so the exception does not apply.

Choice (B) is wrong because, although it reaches the correct conclusion, it does so for the wrong reasons; even if none of the tires came from vehicles used by the state in commercial activities, the federal regulation would still be valid.

Choice (C) is wrong because Congress has power to regulate interstate commerce in a way that binds the states, and there is no exception to this power for regulation of "core state governmental functions" (although as noted above, if Congress were actually ordering the state to enact or enforce a regulatory program, this *would* be beyond Congress's commerce powers).

Choice (D) is wrong because the fact that the unlicensed state disposal facility meets most federal standards is irrelevant; Congress has the power to insist that the state strictly obey the federal requirement that only licensed disposal facilities be used.

2. **Use of state's law-making mechanisms:**

   a. **Enactment of statute:**

   Question: [Same Question as on p. 233.] National statistics revealed a dramatic increase in the number of elementary and secondary school students bringing controlled substances to school for sale. In response, Congress enacted a statute requiring each state legislature to enact a state law making it a crime for any person to sell, within 1,000 feet of any elementary or secondary school, any controlled substance that had previously been transported in interstate commerce.

   Is the federal statute constitutional?

   (A) No, because Congress has no authority to require a state legislature to enact any specified legislation.

   (B) No, because the sale of a controlled substance in close proximity to a school does not have a sufficiently close nexus to interstate commerce to justify its regulation by Congress.

   (C) Yes, because it contains a jurisdictional provision that will ensure, on a case-by-case basis, that any particular controlled substance subject to the terms of this statute will, in fact, affect interstate commerce.

(D) Yes, because Congress possesses broad authority under both the general welfare clause and the commerce clause to regulate any activities affecting education that also have, in inseverable aggregates, a substantial effect on interstate commerce.

[QA084]

Answer: Choice **(A)** is correct. The U.S. Supreme Court held, in *New York v. United States* (1992), that the concept of federalism embedded in the Tenth Amendment prohibits Congress from requiring states to enact laws or to administer federal law. Since Congress is telling each state legislature that it must enact a particular law, Congress is violating this principle. (On the other hand, Congress could itself make it a federal crime to sell a controlled substance near a school if the substance had moved in interstate commerce; see the discussion of Choice (B) for details.)

(B) is wrong because it reaches the correct outcome by incorrect reasoning. The commerce clause of Article I empowers Congress to regulate economic or commercial activity that, in the aggregate, has a substantial effect on interstate commerce. The sale of controlled substances is a commercial activity, even if the particular sale being forbidden occurs entirely within a state. The facts here disclose "a dramatic increase in the number of elementary and secondary school students bringing controlled substances to school for sale," suggesting that, in the aggregate, this activity has a sufficient effect on interstate commerce to bring the regulation within Congress's commerce power. The examiners seem to be trying to trick you into thinking that the case is like *U.S. v. Lopez* (1995), where the Court held that Congress did not have power under the commerce clause to bar the possession of guns near schools. But in *Lopez*, the activity being regulated (possession of guns) was not inherently "commercial," whereas the activity being regulated here (sale of a substance) *is* inherently commercial.

There is a second distinction between the regulation at issue here and the one struck down in *Lopez*. Here, the statute applies only to those controlled substances that have been previously *transported in interstate commerce*. In *Lopez*, by contrast, possession of *any* gun, even one that had not moved in interstate commerce, was prohibited. It's likely that the "jurisdictional hook" here would suffice to make the statute a proper exercise of the commerce power even if no commercial transaction were present. (For instance, if Congress made it a crime to *possess* any controlled substance near a school if the substance had moved in interstate commerce, the statute would likely be a valid exercise of commerce power even though mere possession of such a substance is not itself a commercial activity.) Certainly the *combination* of the requirement that the item have previously moved in commerce, and the requirement that the item be sold rather than just possessed, is easy enough to bring the statute within Congress's commerce power.

(C) is wrong because it ignores the Tenth Amendment problem. It's true that the statutory limitation requiring that any controlled substance must have been previously transported in interstate commerce likely provides a sufficient jurisdictional nexus with interstate commerce to bring Congress's statute within the commerce power. But the statute here is nevertheless unconstitutional because the U.S. Supreme Court held, in *New York v. United States* (1992), that the concept of federalism embedded in the Tenth Amendment disables Congress from requiring states to enact laws or to administer federal law. So although Congress could make it a *federal* crime to sell (or even possess) near a school a controlled substance that had moved in interstate commerce, Congress cannot force a state to use the state's lawmaking mechanism to enact this (or any) criminal prohibition.

(D) is wrong because it both ignores the Tenth Amendment problem and relies on a non-existent power. First, the Tenth Amendment has been interpreted to bar Congress from ordering a state to enact any particular legislation; see Choice (A) for more about this. Second, there is no clause of the Constitution that gives Congress power generally to regulate for the general welfare. (Article I gives Congress the power to *tax and spend* for the general welfare, but there's no taxing or spending that is part of the regulatory scheme here.)

3. **Not a source of state authority:**

    Question: Widgets are manufactured wholly from raw materials mined and processed in the state of Green. The only two manufacturers of widgets in the United States are also located in that state. However, their widgets are purchased by retailers located in every state. The legislature of the state of Green is considering the adoption of a statute that would impose a tax solely on the manufacture of widgets. The tax is to be calculated at 3% of their wholesale value.

    Which of the following arguments would be LEAST helpful to the state in defending the constitutionality of this proposed state tax on widgets?

    (A) At the time widgets are manufactured and taxed they have not yet entered the channels of interstate commerce.

    (B) The economic impact of this tax will be passed on to both in-state and out-of-state purchasers of widgets and, therefore, it is wholly nondiscriminatory in its effect.

    (C) Because of the powers reserved to them by the Tenth Amendment, states have plenary authority to construct their tax system in any manner they choose.

    (D) A tax on the manufacture of widgets may be imposed only by the state in which the manufacturing occurs and, therefore, it is not likely to create the danger of a multiple tax burden on interstate commerce.

    [Q2020]

    Answer: Choice **(C)** is correct. If this tax scheme has a problem, the problem is likely to have to do with the fact that Green is imposing a tax on widgets that are shipped throughout the U.S., and that tax may be a burden on commerce. The Tenth Amendment does not solve this problem for Green — if Green is unduly burdening commerce, the Tenth Amendment won't save it. And it's certainly inaccurate to say that the states "have plenary authority to construct their tax system in any manner they choose" — for instance, if a state intentionally designs its tax system so as to put most of the burden on out-of-staters who derive some revenue from customers in the state and who don't vote in state elections, the scheme would clearly violate the dormant commerce clause.

    (A), (B), and (D) each arguably helps the state rebut the plaintiff's argument that the tax is an undue burden on commerce and that it thus violates the dormant commerce clause. Therefore, each of these arguments might help the state.

III. THE TAXING AND SPENDING POWERS

A. **Taxing power:**

    Question: In order to reduce the federal deficit, Congress enacted a statute imposing a five percent national retail sales tax. The tax was levied upon all retail sales in the United States and applied equally to the sales of all kinds of goods.

    Is this tax constitutional as applied to retail sales of newspapers?

    (A) Yes, because it is within Congress's power to tax.

    (B) Yes, because the tax is necessary to serve the compelling interest of balancing the federal budget.

(C) No, because retail sales taxes are within the taxing power of the states.

(D) No, because the imposition of a tax on the sale of newspapers violates the freedom of the press.

[QA071]

Answer: Choice **(A)** is correct. The tax clause of Article I, Section 8 gives Congress plenary power to raise revenue through taxes. To be a permissible exercise of this power, a tax must merely be a rational way of raising revenue to be used for the general welfare, and must not violate any independent constitutional prohibition. Application of the tax to the sale of newspapers does not violate the freedom of the press protected by the First Amendment, because the tax is generally applicable and in no way singles out press operations.

(B) is wrong because although it reaches the right outcome, it does so by applying the wrong test. The tax clause of Article I, Section 8 gives Congress plenary power to raise revenue through taxes. To be a permissible exercise of this power, a tax must merely be a rational way of raising revenue to be used for the general welfare, and must not violate any independent constitutional prohibition. The choice here applies strict scrutiny, but nothing about this tax would trigger strict scrutiny. In particular, the fact that the tax applies to newspapers — clearly a form of First Amendment expression — does not trigger strict scrutiny, because the tax is generally applicable and in no way singles out press operations.

(C) is incorrect as a statement of law. The Constitution does not reserve retail sales taxes for the states. The tax clause of Article I, Section 8 gives Congress plenary power to raise revenue through taxes. (It's true that the states have the power to establish their own independent tax systems, and a federal statute that barred the states from collecting any taxes of their own probably *would* violate the Tenth Amendment. But the tax here does not interfere with the states' right to tax.)

(D) is wrong because the tax here does not violate the freedom of the press. The Supreme Court has repeatedly held that provisions of general applicability that happen to impose some sort of incidental burden on free expression do not thereby violate the First Amendment. Thus generally-applicable regulations in the area of taxation, litigation discovery, or grand jury subpoenas are all valid even where applied to the press. If the sales tax here had applied *only* to newspapers, this "singling out" *would* have violated the First Amendment. But the tax applies to all retail transactions, and nothing in the First Amendment requires that Congress give a special exemption for newspapers or other speakers.

1. **Regulation:**

   a. **Adverse economic consequences no problem:**

   Question: The Sports Championship Revenue Enhancement Act is a federal statute that was enacted as part of a comprehensive program to eliminate the federal budget deficit. That act imposed, for a period of five years, a 50% excise tax on the price of tickets to championship sporting events. Such events included the World Series, the Super Bowl, major college bowl games, and similar championship sports events.

   This federal tax is probably

   (A) constitutional, because the compelling national interest in reducing the federal budget deficit justifies this tax as a temporary emergency measure.

   (B) constitutional, because an act of Congress that appears to be a revenue raising measure on its face is not rendered invalid because it may have adverse economic consequences for the activity taxed.

(C) unconstitutional, because a 50% tax is likely to reduce attendance at championship sporting events and, therefore, is not rationally related to the legitimate interest of Congress in eliminating the budget deficit.

(D) unconstitutional, because Congress violates the equal protection component of the Fifth Amendment by singling out championship sporting events for this tax while failing to tax other major sporting, artistic, or entertainment events to which tickets are sold.

[Q2033]

Answer: Choice **(B)** is correct; a federal tax that will raise revenue is not rendered invalid by virtue of the fact that it has regulatory consequences, including a lessening of demand for the product or activity being taxed. (That's true, by the way, whether or not Congress intended that lessening of demand.)

(A) is incorrect because the tax would be valid as a revenue-raising measure even in the absence of a compelling national interest.

(C) is incorrect for the same reason that Choice (B) is correct — as long as the tax is on its face a revenue-raiser, it does not even have to be rationally related to some broader federal interest like deficit-reduction (and in any event the tax probably *is* rationally related to deficit-reduction even though sporting attendance may go down — the rational-relation test is very easy to satisfy, and you should beware of any choice that requires you to conclude that a means chosen by government is not rationally related to a particular governmental goal).

(D) is incorrect because where, as here, a legislative classification involves economics and does not implicate any suspect class or fundamental right, equal protection is satisfied as long as the classification is rationally related to the achievement of some legitimate governmental objective; here, the objective is revenue-raising, and the fact that other similar activities are spared the tax does not prevent the tax from being rationally-related to that objective.

b. **No relation needed between activity taxed and how funds are spent:**

Question: In order to provide funds for a system of new major airports near the ten largest cities in the United States, Congress levies a tax of $25 on each airline ticket issued in the United States. The tax applies to every airline ticket, even those for travel that does not originate in, terminate at, or pass through any of those ten large cities.

As applied to the issuance in the United States of an airline ticket for travel between two cities that will not be served by any of the new airports, this tax is

(A) constitutional, because Congress has broad discretion in choosing the subjects of its taxation and may impose taxes on subjects that have no relation to the purpose for which those tax funds will be expended.

(B) constitutional, because an exemption for the issuance of tickets for travel between cities that will not be served by the new airports would deny the purchasers of all other tickets the equal protection of the laws.

(C) unconstitutional, because the burden of the tax outweighs its benefits for passengers whose travel does not originate in, terminate at, or pass through any of the ten largest cities.

(D) unconstitutional, because the tax adversely affects the fundamental right to travel.

[Q1124]

240   Chapter 3 - POWERS OF THE FEDERAL GOVERNMENT; THE SEPARATION OF POWERS

Answer: Choice **(A)** is correct. This choice accurately restates the fundamental rule about Congress's power to tax: as long as Congress can rationally be said to be pursuing the general welfare (not a meaningful constraint), Congress can pick pretty much any activity it wishes as the subject of taxation, and can then spend the funds for a purpose that has no relation to the activity taxed. So here, the fact that Congress is taxing trips that do not involve the 10 large cities, and then spending the funds solely for the benefit of passengers whose travel does involve those 10 cities, makes no difference.

(B) is wrong because, although the main conclusion is correct (that the tax is constitutional), giving an exemption for cities that would not be served would certainly not deny any other purchasers equal protection. In the case of economic regulation not involving a suspect class or fundamental right, the classification scheme merely needs to withstand easy-to-satisfy mere-rationality review, and giving an exemption for travel between cities not involving the new airports would certainly pass this easy test.

(C) is wrong because the burden/benefit analysis used here would not be the proper test for a federally-imposed tax; the burden/benefit analysis would be a proper way to analyze a *state* regulation that might burden interstate travel and thus violate the dormant Commerce Clause, but the regulation here is not by a state.

(D) is wrong because, while the Supreme Court has occasionally recognized a fundamental "right to travel" for equal protection purposes, these cases have involved what would better be called the right to "migrate interstate" (e.g., the right to change one's state of residence and still receive welfare benefits), not the right to take a trip from one state to another.

B. Spending power:

3. Special rule for "direct taxes":

a. Very few taxes are "direct":

i. Nearly all taxes are "indirect":

Question: A federal statute imposes an excise tax of $100 on each new computer sold in the United States. It also appropriates the entire proceeds of that tax to a special fund, which is required to be used to purchase licenses for computer software that will be made available for use, free of charge, to any resident of the United States.

Is this statute constitutional?

(A) No, because the federal government may not impose any direct taxes on citizens of the United States.

(B) No, because this statute takes without just compensation the property of persons who hold patents or copyrights on computer software.

(C) Yes, because it is a reasonable exercise of the power of Congress to tax and spend for the general welfare.

(D) Yes, because the patent power authorizes Congress to impose reasonable charges on the sale of technology and to spend the proceeds of those charges to advance the use of technology in the United States.

[Q7002]

Answer: The correct choice is **(C)**. Article I, Section 8, Clause 1 of the Constitution gives Congress broad power to tax and to spend for the general welfare. Courts defer to reasonable congressional taxing measures, such as the statute at issue in this case, as well as to expenditures that reasonably further the general welfare.

(A) is wrong, because (1) Congress *is* allowed to enact a "direct" tax on citizens if the tax is "apportioned" by state population; and (2) the tax here is not a "direct" tax (an excise tax — which is a tax on a product or activity — would never be deemed to be a direct tax).

(B) is wrong because it relies on an irrelevant concept. It is true that the Fifth Amendment prohibits the taking of private property for public use without just compensation. But no such taking has occurred here. A tax on the sale of a computer takes no property from those who hold patents or copyrights on computer software. Likewise, the software distributed freely under the statute will first be purchased, rather than taken, by the government.

(D) is wrong because, although Article I, Section 8, Clause 8 of the Constitution gives Congress power to provide patent rights to inventors, this clause does not itself authorize federal taxes and appropriations.

5. **General welfare:**

   Question: A newly enacted federal statute appropriates $100 million in federal funds to support basic research by universities located in the United States. The statute provides that "the ten best universities in the United States" will each receive $10 million. It also provides that "the ten best universities" shall be "determined by a poll of the presidents of all the universities in the nation, to be conducted by the United States Department of Education." In responding to that poll, each university president is required to apply the well-recognized and generally accepted standards of academic quality that are specified in the statute. The provisions of the statute are inseverable.

   Which of the following statements about this statute is correct?

   (A) The statute is unconstitutional, because the reliance by Congress on a poll of individuals who are not federal officials to determine the recipients of its appropriated funds is an unconstitutional delegation of legislative power.

   (B) The statute is unconstitutional, because the limitation on recipients to the ten best universities is arbitrary and capricious and denies other high-quality universities the equal protection of the laws.

   (C) The statute is constitutional, because Congress has plenary authority to determine the objects of its spending and the methods used to achieve them, so long as they may reasonably be deemed to serve the general welfare and do not violate any prohibitory language in the Constitution.

   (D) The validity of the statute is nonjusticiable, because the use by Congress of its spending power necessarily involves political considerations that must be resolved finally by those branches of the government that are closest to the political process.

   [Q2145]

   Answer: Choice **(C)** is correct. Although Congress, when it spends, must spend "for the general welfare," this test is extremely easy to satisfy — as the choice correctly states, all that is required is that the spending be "reasonably deemed to serve the general welfare," and that it not violate some specific constitutional ban (e.g., the Establishment Clause's ban on spending for the purpose of advancing religion). Since Congress could rationally have believed that rewarding the "best universities" would promote the country's general welfare, and that determining the "ten best" by this kind of vote was a rational way to go about attaining that end, the spending is constitutional.

   (A) is wrong because the statute here is an acceptable exercise of legislative delegation: Congress has made it reasonably clear to the Dept. of Education what they are to do, and how they are to do it, so there is no "unconstitutional delegation" despite the fact that non-federal officials will be somehow involved in the process.

(B) is wrong, because when a governmental classification does not involve a suspect or semi-suspect class or fundamental right, equal protection requires only a rational relation between the means chosen and a legitimate governmental objective, and the means and end here meet this easy-to-satisfy standard. (To put it another way, limiting the money to the "top ten," and picking the top ten this way, are *not* "arbitrary and capricious" methods.)

(D) is wrong because the mere fact that Congress's use of its spending power is being challenged does not make the matter a nonjusticiable political question.

IV. THE SEPARATION OF POWERS

A. **Separation of powers generally:**

1. **President can't make the laws:**

    d. **Delegation:**

       i. **Requirements for delegation:**

       Question: Congress passed a statute directing the United States Forest Service, a federal agency, to issue regulations to control campfires on federal public lands and to establish a schedule of penalties for those who violate the new regulations. The statute provided that the Forest Service regulations should "reduce, to the maximum extent feasible, all potential hazards that arise from campfires on Forest Service lands." The Forest Service issued the regulations and the schedule of penalties directed by Congress. The regulations include a rule that provides for the doubling of the fine for any negligent or prohibited use of fire if the user is intoxicated by alcohol or drugs.

       Which of the following is the best argument for sustaining the constitutionality of the Forest Service's rule providing for the fines?

       (A) The executive branch of government, of which the Forest Service is part, has inherent rule-making authority over public lands.

       (B) The rule is issued pursuant to a valid exercise of Congress's power to delegate rule-making authority to federal agencies.

       (C) The rule is justified by a compelling governmental interest in safeguarding forest resources.

       (D) The rule relates directly to law enforcement, which is an executive rather than legislative function, and hence it does not need specific congressional authorization.

       [Q7036]

       Answer: Choice **(B)** is correct. Congress can only delegate powers it possesses, so you first have to determine whether Congress itself has power to regulate federal lands. The answer is "yes," because Art. I, Sec. 8, Clause 17 gives Congress power to regulate federal lands. Next, you have to determine whether Congress validly delegated this power that it possesses. Here, too, the answer is "yes." Congress may delegate rule-making authority to federal agencies through statutes that set concrete objectives for the agency, and that list adequate criteria for carrying out those objectives. The Supreme Court has been very deferential in applying these "concrete objectives" and "adequate criteria" requirements. The objective being pursued here (control of campfires on federal lands) is quite concrete, and the criteria specified by Congress for achieving that objective (use of a penalty schedule for rule violators) seem quite adequate. Therefore, the statute's provision of authority to the Forest Service would likely be held to satisfy the requirements.

(A) is incorrect, because the executive branch does not have inherent rule-making authority over public lands. The only source of federal power to regulate public lands is the grant in Art. I, Sec. 8, Cl. 17, to *Congress* to regulate such lands, as discussed above. So the executive's rule-making authority over public lands comes from delegation by Congress, not from any inherent authority.

(C) is wrong because the compelling nature of the government's regulatory interest is neither necessary nor sufficient to justify the Forest Service's regulation. The constitutional requirement is merely that the regulation be pursuant to a valid act of Congress, and that it not violate any specific constitutional prohibition. Since the act is a valid exercise of Congress's power to regulate federal lands, and since the delegation was validly done (as described in (B) above), that's the end of the matter, and the strength of the federal interest never becomes relevant.

(D) is wrong because, although law enforcement is an executive function, the constitutional exercise of that function requires that the executive act pursuant to congressional authorization provided by law.

5. **Presidential Commissions:**

    Question: The vaccination of children against childhood contagious diseases (such as measles, diphtheria, and whooping cough) has traditionally been a function of private doctors and local and state health departments. Because vaccination rates have declined in recent years, especially in urban areas, the President proposes to appoint a Presidential Advisory Commission on Vaccination which would be charged with conducting a national publicity campaign to encourage vaccination as a public health measure. No federal statute authorizes or prohibits this action by the President. The activities of the Presidential Advisory Commission on Vaccination would be financed entirely from funds appropriated by Congress to the Office of the President for "such other purposes as the President may think appropriate."

    May the President constitutionally create such a commission for this purpose?

    (A) Yes, because the President has plenary authority to provide for the health, safety, and welfare of the people of the United States.

    (B) Yes, because this action is within the scope of executive authority vested in the President by the Constitution, and no federal statute prohibits it.

    (C) No, because the protection of children against common diseases by vaccination is a traditional state function and, therefore, is reserved to the states by the Tenth Amendment.

    (D) No, because Congress has not specifically authorized the creation and support of such a new federal agency.

    [Q3109]

    Answer: Choice **(B)** is correct. The setting up of a presidential advisory commission, such as the one here, falls within the President's executive powers — nothing in the facts indicates that the commission will have legislative or judicial powers, so the commission is a proper delegation by the President of his executive power. As to funding: Congress has the right to earmark specified federal monies to be spent as the President shall determine. Therefore, nothing about this arrangement violates any constitutional provision.

(A) is wrong, because the President does *not* have "plenary power to provide for the health, safety, and welfare of the people..." For instance, the President does not have power to spend federal money for what he determines to be the health needs of "the people." This answer ignores both the source of the President's authority (which is limited to the executive power, that is, the power to see that the laws are carried out) and the need for all funding to be appropriated by Congress.

(C) is wrong because it incorrectly states the effect of the Tenth Amendment. The Tenth Amendment states that the powers not delegated to the federal government by the Constitution, and not prohibited to the states, are reserved to the states. The Tenth Amendment has relatively little force today as a limit on federal power. (About the only force it has as a limit on federal powers is to prevent Congress from directly forcing the states to enact or enforce federal policies.) The Amendment does not mean that the federal government may not exercise power over a "traditional state function." So the fact that vaccination has traditionally been a function handled by the states does not mean that the Tenth Amendment bars the federal government from taking action with respect to vaccinations.

(D) is wrong, because Congress does not need to authorize the creation of a temporary commission. An Advisory Commission on Vaccination is not a new federal agency — it is an advisory group, set up for a specific purpose and having a temporary existence. The President does not need congressional approval to create such an organization. Nor has Congress prohibited its creation (which if it had happened might bar creation of the Commission), because as the facts state no federal statute authorizes or prohibits this action.

6. **Appointment and removal of executive personnel:**

   b. **Congress can't appoint federal executives:**

      Question: A federal statute with inseverable provisions established a new five-member National Prosperity Board with broad regulatory powers over the operation of the securities, banking, and commodities industries, including the power to issue rules with the force of law. The statute provides for three of the board members to be appointed by the President with the advice and consent of the Senate. They serve seven-year terms and are removable only for good cause. The other two members of the board were designated in the statute to be the respective general counsel of the Senate and House of Representatives Committees on Government Operations. The statute stipulated that they were to serve on the board for as long as they continued in those positions.

      Following all required administrative procedures, the board issued an elaborate set of rules regulating the operations of all banks, securities dealers, and commodities brokers. The Green Light Securities Company, which was subject to the board's rules, sought a declaratory judgment that the rules were invalid because the statute establishing the board was unconstitutional.

      In this case, the court should rule that the statute establishing the National Prosperity Board is

      (A) unconstitutional, because all members of federal boards having broad powers that are quasi-legislative in nature, such as rulemaking, must be appointed by Congress.

      (B) unconstitutional, because all members of federal boards exercising executive powers must be appointed by the President or in a manner otherwise consistent with the appointments clause of Article II.

      (C) constitutional, because the necessary and proper clause authorizes Congress to determine the means by which members are appointed to boards created by Congress under its power to regulate commerce among the states.

(D) constitutional, because there is a substantial nexus between the power of Congress to legislate for the general welfare and the means specified by Congress in this statute for the appointment of board members.

[Q3084]

Answer: The correct choice is **(B)**, because Congress cannot constitutionally designate two members of this board. Under the Appointments Clause, the President, not Congress, is given the power to appoint federal officers. So Congress itself may not make any appointments of federal officials who exercise executive power. The statute here endowed the board with broad rule-making powers. In *Buckley v. Valeo* (1976), the Court held that rule-making is an executive function, so that the members of a board or agency with rule-making powers are federal officers who must be appointed by the President. So here, the fact that two of the board's five members are directly designated by Congress violates the Appointments Clause.

(A) is wrong because the powers here are not "quasi-legislative." Congress may make its own appointments of persons to exercise powers that are essentially of an investigative or informative nature — such powers would be "quasi-legislative." But where the appointee's powers are essentially rule-making rather than investigative, this is an executive function, not a legislative function. Consequently, as described in Choice (B) above, it is the President, not Congress, that has the right of appointment. So this choice is correct that the statute is unconstitutional on account of separation-of-powers problems, but incorrect about what those problems are.

(C) is wrong because although the Necessary and Proper Clause gives the Congress the power to create the board, it does not give Congress the power to appoint the board's members. It's true that where Congress is exercising one of its enumerated powers, it may enact any law which is "necessary and proper for carrying into execution" that power. So Congress can regulate the securities and banking industries pursuant to its commerce power, and it can enact laws to carry out that regulation. But as explained in the discussion of Choice (B), the Appointments Clause means that the power to appoint members of the board (who are exercising rulemaking authority and are thus "federal officers") falls to the President under the Appointments Clause. Nothing in the Necessary and Proper Clause overcomes this Appointments-Clause problem.

(D) is wrong because (1) it ignores the Appointments-Clause problem described in the discussion of Choice (B); and (2) it falsely indicates that Congress has a free-standing power to pass laws that are for the "general welfare." As to (1), the Appointments Clause, as interpreted by the Court, means that "Officers of the United States" must be appointed by the President, not Congress. The board members here are exercising rule-making powers, which makes them executive-branch members (i.e., "federal officers), so the fact that two of them are appointed by Congress violates this Clause. As to (2), the General Welfare clause, Article 1, §8, states that Congress shall have the power to lay and collect taxes, to pay debts and to provide for the common defense and the general welfare. This clause gives Congress the substantive power to tax and appropriate money. But it does not confer on Congress a free-standing power to regulate to achieve the general welfare. So Congress's General Welfare power is irrelevant to the constitutionality of the regulatory statute here.

Chapter 4
TWO LIMITS ON STATE POWER: THE DORMANT COMMERCE CLAUSE AND CONGRESSIONAL ACTION

I. THE DORMANT COMMERCE CLAUSE

A. Dormant Commerce Clause generally:

3. **Two things to look out for:**

    a. **Protectionism:**

    Question: A toy manufacturer that has its headquarters and sole manufacturing plant in the state of Green developed a "Martian" toy that simulates the exploration of Mars by a remote-controlled vehicle. It accurately depicts the Martian landscape and the unmanned exploratory vehicle traversing it. The toy is of high quality, safe, durable, and has sold very well. Other toy manufacturers, all located outside Green, developed similar toys that are lower in price. These manufacturers have contracts to sell their Martian toys to outlets in Green. Although these toys are safe and durable, they depict the Martian landscape less realistically than the toys manufactured in Green. Nevertheless, because of the price difference, sales of these toys have cut severely into the sales of the Martian toys manufactured in Green. The Green legislature subsequently enacted a law "to protect the children of Green from faulty science and to protect Green toy manufacturers from unfair competition." This law forbids the sale in Green of any toy that purports to represent extraterrestrial objects and does not satisfy specified scientific criteria. The Martian toy manufactured in Green satisfies all of these criteria; none of the Martian toys of the competing manufacturers meets the requirements.

    Is the Green law constitutional?

    A) No, because it abrogates the obligations of the contracts between the other toy manufacturers and their Green outlets who have agreed to sell their Martian toys.

    (B) No, because it imposes an undue burden on interstate commerce.

    (C) Yes, because it deals only with a local matter, the sale of toys in Green stores.

    (D) Yes, because the state's interest in protecting the state's children from faulty science justifies this burden on interstate commerce.

    [Q7008]

    Answer: Choice **(B)** is correct. The Commerce Clause gives Congress the power to regulate commerce among the states and, by negative implication, restricts the regulatory power of the states with respect to interstate commerce. Any state law that has a substantial effect on interstate commerce must not be protectionist (i.e., must not benefit in-state interests at the expense of out-of-state interests) or otherwise impose an undue burden on interstate commerce. A state law that discriminates against interstate commerce is protectionist unless it serves a legitimate local interest that cannot be served by nondiscriminatory legislation. By barring the sale in Green of the Martian toys manufactured in other states, the state law here has a substantial negative effect on interstate commerce. Although the law does not explicitly discriminate against the out-of-state toy manufacturers, it has a purely discriminatory effect against them, and the state has less discriminatory alternatives available to protect the legitimate interests cited in the law (e.g., better public education about the nonsensicality of extraterrestrialism). The state law therefore violates the negative implications of the Commerce Clause.

(A) is wrong because, while it is true that the Green law is unconstitutional, this answer misstates the basis for this conclusion. The contracts clause (Article I, Section 10, Clause 1 of the Constitution) does not forbid state laws affecting contractual relations between private parties so long as they are reasonably related to a legitimate state interest. Because the courts typically defer to state regulations of private contracts as reasonable, the statute at issue here is not likely to be found unconstitutional under the contracts clause.

(C) is wrong because the fact that the matter being regulated is arguably a "local matter" is not a defense to a dormant Commerce Clause claim, if the state's form of regulation discriminates against out-of-state producers. So the fact that education is arguably a "local" state matter won't protect the obviously-protectionist statute here.

(D) is wrong because it is not a defense to protectionist legislation (i.e., legislation that intends to protect in-state economic interests at the expense of out-of-staters, or has that clear effect) that the state is also attempting to achieve some otherwise-permissible state objective. So here, although the state's interest in protecting children from faulty science is legitimate, that interest does not justify the law's intentional discrimination against out-of-staters where the state has less discriminatory alternatives available to protect that interest (e.g., better science education).

Question: Small retailers located in the state of Yellow were concerned about the loss of business to certain large retailers located nearby in bordering states. In an effort to deal with this concern, the legislature of Yellow enacted a statute requiring all manufacturers and wholesalers who sell goods to retailers in Yellow to do so at prices that are no higher than the lowest prices at which they sell them to retailers in any of the states that border Yellow. Several manufacturers and wholesalers who are located in states bordering Yellow and who sell their goods to retailers in those states and in Yellow bring an action in federal court to challenge the constitutionality of this statute.

Which of the following arguments offered by these plaintiffs is likely to be most persuasive in light of applicable precedent?

The state statute

(A) deprives them of their property or liberty without due process of law.

(B) imposes an unreasonable burden on interstate commerce.

(C) deprives them of a privilege or immunity of national citizenship.

(D) denies them the equal protection of the laws.

[Q1190]

Answer: Choice **(B)** is correct. This is a classic case of protectionism: the in-state retailers have persuaded the legislature to strengthen the in-staters' economic position vis-à-vis out-of-state retailers (since small in-state retailers now get an advantage that small out-of-state retailers don't get, and get an unearned cost-equality with large out-of-state retailers). So out-of-state retailers are being discriminated against (treated less favorably by virtue of their out-of-state status). This sort of protectionism is virtually a per se violation of the dormant commerce clause, and is certainly an undue burden on commerce.

(A) is wrong because economic regulation that does not involve a suspect class or fundamental right (and the regulation here involves neither) will receive only mere-rationality review under the Due Process Clause, and the measure here would pass that review.

(C) is wrong because the privileges and immunities of "national" (as opposed to state) citizenship are guaranteed by the Fourteenth Amendment, Sec. 1; that P&I Clause would not protect the plaintiffs because only a few rights have been recognized as rights of national citizenship for purposes of the clause (e.g., the right to travel physically from state to state, to move from state to state, and to vote in national elections), and the right of an out-of-stater to be free of economic discrimination is not one of them. (The plaintiffs might win with an argument based on Art. *IV*'s P&I Clause, which protects against discrimination by a state against out-of-staters; however, that clause doesn't protect the rights of "national citizenship," but rather, the rights of state citizenship.)

(D) is wrong because economic regulations that do not involve a suspect or semi-suspect class or fundamental right receive only easy-to-satisfy mere-rationality review under the equal protection clause, and the statute here would pass that review (since the legislature could reasonably have believed that its citizens would fare better, overall, if small local retailers were not at a disadvantage to large out-of-state retailers).

4. **Lack of uniformity:**

    a. **Converse:**

    Question: In recent years, several large corporations incorporated and headquartered in State A have suddenly been acquired by out-of-state corporations that have moved all of their operations out of State A. Other corporations incorporated and headquartered in State A have successfully resisted such attempts at acquisition by out-of-state corporations, but they have suffered severe economic injury during those acquisition attempts.

    In an effort to preserve jobs in State A and to protect its domestic corporations against their sudden acquisition by out-of-state purchasers, the legislature of State A enacts a statute governing acquisitions of shares in all corporations incorporated in State A. This statute requires that any acquisition of more than 25% of the voting shares of a corporation incorporated in State A that occurs over a period of less than one year must be approved by the holders of record of a majority of the shares of the corporation as of the day before the commencement of the acquisition of those shares. The statute expressly applies to acquisitions of State A corporations by both in-state and out-of-state entities.

    Assume that no federal statute applies.

    Is this statute of State A constitutional?

    (A) No, because one of the purposes of the statute is to prevent out-of-state entities from acquiring corporations incorporated and headquartered in State A.

    (B) No, because the effect of the statute will necessarily be to hinder the acquisition of State A corporations by other corporations, many of whose shareholders are not residents of State A and, therefore, it will adversely affect the interstate sale of securities.

    (C) Yes, because the statute imposes the same burden on both in-state and out-of-state entities wishing to acquire a State A corporation, it regulates only the acquisition of State A corporations, and it does not create an impermissible risk of inconsistent regulation on this subject by different states.

    (D) Yes, because corporations exist only by virtue of state law and, therefore, the negative implications of the commerce clause do not apply to state regulations governing their creation and acquisition.
    [Q3092]

    Answer: The correct choice is **(C)**, because State A's statute does not violate the dormant Commerce Clause, in that it neither unduly burdens, nor intentionally discriminates against, out-of-state economic interests. Under the dormant Commerce Clause, a regulation will be valid if it: (1) does not intentionally discriminate against out-of-state competition to benefit local economic interests; and (2) it is not unduly burdensome, in that the incidental burden on interstate commerce does not outweigh the legitimate local benefits produced by the regulation. The statute here is constitutional because it passes both tests. As to the first test: although the statute seeks to benefit local economic interests, it does not discriminate against out-of-state competition in the method it employs to protect domestic corporations. That is so because the statute, by requiring that any acquisition of more than 25% of the voting shares of a corporation incorporated in State A be approved by the holders of record of a majority of the corporation, imposes exactly the same burden on both in-state and out-of-state entities wishing to acquire a State A corporation.

The second requirement is that the regulation not be "unduly burdensome" to interstate commerce. The State A statute regulates only the acquisition of State A corporations, and there is no obvious large burden on out-of-staters that want to acquire in-state corporations. Since only corporations incorporated in State A are covered by the statute, one important form of undue burden — the inconsistent state-by-state regulation of a corporation incorporated in another state — does not occur. Thus the second prong of the test is satisfied.

The act here is similar to one upheld by the Court against Commerce Clause attack in *CTS Corp. v. Dynamics Corp. of Amer.* (1987) (statute making it harder to acquire a corporation incorporated in the state upheld because, "to the limited extent that the Act affects interstate commerce, this is justified by the State's interests in defining the attributes of shares in its corporations and in protecting shareholders").

(A) is wrong because dormant Commerce Clause attacks generally won't succeed unless the plaintiff shows either a discriminatory intent (less-favored treatment of out-of-staters than in-staters) or an "undue burden" on commerce. (See the discussion of Choice (C) above.) The mere fact that one of the regulation's purposes is to prevent out-of-staters from doing something unsatisfactory won't be enough, if in-staters are also prevented (since then there is no discrimination).

(B) is wrong because the presence of an "adverse effect" on an interstate market does not suffice for a violation of the dormant commerce clause. As is discussed more fully in the treatment of Choice (C) above, a plaintiff in a dormant commerce clause case must generally show either discrimination against interstate commerce, or a "substantial burden" on it. (B), by making the test be whether there is any sort of "adverse effect" at all, is not the right test.

(D) is wrong because it's an incorrect statement about what the dormant commerce clause prohibits. It's true that corporations exist only by virtue of state law. It's also true that a state probably has greater freedom in how it regulates its own domestic (i.e., state-chartered) corporations than in some other areas of regulation. But an anti-takeover statute, even if applied only to state-chartered targets, would still violate the dormant commerce clause if it *discriminated against* — i.e., treated less favorably — out-of-state acquirers than in-state acquirers (for instance, by requiring a higher percentage of target stockholders to approve an out-of-state takeover than a domestic takeover). So when (D) says that the "negative implications of the commerce clause" (an accurate way to refer to the dormant commerce clause) "do not apply to state regulations governing [domestic corporations'] creation and acquisition," the choice is not stating the law correctly.

8. **Discrimination against foreign commerce:**

    Question: In response to massive layoffs of employees of automobile assembly plants located in the state of Ames, the legislature of that state enacted a statute which prohibits the parking of automobiles manufactured outside of the United States in any parking lot or parking structure that is owned or operated by the state or any of its instrumentalities. This statute does not apply to parking on public streets.

Which of the following is the strongest argument with which to challenge the constitutionality of this statute?

(A) The statute imposes an undue burden on foreign commerce.

(B) The statute denies the owners of foreign-made automobiles the equal protection of the laws.

(C) The statute deprives the owners of foreign-made automobiles of liberty or property without due process of law.

(D) The statute is inconsistent with the privileges and immunities clause of the Fourteenth Amendment.

[Q2069]

Answer: The correct choice is **(A)**. Ames is making foreign cars materially less attractive to Ames residents, so residents are likely to buy fewer of them. Therefore, Ames is discriminating against foreign imports and in favor of U.S.-made cars. Since such a rule would clearly be held to be an undue burden on "domestic" interstate commerce if it were applied to the parking of cars made in U.S. states other than Ames, it will found to be an undue burden here, since restraints on foreign commerce are if anything scrutinized more strictly than restraints on domestic interstate commerce.

(B) is wrong because this is an economic regulation not involving a suspect class or fundamental right (there's no fundamental right to park in state-operated parking facilities), so it will be upheld as long as it's rationally related to achievement of a legitimate state objective; the measure here would meet this easy-to-satisfy test, since it's at least rational to believe that making it harder to park will cut down on the number of foreign cars sold in Ames and thus make in-state-produced cars more economically viable.

(C) is wrong, because (1) it's not clear that a person has *any* liberty or property interest in being able to park in a state-owned facility; and (2) even if there is such an interest, the interest is not "fundamental" (parking in state-owned facilities has not been held to be a fundamental right for due process purposes — only some privacy/autonomy-related rights have this status), so the measure would merely need to satisfy the easy rational-relation test, which it does.

(D) is wrong because the Fourteenth Amendment P&I Clause protects only the rights of "national citizenship," and the right to park in a state-owned facility is certainly not a right of national citizenship.

B. **State taxation of interstate commerce:**

1. **Discrimination:**

   a. **Tax favoring local components:**

   Question: Central City in the state of Green is a center for businesses that assemble personal computers. Components for these computers are manufactured elsewhere in Green and in other states, then shipped to Central City, where the computers are assembled. An ordinance of Central City imposes a special license tax on all of the many companies engaged in the business of assembling computers in that city. The tax payable by each such company is a percentage of the company's gross receipts.

   The Green statute that authorizes municipalities to impose this license tax has a "Green content" provision. To comply with this provision of state law, the Central City license tax ordinance provides that the tax paid by any assembler of computers subject to this tax ordinance will be reduced by a percentage equal to the proportion of computer components manufactured in Green.

The plaintiff is a company that assembles computers in Central City and sells them from its offices in Central City to buyers throughout the United States. All of the components of its computers come from outside the state of Green. Therefore, the plaintiff must pay the Central City license tax in full without receiving any refund. Other Central City computer assemblers use components manufactured in Green in varying proportions and, therefore, are entitled to partial reductions of their Central City license tax payments.

Following prescribed procedure, the plaintiff brings an action in a proper court asking to have Central City's special license tax declared unconstitutional on the grounds that it is inconsistent with the negative implications of the commerce clause.

In this case, the court should rule

(A) against the plaintiff, because the tax falls only on companies resident in Central City and, therefore, does not discriminate against or otherwise adversely affect interstate commerce.

(B) against the plaintiff, because the commerce clause does not interfere with the right of a state to foster and support businesses located within its borders by encouraging its residents to purchase the products of those businesses.

(C) for the plaintiff, because any tax on a company engaged in interstate commerce, measured in whole or in part by its gross receipts, is a per se violation of the negative implications of the commerce clause.

(D) for the plaintiff, because the tax improperly discriminates against interstate commerce by treating in-state products more favorably than out-of-state products.

[Q3114]

Answer: Choice **(D)** is correct. When a state or local government uses its taxing powers (just as when it regulates), the state violates the dormant Commerce Clause if the tax: (1) intentionally discriminates against (i.e., treats less favorably) out-of-state competition to the benefit of local economic interests; or (2) unduly burdens interstate commerce. By reducing the amount of taxes paid by assemblers of computers in an amount equal to the portion of computer components manufactured in Green, Central City is discriminating against out-of-state component-makers to benefit local component-makers (the in-state makers get an effective price advantage). This discrimination causes the tax measure to violate test (1) above.

(A) is not the best response, because the ordinance has the effect of making parts manufactured outside of Green more expensive. It is true that the tax directly falls only on companies resident in Central City. But the *effect* of the tax is to make components manufactured in Green less expensive than those manufactured outside of Green, making this intentional discrimination against out-of-staters, even though the out-of-staters aren't being directly taxed.

(B) is not the best response, because the dormant Commerce Clause *does* place some limits on a state's right to foster resident corporations. Although a state may sometimes foster local businesses by encouraging its residents to "buy local," some methods of encouragement violate the dormant Commerce Clause. Where a state uses its tax system to confer a direct financial benefit to those who buy locally-manufactured goods, at the expense of out-of-state makers, the state crosses the line into forbidden "economic protectionism," and violates the dormant Commerce Clause. That's what the tax here does.

(C) is not the best response, because taxes based on gross receipts are not a per se violation of dormant Commerce Clause principles. Some tax schemes violate the dormant Commerce Clause because they either discriminate against, or unduly burden, interstate commerce. But the mere fact that a tax is "measured in whole or in part by [the taxpayer's] gross receipts" does not automatically mean that either forbidden discrimination or an undue burden on commerce is present. It's true that if a state enacted a tax on a multi-state taxpayer's gross receipts, and made no distinction between receipts from in-state activities and those from out-of-state activities, that tax might well be found to be an undue burden on commerce, and thus a violation of the dormant Commerce Clause. But Choice (C) goes way beyond this principle, and doesn't tie in to the problem with the tax here (which is that it intentionally discriminates against out-of-state component makers).

II. CONGRESSIONAL PRE-EMPTION AND CONSENT; THE SUPREMACY CLAUSE

B. **The Supremacy Clause and federal pre-emption:**

1. **Direct conflict:**

b. **Congress forbids, state allows:**

Question: Congressional hearings determined that the use of mechanical power hammers is very dangerous to the persons using them and to persons in the vicinity of the persons using them. As a result, Congress enacted a statute prohibiting the use of mechanical power hammers on all construction projects in the United States. Subsequently, a study conducted by a private research firm concluded that nails driven by mechanical power hammers have longer-lasting joining power than hand-driven nails. After learning about this study, the city council of the city of Green enacted an amendment to its building safety code requiring the use of mechanical power hammers in the construction of all buildings intended for human habitation.

This amendment to the city of Green's building safety code is

(A) unconstitutional, because it was enacted subsequent to the federal statute.

(B) unconstitutional, because it conflicts with the provisions of the federal statute.

(C) constitutional, because the federal statute does not expressly indicate that it supersedes inconsistent state or local laws.

(D) constitutional, because the long-term safety of human habitations justifies some additional risk to the people engaged in their construction.

[Q1016]

Answer: The correct choice is **(B)**. This is a relatively easy case in which Congress is forbidding action X (use of mechanical power hammers) and the state is purporting to allow that very same action X. So this is about as simple a case of preemption by operation of the Supremacy Clause as could be imagined.

(A) is wrong because where federal and state rules conflict, the Supremacy Clause causes the state regulation to be invalid even if it was enacted subsequent to the federal rule.

(C) is wrong because state rules that directly conflict with federal rules are invalid even though the federal pronouncement does not expressly indicate that it supersedes inconsistent state or local laws.

(D) is wrong because whether or not a state regulation might represent a better balance of risk and reward than a directly-conflicting federal regulation, the state law must yield on account of the Supremacy Clause.

c. **Conflict between aims:**

Question: The United States Department of the Interior granted the plaintiff the food and drink concession in a federal park located in the state of Purple. The plaintiff operated his concession out of federally owned facilities in the park. The federal statute authorizing the Interior Department to grant such concessions provided that the grantees would pay only a nominal rental for use of these federal facilities because of the great benefit their concessions would provide to the people of the United States.

The legislature of the state of Purple enacted a statute imposing an occupancy tax on the occupants of real estate within that state that is not subject to state real estate taxes. The statute was intended to equalize the state tax burden on such occupants with that on people occupying real estate that is subject to state real estate taxes. Pursuant to that statute, the Purple Department of Revenue attempted to collect the state occupancy tax from the plaintiff because the federal facilities occupied by the plaintiff were not subject to state real estate taxes. The plaintiff sued to invalidate the state occupancy tax as applied to him.

The strongest ground upon which the plaintiff could challenge the occupancy tax is that it violates the

(A) commerce clause by unduly burdening the interstate tourist trade.

(B) privileges and immunities clause of the Fourteenth Amendment by interfering with the fundamental right to do business on federal property.

(C) equal protection of the laws clause of the Fourteenth Amendment because the tax treats him less favorably than federal concessionaires in other states who do not have to pay such occupancy taxes.

(D) supremacy clause of Article VI and the federal statute authorizing such concessions.

[Q2150]

Answer: Choice **(D)** is correct. The federal concession statute, by requiring a nominal rental on account of the great public benefit from concessions, shows a federal intent to keep the total occupancy costs for concessionaires low. The state occupancy tax has the effect (and purpose) of making occupancy costs higher for the affected taxpayers than it would otherwise be. This fact is coupled with the fact that the state is singling out taxpayers on non-state-taxed property, including federally-owned property, so the interference with federal interests is especially acute. Therefore, a court might well hold that the state law so undermines the federal purposes as to be invalid under the Supremacy Clause. The court would not *necessarily* reach this conclusion, but this is the most powerful of the four arguments.

(A) is wrong because the occupancy tax does not discriminate against interstate commerce (since the effect on tourists from inside Purple is the same as on out-of-state tourists), and it is unlikely that subjecting the plaintiff to the same overall level of overall taxation as businesses located in state-taxable facilities would be found to be an "undue burden."

(B) is wrong because the Fourteenth Amendment's Privileges and Immunities Clause protects only certain very limited rights of "national citizenship" (mostly the right to travel from state to state), and the Clause has never been interpreted to protect a "fundamental right to do business on federal property." (It's true that the P&I Clause of Art. *IV* protects the fundamental right to pursue one's business or profession, but the examiners have tried to trick you here by using the Fourteenth Amendment's P&I Clause, not the Art. IV Clause.)

(C) is wrong because the Fourteenth Amendment Equal Protection Clause protects only against a given state's unfair classification of multiple persons, not against one state's treating a person less favorably than other states treat similarly-situated persons. (Also, any classification being done by Purple here does not involve a suspect or semi-suspect class or a fundamental right, so the classification merely has to be rationally related to the achievement of a legitimate state objective, and the occupancy tax here meets this easy-to-satisfy standard.)

Question: Road Lines is an interstate bus company operating in a five-state area. A federal statute authorizes the Interstate Commerce Commission (ICC) to permit interstate carriers to discontinue entirely any unprofitable route. Road Lines applied to the ICC for permission to drop a very unprofitable route through the sparsely populated Shaley Mountains. The ICC granted that permission even though Road Lines provided the only public transportation into the region.

Foley is the owner of a mountain resort in the Shaley Mountains, whose customers usually arrived on vehicles operated by Road Lines. After exhausting all available federal administrative remedies, Foley filed suit against Road Lines in the trial court of the state in which the Shaley Mountains are located to enjoin the discontinuance by Road Lines of its service to that area. Foley alleged that the discontinuance of service by Road Lines would violate a statute of that state prohibiting common carriers of persons from abandoning service to communities having no alternate form of public transportation.

The state court should

(A) dismiss the action, because Foley lacks standing to sue.

(B) direct the removal of the case to federal court, because this suit involves a substantial federal question.

(C) hear the case on its merits and decide for Foley because, on these facts, a federal agency is interfering with essential state functions.

(D) hear the case on its merits and decide for Road Lines, because a valid federal law preempts the state statute on which Foley relies.

[Q1008]

Answer: The correct choice is **(D)**. There is a *direct conflict* between the federal and state regulations in this case, and it is impossible for the regulated party (Road Lines) to obey both regulations simultaneously. That is, the ICC has expressly permitted Road Lines to drop its route, and the state statute appears to prohibit Road Lines from dropping the route. Since the federal action is constitutional (it falls within Congress's commerce power), under the supremacy clause the federal action preempts the state action.

(A) is wrong, because Foley *does* have standing. It's true that the ICC, in taking the challenged action (letting Road Lines drop the service), was not intending to affect Foley and probably was not even aware of Foley's interest in the matter. But since Foley would suffer imminent and concrete economic harm from the challenged action, and since the injury he would suffer will be at least somewhat different from that suffered by every local resident, Foley has standing even though the challenged action was not directed at him.

(B) is incorrect because the state court does not have power to order a removal to the federal courts. There is no process by which a state court judge (rather than the defendant) can compel a pending state-court case to be removed to the federal courts. And that's true whether the case falls within the state court's jurisdiction or not. So the case will not be removed unless the defendant takes action to remove it.

(C) is wrong because (1) there is probably no constitutional rule that prevents the federal government from interfering with any "essential state function"; and (2) even if there were such a rule, it's highly unlikely that such an interference is happening here (since the federal government is merely allowing a private party to do something, not, for instance, ordering the state to change or eliminate any state function).

2. Congressional pre-emption:

a. Federal occupation of field:

i. State common law:

Question: Lee contracted with Mover, an interstate carrier, to ship household goods from the state of Green to his new home in the state of Pink. A federal statute provides that all liability of an interstate mover to a shipper for loss of or damage to the shipper's goods in transit is governed exclusively by the contract between them. The statute also requires the mover to offer a shipper at least two contracts with different levels of liability. In full compliance with that federal statute, Mover offered Lee a choice between two shipping agreements that provided different levels of liability on the part of Mover. The more expensive contract provided that Mover was fully liable in case of loss or damage. The less expensive contract limited Mover's liability in case of loss or damage to less than full value. Lee voluntarily signed the less expensive contract with Mover, fixing Mover's liability at less than the full value of the shipment.

Mover's truck was involved in an accident in the state of Pink. The accident was entirely a product of the negligence of Mover's driver. Lee's household goods were totally destroyed. In accordance with the contract, Mover reimbursed Lee for less than the full value of the goods. Lee then brought suit against Mover under the tort law of the state of Pink claiming that he was entitled to be reimbursed for the full value of the goods. Mover filed a motion to dismiss.

In this suit, the court should

(A) dismiss the case, because the federal statute governing liability of interstate carriers is the supreme law of the land and preempts state tort law.

(B) dismiss the case, because the contractual relationship between Lee and Mover is governed by the obligation of contracts clause of the Constitution.

(C) deny the motion to dismiss, because the full faith and credit clause of the Constitution requires that state tort law be given effect.

(D) deny the motion to dismiss, because it is unconstitutional for a federal statute to authorize Mover to contract out of any degree of liability for its own negligence.

[Q1136]

Answer: Choice **(A)** is correct. When Congress passed the statute saying that all liability of interstate movers would be "governed exclusively" by the contract between the two parties, this manifested Congress's intent to preempt the entire field of regulation of liability of such movers, and to block any non-contract form of recovery (such as recovery in tort). If Lee were permitted to recover under Pink tort law, the results would be at odds with this clear congressional intent to occupy the field. This is, therefore, a classic illustration of the supremacy of federal law over conflicting state law.

(B) is wrong because (in part) the obligation-of-contracts clause blocks the *states* from modifying contracts in some circumstances, and does not serve as any kind of a limit on when *Congress* may modify contracts. (Also, no contract is being modified here, so even if the state had said by statute what Congress said here, there would be no obligation-of-contracts problem.)

(C) is wrong, because (in part) the Full Faith and Credit Clause does not act as a limit on what Congress may do (and in any event no state is refusing to enforce another court's judgment, which is what the FF&C Clause requires states to do).

(D) is wrong because nothing in constitutional law prevents Congress from authorizing private parties to "contract out of ... liability for [their] own negligence," assuming Congress was acting pursuant to some enumerated power (such as, here, the power to regulate interstate commerce).

3. **No conflict:**

   a. **More stringent state regulations:**

   Question: Radon is a harmful gas found in the soil of certain regions of the United States. A statute of the state of Magenta requires occupants of residences with basements susceptible to the intrusion of radon to have their residences tested for the presence of radon and to take specified remedial steps if the test indicates the presence of radon above specified levels. The statute also provides that the testing for radon may be done only by testers licensed by a state agency. According to the statute, a firm may be licensed to test for radon only if it meets specified rigorous standards relating to the accuracy of its testing. These standards may easily be achieved with current technology; but the technology required to meet them is 50% more expensive than the technology required to measure radon accumulations in a slightly less accurate manner.

   The United States Environmental Protection Agency (EPA) does not license radon testers. However, a federal statute authorizes the EPA to advise on the accuracy of various methods of radon testing and to provide to the general public a list of testers that use methods it believes to be reasonably accurate.

   WeTest, a recently established Magenta firm, uses a testing method that the EPA has stated is reasonably accurate. WeTest is also included by the EPA on the list of testers using methods of testing it believes to be reasonably accurate. WeTest applies for a Magenta radon testing license, but its application is denied because WeTest cannot demonstrate that the method of testing for radon it uses is sufficiently accurate to meet the rigorous Magenta statutory standards. WeTest sues appropriate Magenta officials in federal court claiming that Magenta may not constitutionally exclude WeTest from performing the required radon tests in Magenta.

   In this suit, the court will probably rule in favor of

   (A) WeTest, because the full faith and credit clause of the Constitution requires Magenta to respect and give effect to the action of the EPA in including WeTest on its list of testers that use reasonably accurate methods.

   (B) WeTest, because the supremacy clause of the Constitution requires Magenta to respect and give effect to the action of the EPA in including WeTest on its list of testers that use reasonably accurate methods.

   (C) Magenta, because the federal statute and the action of the EPA in including WeTest on its list of testers that use reasonably accurate methods are not inconsistent with the more rigorous Magenta licensing requirement, and that requirement is reasonably related to a legitimate public interest.

(D) Magenta, because radon exposure is limited to basement areas, which, by their very nature, cannot move in interstate conmerce.

[Q2170]

Answer: The correct choice is **(C)**. The question, of course, is whether the federal regulation on radon detectors preempts the state regulation. The issue is always one of intent: if the federal government did not intend to preempt the state, or to occupy the entire field, then the state regulation will survive if it does not violate any independent constitutional prohibition. Here, there are strong clues that neither Congress nor the EPA intended to displace more-rigorous state regulation of radar detection: the federal government has not chosen to actually license radon testers, and the EPA is merely purporting to give useful information to the public, not to "regulate." Furthermore, it appears that a radon tester can comply simultaneously with both the federal "reasonably accurate" standard and the more-rigorous Magenta standard. All of this justifies the conclusion that the EPA's maintenance of its reasonably-accurate-methods list was not intended to displace more-rigorous state licensing standards.

Choice (A) is wrong because (among other reasons) the Full Faith and Credit Clause applies only to require a state to honor the statutes and judgments of *another state*, not those of the federal government. Choice (B) is wrong because, for the reasons described above, the EPA's list was not intended to displace or preempt more-rigorous state licensing methods, so the supremacy clause never came into action. Choice (D) is wrong because the fact that what is being regulated cannot "move in interstate commerce" does not dispose of the issue of whether federal regulation has preempted the state regulation. For instance, Congress could have (but did not) authorized the EPA to enact radon-testing regulations that would displace any more-stringent state regulation; in doing so Congress could have used its commerce power based on the fact that radon *detectors* move in or affect interstate commerce even though the basement areas being measured do not themselves move in interstate commerce.

C. Consent by Congress:

Question: A state legislature conducted an investigation into a series of fatal accidents in the state involving commercial trucks with trailer exteriors made of polished aluminum. The investigation revealed that the sun's glare off of these trucks blinded the drivers of other vehicles. The state's legislature then enacted a law prohibiting commercial trucks with polished aluminum trailer exteriors from traveling on the state's highways.

Litigation over the state law resulted in a final decision by the United States Supreme Court that the law impermissibly burdened interstate commerce and, therefore, was unconstitutional. Congress later enacted a statute permitting any state to enact a law regulating the degree of light reflectiveness of the exteriors of commercial trucks using the state's highways.

Is this federal statute constitutional?

(A) No, because the U.S. Supreme Court has already determined that state laws of this type impermissibly burden interstate commerce.

(B) No, because Article III vests the judicial power in the federal courts, the essence of judicial power is the ability to render a final judgment, and this statute overrules a final judgment of the federal Supreme Court.

(C) Yes, because Article I, Section 8 grants Congress authority to enact statutes authorizing states to impose burdens on interstate commerce that would otherwise be prohibited.

(D) Yes, because Article I, Section 8 grants Congress authority to enact statutes for the general welfare, and Congress could reasonably believe that state laws regulating the light reflectiveness of the exteriors of trucks promote the general welfare.

[QA047]

Answer: Choice **(C)** is correct. Congress has the power to consent to state conduct that would, in the absence of congressional consent, violate the dormant commerce clause. That's what has happened here. And the usual rule prohibiting Congress from enacting a statute overruling a constitutional decision of the U.S. Supreme Court does not apply here: Congress is not "overruling" the Court's judgment, it's simply changing the law for future cases, which is an action that is within the legislative power of Congress and that doesn't encroach on the Court's power to decide cases.

(A) is wrong because this is one area in which Congress may reverse the impact of prior Supreme Court decisions. In many areas of constitutional law (e.g., the meaning of the equal protection, due process and free speech guarantees), Congress does not have power to prospectively overrule decisions of the Supreme Court. But that is not true of the Court's decisions in some other areas. In particular, Congress has the power to authorize state conduct that would otherwise violate the dormant commerce clause, and the fact that the Supreme Court has already held that particular state conduct violates the dormant commerce clause does not negate this power.

(B) is wrong because it mischaracterizes what the statute did. The congressional statute permitting any state to regulate the degree of light reflectiveness of the exteriors of trucks using the state's highways did not overrule the U.S. Supreme Court's judgment. If the Court had, for example, awarded damages or attorney's fees to the prevailing party in that earlier suit, those awards would remain in effect after Congress enacted the statute, and Congress would not have had the power to reverse those litigant-specific outcomes. But here, Congress's statute simply changed the law for *future cases*, which is an action that is within the legislative power of Congress and that does not encroach on the Court's judicial power to decide cases within its jurisdiction.

(D) is wrong because it relies on a non-existent source of congressional power. While the Constitution gives Congress the power to *appropriate money* to promote the general welfare of the United States (i.e., to "tax and spend" for the general welfare), it does not give Congress the power generally to enact *regulatory*-type statutes on the basis that they promote the general welfare. Since there is no taxing or spending being done by the statute here, the concept of "general welfare" is irrelevant.

Question: A federal statute provides that the cities in which certain specified airports are located may regulate the rates and services of all limousines that serve those airports, without regard to the origin or destination of the passengers who use the limousines.

The cities of Redville and Greenville are located adjacent to each other in different states. The airport serving both of them is located in Redville and is one of those airports specified in the federal statute. The Redville City Council has adopted a rule that requires any limousines serving the airport to charge only the rates authorized by the Redville City Council.

Airline Limousine Service has a lucrative business transporting passengers between Greenville and the airport in Redville, at much lower rates than those required by the Redville City Council. It transports passengers in interstate traffic only; it does not provide local service within Redville. The new rule adopted by the Redville City Council will require Airline Limousine Service to charge the same rates as limousines operating only in Redville.

Must Airline Limousine Service comply with the new rule of the Redville City Council?

(A) Yes, because the airport is located in Redville and, therefore, its city council has exclusive regulatory authority over all transportation to and from the airport.

(B) Yes, because Congress has authorized this form of regulation by Redville and, therefore, removed any constitutional impediments to it that may have otherwise existed.

(C) No, because the rule would arbitrarily destroy a lucrative existing business and, therefore, would amount to a taking without just compensation.

(D) No, because Airline Limousine Service is engaged in interstate commerce and this rule is an undue burden on that commerce.

[Q3079]

Answer: The correct choice is **(B)**. The Redville rule, by requiring higher limo prices for interstate trips than would be set by the market, might well be an undue burden on interstate commerce (and thus a violation of the dormant Commerce Clause) if there were no federal legislation on the subject. But Congress has the power to allow state regulation that would otherwise violate the dormant Commerce Clause, and that's what happened here: Congress gave the city containing the airport the right to set limo rates without respect to the rates' effect on commerce, so there is no dormant Commerce Clause problem.

(A) is wrong because it incorrectly explains the correct result. If Congress had not specifically allowed the city in which any specified airport is located to regulate limos serving that city, Redville would be acting unconstitutionally by burdening interstate commerce. That is, as a general principle it is not correct to say that a city has exclusive regulatory authority over all transportation to and from an airport located within the city. (Under the dormant commerce clause, no city or state may intentionally discriminate against, or unduly burden, interstate commerce, even if that commerce relates to a facility located within the city or state that's doing the regulating.) Only the special congressional authorization validates the Redville regulation.

(C) is wrong because what Redville is doing here is regulating, not "taking." Only if a regulation destroys all economic value of a business will it be deemed to be a Fifth Amendment "taking" for which compensation must be paid. And there's no evidence here that the regulation here will destroy all economic value of the plaintiff's business. Furthermore, even in the exceptionally unlikely event that a court would conclude that there had been a taking, the proper remedy would be an order that Redville pay "just compensation," not a decree holding the regulation itself invalid.

(D) is wrong because Congress has authorized the regulation in question. If Congress had not expressly authorized the type of regulation at issue here (limo rates for airport traffic, imposed by the city where the airport is located), this choice would likely be correct, because the uniform-rate regulation probably would unduly burden (and discriminate against) out-of-state-based limo companies. But Congress always has the power to authorize what would otherwise be a violation of dormant-commerce-clause principles, and that's what it has done here.

Question: The United States Congress enacted a federal statute providing that any state may "require labeling to show the state or other geographic origin of citrus fruit that is imported into the receiving state." Pursuant to the federal statute, a state that produced large quantities of citrus fruit enacted a law requiring all citrus fruit imported into the state to be stamped with a two-letter postal abbreviation signifying the state of the fruit's origin. The law did not impose any such requirement for citrus fruit grown within the state. When it adopted the law, the state legislature declared that its purpose was to reduce the risks of infection of local citrus crops by itinerant diseases that have been found to attack citrus fruit. A national association of citrus growers sued to have the state law declared unconstitutional. The association claims that the law is prohibited by the negative implications of the commerce clause of the Constitution.

Which of the following is the best argument in favor of the state's effort to have this lawsuit dismissed?

(A) Any burden on interstate commerce imposed by the state law is outweighed by a legitimate state interest.

(B) Congress has the authority to authorize specified state regulations that would otherwise be prohibited by the negative implications of the commerce clause, and it has done so in this situation.

(C) The state law does not discriminate against out-of-state citrus growers or producers.

(D) The state law furthers a legitimate state interest, the burden it imposes on interstate commerce is only incidental, and the state's interest cannot be satisfied by other means that are less burdensome to interstate commerce.

[Q7084]

Answer: Choice **(B)** is correct. In the absence of congressional action, the state rule here probably would be a violation of the dormant Commerce Clause (what the question calls the "negative implications of the commerce clause"), because it discriminates against out-of-state growers. But Congress may use its commerce power to permit states to discriminate against interstate commerce. The federal statute here explicitly authorizes states to enact state-of-origin labeling requirements on imported citrus fruit.

(A) is incorrect, because the balancing argument would work only if: (1) Congress had not enacted a statute authorizing the state regulation at issue; and (2) the state law did not discriminate against interstate commerce. In this case, however, neither of these conditions is satisfied: Congress *has* authorized state-of-origin labeling requirements on imported citrus fruit, and the state law *is* discriminatory.

(C) is incorrect, because the state law *does* discriminate against out-of-state citrus growers, in that the law requires that all citrus fruit "imported" into the state be stamped with the state of origin, while the law imposes no such requirement on citrus fruit grown within the state.

(D) is incorrect, because although this argument correctly paraphrases the burden on the state to justify a law that discriminates against interstate commerce, the argument would be less likely to succeed than the "Congress authorized it" argument: in the absence of congressional authorization, the burden on a state to justify its discriminatory regulation is a heavy one, and states only rarely succeed in carrying it. Here, the availability of less-discriminatory alternatives (e.g., requiring in-state growers, not just out-of-staters, to stamp the state's two-letter code on the fruit) makes it unlikely that the state would win with this argument.

CHAPTER 5

INTERGOVERNMENTAL IMMUNITIES; INTERSTATE RELATIONS

I. TAX AND REGULATORY IMMUNITIES

A. **Several types of immunities:**

  1. **Federal immunity from state taxation:**

a. **"Legal incidence" standard:**

i. **Tax on private contractors:**

Question: The childhood home of a former U.S. president is part of a national park located in a city. The National Park Service entered into a contract with an independent antique collector to acquire items owned by residents of the city during the president's lifetime. According to the contract, the collector purchases items and then sells them to the Park Service at a price equal to the collector's cost plus a 10% commission. Purchases by antique collectors are ordinarily subject to the sales tax of the state in which the city is located. The collector files suit in state court to enjoin collection of the tax on these purchases, claiming that the sales tax is unconstitutional as applied to them.

Should the state court issue the injunction?

(A) No, because as the purchaser of these antiques, the collector rather than the federal government is liable for the tax.

(B) No, because the suit is within the exclusive jurisdiction of the federal courts.

(C) Yes, because the federal government is contractually obligated to pay the amount of the sales tax when it covers the collector's cost of these antiques.

(D) Yes, because under the supremacy clause, the federal program to acquire these antiques preempts the state sales tax on the purchase of these items.

[Q7073]

Answer: Choice **(A)** is correct. The federal government has immunity from taxation by the states. But the immunity applies only where the legal incidence of the tax (not just the economic impact of the tax) is on the federal government. Here, the legal incidence of the state sales tax on the collector's purchases of antiques is on the collector, who is independent of the National Park Service. The fact that the federal government ends up paying an extra amount, under the cost-plus-commission arrangement, that exactly matches the tax on the collector, is irrelevant.

(B) is wrong because, while this answer correctly states that the court should not issue the injunction, it misstates the legal basis for that conclusion. State courts generally have concurrent jurisdiction with federal courts over cases arising under federal law, and no exception to that general rule is presented on these facts.

(C) is wrong because the incidence of the state sales tax on the collector's purchases of antiques is on the collector, who is independent of the National Park Service. The fact that the collector passes the cost of the tax on to a federal agency when the collector sells an item to the agency does not change the fact that the incidence of the tax is on the collector's purchase. And the rule is that federal immunity from state taxation applies only where the legal incidence of the tax (not just the economic impact of the tax) is on the federal government. Accordingly, the court should not issue an injunction.

(D) is wrong because there is no indication in the facts that the sales tax on the collector's purchases conflicts with any federal law governing the Park Service's program.

3. **Federal immunity from state regulation:**

a. **Applies to generally-applicable rules:**

Question: A federally owned and operated office building in the state of Red is heated with a new, pollution-free heating system. However, in the coldest season of the year, this new system is sometimes insufficient to supply adequate heat to the building. The appropriation statute providing the money for construction of the new heating system permitted use of the old, pollution-generating system when necessary to supply additional heat. When the old heating system operates (only about two days in any year), the smokestack of the building emits smoke that exceeds the state of Red's pollution-control standards.

May the operators of the federal office building be prosecuted successfully by Red authorities for violating that state's pollution control standards?

(A) Yes, because the regulation of pollution is a legitimate state police power concern.

(B) Yes, because the regulation of pollution is a joint concern of the federal government and the state and, therefore, both of them may regulate conduct causing pollution.

(C) No, because the operations of the federal government are immune from state regulation in the absence of federal consent.

(D) No, because the violations of the state pollution-control standards involved here are so *de minimis* that they are beyond the legitimate reach of state law.

[Q1195]

Answer: Choice **(C)** is correct. The operations of the federal government are indeed immune from state regulation, no matter how reasonable the state regulation, and even though the regulation is a generally-applicable one that treats the federal government no differently than anyone else. Since the office building is owned by and operated by the federal government, this regulatory immunity applies.

(A) is wrong, because even though the regulation of pollution may be a legitimate state police power concern, that regulation must give way to federal regulatory immunity.

(B) is wrong because, even if regulation of pollution is a joint concern of the federal and state governments, and even though both governments can regulate private parties (assuming that the state regulation is not inconsistent with the federal regulation), it does not follow that the state can regulate the federal government — under the principles of regulatory immunity, the state cannot do so.

(D) is wrong because there is no "de minimis" exception to the principle that states may regulate pursuant to their inherent police power. (The sole problem here is the federal immunity from regulation, which applies whether the asserted violation of the state's regulation is de minimis or not.)

Question: The United States Department of Energy regularly transports nuclear materials through Centerville on the way to a nuclear weapons processing plant it operates in a nearby state. The city of Centerville recently adopted an ordinance prohibiting the transportation of any nuclear materials in or through the city. The ordinance declares that its purpose is to protect the health and safety of the residents of that city.

May the Department of Energy continue to transport these nuclear materials through the city of Centerville?

(A) No, because the ordinance is rationally related to the public health and safety of Centerville residents.

(B) No, because the Tenth Amendment reserves to the states certain unenumerated sovereign powers.

(C) Yes, because the Department of Energy is a federal agency engaged in a lawful federal function and, therefore, its activities may not be regulated by a local government without the consent of Congress.

(D) Yes, because the ordinance enacted by Centerville is invalid because it denies persons transporting such materials the equal protection of the laws.

[Q2049]

Answer: Choice **(C)** is correct — the federal government, including the operations of federal agencies, are essentially immune from state regulation. Notice that the answer does not use the word "immunity" — it's up to you to recognize that when the choice says "may not be regulated," what's being referred to is the concept of immunity.

(A) is incorrect, because of federal immunity; note that if there were no federal immunity involved (e.g., the entity being regulated was a private company pursuing its own interests), this choice would be correct, at least if the regulation were challenged on equal protection grounds.

(B) is wrong because the Tenth Amendment has no relevance here. The Tenth Amendment does not restrict the powers of the federal government as long as the latter is not purporting to require the state to enact laws or regulations. Here, the Dept. of Energy isn't requiring the state to enact a federal regulatory program — the DOE is merely pursuing its own regulatory program. And the Tenth Amendment doesn't limit DOE's ability to do that.

(D) is wrong because the equal protection clause would not invalidate this ordinance. The ordinance is an economic regulation, and clearly satisfies the applicable rational-basis test (see the discussion of Choice (A) above). It's only federal immunity from state regulation that causes the ordinance not to be enforceable against the DOE's activities.

II. THE INTERSTATE PRIVILEGES AND IMMUNITIES CLAUSE

A. **Interstate Privileges and Immunities:**

1. **Standard:**

   a. **What rights are fundamental:**

   Question: A doctor, a resident of the city of Greenville in the state of Green, is a physician licensed to practice in both Green and the neighboring state of Red. The doctor finds that the most convenient place to treat her patients who need hospital care is in the publicly owned and operated municipal hospital of the city of Redville in the state of Red, which is located just across the state line from Greenville. For many years the doctor had successfully treated her patients in that hospital. Early this year she was notified that she could no longer treat patients in the Redville hospital because she was not a resident of Red, and a newly adopted rule of the Redville hospital, which was adopted in conformance with all required procedures, stated that every physician who practices in that hospital must be a resident of Red.

   Which of the following constitutional provisions would be most helpful to the doctor in an action to challenge her exclusion from the Redville hospital solely on the basis of this hospital rule?

   (A) The bill of attainder clause.

   (B) The privileges and immunities clause of Article IV.

   (C) The due process clause of the Fourteenth Amendment.

   (D) The ex post facto clause.

   [Q3190]

Answer: Choice **(B)** is correct. When a state (or subdivision of a state, like a city and its municipally-owned operations) regulates a right that is "fundamental to national unity," and does so in a way that disadvantages out-of-staters, that regulation will essentially be subject to strict scrutiny under the Art. IV Privileges and Immunities Clause. (Among other things, the state must show that the discrimination against non-residents bears a "substantial relationship" to the problem the state is attempting to solve.) Practice of one's business or profession is a right "fundamental to national unity" for P&I purposes.

The case here is on all fours with *New Hampshire v. Piper* (1985), where the Court held that New Hampshire's attempt to restrict the right to practice law to state residents violated the Art. IV P&I Clause. Applying *Piper*, since there's no showing that out-of-state doctors are the peculiar source of any special problem that the hospital is trying to solve, the restriction violates the P&I Clause.

(By the way, there's no exception under the P&I Clause for activities in which the city or state is a "market participant," as there is under the dormant Commerce Clause. *United Bldg. and Constr. Trades Counc. v. Camden* (1984). So the fact that the city owns the hospital that's making the rule doesn't help it, as it would against a Commerce Clause attack.)

(A) is wrong because the legislature of state Red was not trying to punish the doctor. A bill of attainder is a legislative act that attempts to inflict punishment without a judicial trial upon individuals who are designated by name or in terms of past conduct. The constitutional prohibition against a bill of attainder would not be helpful to the doctor because the hospital here merely took the purely regulatory action of changing the residency requirement for practicing medicine at the hospital — no public entity named the doctor as a criminal, or attempted to punish or stigmatize him, which is what a bill of attainder would have done.

(C) is wrong because the doctor would have to show that the licensing requirement was not rationally related to a legitimate government interest, a showing the doctor probably couldn't make. The Due Process Clause of the Fourteenth Amendment provides that no state shall make or enforce any law which shall deprive any person of life, liberty, or property, without due process of law. When a fundamental right is not involved, substantive due process requires only that a law be "rationally related" to the achievement of a "legitimate government interest." So to win on due process, the doctor would have to prove that Red's new residency requirement was not rationally related to some legitimate government purpose. This standard is very lenient and easy-to-satisfy. Here, for instance, the hospital could plausibly claim that it wants to have on staff only doctors who live very nearby, and that it's entitled to use state of residence as a proxy for nearby-ness. Although the fit between means and end isn't very tight under this rationale, it's almost certainly tight enough to meet the extremely lenient rational-relation standard.

(D) is wrong because state Red was not legislating against past acts. The Ex Post Facto clauses, Article I, § 9 and § 10, prohibit both the federal government and the state, respectively, from passing legislation that retroactively alters the criminal law as to offenses or punishments, in a substantially prejudicial manner. A retroactive change in civil regulations, such as licensing requirements, cannot violate the prohibition, since the prohibition applies only to "penal," i.e., punitive, measures. Here, the facts make it clear that the hospital was not making a rule penalizing past acts, but merely affecting civil relationships (the woman's right to practice at the hospital).

2. **Only protects non-residents:**

   Question: The United States government demonstrated that terrorist attacks involving commercial airliners were perpetrated exclusively by individuals of one particular race. In response, Congress enacted a statute imposing stringent new airport and airline security measures only on individuals of that race seeking to board airplanes in the United States.

Which of the following provides the best ground for challenging the constitutionality of this statute?

(A) The commerce clause of Article I, Section 8.

(B) The due process clause of the Fifth Amendment.

(C) The privileges and immunities clause of Article IV.

(D) The privileges or immunities clause of the Fourteenth Amendment.

[QA041]

Answer: Choice **(C)** is **incorrect** because the privileges and immunities clause of Article IV prohibits only actions by states that improperly discriminate against the citizens of other states. The clause does not apply to actions of the federal government. (For an analysis of all choices, see *infra*, p. 280.)

Question: Congressional committees heard testimony from present and former holders of licenses issued by state vocational licensing boards. According to the testimony, the boards had unfairly manipulated their disciplinary proceedings in order to revoke the licenses of some license holders as a means of protecting favored licensees from competition.

In response, Congress enacted a statute prescribing detailed procedural requirements for the disciplinary proceedings of all state vocational licensing boards. For example, the statute required the state boards to provide licensees with adequate notice and opportunity for an adjudicatory hearing in all disciplinary proceedings. The statute also prescribed criteria for the membership of all state vocational licensing boards that were designed to ensure that the boards were likely to be neutral.

Which of the following provides the best source of authority for this federal statute?

(A) Section 5 of the Fourteenth Amendment.

(B) The general welfare clause of Article I, Section 8.

(C) The privileges and immunities clause of Article IV, Section 2.

(D) The takings clause of the Fifth Amendment.

[QA043]

Answer: Choice (C) is **incorrect** because the privileges and immunities clause of Article IV, Section 2 prohibits actions by states that improperly discriminate against the citizens of other states. The clause does not apply to actions of the federal government. (For an analysis of all choices, see *infra*, p. 294.)

III. THE FULL FAITH AND CREDIT CLAUSE

A. **How tested on MBE:**

    2. **Effect of Clause:**

        a. **Collection of money judgments:**

        Question: The state of Red sent three of its employees to a city located in the state of Blue to consult with a chemical laboratory there about matters of state business. While in the course of their employment, the three employees of Red negligently released into local

Blue waterways some of the chemical samples they had received from the laboratory in Blue.

Persons in Blue injured by the release of the chemicals sued the three Red state employees and the state of Red in Blue state courts for the damages they suffered. After a trial in which all of the defendants admitted jurisdiction of the Blue state court and fully participated, plaintiffs received a judgment against all of the defendants for $5 million, which became final.

Subsequently, plaintiffs sought to enforce their Blue state court judgment by commencing a proper proceeding in an appropriate court of Red. In that enforcement proceeding, the state of Red argued, as it had done unsuccessfully in the earlier action in Blue state court, that its liability is limited by a law of Red to $100,000 in any tort case. Because the three individual employees of Red are able to pay only $50,000 of the judgment, the only way the injured persons can fully satisfy their Blue state court judgment is from the funds of the state of Red.

Can the injured persons recover the full balance of their Blue state court judgment from the state of Red in the enforcement proceeding they filed in a court of Red?

(A) Yes, because the final judgment of the Blue court is entitled to full faith and credit in the courts of Red.

(B) Yes, because a limitation on damage awards against Red for tortious actions of its agents would violate the equal protection clause of the Fourteenth Amendment.

(C) No, because the Tenth Amendment preserves the right of a state to have its courts enforce the state's public policy limiting its tort liability.

(D) No, because the employees of Red were negligent and, therefore, their actions were not authorized by the state of Red.

[Q3151]

Answer: Choice **(A)** is correct. The Blue court issued a valid judgment against the plaintiffs. Therefore, the Red state court was required by the Full Faith and Credit Clause to enforce that judgment, even though the only solvent defendant in the Blue proceeding is the state of Red itself. The constitutional requirement of Full Faith and Credit does not recognize any exception just because the state in which enforcement is sought happens to itself be the defendant against which the original judgment was issued. (By the way, it's important that all the defendants admitted jurisdiction in the original Blue proceedings — if the Blue courts had not had jurisdiction, the defendants could make a "collateral attack" on the original judgment in Red court, and Full Faith and Credit would not have applied.)

(B) is wrong because it gives an incorrect reason for the current result. A state may, without violating the equal protection clause, cap (or even abolish entirely) its liability for torts by its employees or agents. The correct reason Red must pay the judgment is as given in (A).

(C) is wrong because (1) although a state does, as a general rule, have the right to enforce a public policy limiting its tort liability, this right does not derive from the Tenth Amendment; and (2) in any event, a state's obligation to enforce an out-of-state judgment under the Full Faith and Credit clause takes priority over the state's own public policy, at least where the out-of-state judgment came after all defendants had a full and fair opportunity to litigate in a court that had jurisdiction over them.

(D) is wrong because the Red courts must enforce the Blue court's judgment, regardless of whether a Red court would have reached the same conclusion on the merits as the Blue court did about whether Red as employer is liable for these torts by its agents.

b. **First state's error of law:**

Question: A man bought an antique car from a car dealer in State A. Under State A law, a person who buys from such a dealer acquires good title, even if the property was stolen from a previous owner. The man showed the car at an antique car show in State B. A woman recognized the car as having been stolen from her. Under State B law, a person whose property is stolen may reclaim it, even if the current possessor is an innocent purchaser. The woman sued the man in a State B court to reclaim the car. The man defended, claiming that he had good title under the law of State A. Nevertheless, the State B court applied State B law, and the woman prevailed. The man did not appeal. The sheriff gave the woman possession of the car. Several months later, the woman drove the car to State A. The man brought a new suit against the woman, claiming that the State B court in the prior suit should have applied the State A law, which protected innocent purchasers. The woman appeared and moved to dismiss the suit.

What should the State A court do?

(A) Apply the federal law of sale of goods, because the car has moved in interstate commerce.

(B) Apply the State A law, because the car is currently located in State A.

(C) Dismiss the suit, because the State A court must give full faith and credit to the State B judgment.

(D) Remove the case to federal court, because the car has moved in interstate commerce, and therefore the case raises a federal question.

[Q7051]

Answer: Choice **(C)** is correct. The Full Faith & Credit (FF&C) clause prohibits state courts from re-litigating cases in which the courts of another state have rendered final judgment. Even if the first court should have applied the second court's laws under standard conflict rules, the FF&C clause bars the second court from re-hearing the case. (If the State B courts had not had jurisdiction over the man, and the jurisdiction issue had not been litigated or waived, the FF&C clause might not bar the State A courts from hearing the new suit. But the facts tell us that the man "defended" on the merits, thus waiving any claim he might have had that the State B courts lacked jurisdiction over him.) Accordingly, the court in State A was required to dismiss the suit.

(A) is incorrect, because the FF&C clause prevents the court in State A from relitigating the merits, and the fact that the woman drove the car to State A has no effect on the constitutional analysis.

(B) is, similarly, wrong because the location of the car has no effect on the constitutional analysis.

(D) is wrong because the movement of the car across state lines did not create a federal question.

CHAPTER 6
THE DUE PROCESS CLAUSE

III. SUBSTANTIVE DUE PROCESS — ECONOMIC AND SOCIAL WELFARE REGULATION

C. Economic and social-welfare regulation:

2. Easy to satisfy:

Question: A state statute requires each insurance company that offers burglary insurance policies in the state to charge a uniform rate for such insurance to all of its customers residing within the same county in that state. So long as it complies with this requirement, a company is free to charge whatever rate the market will bear for its burglary insurance policies.

An insurance company located in the state files suit in federal district court against appropriate state officials to challenge this statute on constitutional grounds. The insurance company wishes to charge customers residing within the same county in the state rates for burglary insurance policies that will vary because they would be based on the specific nature of the customer's business, on its precise location, and on its past claims record.

In this suit, the court should

(A) hold the statute unconstitutional, because the statute deprives the insurance company of its liberty or property without due process of law.

(B) hold the statute unconstitutional, because the statute imposes an undue burden on interstate commerce.

(C) hold the statute constitutional, because the statute is a reasonable exercise of the state's police power.

(D) abstain from ruling on the merits of this case until the state courts have had an opportunity to pass on the constitutionality of this state statute.

[Q2008]

Answer: Choice **(C)** is correct. This is a classic illustration of a state regulation in the economic or social-welfare area, where no fundamental right is involved. (Insurers don't have a fundamental right to adopt any particular pricing mechanism.) Since the "one price for all" scheme is rationally related to achieving one or more legitimate state objectives (e.g., promoting a sense of fairness and non-discrimination among insurance customers living in a particular county, or avoiding race-based redlining), the scheme does not violate the insurer's due process rights.

(A) is wrong for the same reason (C) is right — the company may have a due process right not to be irrationally deprived of its desired pricing mechanism, but the requirement of uniform pricing here is not irrational.

(B) is wrong, because the statute does not unduly burden interstate commerce (it only applies to policies written in-state, and it does not discriminate against out-of-state insurers).

(D) is wrong because federal courts do not have a duty to abstain from passing on the case until the state courts have had an opportunity to pass on the constitutionality of this state statute. When a litigant believes that a state statute violates the federal constitution, the litigant may sue immediately in federal court for a determination that this is so, as long as the requirements of justiciability (e.g., ripeness, actual injury to the plaintiff, etc.) are met. In other words, there is no sense in which state courts get "first shot" to determine the federal constitutionality of a state statute.

IV. SUBSTANTIVE DUE PROCESS — REGULATIONS AFFECTING FUNDAMENTAL RIGHTS

C. Abortion:

3. Consent:

b. **Parental consent:**

   ii. **Emancipation or maturity:**

   Question: A state statute requires, without exception, that a woman under the age of 18 notify one of her parents at least 48 hours before having an abortion. A proper lawsuit challenges the constitutionality of this state statute.

   In that suit, should the court uphold the constitutionality of the statute?

   (A) No, because a 48-hour waiting period is excessively long and, therefore, it imposes an undue burden on a woman's right to procure an abortion.

   (B) No, because the state law does not provide a bypass procedure that would allow a court to authorize a minor to obtain an abortion without prior parental notification under appropriate circumstances.

   (C) Yes, because parents' rights to supervise their minor daughter's health care outweighs any individual right she may have.

   (D) Yes, because such parental notification and waiting-period requirements do not impose an undue burden on a minor's right to procure an abortion.

   [Q7056]

   Answer: Choice **(B)** is correct. The Supreme Court has held that parental notification requirements constitute an undue burden on the minor's right to abortion, and thus violate the minor's due substantive right to due process, unless there is a satisfactory judicial bypass procedure. Such a procedure must allow a court to approve an abortion for a minor without parental notification if the court finds either that: (1) the minor is sufficiently mature and informed to make an independent decision to obtain an abortion; or (2) the abortion would be in the minor's best interest. Because no such bypass procedure is included in the statute at issue, the court will hold the statute unconstitutional.

   (A) is wrong because although it is true that the statute at issue is unconstitutional, this answer misstates the basis for this conclusion — the Supreme Court has held that a short waiting period does not constitute an undue burden on a woman's right to an abortion.

   (C) is incorrect, because the rights of parents to supervise the health care of their minor children do not always prevail over the individual rights of their children — as discussed above, the Court has held that parental notification requirements violate a minor's right to an abortion unless there is a satisfactory judicial bypass procedure, which is not included in the statute at issue.

   (D) is incorrect, because the Court has held that parental notification requirements are an undue burden, and violate a minor's right to an abortion, unless there is a satisfactory judicial bypass procedure.

4. **Public funding:**

   Question: A state statute prohibits the use of state-owned or state-operated facilities for the performance of abortions that are not "necessary to save the life of the mother." That statute also prohibits state employees from performing any such abortions during the hours they are employed by the state.

   A woman was in her second month of pregnancy. She sought an abortion at a state-owned and state-operated hospital. The woman did not claim that the requested abortion was necessary to save her life. The officials in charge of the hospital refused to perform the requested abortion solely on the basis of the state statute. The woman immediately filed suit against those officials in an appropriate federal district court. She challenged the constitutionality of the state statute and requested the court to order the hospital to perform the abortion she sought. In this case, the court will probably hold that the state statute is

(A) unconstitutional, because a limit on the availability of abortions performed by state employees or in state-owned or state-operated facilities to situations in which it is necessary to save the life of the mother impermissibly interferes with the fundamental right of the woman to decide whether to have a child.

(B) unconstitutional, because it impermissibly discriminates against poor persons who cannot afford to pay for abortions in privately owned and operated facilities and against persons who live far away from privately owned and operated abortion clinics.

(C) constitutional, because it does not prohibit a woman from having an abortion or penalize her for doing so, it is rationally related to the legitimate governmental goal of encouraging childbirth, and it does not unduly burden the voluntary performance of abortions by private physicians in private facilities.

(D) constitutional, because the use of state-owned or state-operated facilities and access to the services of state employees are privileges and not rights and, therefore, a state may condition them on any basis it chooses.

[Q2162]

Answer: Choice **(C)** is correct. The Court held in *Webster v. Reproductive Health Services* (1989) that a state could constitutionally forbid the use of all public facilities and publicly-employed staff in abortions, without thereby violating the substantive due process right to abortion. If the state forbade all facilities in the state — public or private — from performing abortions, that would be an unconstitutional "undue burden" on abortion, but the availability of private-facility abortions here prevents an undue burden from occurring. And the fact that the state here is allowing the use of public facilities for those abortions necessary to save the life of the mother makes it even more clear that the regulation is constitutional. (Probably under *Webster* such an exception is not even required.)

(A) is wrong because the Court has held (in *Webster*, supra) that the availability of private-facility abortions means that a ban on the use of public facilities does not impermissibly interfere with the right of abortion.

(B) is wrong because the Court has held (in *Harris v. McRae* (1980)) that government's refusal to fund abortions for patients who cannot afford them does not constitute an interference with the constitutionally-protected right to abortion.

(D) is wrong because the Court no longer uses the privilege/right distinction in deciding cases involving the exercise of the important constitutional interests, and it is certainly not the case that the state may condition access to public facilities for an abortion "on any basis it chooses." (For instance, the state could not say that it will fund abortions at state-owned facilities for white women but not black women.)

V. PROCEDURAL DUE PROCESS

A. Introduction:

1. Life, liberty or property:

Question: A city ordinance requires a taxicab operator's license to operate a taxicab in King City. The ordinance states that the sole criteria for the issuance of such a license are driving ability and knowledge of the geography of King City. An applicant is tested by the city for these qualifications with a detailed questionnaire, written and oral examinations, and a practical behind-the-wheel demonstration.

The ordinance does not limit the number of licenses that may be issued. It does, however, allow any citizen to file an objection to the issuance of a particular license, but only on the ground that an applicant does not possess the required qualifications. City licensing officials are also authorized by the ordinance to determine, in their discretion, whether to hold an evidentiary hearing on an objection before issuing a license.

Sandy applies for a taxicab operator's license and is found to be fully qualified after completing the usual licensing process. Her name is then posted as a prospective licensee, subject only to the objection process. John, a licensed taxicab driver, files an objection to the issuance of such a license to Sandy solely on the ground that the grant of a license to Sandy would impair the value of John's existing license. John demands a hearing before a license is issued to Sandy so that he may have an opportunity to prove his claim. City licensing officials refuse to hold such a hearing, and they issue a license to Sandy. John petitions for review of this action by city officials in an appropriate court, alleging that the Constitution requires city licensing officials to grant his request for a hearing before issuing a license to Sandy.

In this case, the court should rule for

(A) John, because the due process clause of the Fourteenth Amendment requires all persons whose property may be adversely affected by governmental action to be given an opportunity for a hearing before such action occurs.

(B) John, because the determination of whether to hold a hearing may not constitutionally be left to the discretion of the same officials whose action is being challenged.

(C) city officials, because John had the benefit of the licensing ordinance and, therefore, may not now question actions taken under it.

(D) city officials, because the licensing ordinance does not give John any property interest in being free of competition from additional licensees.

[Q3058]

Answer: The correct choice is **(D)**, because there is no right to a hearing unless one has been deprived of liberty or property, and John hasn't been so deprived. A person who is affected by governmental action doesn't thereby automatically get the right to a hearing. Instead, only those whose "property" or "liberty" are being affected have the right to due process (and even then, these due process rights won't necessarily entail the right to a formal hearing). Here, nothing the city has ever done has created in John a property interest in being free of additional taxi competition. Indeed, the facts demonstrate the contrary — there is no limit to the number of licenses that may be issued, and the only required qualifications are driving ability and geographic knowledge. So John has not been deprived of a property (or liberty) interest, and the court will never even reach the issue of what procedures (such as a hearing) were due to him — none were.

(A) is wrong because it is not a correct statement of who gets the protection of due process. For the reason stated in Choice (D) above, Choice (A) is exactly wrong about when the Due Process Clause applies — only those deprived of "property" or "liberty" by the government, not all those "adversely affected by government action," have a due process interest.

(B) is wrong because John never had a right to a hearing at all. For the reasons stated in Choice (D), John had no due process rights that were implicated here, and therefore had no right to a hearing. Thus the court would never reach the issue of who may decide whether he gets a hearing.

(C) is wrong because the fact that John once got the benefit of the ordinance has nothing to do with whether his due process rights have been violated here. The licensing ordinance might have been written in such a way that John would get a property interest in not having new competition. (For instance, this would probably be so if the ordinance set the number of licenses at a fixed total, and charged a substantial fee for each one.) In that event, John would be permitted to assert his due process claim even though he originally benefitted from the same ordinance. The reason John loses is because he had no property interest in being free from additional competition (see the discussion of Choice (D) above), not because he previously benefitted from the ordinance.

D. Process required:

2. Non-judicial proceeding:

Question: John is a licensed barber in State A. The State A barber licensing statute provides that the Barber Licensing Board may revoke a barber license if it finds that a licensee has used his or her business premises for an illegal purpose.

John was arrested by federal narcotics enforcement agents on a charge of selling cocaine in his barbershop in violation of federal laws. However, the local United States Attorney declined to prosecute and the charges were dropped.

Nevertheless, the Barber Licensing Board commenced a proceeding against John to revoke his license on the ground that John used his business premises for illegal sales of cocaine. At a subsequent hearing before the board, the only evidence against John was affidavits by unnamed informants, who were not present or available for cross-examination. Their affidavits stated that they purchased cocaine from John in his barbershop. Based solely on this evidence, the board found that John used his business premises for an illegal purpose and ordered his license revoked.

In a suit by John to have this revocation set aside, his best constitutional argument is that

(A) John's inability to cross-examine his accusers denied him a fair hearing and caused him to be deprived of his barber license without due process of law.

(B) the administrative license revocation proceeding was invalid, because it denied full faith and credit to the dismissal of the criminal charges by the United States Attorney.

(C) Article III requires a penalty of the kind imposed on John to be imposed by a court rather than an administrative agency.

(D) the existence of federal laws penalizing the illegal sale of cocaine preempts state action relating to drug trafficking of the kind involved in John's case.

[Q3148]

Answer: The correct choice is **(A)**, because John's barber license was "property," which the state could not take away from him without due process. Where a state-issued license is required to pursue a business or profession, a person who has already obtained the license normally has a "property" interest in that license for Fourteenth Amendment due process purposes. Consequently, that property may not be taken away without due process of law.

Precisely what procedural safeguards John is entitled to is not certain, but the more serious the threatened loss of property or liberty, the wider the array of procedural safeguards required. Here, the threatened loss (right to practice one's profession) is serious, so extensive safeguards ought to be given. Since the proceeding is analogous to a criminal trial — the Board is determining whether John used his premises to commit a crime — he's got a strong claim of entitlement to the sorts of procedures used in criminal trials, including the right to cross-examine his accusers. There's no guarantee that John would win with this due process argument, but it's clearly the most likely to succeed of the choices.

(B) is wrong because there was no final judgment here. Article IV, §1 states that Full Faith and Credit shall be given by each state to public acts and judicial proceedings of every other state. By extension of this principle, the states must give full faith and credit to federal proceedings as well. However, the decision by the local United States Attorney not to prosecute John was not a judicial decision deserving full faith and credit, because it was not the final outcome of a judicial proceeding. (The case was dropped, not decided, so there would be nothing to give full faith and credit to.)

(C) is wrong because Article III has nothing to do with state proceedings (it describes the federal judiciary's authority), and anyway this is not the sort of "penalty" that must be conferred by a court rather than an agency. Article III prescribes the judicial power of the United States, i.e., the limits of the power of the *federal* judiciary. It says nothing about how the states must exercise their judicial power. Since this is a state proceeding, Article III is irrelevant.

(D) is wrong because federal drug laws are not so extensive as to force aside state laws. Under the Supremacy Clause of Article IV, §2, even absent explicit language, Congress's intent to supersede state law altogether may be found from a scheme of federal regulation so pervasive as to make reasonable the inference that Congress left no room to supplement it. However, there's nothing in the facts here to suggest that when Congress made it a federal crime to sell cocaine, it intended to preempt the states from also criminalizing cocaine sales. (Indeed, as to virtually all federal drug crimes, the states have concurrent jurisdiction to criminalize the same conduct.) So the states would even be free to prosecute John for the state crime of cocaine selling. Beyond that, the state proceeding here is a non-penal civil proceeding, so it certainly wouldn't be preempted by the existence of a federal statute criminalizing the same conduct.

3. **Time for hearing:**

    Question: A state statute declares that after five years of continuous service in their positions all state employees, including faculty members at the state university, are entitled to retain their positions during "good behavior." The statute also contains a number of procedural provisions. Any state employee who is dismissed after that five-year period must be given reasons for the dismissal before it takes effect. In addition, such an employee must, upon request, be granted a post-dismissal hearing before an administrative board to seek reinstatement and back pay. The statute precludes any other hearing or opportunity to respond to the charges. That post-dismissal hearing must occur within six months after the dismissal takes effect. The burden of proof at such a hearing is on the state, and the board may uphold the dismissal only if it is supported by a preponderance of the evidence. An employee who is dissatisfied with a decision of the board after a hearing may appeal its decision to the state courts. The provisions of this statute are inseverable.

    A teacher who had been employed continuously for seven years as a faculty member at the state university was dismissed. A week before the dismissal took effect, she was informed that she was being dismissed because of a charge that she accepted a bribe from a student in return for raising the student's final grade in her course. At that time she requested an immediate hearing to contest the propriety of her dismissal.

    Three months after her dismissal, she was granted a hearing before the state administrative board. The board upheld her dismissal, finding that the charge against her was supported by a preponderance of the evidence presented at the hearing.

The faculty member did not appeal the decision of the state administrative board to the state courts. Instead, she sought a declaratory judgment in federal district court to the effect that the state statute prescribing the procedures for her dismissal is unconstitutional.

In this case, the federal district court should

(A) dismiss the suit, because a claim that a state statute is unconstitutional is not ripe for adjudication by a federal court until all judicial remedies in state courts provided for by state law have been exhausted.

(B) hold the statute unconstitutional, because the due process clause of the Fourteenth Amendment requires a state to demonstrate beyond a reasonable doubt the facts constituting good cause for termination of a state employee.

(C) hold the statute unconstitutional, because a state may not ordinarily deprive an employee of a property interest in a job without giving the employee an opportunity for some kind of predismissal hearing to respond to the charges against that employee.

(D) hold the statute constitutional, because the due process clause of the Fourteenth Amendment entitles state employees who have a right to their jobs during good behavior only to a statement of reasons for their dismissal and an opportunity for a post-dismissal hearing.

[Q1152]

Answer: Choice **(C)** is correct. Since the government had previously agreed that the teacher could only be fired if she were shown not to have had "good behavior," she had a due process "property" interest in maintaining her job. The Supreme Court has held that once a person has a property interest in a job or benefit, only the courts, not the government, may prescribe the procedures that are to be used to terminate that job or benefit. So the fact that the statute provides only for a post-discharge hearing does not mean that this is all the teacher is due. Instead, the Court has held that the job holder is entitled to a hearing before the termination (or at least before the termination of salary). *Cleveland Bd. of Ed. v. Loudermill* (1985). Since the statute here did not give the teacher such a pre-termination hearing, the statute was unconstitutional. And the statute did not get saved by the government's holding a hearing three months after the termination.

(A) is wrong because it is not true that a claim that a state statute is unconstitutional is not ripe until all state-court remedies have been exhausted. When a litigant believes that a state statute violates the federal constitution, the litigant may sue immediately in federal court for a determination that this is so, as long as the requirements of justiciability are met. And although it's true that one of the requirements of justiciability is that the case be "ripe," ripeness merely means that the plaintiff has already suffered, or imminently faces, actual injury.

(B) is wrong for at least two reasons: (1) not all state employees have the right not to be dismissed except for good cause (and this choice implies that all of them do); and (2) even if an employee such as the teacher here had a right not to be dismissed except for good cause, the burden of proof on the government would be just a preponderance-of-the-evidence standard, not the hard-to-satisfy "beyond a reasonable doubt" standard.

(D) is wrong because the Supreme Court has held that, where a state employee has a right to hold her job during good behavior, the employee is entitled not only to a pre-dismissal statement of reasons but a pre-dismissal hearing (and the fact that the statute provides only for a post-dismissal hearing does not change the constitutional requirement of a pre-dismissal one). Cf. *Loudermill, supra.*

CHAPTER 7
EQUAL PROTECTION

I. EQUAL PROTECTION GENERALLY

A. Text of clause:

2. State and federal:

Question: The United States government demonstrated that terrorist attacks involving commercial airliners were perpetrated exclusively by individuals of one particular race. In response, Congress enacted a statute imposing stringent new airport and airline security measures only on individuals of that race seeking to board airplanes in the United States.

Which of the following provides the best ground for challenging the constitutionality of this statute?

(A) The commerce clause of Article I, Section 8.

(B) The due process clause of the Fifth Amendment.

(C) The privileges and immunities clause of Article IV.

(D) The privileges or immunities clause of the Fourteenth Amendment.

[QA041]

Answer: Choice **(B)** is correct. What makes this question slightly challenging is that you're expecting a choice that uses the phrase "equal protection" (since the government is treating members of one race differently than those of other races). But the key is that the way equal protection principles apply to the federal government is via the *Fifth Amendment's Due Process Clause* — the Supreme Court held, in *Bolling v. Sharpe* (1954), that the equal protection principles of the Fourteenth Amendment apply to actions of the federal government through incorporation into the Due Process Clause of the Fifth Amendment. The new security measures presumptively violate equal protection because they contain a racial classification: the new measures apply only to individuals of one race. A court therefore would uphold the measures only if the government could prove that they are necessary to serve a compelling public interest, a standard that the government typically cannot meet and would be very unlikely to meet here. (For a full analysis of all choices, see *infra*, p. 280.)

a. Government action only:

Question: Congress wishes to enact legislation prohibiting discrimination in the sale or rental of housing on the basis of the affectional preference or sexual orientation of the potential purchaser or renter. Congress wishes this statute to apply to all public and private vendors and lessors of residential property in this country, with a few narrowly drawn exceptions.

The most credible argument for congressional authority to enact such a statute would be based upon the

(A) general welfare clause of Article I, Sec. 8, because the conduct the statute prohibits could reasonably be deemed to be harmful to the national interest.

(B) commerce clause of Article I, Sec. 8, because, in inseverable aggregates, the sale or rental of almost all housing in this country could reasonably be deemed to have a substantial effect on interstate commerce.

(C) enforcement clause of the Thirteenth Amendment, because that amendment clearly prohibits discrimination against the class of persons protected by this statute.

(D) enforcement clause of the Fourteenth Amendment, because that amendment prohibits all public and private actors from engaging in irrational discrimination.

[Q3170]

Answer: (D) is **incorrect**, because it is a misstatement of law, in that the Fourteenth Amendment does not prohibit private actors from engaging in discrimination (whether irrational or not). The Equal Protection clause of the Fourteenth Amendment bars discrimination when there is state action. When a purely private actor practices discrimination, Congress's Fourteenth Amendment § 5 remedial powers do not permit it to prohibit that discrimination. So although Congress could probably rely on its § 5 powers to prohibit public entities (states and cities, for instance) from discriminating on grounds of sexual orientation, it cannot do so with respect to purely private discrimination. See, e.g., *U.S. v. Morrison* (2000) (Congress can't use its Fourteenth Amendment § 5 powers to let victims of gender-motivated violent crimes sue in federal court.) (The correct answer is (B); see *supra*, p. 232.)

II. ECONOMIC AND SOCIAL LAWS — THE "MERE RATIONALITY" TEST

A. **Non-suspect, non-fundamental rights (economic and social legislation):**

1. **Mere rationality:**

    Question: In one state, certain kinds of advanced diagnostic medical technology were located only in hospitals, where they provided a major source of revenue. In many other states, such technology was also available at "diagnostic centers" that were not affiliated with hospitals.

    A group of physicians announced its plan to immediately open in the state a diagnostic center that would not be affiliated with a hospital. The state hospital association argued to the state legislature that only hospitals could reliably handle advanced medical technologies. The legislature then enacted a law prohibiting the operation in the state of diagnostic centers that were not affiliated with hospitals.

    The group of physicians filed suit challenging the constitutionality of the state law.

    What action should the court take?

    (A) Uphold the law, because the provision of medical services is traditionally a matter of legitimate local concern that states have unreviewable authority to regulate.

    (B) Uphold the law, because the legislature could rationally believe that diagnostic centers not affiliated with hospitals would be less reliable than hospitals.

    (C) Invalidate the law, because it imposes an undue burden on access to medical services in the state.

    (D) Dismiss the suit without reaching the merits, because the suit is not ripe.

    [QA066]

    Answer: Choice **(B)** is correct. First, notice that the plaintiff's best attack on the statute would be based on equal protection, since the state is classifying providers of advanced diagnostic technology by dividing them into ones that are hospital-based and ones that are not. In equal protection cases, the court uses heightened judicial scrutiny only where the classification either (1) is based on a suspect category (e.g., race or ethnicity) or a semi-suspect one (e.g., gender); or (2) burdens the exercise of a fundamental right (e.g., the right to vote). The classification here does not involve a suspect or semi-suspect class, nor does it burden the exercise of a fundamental right (since access to medical services has never been identified by the Supreme Court as a fundamental right for equal protection purposes). Therefore, this is a garden-variety economic or social-welfare classification scheme, and will be upheld as long as it is rationally related to achieving a legitimate governmental interest. That easy-to-pass standard is satisfied here, since the legislature's belief that diagnostic centers not affiliated with hospitals would be less reliable than hospitals is a rational belief, regardless of whether it is in fact a correct belief.

(A) is wrong because, even if the provision of medical services is traditionally a matter of legitimate local concern, states do not have "unreviewable authority" to regulate that area — state regulation is *always* subject to constitutional limits. The appropriate constitutional standard of review is whether the law is rationally related to a legitimate government interest, as described further in the discussion of Choice (B).

(C) is wrong because it applies an incorrect standard. The U.S. Supreme Court has not held access to medical services to be a fundamental right for equal protection (or any other) purposes. (If such access *were* a fundamental right, then the court would strictly scrutinize any substantial burden on that right.) Thus, even if the law unduly burdens such access, the court would not use heightened judicial scrutiny. The appropriate constitutional standard of review therefore is whether the law is rationally related to a legitimate government interest, as further discussed in Choice (B).

(D) is wrong because the suit *is* ripe. The suit is ripe because the facts state that the physicians' group has immediate plans to open a diagnostic center in the state; whenever the plaintiff is proposing an immediate course of action that would be rendered illegal by government regulation, an attack on the regulation's legality presents an immediate case or controversy, and is thus ripe for adjudication.

Question: A statute of the state of Texona prohibits any retailer of books, magazines, pictures, or posters from "publicly displaying or selling to any person any material that may be harmful to minors because of the violent or sexually explicit nature of its pictorial content." Violation of this statute is a misdemeanor.

Corner Store displays publicly and sells magazines containing violent and sexually explicit pictures. The owner of this store is prosecuted under the above statute for these actions.

In defending against this prosecution in a Texona trial court, the argument that would be the best defense for Corner Store is that the statute violates the

(A) First Amendment as it is incorporated into the Fourteenth Amendment, because the statute is excessively vague and overbroad.

(B) First Amendment as it is incorporated into the Fourteenth Amendment, because a state may not prohibit the sale of violent or sexually explicit material in the absence of proof that the material is utterly without any redeeming value in the marketplace of ideas.

(C) equal protection of the laws clause, because the statute irrationally treats violent and sexually explicit material that is pictorial differently from such material that is composed wholly of printed words.

(D) equal protection of the laws clause, because the statute irrationally distinguishes between violent and sexually explicit pictorial material that may harm minors and such material that may harm only adults.

[Q3199]

Answer: Choice **(C)** is **incorrect**, because the distinction between written and pictorial material would not be found to be wholly irrational. Where a statute treats two different classes of things or people in two different ways, unless a suspect class or fundamental right is involved, only a completely irrational classification will be found to violate equal protection. Here, is very unlikely that a court would agree that there's no rational relation between any legitimate legislative objective and the picture/text distinction. For instance, it would certainly be a legitimate legislative objective for a state to try to reduce the infliction of sexually-sadistic violence on women. And a court would be very unlikely to find that it is wholly irrational for the legislature to believe that sexually explicit or violent images may be more likely to spark sexually-sadistic violence than sexually explicit or violent words. (The correct answer is (A); see infra, p. 297.)

3. **"Grandfather clause" as rational classification:**

   Question: A city has had a severe traffic problem on its streets. As a result, it enacted an ordinance prohibiting all sales to the public of food or other items by persons selling directly from trucks, cars, or other vehicles located on city streets. The ordinance included an inseverable grandfather provision exempting from its prohibition vendors who, for 20 years or more, have continuously sold food or other items from such vehicles located on the streets of the city.

   A retail ice cream vendor qualifies for this exemption and is the only food vendor that does. A yogurt company is a business similar to the ice cream company, but the yogurt company has been selling to the public directly from trucks located on the streets of the city only for the past ten years. The yogurt company filed suit in an appropriate federal district court to enjoin enforcement of this ordinance on the ground that it denies the yogurt company the equal protection of the laws.

   In this case, the court will probably rule that the ordinance is

   (A) constitutional, because it is narrowly tailored to implement the city's compelling interest in reducing traffic congestion and, therefore, satisfies the strict scrutiny test applicable to such cases.

   (B) constitutional, because its validity is governed by the rational basis test, and the courts consistently defer to economic choices embodied in such legislation if they are even plausibly justifiable.

   (C) unconstitutional, because the nexus between the legitimate purpose of the ordinance and the conduct it prohibits is so tenuous and its provisions are so underinclusive that the ordinance fails to satisfy the substantial relationship test applicable to such cases.

   (D) unconstitutional, because economic benefits or burdens imposed by legislatures on the basis of grandfather provisions have consistently been declared invalid by courts as per se violations of the equal protection clause of the Fourteenth Amendment.

   [Q1021]

   Answer: Choice **(B)** is correct. The city here is engaging in economic regulation, and no suspect class or fundamental right is involved. The "even plausibly justifiable" standard is a good summary of the extreme deference that courts give to government choices in the economic-regulatory area where no suspect class or fundamental right is at issue. Grandfather schemes in which people with longtime track records of pursuing an activity are treated more favorably than newcomers to that activity are a good illustration of classifications that are very likely to be upheld.

(A) is wrong because it incorrectly applies strict scrutiny; strict scrutiny would be appropriate for a regulation that intentionally disfavored a suspect class (e.g., persons of a particular race) or substantially impaired a fundamental right (e.g., the right to vote), but the classification here does not do either of these things.

(C) is wrong because the grandfather scheme here would not be found to be so "tenuous" or "underinclusive" as to fail the easy-to-satisfy rational-basis test.

(D) is wrong as a statement of law; so long as no suspect class or fundamental right is impaired, grandfather clauses are usually found valid, and are certainly not "per se violations" of equal protection.

5. **Non-suspect classes:**

e. **Status as convicted criminal:**

Question: A city zoning ordinance requires anyone who proposes to operate a group home to obtain a special use permit from the city zoning board. The zoning ordinance defines a group home as a residence in which four or more unrelated adults reside. An individual applied for a special use permit to operate a group home for convicts during their transition from serving prison sentences to their release on parole. Although the proposed group home met all of the requirements for the special use permit, the zoning board denied the individual's application because of the nature of the proposed use. The individual sued the zoning board seeking declaratory and injunctive relief on constitutional grounds.

Which of the following best states the appropriate burden of persuasion in this action?

(A) Because housing is a fundamental right, the zoning board must demonstrate that denial of the permit is necessary to serve a compelling state interest.

(B) Because the zoning board's action has the effect of discriminating against a quasi-suspect class in regard to a basic subsistence right, the zoning board must demonstrate that the denial of the permit is substantially related to an important state interest.

(C) Because the zoning board's action invidiously discriminates against a suspect class, the zoning board must demonstrate that denial of the permit is necessary to serve a compelling state interest.

(D) Because the zoning board's action is in the nature of an economic or social welfare regulation, the individual seeking the permit must demonstrate that the denial of the permit is not rationally related to a legitimate state interest.

[Q7041]

Answer: Choice **(D)** is correct. Note that the only plausible ground for plaintiff's attack is the equal protection clause — government is saying that certain groups of four or more people can live together without a permit and others can't. Persons convicted of crimes have not been held to constitute either a suspect or a quasi-suspect class for equal protection purposes. Therefore, the zoning board's denial of the permit discriminated against neither a suspect class nor a quasi-suspect class. Nor did it unduly burden the exercise of a fundamental right (since housing has not been held to be a fundamental right for equal protection purposes). The denial therefore triggers rational basis scrutiny.

(A) is wrong because housing has been held not to be a fundamental right for equal protection purposes. *Lindsey v. Normet* (1972). Therefore, the strict scrutiny standard articulated in this choice would not be appropriate.

(B) is wrong because convicts have never been held to be a semi-suspect class. (The only semi-suspect class is recognized by the court to date are gender and illegitimacy.) Nor does housing have any special equal protection status as a "basic subsistence right." Therefore, the intermediate standard of review (which this choice correctly describes as the "substantially related to an important state interest" test) would not apply here.

(C) is wrong because convicts do not constitute a suspect class for equal protection purposes. Therefore, while this would be the correct test if the legislative classification involved a suspect class (e.g., race or national origin), it is not the correct test for this case.

III. SUSPECT CLASSIFICATIONS, ESPECIALLY RACE

A. Suspect classifications:

Question: The United States government demonstrated that terrorist attacks involving commercial airliners were perpetrated exclusively by individuals of one particular race. In response, Congress enacted a statute imposing stringent new airport and airline security measures only on individuals of that race seeking to board airplanes in the United States.

Which of the following provides the best ground for challenging the constitutionality of this statute?

(A) The commerce clause of Article I, Section 8.

(B) The due process clause of the Fifth Amendment.

(C) The privileges and immunities clause of Article IV.

(D) The privileges or immunities clause of the Fourteenth Amendment.

[QA041]

Answer: Choice **(B)** is correct. What makes this question slightly challenging is that you're expecting a choice that uses the phrase "equal protection" (since the government is treating members of one race differently than those of other races). But the key is that the way equal protection principles apply to the federal government is via the Fifth Amendment's Due Process Clause — the Supreme Court held, in *Bolling v. Sharpe* (1954), that the equal protection principles of the Fourteenth Amendment apply to actions of the federal government through incorporation into the Due Process Clause of the Fifth Amendment. The new security measures presumptively violate equal protection because they contain a racial classification: the new measures apply only to individuals of one race. A court therefore would uphold the measures only if the government could prove that they are necessary to serve a compelling public interest, a standard that the government typically cannot meet and would be very unlikely to meet here.

(A) is wrong because the statute here would be a proper exercise of the commerce power, if it did not violate the Due Process Clause. The commerce clause grants Congress plenary power to regulate the safety of air travel because airlines are instrumentalities of interstate commerce. (Instead, the problem is that the new security measures presumptively violate equal protection, as made applicable to the states via the Fifth Amendment's Due Process Clause. See Choice (B) for more details.)

(C) is wrong because the privileges and immunities clause of Article IV prohibits only actions by states that improperly discriminate against the citizens of other states. The clause does not apply to actions of the federal government.

(D) is wrong because the privileges or immunities clause of the Fourteenth Amendment prohibits *states* from depriving individuals of the privileges or immunities of United States citizenship. The U.S. Supreme Court has never applied the clause to actions of the federal government. (Furthermore, even where state rather than federal action is at issue, be skeptical of any choice that finds a governmental action unconstitutional on the grounds that it violates the Fourteenth Amendment P&I Clause. That clause protects only the privileges and immunities of "national citizenship." There are very few privileges and immunities of national citizenship, mainly the right to vote in national elections, the right to travel physically from state to state, and the right not to be discriminated against by virtue of one's having recently moved to the state from a different state.)

V. MIDDLE-LEVEL REVIEW (GENDER, ILLEGITIMACY AND ALIENAGE)

B. Gender:

Question: State Y has a state employee grievance system that requires any state employee who wishes to file a grievance against the state to submit that grievance for final resolution to a panel of three arbitrators chosen by the parties from a statewide board of 13 arbitrators. In any given case, the grievant and the state alternate in exercising the right of each party to eliminate five members of the board, leaving a panel of three members to decide their case. At the present time, the full board is composed of seven male arbitrators and six female arbitrators.

Ellen, a female state employee, filed a sexual harassment grievance against her male supervisor and the state. Anne, the state's attorney, exercised all of her five strikes to eliminate five of the female arbitrators. At the time she did so, Anne stated that she struck the five female arbitrators solely because she believed women, as a group, would necessarily be biased in favor of another woman who was claiming sexual harassment. Counsel for Ellen eliminated four males and one female arbitrator, all solely on grounds of specific bias or conflicts of interest. As a result, the panel was all male.

When the panel ruled against Ellen on the merits of her case, she filed an action in an appropriate state court, challenging the panel selection process as a gender-based denial of equal protection of the laws.

In this case, the court should hold that the panel selection process is

(A) unconstitutional, because the gender classification used by the state's attorney in this case does not satisfy the requirements of intermediate scrutiny.

(B) unconstitutional, because the gender classification used by the state's attorney in this case denies the grievant the right to a jury made up of her peers.

(C) constitutional, because the gender classification used by the state's attorney in this case satisfies the requirements of the strict scrutiny test.

(D) constitutional, because the gender classification used by the state's attorney in this case satisfies the requirements of the rational basis test.

[Q3180]

Answer: (A) is the best response, because peremptory challenges based on gender violate equal protection. Gender-based classifications are subject to intermediate scrutiny, which requires that the government show that the classification be substantially related to an important government objective. The use of peremptory challenges to exclude all women from a jury cannot survive mid-level review because it fails to further the state's legitimate interest in achieving a fair trial, while reinforcing stereotypical assumptions about women.

(*J.E.B. v. Alabama* (1994).) This rationale should apply to invalidate the state's action here, even though a non-jury adjudication method has been used. Anne used all of her peremptory challenges to eliminate women from the arbitrator's panel because she believed that they would necessarily be biased in favor of another woman claiming sexual harassment. Her reasoning reinforced the stereotypical assumption about women. By removing only women from the panel she did not substantially further State Y's legitimate interest in ensuring that the employee grievance system provides a fair trial for employers and employees; therefore, her actions were unconstitutional.

(B) is wrong because a participant in an arbitration does not have a constitutional right to have the arbitration panel made up of the participant's peers. That is a right that is limited to formal jury trials.

(C) is wrong because (1) gender-based classifications are subject to intermediate scrutiny (which requires that the government show that the classification is substantially related to an important government objective) not strict scrutiny; and (2) as described in the analysis of (A), the state's strike-all-female-arbitrators action here does not satisfy even this intermediate-level standard, let alone the strict scrutiny that this choice mentions.

(D) is wrong because gender-based classifications are examined under intermediate scrutiny, not rational-basis review. See the discussion of Choice (A) above. (It probably is true that if rational-basis review were the correct standard, the state would survive that review here, though this is not absolutely certain.)

2. **Male or female plaintiff:**

   Question: A public high school has had a very high rate of pregnancy among its students. In order to assist students who keep their babies to complete high school, the high school has established an infant day-care center for children of its students, and also offers classes in child care. Because the child-care classes are always overcrowded, the school limits admission to those classes solely to students at the high school who are the mothers of babies in the infant day-care center.

   A male student at the high school has legal custody of his infant son. The school provides care for his son in the infant day-care center, but will not allow the male student to enroll in the child-care classes. He brings suit against the school challenging, on constitutional grounds, his exclusion from the child-care classes.

   Which of the following best states the burden of persuasion in this case?

   (A) The student must demonstrate that the admission requirement is not rationally related to a legitimate governmental interest.

   (B) The student must demonstrate that the admission requirement is not as narrowly drawn as possible to achieve a substantial governmental interest.

   (C) The school must demonstrate that the admission policy is the least restrictive means by which to achieve a compelling governmental interest.

   (D) The school must demonstrate that the admission policy is substantially related to an important governmental interest.
   [Q2155]

   Answer: Choice **(D)** is correct. The issue here is the validity of the school's gender-based classification, under which students who are mothers of an infant can use the day-care center but students who are fathers of an infant cannot. For such a gender-based classification, the court uses intermediate-level scrutiny, under which, as Choice (D) recites, the defendant (the government) bears the burden of showing that its classification is "substantially related" to the fulfillment of an "important governmental interest." *Craig v. Boren* (1976). Notice that the standard is the same for a male plaintiff who is disadvantaged by the classification as it would be for a female plaintiff who was disadvantaged.

(A) would be correct if the classification were one that did not involve a suspect or semi-suspect class or fundamental interest (e.g., a garden-variety economic or social-welfare regulation); but since gender is a semi-suspect category, the standard in Choice (A) is insufficiently demanding.

(B) is incorrect mainly because, when the classification is based on gender, the use of semi-strict scrutiny means that the government bears the burden of persuasion. (Also, the key phrases "narrowly drawn as possible" and "substantial governmental interest" are not quite right.)

(C) is wrong because, while it correctly places the burden of persuasion on the government defendant, this choice recites the standard for strict rather than semi-strict scrutiny.

VI. FUNDAMENTAL RIGHTS

B. Voting rights:

3. Fifteenth Amendment:

Question: Twenty percent of the residents of Green City are members of minority racial groups. These residents are evenly distributed among the many different residential areas of the city. The five city council members of Green City are elected from five single-member electoral districts that are nearly equally populated. No candidate has ever been elected to the city council who was a member of a minority racial group.

A group of citizens who are members of minority racial groups file suit in federal district court seeking a declaratory judgment that the single-member districts in Green City are unconstitutional. They claim that the single-member districting system in that city diminishes the ability of voters who are members of minority racial groups to affect the outcome of city elections. They seek an order from the court forcing the city to adopt an at-large election system in which the five candidates with the greatest vote totals would be elected to the city council. No state or federal statutes are applicable to the resolution of this suit.

Which of the following constitutional provisions provides the most obvious basis for plaintiffs' claim in this suit?

(A) The Thirteenth Amendment.

(B) The due process clause of the Fourteenth Amendment.

(C) The privileges and immunities clause of the Fourteenth Amendment.

(D) The Fifteenth Amendment.

[Q2028]

Answer: The correct answer is Choice **(D)**. Direct impairments of the right to vote, based on a person's race or color, may violate the Fifteenth Amendment, even where Congress has not passed a statute banning the impairment.

(A) is wrong because the Thirteenth Amendment bars only slavery. Congress has the power to ban the "badges and incidents" of slavery under this Amendment, and voting rules that have a racially discriminatory impact might qualify as a badge-or-incident, but

Congress has not used its power here (since we're told that there is no applicable federal statute).

(B) is wrong because the Due Process Clause does not directly address voting rights, so any due process violation would be far more tenuous than the Thirteenth Amendment claim. (There might be a valid Fourteenth Amendment *equal protection* claim, but *that's not one of the choices*.)

(C) is wrong because the Fourteenth Amendment's P&I Clause is interpreted to protect only the rights of "national" (not state) citizenship, and the right to vote in a local election is not a right of national citizenship, at least where the local government is not discriminating against those who recently moved there.

C. **Ballot access:**

1. **Two invalid restrictions:**

   a. **Unfair to new parties:**

      Question: A state has a statute providing that an unsuccessful candidate in a primary election for a party's nomination for elected public office may not become a candidate for the same office at the following general election by nominating petition or by write-in votes.

      A woman sought her party's nomination for governor in the May primary election. After losing in the primary, the woman filed nominating petitions containing the requisite number of signatures to become a candidate for the office of governor in the following general election. The chief elections officer of the state refused to certify the woman's petitions solely because of the above statute. The woman then filed suit in federal district court challenging the constitutionality of this state statute.

      As a matter of constitutional law, which of the following is the proper burden of persuasion in this suit?

      (A) The woman must demonstrate that the statute is not necessary to achieve a compelling state interest.

      (B) The woman must demonstrate that the statute is not rationally related to a legitimate state interest.

      (C) The state must demonstrate that the statute is the least restrictive means of achieving a compelling state interest.

      (D) The state must demonstrate that the statute is rationally related to a legitimate state interest.

      [Q1122]

      Answer: Choice **(C)** is correct. Ballot restrictions that are so severe that minor-party and independent candidates have no realistic opportunity to get on the ballot are given strict scrutiny, under both the equal protection clause and the First Amendment's freedom of association clause. *Williams v. Rhodes* (1968). The statute here is such a restriction, because it makes it completely impossible (not just somewhat harder) for someone who fails to get a major-party nomination to then run as an independent or minor-party candidate in the general election, no matter how much public support that person can demonstrate. Consequently, the choice here, by articulating strict scrutiny as the standard, is correct.

      (A) is incorrect because, although it correctly articulates the strict-scrutiny standard, it incorrectly says that the plaintiff who is challenging the government bears the burden of persuasion; in those scenarios triggering strict scrutiny, the burden of persuasion is on the government.

(B) is wrong because it incorrectly uses the easy-to-satisfy mere-rationality standard, when what is at issue is a serious impairment of the fundamental right to be a candidate (and the right of voters to choose the best candidate).

(D) is wrong because, for the reasons stated above, the court would apply the strict scrutiny standard on these facts.

Question: A statute of State X permits a person's name to appear on the general election ballot as a candidate for statewide public office if the person pays a $100 filing fee and provides proof from the State Elections Board that he or she was nominated in the immediately preceding primary election by one of the state's two major political parties. It also permits the name of an independent candidate or a candidate of a smaller party to appear on the general election ballot if that person pays a filing fee of $1,000, and submits petitions signed by at least 3% of the voters who actually cast ballots for the office of governor in the last State X election. State X maintains that these filing requirements are necessary to limit the size of the election ballot, to eliminate frivolous candidacies, and to help finance the high cost of elections.

Historically, very few of State X's voters who are members of racial minority groups have been members of either of the two major political parties. Recently, a new political party has been formed by some of these voters.

Which of the following constitutional provisions would be most helpful to the new political party as a basis for attacking the constitutionality of this statute of State X?

(A) The First Amendment.

(B) The Thirteenth Amendment.

(C) The Fourteenth Amendment.

(D) The Fifteenth Amendment.

[Q3063]

Answer: (C) is the best response, because access to the ballot is protected by the Equal Protection clause of the Fourteenth Amendment. In particular, the Court has strictly scrutinized state burdens that seem to protect major parties at the expense of new parties, minor parties and independent candidates, especially where the disadvantaged voters and/or candidates are racial minorities. *Williams v. Rhodes*, cited above, is one such case. While the equal protection argument might not win (the restrictions here on candidates from new parties are much less severe than the ones struck down in *Williams*, and might not even trigger strict scrutiny), it is the only argument of the four presented that has even a reasonable chance of success.

Choice **(D)** is wrong because the Fifteenth Amendment prohibits the federal and state governments from denying any citizen the right to vote for reasons of race or color, and the state statute here isn't inhibiting anyone's right to vote, it's directed at who may be on the ballot. Traditionally, the Court has viewed ballot-access restrictions as implicating only the Equal Protection Clause, not the Fifteenth Amendment right to vote.

F. Necessities:

1. Education:

Question: Public schools in a state are financed, in large part, by revenue derived from real estate taxes imposed by each school district on the taxable real property located in that district. Public schools also receive other revenue from private gifts, federal grants, student fees, and local sales taxes. For many years, the state has distributed additional funds, which come from the state treasury, to local school districts in order to equalize the funds available on a per-student basis for each public school district. These additional funds are distributed on the basis of a state statutory formula that considers only the number of students in each public school district and the real estate tax revenue raised by that district. The formula does not consider other revenue received by a school district from different sources.

The school boards of two school districts, together with parents and schoolchildren in those districts, bring suit in federal court to enjoin the state from allocating the additional funds from the state treasury to individual districts pursuant to this formula. They allege that the failure of the state, in allocating this additional money, to take into account a school district's sources of revenue other than revenue derived from taxes levied on real estate located there violates the equal protection clause of the Fourteenth Amendment. The complaint does not allege that the allocation of the additional state funds based on the current statutory formula has resulted in a failure to provide minimally adequate education to any child.

Which of the following best describes the appropriate standard by which the court should review the constitutionality of the state statutory funding formula?

(A) Because classifications based on wealth are inherently suspect, the state must demonstrate that the statutory formula is necessary to vindicate a compelling state interest.

(B) Because the statutory funding formula burdens the fundamental right to education, the state must demonstrate that the formula is necessary to vindicate a compelling state interest.

(C) Because no fundamental right or suspect classification is implicated in this case, the plaintiffs must demonstrate that the funding allocation formula bears no rational relationship to any legitimate state interest.

(D) Because the funding formula inevitably leads to disparities among the school districts in their levels of total funding, the plaintiffs must only demonstrate that the funding formula is not substantially related to the furtherance of an important state interest.

[Q1073]

Answer: Choice **(C)** is correct. First, education is not a fundamental right for equal protection purposes. *San Antonio Sch. Dist. v. Rodriguez* (1973). Second, wealth classifications are not a suspect category. This choice therefore correctly asserts that (1) no fundamental right or suspect classification is involved in this case; and (2) where this is true, the plaintiff must bear the very difficult burden of proving that there is no rational relationship between the classification being used and any legitimate state interest. (By the way, it is very unlikely that the plaintiffs would win under this test; a school-funding scheme relying principally on local property taxes was upheld against rational-basis equal protection attack in *San Antonio v. Rodriguez, supra*.)

(A) is wrong because classifications based on wealth are not "inherently suspect" for equal protection purposes, so such classifications do not have to satisfy the strict scrutiny standard that this choice articulates.

(B) is wrong because the Court has held that education (or at least the right to have a public education that goes beyond minimally-adequate standards) is not a fundamental right for equal protection purposes; therefore, the strict scrutiny standard articulated by this choice would not apply.

(D) is wrong because it articulates an intermediate level of scrutiny, and that level is only used in cases involving semi-suspect classifications (e.g., ones based on gender).

Chapter 8
MISCELLANEOUS CLAUSES

I. FOURTEENTH AMENDMENT PRIVILEGES AND IMMUNITIES

A. **Privileges and Immunities Clause (P&I) Generally:**

Question: The United States government demonstrated that terrorist attacks involving commercial airliners were perpetrated exclusively by individuals of one particular race. In response, Congress enacted a statute imposing stringent new airport and airline security measures only on individuals of that race seeking to board airplanes in the United States.

Which of the following provides the best ground for challenging the constitutionality of this statute?

(A) The commerce clause of Article I, Section 8.

(B) The due process clause of the Fifth Amendment.

(C) The privileges and immunities clause of Article IV.

(D) The privileges or immunities clause of the Fourteenth Amendment.

[QA041]

Answer: Choice **(D)** is **incorrect**, because the privileges or immunities clause of the Fourteenth Amendment prohibits *states* from depriving individuals of the privileges or immunities of United States citizenship. The U.S. Supreme Court has never applied the clause to actions of the federal government. (Furthermore, even where state rather than federal action is at issue, be skeptical of any choice that finds a governmental action unconstitutional on the grounds that it violates the Fourteenth Amendment P&I Clause. That clause protects only the privileges and immunities of "national citizenship." There are very few privileges and immunities of national citizenship, mainly the right to vote in national elections, the right to travel physically from state to state, and the right not to be discriminated against by virtue of one's having recently moved to the state from a different state.)

The correct answer is (B); for an analysis of all choices, see *supra*, p. 280.

II. THE "TAKING" CLAUSE

A. **The "Taking" Clause Generally:** The Fifth Amendment contains the "Taking" Clause: "*[N]or shall private property be taken for public use, without just compensation.*"

1. **General meaning:**

Question: Congressional committees heard testimony from present and former holders of licenses issued by state vocational licensing boards. According to the testimony, the boards had unfairly manipulated their disciplinary proceedings in order to revoke the licenses of some license holders as a means of protecting favored licensees from competition.

In response, Congress enacted a statute prescribing detailed procedural requirements for the disciplinary proceedings of all state vocational licensing boards. For example, the statute required the state boards to provide licensees with adequate notice and opportunity for an adjudicatory hearing in all disciplinary proceedings. The statute also prescribed criteria for the membership of all state vocational licensing boards that were designed to ensure that the boards were likely to be neutral.

Which of the following provides the best source of authority for this federal statute?

(A) Section 5 of the Fourteenth Amendment.

(B) The general welfare clause of Article I, Section 8.

(C) The privileges and immunities clause of Article IV, Section 2.

(D) The takings clause of the Fifth Amendment.

[QA043]

Answer: Choice (D) is **incorrect** for two distinct reasons. The takings clause of the Fifth Amendment prohibits the federal government from taking property from an individual without paying fair compensation for the property taken. The takings clause does not apply here because (1) this legislation does not authorize the taking of anyone's property, and (2) in any event the takings clause is never a source of congressional power (which is what the question is asking about), only a limitation on that power. (The correct choice is (A); for an analysis of all choices, see *infra*, p. 294.)

2. **Taking vs. regulation:**

   b. **Guidelines:**

      i. **No denial of economically viable use:**

Question: A purchaser bought land in the mountain foothills just outside a resort town and planned to build a housing development there. Soon thereafter, the county in which the land was located unexpectedly adopted a regulation that, for the first time, prohibited all construction in several foothill and mountain areas, including the area of the purchaser's property. The purpose of the county's regulation was "to conserve for future generations the unique natural wildlife and plant habitats" in the mountain areas. Since the adoption of the regulation, the purchaser has been unable to lease or sell the property at any price. Several realtors have advised the purchaser that the property is now worthless. The purchaser sued the county, claiming that the regulation has taken the purchaser's property and that the county therefore owes the purchaser just compensation.

Is the court likely to rule in favor of the purchaser?

(A) No, because the county did not take title to the property from the purchaser.

(B) No, because the regulation has not caused or authorized any uninvited physical invasion or intrusion onto the property.

(C) Yes, because the conservation objective of the county ordinance is not sufficiently compelling to justify the substantial diminution in the property value.

(D) Yes, because the effect of the county's regulation is to deny the purchaser's investment-backed expectation and essentially all economically beneficial use of the property.

[Q7046]

Answer: Choice **(D)** is correct. A government regulation that totally eliminates the investment-backed expectation and economic value of an individual's property is a "taking" within the meaning of the Fifth Amendment, as applied to the county by the Fourteenth Amendment. Because the regulation has this effect, it constitutes a taking of the purchaser's property, for which the county must pay just compensation.

Choice (A) is incorrect, because the government's acquisition of property is sufficient but is not necessary to establish a taking within the meaning of the Fifth Amendment, as applied to the county by the Fourteenth Amendment — as explained in the discussion of Choice D, a government regulation that totally eliminates the economic value of an individual's property is a taking for which the government must pay just compensation, even though the government has not taken title.

Choice (B) is also incorrect, because physical invasion of or intrusion on property, like the taking of title, is sufficient but is not necessary to establish a taking — a government regulation that completely eliminates the economic value of an individual's property is a taking for which the government must pay just compensation even though government did not physically invade or intrude on the property.

Choice (C) is incorrect, because the Supreme Court does not use a balancing test for determining whether a governmental action is an unconstitutional taking — a government regulation that completely eliminates the economic value of an individual's property is a taking for which the government must pay just compensation no matter how compelling the government's interest in enacting the regulation.

v. "Give-backs":

Question: A company wanted to expand the size of the building it owned that housed the company's supermarket by adding space for a coffeehouse. The company's building was located in the center of five acres of land owned by the company and devoted wholly to parking for its supermarket customers.

City officials refused to grant a required building permit for the coffeehouse addition unless the company established in its store a child care center that would take up space at least equal to the size of the proposed coffeehouse addition, which was to be 20% of the existing building. This action of city officials was authorized by provisions of the applicable zoning ordinance.

In a suit filed in state court against appropriate officials of the city, the company challenged this child care center requirement solely on constitutional grounds. The lower court upheld the requirement even though city officials presented no evidence and made no findings to justify it other than a general assertion that there was a shortage of child care facilities in the city. The company appealed.

The court hearing the appeal should hold that the requirement imposed by the city on the issuance of this building permit is

(A) constitutional, because the burden was on the company to demonstrate that there was no rational relationship between this requirement and a legitimate governmental interest, and the company could not do so because the requirement is reasonably related to improving the lives of families and children residing in the city.

(B) constitutional, because the burden was on the company to demonstrate that this requirement was not necessary to vindicate a compelling governmental interest, and the company could not do so on these facts.

(C) unconstitutional, because the burden was on the city to demonstrate that this requirement was necessary to vindicate a compelling governmental interest, and the city failed to meet its burden under that standard.

(D) unconstitutional, because the burden was on the city to demonstrate a rough proportionality between this requirement and the impact of the company's proposed action on the community, and the city failed to do so.

[Q3162]

Answer: Choice **(D)** is correct. This is the best response, because without the showing of "rough proportionality" specified in this choice, the ordinance violates the Takings clause.

Dolan v. City of Tigard (1994) holds that when a city conditions a building permit on some "give back" by the owner, there must be a "rough proportionality" between the burdens on the public that the building permit would bring about, and the benefits to the public from the give-back. There's nothing in the facts to suggest that the city ever made the required showing here. (Indeed, the facts tell us that city officials presented no evidence of any sort, so they certainly didn't produce evidence either about the size of the public burden from allowing the coffee-house or the size of the corresponding benefit from the new child care facility they were requiring here.)

(A), (B), and (C) are all wrong because they misstate the burden of proof and the standard. When a city demands a "give back" in return for approving construction, the city, not the owner, bears the burden of proof as to rough proportionality (and this burden is probably somewhere between the easy-to-satisfy "rational relation" test of Choice (A) and the strict scrutiny of Choice (D)).

IV. *EX POST FACTO* LAWS

A. **Constitutional prohibition:**

1. **Criminal only:**

    a. **Significance:**

    Question: A doctor, a resident of the city of Greenville in the state of Green, is a physician licensed to practice in both Green and the neighboring state of Red. The doctor finds that the most convenient place to treat her patients who need hospital care is in the publicly owned and operated municipal hospital of the city of Redville in the state of Red, which is located just across the state line from Greenville. For many years the doctor had successfully treated her patients in that hospital. Early this year she was notified that she could no longer treat patients in the Redville hospital because she was not a resident of Red, and a newly adopted rule of the Redville hospital, which was adopted in conformance with all required procedures, stated that every physician who practices in that hospital must be a resident of Red.

    Which of the following constitutional provisions would be most helpful to the doctor in an action to challenge her exclusion from the Redville hospital solely on the basis of this hospital rule?

    (A) The bill of attainder clause.

    (B) The privileges and immunities clause of Article IV.

    (C) The due process clause of the Fourteenth Amendment.

    (D) The ex post facto clause.

    [Q3190]

    Answer: Choice **(B)** is correct. When a state (or subdivision of a state, like a city and its municipally-owned operations) regulates a right that is "fundamental to national unity," and does so in a way that disadvantages out-of-staters, that regulation will essentially be subject to strict scrutiny under the Art. IV Privileges and Immunities clause. (Among other things, the state must show that the discrimination against non-residents bears a "substantial relationship" to the problem the state is attempting to solve.) Practice of one's business or profession is a right "fundamental to national unity" for P&I purposes.

The case here is on all fours with *New Hampshire v. Piper* (1985), where the Court held that New Hampshire's attempt to restrict the right to practice law to state residents violated the Art. IV P&I Clause. Applying *Piper*, since there's no showing that out-of-state doctors are the peculiar source of any special problem that the hospital is trying to solve, the restriction violates the P&I Clause.

(By the way, there's no exception under the P&I Clause for activities in which the city or state is a "market participant," as there is under the dormant Commerce Clause. *United Bldg. and Constr. Trades Counc. v. Camden* (1984). So the fact that the city owns the hospital that's making the rule doesn't help it, as it would against a Commerce Clause attack.)

(A) is wrong because the legislature of state Red was not trying to punish the doctor. A bill of attainder is a legislative act that attempts to inflict punishment without a judicial trial upon individuals who are designated by name or in terms of past conduct. The constitutional prohibition against a bill of attainder would not be helpful to the doctor because the hospital here merely took the purely regulatory action of changing the residency requirement for practicing medicine at the hospital — no public entity named the doctor as a criminal, or attempted to punish or stigmatize him, which is what a bill of attainder would have done.

(C) is wrong because the doctor would have to show that the licensing requirement was not rationally related to a legitimate government interest, a showing the doctor probably couldn't make. The Due Process Clause of the Fourteenth Amendment provides that no state shall make or enforce any law which shall deprive any person of life, liberty, or property, without due process of law. When a fundamental right is not involved, substantive due process requires only that a law be "rationally related" to the achievement of a "legitimate government interest." So to win on due process, the doctor would have to prove that Red's new residency requirement was not rationally related to some legitimate government purpose. This standard is very lenient and easy-to-satisfy. Here, for instance, the hospital could plausibly claim that it wants to have on staff only doctors who live very nearby, and that it's entitled to use state of residence as a proxy for nearby-ness. Although the fit between means and end isn't very tight under this rationale, it's almost certainly tight enough to meet the extremely lenient rational-relation standard.

(D) is wrong because state Red was not legislating against past acts. The Ex Post Facto clauses, Article I, § 9 and § 10, prohibit both the federal government and the state, respectively, from passing legislation that retroactively alters the criminal law as to offenses or punishments, in a substantially prejudicial manner. A retroactive change in civil regulations, such as licensing requirements, cannot violate the prohibition, since the prohibition applies only to "penal," i.e., punitive, measures. Here, the facts make it clear that the hospital was not making a rule penalizing past acts, but was instead making residency a requirement to practice medicine in state Red going forward.

V. BILLS OF ATTAINDER

B. Definition of "punishment":

Question: Two tenured professors at a state university drafted a new university regulation prohibiting certain kinds of speech on campus. Students, staff, and faculty convicted by campus tribunals of violating the regulation were made subject to penalties that included fines, suspensions, expulsions, and termination of employment. The regulation was widely unpopular and there was a great deal of public anger directed toward the professors who drafted it. The following year, the state legislature approved a severable provision in the appropriations bill for the university declaring that none of the university's funding could be used to pay the two professors, who were specifically named in the provision. In the past, the professors' salaries had always been paid from funds appropriated to the university by the legislature, and the university had no other funds that could be used to pay them.

If the professors challenge the constitutionality of the appropriations provision, is the court likely to uphold the provision?

(A) No, because it amounts to the imposition of a punishment by the legislature without trial.

(B) No, because it was based on conduct the professors engaged in before it was enacted.

(C) Yes, because the Eleventh Amendment gives the state legislature plenary power to appropriate state funds in the manner that it deems most conducive to the welfare of its people.

(D) Yes, because the full faith and credit clause requires the court to enforce the provision strictly according to its terms.

[Q7021]

Answer: Choice **(A)** is correct. The provision is a bill of attainder. A bill of attainder is a law that provides for the punishment of a particular person without trial. The challenged provision satisfies this definition because it deprives two named professors of their salaries, and thus, their employment — a court would almost certainly hold that the purpose of the provision was punitive rather than purely regulatory.

(B) is wrong because, while it is true that the court is likely to strike down the provision, this answer misstates the basis for this conclusion. The fact that the professors' conduct preexisted the state law would be significant if the state law provided for a criminal penalty — it would then be unconstitutional as an ex post facto law in violation of Article I, Section 10, Clause 1 of the Constitution. The ex post facto clause, however, does not apply to laws attaching civil consequences to past conduct, which is what the present law does.

(C) is wrong because the Eleventh Amendment provides for state sovereign immunity from certain kinds of adjudications. It does not extend legislative authority of any kind to the states.

(D) is wrong because the full faith and credit clause (Article IV, Section 1 of the Constitution) does not insulate state laws from constitutional challenge. It merely requires state courts to accord due authority to the laws of other states, something that is not at issue here.

CHAPTER 9

THE "STATE ACTION" REQUIREMENT; CONGRESS'S ENFORCEMENT OF THE CIVIL WAR AMENDMENTS

I. STATE ACTION

C. "State involvement" doctrine:

4. Entanglement or entwinement:

b. Licensing:

Question: Insurance is provided in a particular state only by private companies. Although the state insurance commissioner inspects insurance companies for solvency, the state does not regulate their rates or policies. A particular insurance company charges higher rates for burglary insurance to residents of one part of a county in the state than to residents of another section of the same county because of the different crime rates in those areas.

A resident of that county was charged the higher rate by the insurance company because of the location of her residence. The resident sues the insurance company, alleging that the differential in insurance rates unconstitutionally denies her the equal protection of the laws.

Will the resident's suit succeed?

(A) Yes, because the higher crime rate in the resident's neighborhood demonstrates that the county police are not giving persons who reside there the equal protection of the laws.

(B) Yes, because the insurance rate differential is inherently discriminatory.

(C) No, because the constitutional guarantee of equal protection of the laws is not applicable to the actions of these insurance companies.

(D) No, because there is a rational basis for the differential in insurance rates.

[Q1114]

Answer: Choice **(C)** is correct. Although the state does some regulation of the insurance industry (for solvency), the state is not sufficiently involved with the operations of the insurance company here to satisfy the requirement — applicable to any equal protection claim — that there be "state action." Notice that the choice never uses the phrase "state action" — it's up to you to spot the state action issue and to notice that this choice's use of the phrase "not applicable to the actions of these ... companies" captures the state-action concept.

(A) is wrong for several reasons, including most basically the fact that it ignores the state-action requirement for any equal protection claim. (The fact that the *state police* are arguably failing to give equal protection is irrelevant, since the police aren't a party and aren't tightly associated with a party.)

(B) and (D) are wrong, similarly, because they too ignore the state-action requirement for equal protection claims. (If the state-action requirement were satisfied — if, for instance, the state expressly required burglary-insurance rates to be adjusted based on local crime rates — then (D) would be the best answer because it correctly expresses the idea that a governmental classification that does not involve a suspect class or fundamental right needs to be supported only by a rational basis.)

II. CONGRESSIONAL ENFORCEMENT OF CIVIL RIGHTS

B. **Congress's power to enforce:**

Question: Congressional committees heard testimony from present and former holders of licenses issued by state vocational licensing boards. According to the testimony, the boards had unfairly manipulated their disciplinary proceedings in order to revoke the licenses of some license holders as a means of protecting favored licensees from competition.

In response, Congress enacted a statute prescribing detailed procedural requirements for the disciplinary proceedings of all state vocational licensing boards. For example, the statute required the state boards to provide licensees with adequate notice and opportunity for an adjudicatory hearing in all disciplinary proceedings. The statute also prescribed criteria for the membership of all state vocational licensing boards that were designed to ensure that the boards were likely to be neutral.

Which of the following provides the best source of authority for this federal statute?

(A) Section 5 of the Fourteenth Amendment.

(B) The general welfare clause of Article I, Section 8.

(C) The privileges and immunities clause of Article IV, Section 2.

(D) The takings clause of the Fifth Amendment.

[QA043]

Answer: Choice **(A)** is correct. Section 5 of the Fourteenth Amendment gives Congress the power to enforce the provisions of the Fourteenth Amendment by "appropriate legislation." Congressional legislation is appropriate within the meaning of §5 if (1) the legislation seeks to prevent or remedy actions by state or local governments that violate provisions of the Fourteenth Amendment, and (2) the requirements imposed by the legislation are "congruent with" and "proportional to" the Fourteenth Amendment violations it addresses. *Boerne v. Flores* (1997). In this case, the legislation seeks to prevent actions by state agencies that violate the Due Process Clause of the Fourteenth Amendment; and the requirements of the legislation appear to be proportional to and congruent with the Fourteenth Amendment violations Congress has sought to prevent. (Notice that here, Congress has acted based on substantial evidence that prior to the legislation, the states were directly and substantially violating people's due process rights. If the principal wrongdoing had been by *private* parties, and any violations by the states had been sporadic and minor, then the federal statute would, as applied to the regulate the states' conduct, probably *not* have been "congruent and proportional," and would therefore not have been a proper exercise of the §5 power.)

(B) is incorrect because there *is* no "general welfare clause." Article I, Section 8 of the Constitution gives Congress the power to *tax and spend* for the general welfare, but this power is inapplicable here, because the legislation at issue is not a taxing or spending measure.

(C) is wrong because the privileges and immunities clause of Article IV, Section 2 prohibits actions by states that improperly discriminate against the citizens of other states. The clause does not apply to actions of the federal government.

(D) is wrong because the takings clause is a *limit* on federal power, not a *source* of power. The takings clause of the Fifth Amendment prohibits the federal government from taking property from an individual without paying fair compensation for the property taken. The takings clause does not apply here because (1) this legislation does not authorize the taking of anyone's property, and (2) in any event the takings clause is never a source of congressional power (which is what the question is asking about), only a limitation on that power.

C. **Congress's power to reach private conduct:**

2. **Thirteenth Amendment:**

a. **"Badges of slavery":**

Question: A proposed federal statute would prohibit all types of discrimination against black persons on the basis of their race in every business transaction executed anywhere in the United States by any person or entity, governmental or private.

Is this proposed federal statute likely to be constitutional?

(A) Yes, because it could reasonably be viewed as an exercise of Congress's authority to enact laws for the general welfare.

(B) Yes, because it could reasonably be viewed as a means of enforcing the provisions of the Thirteenth Amendment.

(C) No, because it would regulate purely local transactions that are not in interstate commerce.

(D) No, because it would invade the powers reserved to the states by the Tenth Amendment.

[Q2101]

Answer: Choice **(B)** is correct. The Thirteenth Amendment permits Congress to forbid the "badges and incidents" of slavery. This power has been interpreted by the Court to include the power to forbid even private acts of racial discrimination against black people, on the theory that such discrimination is the relic of slavery.

(A) is wrong because Congress does not have any "authority to enact laws for the general welfare" (only the power to "tax and spend" for the general welfare).

(C) is wrong because this might be an explanation of why the statute couldn't be supported by Congress's commerce power, but the Thirteenth Amendment power allows Congress to forbid even purely local racial discrimination (i.e., discrimination that does not involve interstate commerce).

(D) is wrong because if Congress's action falls within a specific grant of power (here, the Thirteenth Amendment grant), the Tenth Amendment acts as a limitation only in the highly specialized case of Congress's attempt to take over state lawmaking mechanisms.

c. **Non-racial grounds:**

Question: Congress wishes to enact legislation prohibiting discrimination in the sale or rental of housing on the basis of the affectional preference or sexual orientation of the potential purchaser or renter. Congress wishes this statute to apply to all public and private vendors and lessors of residential property in this country, with a few narrowly drawn exceptions.

The most credible argument for congressional authority to enact such a statute would be based upon the

(A) general welfare clause of Article I, Sec. 8, because the conduct the statute prohibits could reasonably be deemed to be harmful to the national interest.

(B) commerce clause of Article I, Sec. 8, because, in inseverable aggregates, the sale or rental of almost all housing in this country could reasonably be deemed to have a substantial effect on interstate commerce.

(C) enforcement clause of the Thirteenth Amendment, because that amendment clearly prohibits discrimination against the class of persons protected by this statute.

(D) enforcement clause of the Fourteenth Amendment, because that amendment prohibits all public and private actors from engaging in irrational discrimination.

[Q3170]

Answer: (C) is **incorrect**, because the Thirteenth Amendment almost certainly cannot be used to protect against sexual-orientation discrimination. The Thirteenth Amendment expressly protects against slavery. Its enforcement clause has been interpreted to allow Congress to legislate against the "badges of slavery," and to prohibit even private actors from practicing racial discrimination. The Court has never held that the Amendment may be used outside of the racial area. It's possible (though not certain) that Congress could rely on the Amendment to prohibit private discrimination on the basis of ethnicity and national origin in addition to race, since these are similar to racial discrimination. But it's very unlikely that the Amendment can be used to bar private discrimination on grounds so distinct from slavery as sexual orientation. (Instead, (B) is the best response, because the "substantial effect on commerce" rationale has been accepted by the Supreme Court as a basis for use of the commerce power. See *supra*, p. 232.)

CHAPTER 10
FREEDOM OF EXPRESSION

I. GENERAL THEMES

C. Analysis of content-based government action:

2. Protected category:

a. "Viewpoint neutrality" not enough:

Question: The Federal Family Film Enhancement Act assesses an excise tax of 10% on the price of admission to public movie theaters when they show films that contain actual or simulated scenes of human sexual intercourse.

Which of the following is the strongest argument against the constitutionality of this federal act?

(A) The act imposes a prior restraint on the freedom of speech protected by the First Amendment.

(B) The act is not rationally related to any legitimate national interest.

(C) The act violates the equal protection concepts embodied in the due process clause of the Fifth Amendment because it imposes a tax on the price of admission to view certain films and not on the price of admission to view comparable live performances.

(D) The act imposes a tax solely on the basis of the content of speech without adequate justification and, therefore, it is prohibited by the freedom of speech clause of the First Amendment.

[Q1099]

Answer: Choice **(D)** is correct. The tax applies only to films that show some form of sexual intercourse. This means that the regulation is content-based (it treats different forms of expression differently depending solely on the message being conveyed). Therefore, the court will apply strict scrutiny to it. (Notice, by the way, that the tax is not limited to films that would be "obscene" — not all portrayals of sexual intercourse would be obscene; if only obscene films were taxed, probably strict scrutiny would *not* be used.)

Choice (A) is wrong because a tax is not a "prior restraint"; a legislative act imposes a prior restraint only where government forbids the doing of the act in advance (e.g., a statute forbidding showing of a film without first paying a license fee). Since the tax here kicks in only after the showing of the film, it is not a prior restraint.

Choice (B) is wrong because the regulation here is a content-based regulation on expression, and such a restraint is evaluated based on strict scrutiny, not the easy-to-satisfy rational-relation test.

Choice (C) is wrong because an equal protection attack on a legislative classification that does not involve a suspect or semi-suspect class or fundamental right is evaluated based on the easy-to-satisfy rational-relation standard, and the tax here would likely pass that standard.

E. Overbreadth:

Question: A statute of the state of Texona prohibits any retailer of books, magazines, pictures, or posters from "publicly displaying or selling to any person any material that may be harmful to minors because of the violent or sexually explicit nature of its pictorial content." Violation of this statute is a misdemeanor.

Corner Store displays publicly and sells magazines containing violent and sexually explicit pictures. The owner of this store is prosecuted under the above statute for these actions.

In defending against this prosecution in a Texona trial court, the argument that would be the best defense for Corner Store is that the statute violates the

(A) First Amendment as it is incorporated into the Fourteenth Amendment, because the statute is excessively vague and overbroad.

(B) First Amendment as it is incorporated into the Fourteenth Amendment, because a state may not prohibit the sale of violent or sexually explicit material in the absence of proof that the material is utterly without any redeeming value in the marketplace of ideas.

(C) equal protection of the laws clause, because the statute irrationally treats violent and sexually explicit material that is pictorial differently from such material that is composed wholly of printed words.

(D) equal protection of the laws clause, because the statute irrationally distinguishes between violent and sexually explicit pictorial material that may harm minors and such material that may harm only adults.

[Q3199]

Answer: Choice **(A)** is correct, because the statute bars a substantial amount of protected conduct. A statute is overbroad if, in addition to proscribing activities that may constitutionally be forbidden, it also sweeps within its coverage a substantial amount of speech or conduct which is protected by the guarantees of free speech. The statute here is overbroad because it proscribes a substantial amount of conduct protected by the First Amendment. As the statute is written, if the material might be harmful to minors, it may not be sold to (or displayed to) *adults*, either. And adults have a First Amendment right to read (1) even sexually explicit materials, if they aren't "obscene" (a definition that requires an absence of "serious literary, artistic, political, or scientific value," something the statute here doesn't take into account); and (2) materials of a violent nature, even if these would harm minors. So the statute denies to adults massive amounts of material that they have a constitutional right to buy and read.

(B) is wrong because this is a corrupted version of a now-outmoded test for obscenity, and is therefore not the relevant test. At one time, to sustain an obscenity prosecution, prosecutors had to prove that the material was utterly without "the slightest redeeming social importance," a standard somewhat similar to the one in this choice. But that's no longer the test for obscenity: now, a "patently offensive" portrayal of "sexual conduct" that is "specifically defined" by state law may be prohibited, provided only that the work, taken as a whole, lacks "serious literary, artistic, political, or scientific value." (*Miller v. Cal.* (1973).) So the presence of the smallest "redeeming value in the marketplace of ideas" (as this choice states) wouldn't protect against a finding of obscenity. But even if this choice had the right test for obscenity, it would miss the fact that, as the Court held in *Ginsberg v. N.Y.* (1968), states *may* prohibit the sale *to minors* of sexually explicit material that doesn't meet the definition of obscenity. The big problem with the statute is that (as described in Choice (A)) it bars adults from seeing or buying non-obscene materials on grounds that these might harm minors, and Choice (B) doesn't capture this difficulty at all.

(C) is wrong because the distinction between written and pictorial material would not be found to be wholly irrational. Where a statute treats two different classes of things or people in two different ways, unless a suspect category or fundamental right is involved, only a completely irrational classification will be found to violate equal protection. So here, if a plaintiff could convince the court that it is irrational to treat people who want to buy sexually-explicit pictorial materials differently from those who want to buy sexually-explicit materials consisting solely of words, the plaintiff might prevail with an equal protection argument. The problem is that it is very unlikely that a court would agree that it's completely irrational to distinguish between pictures and words. It might be rational, for example, for a state to conclude that the harmful impact of sexually explicit pictures on men with a latent tendency to impose sexually-sadistic violence on women is greater than the impact on the same men of works consisting solely of words.

(D) is wrong because there *is* a rational distinction that may be made between minors and adults. Where a statute treats two different classes of things or people in two different ways, unless a suspect category or fundamental right is involved, only a completely irrational classification will be found to violate equal protection. So here, if a plaintiff could convince the court that it is wholly irrational to treat violent or sexually-explicit pictorial materials differently depending on whether they harm minors or just adults, the claim might work. But a plaintiff would be exceptionally unlikely to succeed in making such a showing. The Court has previously held (in *Ginsberg v. N.Y.* (1968), a First Amendment case), that the states may prohibit the sale to minors of sexually explicit material that doesn't meet the definition of obscenity, on the grounds that minors are more impressionable. So a court now would be unlikely to conclude that it's wholly irrational for materials that might harm minors in this way to be distinguished from those that would "only" harm adults. (Besides, any materials that would harm adults would be likely to harm minors as well, making the statute's distinction even less irrational.)

III. TIME, PLACE AND MANNER REGULATIONS

A. Time, place and manner generally:

1. Three-part test:

    Question: Residents of a city complained that brightly colored signs detracted from the character of the city's historic district and distracted motorists trying to navigate its narrow streets. In response, the city council enacted an ordinance requiring any "sign or visual display" visible on the streets of the historic district to be black and white and to be no more than four feet long or wide.

    A political party wanted to hang a six-foot-long red, white, and blue political banner in front of a building in the historic district. The party filed suit to challenge the constitutionality of the sign ordinance as applied to the display of its banner.

    Which of the following would be the most useful argument for the political party?

    (A) The ordinance is not the least restrictive means of promoting a compelling government interest.

    (B) The ordinance is not narrowly tailored to an important government interest, nor does it leave open alternative channels of communication.

(C) The ordinance imposes a prior restraint on political expression.

(D) The ordinance effectively favors some categories of speech over others.

[QA055]

Answer: Choice **(B)** is correct. The ordinance here is a "time, place, or manner" regulation of speech occurring in a public forum. As you analyze such a regulation, you must first check that the regulation is content-neutral (since the time-place-or-manner analysis is applied only to content-neutral regulations). If the content-neutrality requirement is satisfied, then the time-place-or-manner restriction will be upheld if and only if the regulation (1) is narrowly tailored to achieve (2) a significant or important governmental interest; and (3) it leaves open alternative channels of communication. This is essentially intermediate-level scrutiny. It's not clear that the plaintiff political party will win with this argument — the court might well hold that preserving historic character and avoiding motorist distraction are important governmental objectives, and that barring large or colored signs is a narrowly tailored means of achieving these objectives. But this choice correctly states what the party will have to establish if it is to prevail.

(A) is wrong because it applies the wrong test. A test that requires government to prove that its regulation is the least restrictive means of promoting a compelling government interest constitutes strict scrutiny. When government regulates speech, the court uses strict scrutiny only where the regulation is content-based rather than content neutral. Here, since the regulation bans large or colored signs regardless of their content, the regulation is content-neutral, and would not trigger strict scrutiny. (Instead, the court will use intermediate-level review, as further described in Choice (B).)

(C) is wrong because no prior restraint is occurring here. A governmental regulation of expression is said to impose a "prior restraint" only where the regulation requires the express permission of a government official (i.e., a permit) before the expression occurs. The ordinance here does not impose a prior restraint because it does not require a permit. (Rather, the person can simply engage in the expression — by posting the sign — and then await punishment.) If the ordinance had imposed a prior restraint, the ordinance would have been subjected to strict scrutiny and probably struck down, so in that event Choice (C) would have supplied a good argument for the party. But since there is no prior restraint, the court will use intermediate-level review, as further described in Choice (B).

(D) is wrong because it mischaracterizes the facts. The text of the city's ordinance restricts signs regardless of their content, and there are no facts to support a claim that the ordinance effectively operates as a content-based restriction on expression. (If the ordinance had applied only, say, to political signs, then this intentional preference of one category over others *would* have caused the ordinance to be viewed as content-based, and would have caused the court to apply strict scrutiny.)

G. **Regulation of "hate speech":**

1. **General rules:**

    Question: A man intensely disliked his neighbors, who were of a different race. One night, intending to frighten his neighbors, he spray-painted their house with racial epithets and threats that they would be lynched. The man was arrested and prosecuted under a state law providing that "any person who threatens violence against another person with the intent to cause that person to fear for his or her life or safety may be imprisoned for up to five years." In defense, the man claimed that he did not intend to lynch his neighbors, but only to scare them so that they would move away.

Can the man constitutionally be convicted under this law?

(A) No, because he was only communicating his views and had not commenced any overt action against the neighbors.

(B) Yes, because he was engaged in trespass when he painted the words on his neighbors' house.

(C) Yes, because his communication was a threat by which he intended to intimidate his neighbors.

(D) Yes, because his communication was racially motivated and thus violated the protections of the Thirteenth Amendment.

[Q7095]

Answer: Choice **(C)** is correct. The Supreme Court has held that a threat communicated with the intent to intimidate the recipient, like the communication in this case, is not protected by the free speech clause of the First Amendment. If the state had singled out only certain types of threats (e.g., ones based on race), there might be a First Amendment problem, but the statute here bans *all* threats of violence, so it is content-neutral and thus acceptable.

(A) is incorrect, because as explained above, threats of violence with intent to intimidate are not protected by the First Amendment, and that's true even if the speaker never acted (and indeed never intended to act) on the threat.

(B) is incorrect because it misstates the legal basis for the correct conclusion that the man may be punished: intimidating threats of violence may be proscribed regardless of whether the threatener was committing a trespass.

(D) is incorrect because the Supreme Court has never held that racially motivated threats can violate the Thirteenth Amendment's prohibition of involuntary servitude.

V. DEFAMATION AND INVASION OF PRIVACY

B. Other state-law tort claims:

1. Can't take whole performance:

Question: Roberts, a professional motorcycle rider, put on a performance in a privately owned stadium during which he leaped his motorcycle over 21 automobiles. Spectators were charged $5 each to view the jump and were prohibited from using cameras. However, the local television station filmed the whole event from within the stadium without the knowledge or consent of Roberts and showed the film in its entirety on the evening newscast that day. Roberts thereafter brought suit to recover damages from the station for the admittedly unauthorized filming and broadcasting of the act. The television station raised only constitutional defenses.

The court should

(A) hold against Roberts, because the First and Fourteenth Amendments authorize press coverage of newsworthy entertainment events.

(B) hold against Roberts, because under the First and Fourteenth Amendments news broadcasts are absolutely privileged.

(C) find the station liable, because its action deprives Roberts of his property without due process.

(D) find the station liable, because the First and Fourteenth Amendments do not deprive an entertainer of the commercial value of his or her performances.

[Q1159]

Answer: Choice **(D)** is correct. While the First Amendment does indeed give the media a privilege to cover newsworthy events, that privilege does not extend to the broadcasting of a performance where this would deprive the performer of the commercial value of that performance. The fact pattern here is on all fours with *Zacchini v. Scripps-Howard Broadcasting*.

(A) is wrong, because while the First Amendment does give a privilege for press coverage of newsworthy events, that privilege does not extend to a broadcast that takes so much of an act that it deprives the performer of much of the commercial value of the act.

(B) is wrong because news broadcasts are not "absolutely privileged"; rather, they receive a qualified privilege, subject to a number of limits (including, here, the limit that the broadcast not appropriate so much of a performance that the commercial value of the performance is taken from the performer).

(C) is wrong, because the Due Process Clause of the Fourteenth Amendment protects only against a taking by a government, and any taking here was by a private party (the TV station), not by the government.

VI. OBSCENITY

C. **Significance:**

1. **Abandonment of "redeeming social value" test:**

    Question: A statute of the state of Texona prohibits any retailer of books, magazines, pictures, or posters from "publicly displaying or selling to any person any material that may be harmful to minors because of the violent or sexually explicit nature of its pictorial content." Violation of this statute is a misdemeanor.

    Corner Store displays publicly and sells magazines containing violent and sexually explicit pictures. The owner of this store is prosecuted under the above statute for these actions.

    In defending against this prosecution in a Texona trial court, the argument that would be the best defense for Corner Store is that the statute violates the

    (A) First Amendment as it is incorporated into the Fourteenth Amendment, because the statute is excessively vague and overbroad.

    (B) First Amendment as it is incorporated into the Fourteenth Amendment, because a state may not prohibit the sale of violent or sexually explicit material in the absence of proof that the material is utterly without any redeeming value in the marketplace of ideas.

    (C) equal protection of the laws clause, because the statute irrationally treats violent and sexually explicit material that is pictorial differently from such material that is composed wholly of printed words.

    (D) equal protection of the laws clause, because the statute irrationally distinguishes between violent and sexually explicit pictorial material that may harm minors and such material that may harm only adults.

    [Q3199]

    Answer: Choice **(B)** is **incorrect**, because this is a corrupted version of a now-outmoded test for obscenity, and is therefore not the relevant test. At one time, to sustain an obscenity prosecution, prosecutors had to prove that the material was utterly without "the slightest redeeming social importance," a standard somewhat similar to the one in this choice. But now, under *Miller*, that's no longer the test for obscenity: today, a "patently offensive" portrayal of "sexual conduct" that is "specifically defined" by state law may be prohibited, provided only that the work, taken as a whole, lacks "serious literary, artistic, political, or scientific value." So the presence of the smallest "redeeming value in the marketplace of ideas" (as this choice states) wouldn't protect against a finding of obscenity. (The correct answer is (A); see *supra*, p. 297.)

G. Regulating secondary effects of adult speech:

1. Regulation of red-light districts:

Question: A city has an ordinance that prohibits the location of "adult theaters and bookstores" (theaters and bookstores presenting sexually explicit performances or materials) in residential or commercial zones within the city. The ordinance was intended to protect surrounding property from the likely adverse secondary effects of such establishments. "Adult theaters and bookstores" are freely permitted in the areas of the city zoned industrial, where those adverse secondary effects are not as likely. A storekeeper is denied a zoning permit to open an adult theater and bookstore in a building owned by him in an area zoned commercial. As a result, the storekeeper brings suit in an appropriate court challenging the constitutionality of the zoning ordinance.

Which of the following statements regarding the constitutionality of this city ordinance is most accurate?

(A) The ordinance is valid, because a city may enforce zoning restrictions on speech-related businesses to ensure that the messages they disseminate are acceptable to the residents of adjacent property.

(B) The ordinance is valid, because a city may enforce this type of time, place, and manner regulation on speech-related businesses, so long as this type of regulation is designed to serve a substantial governmental interest and does not unreasonably limit alternative avenues of communication.

(C) The ordinance is invalid, because a city may not enforce zoning regulations that deprive potential operators of adult theaters and bookstores of their freedom to choose the location of their businesses.

(D) The ordinance is invalid, because a city may not zone property in a manner calculated to protect property from the likely adverse secondary effects of adult theaters and bookstores.

[Q2193]

Answer: Choice **(B)** is correct. The Supreme Court has repeatedly held that even if a city is using its zoning powers to limit or prohibit a speech-related activity, the regulation is acceptable if the city is reasonably targeting the secondary effects of that speech (e.g., crime or lower property values) rather than targeting the expressive content of that speech. See, e.g., *Erie v. Pap's A.M.* (2004) (city may completely ban "nude dancing" to combat the bad secondary effects of such). Since the government is targeting the secondary effects rather than the message, the regulation is to be evaluated based on the test for content-neutral time, place and manner regulations, which as this choice suggests makes such regulations valid as long as they are designed to serve a substantial governmental interest and do not unreasonably limit alternative avenues of expression. Since the interest in preventing blight is "substantial," and since adult uses are permitted in alternative venues (areas zoned commercial), these requirements are easily satisfied.

(A) is wrong because it falsely asserts that the city may use its zoning powers to forbid particular messages based on their content. Such a content-based regulation would have to be strictly scrutinized, and would almost certainly be struck down.

(C) is wrong because it badly misstates the law: cities may indeed use their zoning regulations to prevent operators of adult theaters and the like from choosing their location, as long as the city is acting reasonably to combat the perceived negative secondary effects of the business, rather than out of distaste for the content of the messages transmitted by the business.

(D) is wrong because it exactly misstates present law; cities may (not "may not") "zone property in a manner calculated to protect property from the likely adverse secondary effects of adult theaters and bookstores." *Erie v. Pap's, supra.*

VII. COMMERCIAL SPEECH

A. **Commercial speech generally:**

1. **Truthful speech:**

    a. *Reasonable probability of success:*

    Question: City enacted an ordinance banning from its public sidewalks all machines dispensing publications consisting wholly of commercial advertisements. The ordinance was enacted because of a concern about the adverse aesthetic effects of litter from publications distributed on the public sidewalks and streets. However, City continued to allow machines dispensing other types of publications on the public sidewalks. As a result of the City ordinance, 30 of the 300 sidewalk machines that were dispensing publications in City were removed.

    Is this City ordinance constitutional?

    (A) Yes, because regulations of commercial speech are subject only to the requirement that they be rationally related to a legitimate state goal, and that requirement is satisfied here.

    (B) Yes, because City has a compelling interest in protecting the aesthetics of its sidewalks and streets, and such a ban is necessary to vindicate this interest.

    (C) No, because it does not constitute the least restrictive means with which to protect the aesthetics of City's sidewalks and streets.

    (D) No, because there is not a reasonable fit between the legitimate interest of City in preserving the aesthetics of its sidewalks and streets and the means it chose to advance that interest.

    [Q3043]

    Answer: (D) is the best response, because the ordinance removes only one box in ten from the streets, and thus does not have a reasonable probability of materially improving the litter problem. Commercial speech, if it is not misleading or concerning unlawful activity, is covered by the First Amendment and may be regulated only if the state shows that the regulation (1) directly advances, (2) a substantial governmental interest, (3) in a way that is reasonably tailored to achieve that objective. *Edenfield v. Fane* (1993). While the ordinance here (which regulates commercial speech) directly advances City's substantial governmental interest in preventing the adverse effects of publication-caused litter on public sidewalks and streets, the ordinance fails the requirement that the regulation be reasonably tailored to achievement of the state's interest. The facts state that the ordinance caused the removal of just 30 of the existing 300 sidewalk machines that were dispensing publications. And there's no indication that publications containing solely advertising will result in more litter per publication than those that have some non-advertising content. An ordinance which removes only one box in ten, and with no indication why that one poses more of a litter problem, is not reasonably tailored to achieving the city's legitimate interest in reducing litter.

(A) is wrong because this choice states the wrong test. As is described in Choice (D) above, the Court applies what is essentially mid-level review to regulations of commercial speech. Since (A) says that the review is the easy-to-satisfy rational-relation standard, it's wrong.

(B) is wrong because the answer is based on a test that is inapplicable to the facts. This choice propounds the strict-scrutiny standard used for content-based restrictions. What's at issue here, however, is a time-place-and-manner regulation aimed at the secondary effects (litter) of a certain method of disseminating written material. The appropriate standard is the intermediate-level review described in Choice (D). Furthermore, if strict-scrutiny *were* the correct standard, the ordinance here would clearly not satisfy the standard, since it's attacking only one-tenth of the problem (by removing only one-tenth of the boxes), meaning that the means chosen are not a very good method of achieving the objective.

(C) is wrong because the applicable test is reasonable-fit, not least-restrictive means. Commercial speech, if it is not misleading or concerning unlawful activity, is covered by the 1st Amendment and may be regulated only if the state shows that the regulation (1) directly advances, (2) a substantial governmental interest, (3) in a way that is reasonably tailored to achieve that objective. (See (D) above for more details.) The Court has indicated that showing (3) does not require that there not be any less-restrictive alternative, merely that there be a fairly close relationship between means and end. In fact, the scheme here doesn't even meet this reasonably-tailored test, but (C) is wrong because it states an incorrectly-strict test for the means-end fit.

C. Lawyers

3. *Solicitation by other professionals:*

Question: A state legislature received complaints from accident victims who, in the days immediately following their accidents, had received unwelcome and occasionally misleading telephone calls on behalf of medical care providers. The callers warned of the risks of not obtaining prompt medical evaluation to detect injuries resulting from accidents and offered free examinations to determine whether the victims had suffered any injuries.

In response to these complaints, the legislature enacted a law prohibiting medical care providers from soliciting any accident victim by telephone within 30 days of his or her accident.

Which of the following is the most useful argument for the state to use in defending the constitutionality of the law?

(A) Because the commercial speech that is the subject of this law includes some speech that is misleading, the First Amendment does not limit the power of the state to regulate that speech.

(B) Because the law regulates only commercial speech, the state need only demonstrate that the restriction is rationally related to achieving the state's legitimate interests in protecting the privacy of accident victims and in regulating the medical profession.

(C) The state has substantial interests in protecting the privacy of accident victims and in regulating the practice of medical care providers, and the law is narrowly tailored to achieve the state's objectives.

(D) The law is a reasonable time, place, and manner regulation.

[QA014]

Answer: Choice **(C)** is correct. The statute regulates only commercial speech, and the First Amendment invalidates any law regulating such speech unless the law is narrowly tailored to serve a substantial government interest (essentially a mid-level review standard). The U.S. Supreme Court has held that a law barring the solicitation of accident victims within a limited time period following an accident was narrowly tailored to serve the state's substantial interest in protecting the privacy of the victims. *Florida Bar v. Went For It, Inc.* (1995). While *Florida Bar* involved solicitation by tort lawyers, the same test would clearly apply to solicitation by medical-care providers. Although the question does not ask you to say how the case will come out (only to supply the argument most helpful to the state), it's pretty clear that the outcome of this test would be the same as in the lawyer-solicitation scenario (i.e., that the restriction would be upheld as narrowly tailored to serve the state's substantial privacy-protection interest).

(A) is wrong because it relies on a factor that does not apply to these facts. It's true that the law regulates only commercial speech, and it's also true that the First Amendment does not protect commercial speech that is misleading. So if the statute only barred misleading statements, it would be constitutional. But the facts state that the phone calls only "occasionally" were misleading. The Court has held that even commercial speech (as long as it is not fraudulent or misleading) is protected against government regulation unless the regulation is narrowly tailored to serve a substantial government interest. Banning of *all* speech in a category (here, all direct mail to the recently-injured) would not be found to be a "narrowly tailored" method of pursuing the admittedly-substantial interest in avoiding occasional misleading speech in that category.

(B) is wrong because it misstates the law governing regulation of commercial speech. The First Amendment invalidates any law regulating commercial speech unless the law is narrowly tailored to serve a substantial government interest. So the fact that there is a rational relationship between the restrictions imposed by the law and a legitimate state interest is not sufficient to satisfy this "mid-level" standard.

(D) is wrong because it mischaracterizes the nature of the regulation. The law at issue is not a "time, place, and manner regulation," because that phrase is used to describe content-neutral regulations, and the regulation here restricts speech based on its content. (It forbids only solicitations to provide medical care, and thus regulates some advertising messages but not others, based solely on the message's content.) Because the law is a content-based regulation of commercial speech, it is valid only if it is narrowly tailored to serve a substantial government interest (a test which, as described in Choice (C), the law satisfies).

IX. FREEDOM OF ASSOCIATION, AND DENIAL OF PUBLIC BENEFITS OR JOBS

C. Denial of public benefit or job:

1. Non-illegal activities:

a. Licenses:

Question: An ordinance of Central City requires every operator of a taxicab in the city to have a license and permits revocation of that license only for "good cause." The Central

City taxicab operator's licensing ordinance conditions the issuance of such a license on an agreement by the licensee that the licensee "not display in or on his or her vehicle any bumper sticker or other placard or sign favoring a particular candidate for any elected municipal office." The ordinance also states that it imposes this condition in order to prevent the possible imputation to the city council of the views of its taxicab licensees and that any licensee who violates this condition shall have his or her license revoked.

Driver, the holder of a Central City taxicab operator's license, decorates his cab with bumper stickers and other signs favoring specified candidates in a forthcoming election for municipal offices. A proceeding is initiated against him to revoke his taxicab operator's license on the sole basis of that admitted conduct.

In this proceeding, does Driver have a meritorious defense based on the United States Constitution?

(A) No, because he accepted the license with knowledge of the condition and, therefore, has no standing to contest it.

(B) No, because a taxicab operator's license is a privilege and not a right and, therefore, is not protected by the due process clause of the Fourteenth Amendment.

(C) Yes, because such a proceeding threatens Driver with a taking of property, his license, without just compensation.

(D) Yes, because the condition imposed on taxicab operators' licenses restricts political speech based wholly on its content, without any adequate governmental justification.

[Q3120]

Answer: (D) is the best response, because the operator's ordinance is a content-based restriction on core political speech, and cannot survive strict scrutiny. Central City would not be permitted to simply ban all citizens from displaying political bumper sticks on their cars (that would be a content-based restriction on core political speech, which would be strictly scrutinized, and struck down because no compelling governmental interest has been shown). What the government cannot do directly, it cannot do indirectly by conditioning a government benefit (a cab license) on the licensee's agreement not to exercise the speech right in question. And nothing about the taxicab-licensing process changes the fact that the restriction cannot survive strict scrutiny: there is no indication of any meaningful risk that members of the public might incorrectly think that the slogans were attributable to council members, and even if there were such risk, avoiding it would hardly rise to the level of a "compelling" interest.

(A) is wrong because the ordinance is unconstitutional and Driver has not waived his rights to challenge it. It is presumptively unconstitutional for the government to place burdens on speech because of its content. To justify such content-based regulation of speech, the government must show that the regulation is necessary to achieve a compelling state interest and is narrowly defined to achieve that end. The fact that Central City has not made display of all political messages a crime, and has instead used its power to deny a hack license as a "club" to induce some people (cab drivers) to "voluntarily" surrender their right to transmit those messages, is no defense. And the fact that Driver knew of the condition when he applied for his license would not cause him to lose standing to contest this clear unconstitutionality.

(B) is wrong because calling a government-bestowed benefit a "privilege" does not entitle the government to condition that benefit on the beneficiary's renunciation of the right to constitutionally-protected speech. As a general matter (subject to some exceptions not relevant here), government may not condition the receipt of a government-conferred benefit upon the beneficiary's willingness to forego the exercise of some constitutional right. So, for instance, government can't say, "We hereby fire any public employee who is a member of the Communist

Party," if government wouldn't have the power under the First Amendment to ban Communist Party membership. *Elfbrandt v. Russell* (1966). Here, since the display of political messages on bumper stickers is protected by the First Amendment, the City cannot condition a government-bestowed "privilege" (a cab license) on the driver's willingness to forego the right to make such a display.

(C) is wrong because the ordinance is merely a regulation, not a "taking." The 5th Amendment provides that private property shall not be taken for public use without paying just compensation to the owner. If Central City confiscated cab licenses so that, say, it could operate all cabs itself for profit — and then refused to pay the former license-holders anything — the licensees might have a "taking" argument. But here, what is occurring is merely regulation, and it's regulation of a sort that falls far short of denying the licensee all economically viable use of his property (the standard for when a "taking" is deemed to have occurred). Therefore, the takings clause has not been violated.

5. **Some exceptions:**

   c. **Speech critical of superiors or otherwise inappropriate:**

      i. **Non-policy-making role:**

      Question: A clerical worker has been employed for the past two years in a permanent position in the Public Records Office of a county. The clerk has been responsible for copying and filing records of real estate transactions in that office. The clerk works in a non-public part of the office and has no contact with members of the public. However, state law provides that all real estate records in that office are to be made available for public inspection.

      On the day an attempted assassination of the governor of the state was reported on the radio, the clerk remarked to a coworker, "Our governor is such an evil man, I am sorry they did not get him." The clerk's coworker reported this remark to the clerk's employer, the county recorder. After the clerk admitted making the remark, the county recorder dismissed him stating that "there is no room in this office for a person who hates the governor so much."

      The clerk sued for reinstatement and back pay. His only claim is that the dismissal violated his constitutional rights.

      In this case, the court should hold that the county recorder's dismissal of the clerk was

      (A) unconstitutional, because it constitutes a taking without just compensation of the clerk's property interest in his permanent position with the county.

      (B) unconstitutional, because in light of the clerk's particular employment duties his right to express himself on a matter of public concern outweighed any legitimate interest the state might have had in discharging him.

      (C) constitutional, because the compelling interest of the state in having loyal and supportive employees outweighs the interest of any state employee in his or her job or in free speech on a matter of public concern.

      (D) nonjusticiable, because public employment is a privilege rather than a right and, therefore, the clerk lacked standing to bring this suit.
      [Q2184]

      Answer: Choice **(B)** is correct. The mortgage attached to the entire property, and payment of 1/2 the total amount therefore did not "free up" a 1/2 undivided interest. The investor as mortgagee has a lien on the *entire property*. That is, the investor received a security interest on the full property — and the concomitant right upon default to conduct a judicial sale of the full property to get her debt repaid — regardless of whether one party paid that party's full share. A.L.P. § 16.172. In other words, the investor is entitled to say, "Who paid what is between the two of you — I've got the right to have the whole property sold at foreclosure if any part of my loan is in default and the default is not wholly cured." That's what happened here. (The sister's remedy is a suit in contribution against the brother for 1/2 the amount she paid to the investor.)

(A) is wrong, because the investor did not have title to the property. A mortgage is a security interest in a property securing a loan. The fact that the mortgage instrument contained a clause in which the brother and sister warranted that they owned the property free of encumbrances (which is what the general warranty clause did) is irrelevant to the issue of whether the sister is entitled to quiet title.

(C) is wrong, because the equitable doctrine of marshaling does not apply to these facts. Marshalling is the ranking of assets in a certain order toward the payment of debts. The concept arises in equity, and means that where there are two creditors, with the senior one having two funds to satisfy his debt, that senior creditor must resort first to the fund which is not subject to demand of the junior creditor. The concept is misapplied to this fact pattern, because the doctrine would be one a second mortgagee invoked to protect his interest from the first mortgagee's foreclosure. Under these facts there is only one mortgage on the property, and as a party who joined with the brother in making the mortgage on the property, the sister would not be able to have her interest released.

(D) is wrong, because the sister would lose even if the cotenancy was joint. Joint tenancy differs from tenancy in common only with respect to the right of survivorship, which exists as to the former but not the latter. There is no difference in the legal analysis here between the joint-tenancy and tenancy-in-common scenarios.

ii. Interferes with job:

Question: A city ordinance makes the city building inspector responsible for ensuring that all buildings in that city are kept up to building code standards, and requires the inspector to refer for prosecution all known building code violations. Another ordinance provides that the city building inspector may be discharged for "good cause." The building inspector took a newspaper reporter through a number of rundown buildings in a slum neighborhood. After using various epithets and slurs to describe the occupants of these buildings, the building inspector stated to the reporter: "I do not even try to get these buildings up to code or to have their owners prosecuted for code violations because if these buildings are repaired, the people who live in them will just wreck them again." The reporter published these statements in a story in the local newspaper. The building inspector admitted he made the statements.

On the basis of these statements, the city council discharged the building inspector.

Is the action of the city council constitutional?

(A) Yes, because the statements demonstrate that the building inspector has an attitude toward a certain class of persons that interferes with the proper performance of the obligations of his job.

(B) Yes, because the building inspector is a government employee and a person holding such a position may not make public comments inconsistent with current governmental policy.

(C) No, because the statements were lawful comments on a matter of public concern.

(D) No, because the statements were published in a newspaper that is protected by the First and Fourteenth Amendments.

[Q1103]

Answer: Choice **(A)** is correct. When a public employee speaks on a matter that is arguably one of public concern, the employee gets limited protection against dismissal or discipline. However, where the content of the speech interferes with the speaker's proper performance of his job (or indicates that the speaker has underlying attitudes that would interfere with job performance), the balance is tipped heavily toward the employer's right to discharge or discipline the employee. Here, given that the inspector is required to enforce the building codes, and given that he has publicly stated that he does not even try to do this core job function on account of his attitudes towards slumdwellers, the city council was clearly justified in firing him.

Choice (B) is wrong because it is overbroad; even a government employee may make public comments inconsistent with current governmental policy, if the speaker is not in a public role and/or the comments do not interfere with the speaker's ability to perform his job adequately.

Choice (C) is wrong because, although the comments may have been "lawful" and on a "matter of public concern," these two facts do not give the speaker immunity from being punished for the comments, for the reasons given above in the discussion of the correct choice.

Choice (D) is wrong because the fact that the comments were published in a newspaper that was in turn protected by the First and Fourteenth Amendments, is irrelevant to the question of whether the speaker may be punished; as described above, government may discharge a government employee for making statements (even ones published in a First-Amendment-protected newspaper) that seriously interfere with the employee's proper performance of her job.

X. SPECIAL PROBLEMS OF THE MEDIA

A. **The media (and its special problems):**

   3. **Right of access:**

      a. **No right to compel disclosure of government information:**

         i. **Right to publish information held in private hands:**

         Question: The state of Brunswick enacted a statute providing for the closure of the official state records of arrest and prosecution of all persons acquitted of a crime by a court or against whom criminal charges were filed and subsequently dropped or dismissed. The purpose of this statute is to protect these persons from further publicity or embarrassment relating to those state proceedings. However, this statute does not prohibit the publication of such information that is in the possession of private persons.

         A prominent businessman in Neosho City in Brunswick was arrested and charged with rape. Prior to trial, the prosecutor announced that new information indicated that the charges should be dropped. He then dropped the charges without further explanation, and the records relating thereto were closed to the public pursuant to the Brunswick statute.

         The Neosho City *Times* conducted an investigation to determine why the businessman was not prosecuted, but was refused access to the closed official state records. In an effort to determine whether the law enforcement agencies involved were properly doing their duty, the *Times* filed suit against appropriate state officials to force opening of the records and to invalidate the statute on constitutional grounds.

Which of the following would be most helpful to the state in defending the constitutionality of this statute?

(A) The fact that the statute treats in an identical manner the arrest and prosecution records of all persons who have been acquitted of a crime by a court or against whom criminal charges were filed and subsequently dropped or dismissed.

(B) The argument that the rights of the press are no greater than those of citizens generally.

(C) The fact that the statute only prohibits public access to these official state records and does not prohibit the publication of information they contain that is in the possession of private persons.

(D) The argument that the state may seal official records owned by the state on any basis its legislature chooses.

[Q3046]

Answer: Choice **(C)** is the best response, because there is no constitutional principle requiring the government to divulge information it possesses. The suit here is claiming that some constitutional principle (presumably the First Amendment) is violated by the statute. This amounts to a claim that government is sometimes required by the First Amendment to divulge information that it possesses. However, the Supreme Court has never squarely found that the First Amendment ever requires the release of government information.

The First Amendment does, however, prevent government from imposing a "prior restraint," that is, from prohibiting private individuals (including the media) from publishing information that they possess, except in the most extraordinary instances (e.g., troop movements in time of war). So if the statute did prohibit newspapers from publishing information it already possessed about the businessman (or about the prosecution's decision not to prosecute him), the statute would almost certainly violate this prohibition on prior restraints. Since (C) is the only choice that distinguishes between compelling the disclosure by the government of information it holds, and publication of privately-held information that originally comes from government records, it is the correct choice.

(A) is wrong because the answer doesn't address the issue the court would address. This choice sounds as though it would be relevant in defending against an equal protection claim, but it is irrelevant to defending against a First Amendment claim. For instance, if the statute prohibited newspapers from publishing the name of any person prosecuted and not convicted, the fact that it treated those who are acquitted the same as those against whom filed charges are dropped would be completely irrelevant — the statute would still be a prior restraint that violated the First Amendment.

(B) is wrong because even if the press doesn't have greater rights than citizens generally, this would not be a defense against the claim here. First, it's not clear whether the press has greater rights than those of citizens generally — the Court has never definitively decided this. Second, even if the press didn't have greater rights, that wouldn't necessarily help the state defend the statute; for instance, a court might hold that anyone — newspaper or private citizen — had the right to compel disclosure of this information. So the argument is irrelevant to the attack that's been made here.

(D) is wrong because it represents a more extreme position than the Court has ever endorsed. There are a few Court cases (e.g., *Richmond Newspapers v. Virginia*) that seem to suggest that the press may have some limited right of access to certain types of government-controlled information (e.g., contents of certain trials), if the state interest in non-disclosure is weak. So Choice (D), by indicating that no legislative objective is ever too weak to justify a sealing of governmental records, probably goes too far.

4. *Laws of general applicability:*

Question: In order to reduce the federal deficit, Congress enacted a statute imposing a five percent national retail sales tax. The tax was levied upon all retail sales in the United States and applied equally to the sales of all kinds of goods.

Is this tax constitutional as applied to retail sales of newspapers?

(A) Yes, because it is within Congress's power to tax.

(B) Yes, because the tax is necessary to serve the compelling interest of balancing the federal budget.

(C) No, because retail sales taxes are within the taxing power of the states.

(D) No, because the imposition of a tax on the sale of newspapers violates the freedom of the press.

[QA071]

Answer: Choice **(D)** is **incorrect**, because the tax here does not violate the freedom of the press. The Supreme Court has repeatedly held that provisions of general applicability that happen to impose some sort of incidental burden on free expression do not thereby violate the First Amendment. Thus generally-applicable regulations in the area of taxation, litigation discovery, or grand jury subpoenas are all valid even where applied to the press. If the sales tax here had applied *only* to newspapers, this "singling out" *would* have violated the First Amendment. But the tax applies to all retail transactions, and nothing in the First Amendment requires that Congress give a special exemption for newspapers or other speakers. (The correct choice is (A); see *supra*, p. 238.)

Chapter 11
FREEDOM OF RELIGION

II. THE ESTABLISHMENT CLAUSE

B. Three-part test:

1. Incidental benefit not fatal:

Question: A city operates a cemetery pursuant to a city ordinance. The ordinance requires the operation of the city cemetery to be supported primarily by revenues derived from the sale of cemetery lots to individuals. The ordinance further provides that the purchase of a cemetery lot entitles the owner to perpetual care of the lot, and entitles the owner to erect on the lot, at the owner's expense, a memorial monument or marker of the owner's choice, subject to certain size restrictions. The ordinance requires the city to maintain the cemetery, including mowing the grass, watering flowers, and plowing snow, and provides for the expenditure of city tax funds for such maintenance if revenues from the sale of cemetery lots are insufficient. Although cemetery lots are sold at full fair market value, which includes the current value of perpetual care, the revenue from the sale of such lots has been insufficient in recent years to maintain the cemetery. As a result, a small amount of city tax funds has also been used for that purpose.

A group of city taxpayers brings suit against the city challenging the constitutionality of the city ordinance insofar as it permits the owner of a cemetery lot to erect a religious memorial monument or marker on his or her lot.

Is this suit likely to be successful?

(A) No, because only a small amount of city tax funds has been used to maintain the cemetery.

(B) No, because the purpose of the ordinance is entirely secular, its primary effect neither advances nor inhibits religion, and it does not foster an excessive government entanglement with religion.

(C) Yes, because city maintenance of any religious object is a violation of the establishment clause of the First Amendment as incorporated into the Fourteenth Amendment.

(D) Yes, because no compelling governmental interest justifies authorizing private persons to erect religious monuments or markers in a city-operated cemetery.

[Q1138]

Answer: Choice **(B)** is correct. This choice correctly states the three-part *Lemon v. Kurtzman* (1970) test for government action that is alleged to benefit some religious interest. On the facts here, the statute passes all three parts: there is no evidence that the city's decision to operate the cemetery under these rules was intended to benefit religious groups; the primary effect of the cemetery operation is not to benefit those who put religious monuments on their plot; and the city's work in maintaining the religious monuments is so incidental to the overall operation of the cemetery — and so comparable to the work needed to maintain non-religious monuments — that there is no excessive entanglement between government and religion.

(A) is wrong because the amount of government funds spent is not dispositive; if the city was intending to benefit only religion (e.g., by providing a $20 reimbursement to the first 100 people who bought a piece of religious jewelry), the fact that only a "small amount" of city funds was spent would not save the expenditure from being a violation of the Establishment Clause.

(C) is wrong because it misstates the test for Establishment Clause violations; a city may maintain a "religious object" if the maintenance is part of a religiously-neutral program that is not intended to, and does not have the primary effect of, benefiting religion.

(D) is wrong because, if the government acts neutrally as to religion (as it has done here), there is no Establishment Clause violation whether the government has pursued a compelling interest or not.

F. **Ceremonies and displays:**

2. **Religious displays:**

    a. **Context:**

    Question: The governor of a state proposes to place a Christmas nativity scene, the components of which would be permanently donated to the state by private citizens, in the state Capitol Building rotunda where the state legislature meets annually. The governor further proposes to display this state-owned nativity scene annually from December 1 to December 31, next to permanent displays that depict the various products manufactured in the state. The governor's proposal is supported by all members of both houses of the legislature.

    If challenged in a lawsuit on establishment clause grounds, the proposed nativity scene display would be held

    (A) unconstitutional, because the components of the nativity scene would be owned by the state rather than by private persons.

    (B) unconstitutional, because the nativity scene would not be displayed in a context that appeared to depict and commemorate the Christmas season as a primarily secular holiday.

    (C) constitutional, because the components of the nativity scene would be donated to the state by private citizens rather than purchased with state funds.

(D) constitutional, because the nativity scene would be displayed alongside an exhibit of various products manufactured in the state.

[Q3165]

Answer: Choice **(B)** is correct. In judging the constitutionality of the display of a religious symbol such as a nativity scene, the most important single factor seems to be the context in which the religious symbol is displayed: If the religious symbol is presented by itself in what is clearly a space reserved by the government for its own property and its own messages, the Court is likely to conclude that a reasonable observer would believe that the government was endorsing the religious message. Conversely, the presence of other non-religious symbols nearby, or the existence of a sign indicating that the display was furnished by private parties, may well be enough to lead a reasonable observer to the conclusion that the government was *not* endorsing religion. *Allegheny County v. ACLU*.

On this standard, the proposed display of the nativity scene here would be unconstitutional. The nativity scene would not be surrounded by non-religious symbols having to do with the holiday season (symbols that would make it seem that the nativity scene was just part of a secular celebration of the holiday season). The whole presentation here — and the fact that the governor and legislature supported it — would create in a reasonable observer the impression that the government was endorsing a religious message. And the fact that the display components would be contributed by private citizens would not be enough to prevent the reasonable observer from believing that the government was endorsing religion.

(A) is wrong because the ownership of the display would not be dispositive on the issue of whether government seemed to be endorsing religion. If the scene here seemed to be a celebration of Christmas as a primarily secular holiday, the fact that the government owned the display would not be fatal. But, for the reasons discussed in Choice (B) above, the context of the display here would suggest to a reasonable observer that the state was endorsing religion. Consequently, the display violates the Establishment Clause.

(C) is wrong because donation would be only one element considered in the total context of the display. If the display made it clear to the public that private citizens had donated the components, this would indeed be one factor (but just one) tending to demonstrate that the display was not a forbidden government endorsement of religion. But there's no indication here that the fact of private donations would be disclosed to the public. Furthermore, this fact, even if disclosed, probably wouldn't be enough to overcome the otherwise-powerful impression that the government is endorsing a religious message.

(D) is wrong because displaying the scene next to the products would not rebut the impression that the state was endorsing the nativity scene's religious message. When a religious symbol such as a nativity scene is displayed in a public place, the issue is whether a reasonable observer would believe that the government is endorsing a religious method. Context is all-important. If the nativity scene were displayed next to other objects that pertain to December as a primarily secular holiday (e.g., a Santa Claus figure), the impression of an endorsement of religion would be rebutted. But putting the scene next to the year-round display of in-state-manufactured products would not rebut the impression of an endorsement of religion, because an observer would realize that the two displays were separate, and that the nativity scene was its own stand-alone display on an explicitly religious topic.

III. THE FREE EXERCISE CLAUSE

E. **Generally-applicable laws:**

1. **Criminal prohibitions:**

    Question: A generally applicable state statute requires an autopsy by the county coroner in all cases of death that are not obviously of natural causes. The purpose of this law is to ensure the discovery and prosecution of all illegal activity resulting in death. In the 50 years since its enactment, the statute has been consistently enforced.

    The plaintiffs, a married couple, are sincere practicing members of a religion that maintains it is essential for a deceased person's body to be buried promptly and without any invasive procedures, including an autopsy. When the plaintiffs' son died of mysterious causes and an autopsy was scheduled, the plaintiffs filed an action in state court challenging the constitutionality of the state statute, and seeking an injunction prohibiting the county coroner from performing an autopsy on their son's body. In this action, the plaintiffs claimed only that the application of this statute in the circumstances of their son's death would violate their right to the free exercise of religion as guaranteed by the First and Fourteenth Amendments. Assume that no federal statutes are applicable.

    As applied to the plaintiffs' case, the court should rule that the state's autopsy statute is

    (A) constitutional, because a dead individual is not a person protected by the due process clause of the Fourteenth Amendment.

    (B) constitutional, because it is a generally applicable statute and is rationally related to a legitimate state purpose.

    (C) unconstitutional, because it is not necessary to vindicate a compelling state interest.

    (D) unconstitutional, because it is not substantially related to an important state interest.
    [Q3008]

    Answer: Choice **(B)** is correct. Under the rule of *Employment Div. v. Smith* (1990), "the right of free exercise does not relieve an individual of the obligation to comply with a *valid and neutral law of general applicability* on the ground that the law proscribes ... conduct that his religion prescribes." Here, the law states that "there must be an autopsy" (in certain cases), and the plaintiffs claim that their religion prohibits autopsies. So *Smith* applies: we have a "valid and neutral law of general applicability" (i.e., a law that's not motivated by anti-religious bias, that applies to all cases of non-natural death, and that's rationally related to the legitimate state purpose of detecting illegal activity). That law is proscribing certain conduct (refusing an autopsy), and it's applicable to conduct that the plaintiff's religion prescribes, or requires (refusing an autopsy). So *Smith* requires that the law be enforced notwithstanding the plaintiffs' objection, even though the effect would be to impair their free exercise of their religion.

    (A) is wrong because while the statute is constitutional, it is not constitutional for the reason stated in this choice. It's in a sense true that a "dead individual is not a person protected by the Due Process Clause..." But the plaintiffs' claim is not based on their son's due process rights, but on their own free-exercise rights (as made applicable to the states through the Fourteenth Amendment's Due Process Clause). So the fact that the son has no relevant rights is irrelevant. Instead, the statute is constitutional for the reason discussed in Choice (B).

    (C) is wrong because strict scrutiny is not the appropriate standard for the statute here. *Employment Div. v. Smith* (see Choice (B)) says that where a valid generally-applicable statute requires certain conduct, the statute must be obeyed even by a person whose religion proscribes that conduct. So the Court does not strictly scrutinize the statute, as this choice implies that it should; instead, the Court gives just the lowest-level mere-rationality review, which the statute here easily passes.

(D) is wrong because mid-level review is not the appropriate standard for the statute here. *Employment Div. v. Smith* (see Choice (B)) says that where a valid generally-applicable statute requires certain conduct, the statute must be obeyed even by a person whose religion proscribes that conduct. So the Court does not give mid-level review to the statute, as this choice implies that it should (just the lowest-level mere-rationality review, which the statute here easily passes).

2. ***State need not tolerate serious impairment of important state interest:***

   Question: Members of a religious group believe in Lucifer as their Supreme Being. The members of this group meet once a year on top of Mt. Snow, located in a U.S. National Park, to hold an overnight encampment and a midnight dance around a large campfire. They believe this overnight encampment and all of its rituals are required by Lucifer to be held on the top of Mt. Snow. U.S. National Park Service rules that have been consistently enforced prohibit all overnight camping and all campfires on Mt. Snow because of the very great dangers overnight camping and campfires would pose in that particular location. As a result, the park Superintendent denied a request by the group for a permit to conduct these activities on top of Mt. Snow. The park Superintendent, who was known to be violently opposed to cults and other unconventional groups had, in the past, issued permits to conventional religious groups to conduct sunrise services in other areas of that U.S. National Park.

   The group brought suit in Federal Court against the U.S. National Park Service and the Superintendent of the park to compel issuance of the requested permit.

   As a matter of constitutional law, the most appropriate result in this suit would be a decision that denial of the permit was

   (A) invalid, because the free exercise clause of the First Amendment prohibits the Park Service from knowingly interfering with religious conduct.

   (B) invalid, because these facts demonstrate that the action of the Park Service purposefully and invidiously discriminated against the group.

   (C) valid, because the establishment clause of the First Amendment prohibits the holding of religious ceremonies on federal land.

   (D) valid, because religiously motivated conduct may be subjected to nondiscriminatory time, place, and manner restrictions that advance important public interests.

   [Q2112]

   Answer: Choice **(D)** is correct. Government may take generally-applicable actions that advance important public interests, without giving an exemption to those whose religious beliefs are thereby burdened. The facts tell us that the rules against overnight camping and campfires are "consistently enforced" because of "very great dangers," so the "generally applicable" and "advancement of important public interests" standards are met here. The fact that the Superintendent doesn't like cults doesn't matter, because there is no indication that his decision to deny the permit here was motivated by anything other than a desire to enforce these generally-applicable rules.

   (A) is wrong, for the same reason that (D) is right: government may impose a generally-applicable rule to promote an important interest, even if government knows that its enforcement of that rule will interfere with religious conduct.

(B) is wrong because the Park Service's action did not "purposely and invidiously discriminate" against the group — what was being enforced was a generally-applicable rule that was not enacted for anti-religious purposes.

(C) is wrong because it misstates the law governing the Establishment Clause as well as the facts — if non-religious groups were permitted to take the same general type of action in question (here, overnight camping and campfires), which they are not, then it would not be a violation of the Establishment Clause for the government to allow a religious group to do the same thing (and, indeed, it would probably be a violation of the Free Exercise Clause for the government *not* to allow the religious group to do the same thing that the non-religious are permitted to do).

Chapter 12
JUSTICIABILITY

III. STANDING

D. Cases not based on taxpayer or citizen status:

2. "Injury in fact":

b. Imminent harm:

i. P hasn't made relevant decision:

Question: An ordinance of a city requires that its mayor must have been continuously a resident of the city for at least five years at the time he or she takes office. The plaintiff, who is thinking about running for mayor in an election that will take place next year, will have been a resident of the city for only four and one-half years at the time the mayor elected then takes office. Before he decides whether to run for the position of mayor, the plaintiff wants to know whether he could lawfully assume that position if he were elected. As a result, the plaintiff files suit in the local federal district court for a declaratory judgment that the five-year-residence requirement is unconstitutional and that he is entitled to a place on his political party's primary election ballot for mayor. He names the chairman of his political party as the sole defendant but does not join any election official. The chairman responds by joining the plaintiff in requesting the court to declare the residence requirement invalid.

In this case, the court should

(A) refuse to determine the merits of this suit, because there is no case or controversy.

(B) refuse to issue such a declaratory judgment, because an issue of this kind involving only a local election does not present a substantial federal constitutional question.

(C) issue the declaratory judgment, because a residency requirement of this type is a denial of the equal protection of the laws.

(D) issue the declaratory judgment, because the plaintiff will have substantially complied with the residency requirement.

[Q2153]

Answer: Choice **(A)** is correct. The plaintiff does not meet the requirement of "injury in fact." He clearly has not been injured yet; the real question is whether he faces sufficiently imminent injury from the residency requirement. A court would likely hold that because the plaintiff has not yet even made the decision to run, and could not be injured unless he decided to run, any threatened injury to him is too uncertain and speculative to meet the requirement that prospective injury be reasonably concrete and imminent. The fact that the chairman has joined the suit does not change this, since the chairman (and the chairman's party) would not be injured unless some actual candidate was blocked by the residency requirement, and there is no such candidate now.

(B) is wrong because: (1) the absence of a case or controversy would prevent the court even from getting to the issue of whether there was a substantial federal constitutional question in the case; and (2) the fact that something is a local election does not prevent it from presenting a substantial federal constitutional question (for instance, an unduly long residency requirement probably *would* constitute a violation of an actual candidate's equal protection rights).

(C) is wrong because, while the residency restriction might well constitute an equal protection violation of the rights of an actual candidate, the plaintiff's lack of actual-candidate status prevents him from raising a case or controversy.

(D) is wrong because there is no basis (certainly not a federal constitutional basis) for the court to conclude that "substantially complying," rather than fully complying, with the residency requirement here would be sufficient.

3. **Individuated harm:**

   b. **Organizations and associations:**

   Question: Congress recently enacted a statute imposing severe criminal penalties on anyone engaged in trading in the stock market who, in the course of that trading, takes "unfair advantage" of other investors who are also trading in the stock market. The statute does not define the term "unfair advantage." There have been no prosecutions under this new statute. The members of an association of law school professors that is dedicated to increasing the clarity of the language used in criminal statutes believe that this statute is unconstitutionally vague. Neither the association nor any of its members is currently engaged in, or intends in the future to engage in, trading in the stock market. The association and its members bring suit against the Attorney General of the United States in a federal district court, seeking an injunction against the enforcement of this statute on the ground that it is unconstitutional.

   May the federal court determine the merits of this suit?

   (A) Yes, because the suit involves a dispute over the constitutionality of a federal statute.

   (B) Yes, because the plaintiffs seek real relief of a conclusive nature — an injunction against enforcement of this statute.

   (C) No, because the plaintiffs do not have an interest in the invalidation of this statute that is adequate to ensure that the suit presents an Article III controversy.

   (D) No, because a suit for an injunction against enforcement of a criminal statute may not be brought in federal court at any time prior to a *bona fide* effort to enforce that statute.

   [Q3034]

   Answer: Choice **(C)** is correct. This is the best response, because none of the members of the association has been injured or will be injured, making the organization lack standing.

   Standing is an interest in the outcome of a controversy. One requirement for an organization to have standing to challenge government actions that cause an injury in fact to its members is that the organization be able to demonstrate that there is an injury in fact to at least *some* members of the organization that would give these individual members a right to sue on their own behalf. Here, the organization cannot satisfy this requirement: The facts carefully specify that no member currently trades or expects to do so in the future. Consequently, no member could either be prohibited by the statute from conduct they would otherwise engage in, or even benefit from the statute's protections. Therefore, no member has standing to bring an individual action, and thus the organization does not have standing either.

(A) is wrong because the mere fact that a suit involves a "dispute over the constitutionality of a federal statute" does not dispense with the need for standing. It's true that, as this choice suggests, a federal suit (at least one not based on diversity) must involve a federal question, that is, a question arising under the constitution or under a federal statute. So the fact that the constitutionality of a federal statute is at issue certainly satisfies the "must pose a federal question" requirement. But there is an additional requirement that the plaintiffs have standing, and for the reasons discussed in Choice (C) above, that requirement is not satisfied.

(B) is wrong because the fact that the suit seeks "relief of a conclusive nature" is irrelevant. Where plaintiffs lack standing, the fact that they are seeking "relief of a conclusive nature" does not nullify the non-justiciability of their claim. This organization lacks standing for the reasons discussed in Choice (C). If Choice (B) were correct, it would follow that any person or organization, no matter how little their practical stake in the outcome, could sue for an injunction against any statute's enforcement. This would effectively nullify the constitutional requirement that each federal suit involve a "case or controversy."

(D) is not the best response, because a suit for an injunction preventing enforcement of the statute *could* be brought. It's true that if the court were convinced that enforcement of the statute was extremely unlikely to occur in the reasonable future, the court might exercise its discretion to conclude that the suit shouldn't be heard because it wasn't ripe. But this choice says far more than that — it asserts that the mere fact that there has not yet been a "bona fide effort" to enforce the statute means an injunction suit can't be brought. And that's clearly not true. See, e.g., *Epperson v. Arkansas* (1968) (Court hears case involving ban on teaching evolution, which ban hadn't ever been enforced during its entire 40 years on the books.)

5. **Claimed violation need not be directed at P:**

    Question: Road Lines is an interstate bus company operating in a five-state area. A federal statute authorizes the Interstate Commerce Commission (ICC) to permit interstate carriers to discontinue entirely any unprofitable route. Road Lines applied to the ICC for permission to drop a very unprofitable route through the sparsely populated Shaley Mountains. The ICC granted that permission even though Road Lines provided the only public transportation into the region.

    Foley is the owner of a mountain resort in the Shaley Mountains, whose customers usually arrived on vehicles operated by Road Lines. After exhausting all available federal administrative remedies, Foley filed suit against Road Lines in the trial court of the state in which the Shaley Mountains are located to enjoin the discontinuance by Road Lines of its service to that area. Foley alleged that the discontinuance of service by Road Lines would violate a statute of that state prohibiting common carriers of persons from abandoning service to communities having no alternate form of public transportation.

    The state court should

    (A) dismiss the action, because Foley lacks standing to sue.

    (B) direct the removal of the case to federal court, because this suit involves a substantial federal question.

    (C) hear the ease on its merits and decide for Foley because, on these facts, a federal agency is interfering with essential state functions.

(D) hear the case on its merits and decide for Road Lines, because a valid federal law preempts the state statute on which Foley relies.

[Q1008]

Answer: Choice **(A)** is **incorrect**. It's true that the ICC, in taking the challenged action (letting Road Lines drop the service), was not intending to affect Foley and probably was not even aware of Foley's interest in the matter. But since Foley would suffer imminent and concrete economic harm from the challenged action, and since the injury he would suffer will be at least somewhat different from that suffered by every local resident, Foley has standing even though the challenged action was not directed at him. (The correct choice is (D); see the explanation on p. 254.)

E. **Third-party standing:**

Question: City police officers shot and killed the plaintiff's friend as he attempted to escape arrest for an armed robbery he had committed. The plaintiff brought suit in federal district court against the city police department and the city police officers involved, seeking only a judgment declaring unconstitutional the state statute under which the police acted. That newly enacted statute authorized the police to use deadly force when necessary to apprehend a person who has committed a felony. In his suit, the plaintiff alleged that the police would not have killed his friend if the use of deadly force had not been authorized by the statute.

The federal district court should

(A) decide the case on its merits, because it raises a substantial federal question.

(B) dismiss the action, because it involves a nonjusticiable political question.

(C) dismiss the action, because it does not present a case or controversy.

(D) dismiss the action, because the Eleventh Amendment prohibits federal courts from deciding cases of this type.

[Q1133]

Answer: Choice **(C)** is correct. Because the only person whose rights have been arguably affected by the new statute is the friend, who is not a claimant, there is no live case or controversy between the litigants, so standing rules prevent the court from hearing it.

(A) is wrong because the lack of standing prevents the court from deciding the case on its merits even though the plaintiff is claiming that the Constitution has been violated (which would of course raise a federal question if there were a case or controversy before the court).

(B) is wrong because, if there were not any standing problem, the question of the constitutionality of the statute would not be a nonjusticiable political question (a category limited to a few special situations, none of which applies here).

(D) is wrong, because the Eleventh Amendment bars only suits seeking money damages against states, and the suit here is seeking a declaratory judgment rather than money damages.

IV. MOOTNESS

B. **Exceptions:**

2. **Voluntary cessation by defendant:**

a. **Injunction:**

i. **No reasonable likelihood of revival of conduct:**

Question: The plaintiff contracted for expensive cable television service for a period of six months solely to view the televised trial of Clark, who was on trial for murder in a court of the state of Green.

In the midst of the trial, the judge prohibited any further televising of Clark's trial because he concluded that the presence of television cameras was disruptive.

The plaintiff brought an action in a federal district court against the judge in Clark's case asking only for an injunction that would require the judge to resume the televising of Clark's trial. The plaintiff alleged that the judge's order to stop the televising of Clark's trial deprived him of property—his investment in cable television service—without due process of law.

Before the plaintiff's case came to trial, Clark's criminal trial concluded in a conviction and sentencing. There do not appear to be any obvious errors in the proceeding that led to the result in Clark's case. After Clark's conviction and sentencing, the defendant in the plaintiff's case moved to dismiss that suit.

The most proper disposition of this motion by the federal court would be to

(A) defer action on the motion until after any appellate proceedings in Clark's case have concluded, because Clark might appeal, his conviction might be set aside, he might be tried again, and television cameras might be barred from the new trial.

(B) defer action on the motion until after the Green Supreme Court expresses a view on its proper disposition, because the state law of mootness governs suits in federal court when the federal case is inexorably intertwined with a state proceeding.

(C) grant the motion, because the subject matter of the controversy between the plaintiff and the defendant has ceased to exist and there is no strong likelihood that it will be revived.

(D) deny the motion, because the plaintiff has raised an important constitutional question — whether his investment in cable service solely to view Clark's trial is property protected by the due process clause of the Fourteenth Amendment.

[Q3160]

Answer: Choice **(C)** is correct. The plaintiff was seeking only an injunction (not, for instance, damages). And the facts tell us that this is the only criminal trial he was counting on seeing via cable TV. So unless this criminal trial has a significant likelihood of continuing, there is no ongoing damage to the plaintiff, and thus no need for an injunction. That is, if there will never be a criminal trial, the case is moot, preventing it from posing the required "case or controversy" within the meaning of Art. III. The facts tell us that there were no obvious errors in the trial, so it's unlikely that the case will be reversed and remanded for a new trial. Consequently, it's unlikely that there will be new proceedings that could be televised, and thus no live controversy about whether the injunction sought by the plaintiff should be granted.

(A) is not the best response, because the likelihood of a live controversy is remote, thus dictating dismissal rather than deferral. It is appropriate for a court to defer decision in a case where later events will or may likely occur that would make the case more suitable for decision than it is now. So if there were a good likelihood that a new trial would occur, deferral might be the right course. But here, we're told that there are no obvious errors, so it's unlikely that there will be an appellate reversal and a new criminal trial. Since likelihood of a new trial that would raise the "Do we televise?" issue is remote, the court should dismiss rather than merely defer.

(B) is wrong because the Green Supreme Court will not have occasion to say anything about the case's merits. The plaintiff's case presents a pure question of federal (constitutional) law. While principles of concurrent jurisdiction would probably have permitted him to bring the case in state court, he didn't choose to do that. Therefore, the Green Supreme Court won't ever have occasion to express an opinion. In any event, this choice's statement that "state law of mootness governs suits in federal court..." is basically gibberish — it's up to the federal courts to say, as a federal constitutional matter, when a controversy is moot.

(D) is wrong because, however important the constitutional question raised by the plaintiff, it's moot due to the fact that there's no longer a criminal trial about which to grant the requested injunctive relief. A case will be dismissed as moot if the relief sought no longer makes sense. That's true even if, in the abstract, the case presents "an important constitutional question." So Choice (D), by ignoring the mootness problem and relying solely on the importance of the issue, is wrong.

V. RIPENESS

A. Ripeness problem generally:

1. **Remedy is dismissal:**

    Question: A federal statute required the National Bureau of Standards to establish minimum quality standards for all beer sold in the United States. The statute also provided that public proceedings must precede adoption of the standards, and that once they were adopted, the standards would be subject to judicial review. No standards have yet been adopted. Several officials of the National Bureau of Standards have indicated their personal preference for beer produced by a special brewing process commonly referred to as pasteurization. However, these officials have not indicated whether they intend to include a requirement for pasteurization in the minimum beer quality standards to be adopted by the Bureau. A brewery that produces an unpasteurized beer believes that its brewing process is as safe as pasteurization. The brewery is concerned that, after the appropriate proceedings, the Bureau may adopt quality standards that will prohibit the sale of any unpasteurized beer. As a result, the brewery sued in federal district court to enjoin the Bureau from adopting any standards that would prohibit the sale of unpasteurized beer in this country.

    How should the district court dispose of the suit?

    (A) Determine whether the Bureau could reasonably believe that pasteurization is the safest process by which to brew beer, and if the Bureau could reasonably believe that, refuse to issue the injunction against the Bureau.

    (B) Determine whether the process used by the brewery is as safe as pasteurization and, if it is, issue the injunction against the Bureau.

    (C) Refuse to adjudicate the merits of the suit at this time and stay the action until the Bureau has actually issued beer quality standards.

    (D) Refuse to adjudicate the merits of the suit, because it does not involve a justiciable case or controversy.

    [Q7080]

    Answer: Choice **(D)** is correct. The federal courts lack power to entertain a suit that is not ripe for adjudication, because such a suit does not present a "case" or "controversy." The court should dismiss the suit because the Bureau has yet to announce the beer-quality standards, and therefore the case is not ripe.

(A) and (B) are both wrong because the court may not hear the case at all, due to the lack of a case or controversy, as explained in the discussion of (D) above.

(C) is wrong because the court may not maintain jurisdiction over the suit by issuing a stay — the absence of a live case or controversy means that the court lacks the constitutional authority even to retain control over the suit without deciding it.

C. Reasonable probability of harm required:

1. Specificity required:

Question: In response to the need for additional toxic waste landfills in a state, the state's legislature enacted a law authorizing a state agency to establish five new state-owned and state-operated toxic waste landfills. The law provided that the agency would decide the locations and sizes of the landfills after an investigation of all potential sites and a determination that the particular sites chosen would not endanger public health and would be consistent with the public welfare.

A community in the state was scheduled for inspection by the agency as a potential toxic waste landfill site. Because the community's residents obtained most of their drinking water from an aquifer that ran under the entire community, a citizens' group, made up of residents of that community, sued the appropriate officials of the agency in federal court. The group sought a declaratory judgment that the selection of the community as the site of a toxic waste landfill would be unconstitutional and an injunction preventing the agency from selecting the community as a site for such a landfill. The agency officials moved to dismiss.

Which of the following is the most appropriate basis for the court to dismiss this suit?

(A) The case presents a nonjusticiable political question.

(B) The interest of the state in obtaining suitable sites for toxic waste landfills is sufficiently compelling to justify the selection of the community as a location for such a facility.

(C) The Eleventh Amendment bars suits of this kind in the federal courts.

(D) The case is not ripe for a decision on the merits.

[QA079]

Answer: Choice **(D)** is correct. The defendant agency has a strong argument that the case is not ripe for adjudication because the agency's inspection does not itself pose any risk of harm to residents of the community. A case meets the constitutional requirement of ripeness only when the plaintiff has already suffered some harm, or faces future harm that is reasonably specific and reasonably imminent. Here, the residents would face a risk of imminent harm only if the agency were to select their community as a site for a landfill, but on these facts it is unclear whether or when the community will eventually be selected. It's not certain that this ripeness argument would prevail, but the question asks you only what the "most appropriate" basis is, and this is the only choice that could even theoretically prevail.

(A) is wrong because the political question doctrine doesn't apply. The political question doctrine insulates from federal judicial review certain constitutional questions that the Constitution has committed either to the legislative branch or to the executive branch of the federal government. No such question is presented on these facts, which concern actions by a state government.

(B) is wrong because it states an inappropriate test. When a choice turns on whether a governmental interest is "compelling," that test is applying a form of strict scrutiny. Here, nothing in the facts suggests that strict judicial scrutiny of the state's site-selection decision is warranted. (For instance, the state is not making a classification that is based on a suspect category or that impairs a fundamental right.) Rather, the state is engaged in ordinary social-welfare legislation, which would be evaluated based on the rational-relation standard.

An additional clue that this is not the right answer comes from the language of the question: you are asked for the most appropriate basis for the court to "dismiss" the suit. "Dismissal" implies that the litigation would be ended without the court's reaching the merits. So any choice that relies on determining whether a state interest is "compelling" would require the court to decide the underlying merits of the state's action, rather than issuing a "dismissal."

(C) is wrong because the Eleventh Amendment does not bar this type of suit. The Eleventh Amendment bars federal-court suits for *money damages* against a state, and it also bars federal-court attempts to have a *state itself enjoined* from acting in a particular way. But the amendment does *not* bar suits against state *officials* for an injunction, even if the injunction would, if granted, have the effect of barring implementation of an official state policy. Cf. *Ex parte Young* (1908); Chemerinsky, *Constitutional Law* (2d Ed., Aspen, 2005), p. 223. Since the question carefully specifies that the citizens' group sued "the appropriate officials of the agency" (not the state itself), the Eleventh Amendment does not apply.

Question: The legislature of the state of Gray recently enacted a statute forbidding public utilities regulated by the Gray Public Service Commission to increase their rates more than once every two years. Economy Electric Power Company, a public utility regulated by that commission, has just obtained approval of the commission for a general rate increase. Economy Electric has routinely filed for a rate increase every 10 to 14 months during the last 20 years. Because of uncertainties about future fuel prices, the power company cannot ascertain with any certainty the date when it will need a further rate increase; but it thinks it may need such an increase sometime within the next 18 months.

Economy Electric files an action in the federal district court in Gray requesting a declaratory judgment that this new statute of Gray forbidding public utility rate increases more often than once every two years is unconstitutional. Assume no federal statute is relevant.

In this case, the court should

(A) hold the statute unconstitutional, because such a moratorium on rate increases deprives utilities of their property without due process of law.

(B) hold the statute constitutional, because the judgment of a legislature on a matter involving economic regulation is entitled to great deference.

(C) dismiss the complaint, because this action is not ripe for decision.

(D) dismiss the complaint, because controversies over state-regulated utility rates are outside of the jurisdiction conferred on federal courts by Article III of the Constitution.
[Q2175]

Answer: The correct choice is **(C)**. This is a classic ripeness issue: Economy does not know that it will certainly (or even more-probably-than-not) need another rate increase in less than the now-required two-year minimum. All we know is that Economy "may" need the increase sometime in the next 18 months. Therefore, it is highly uncertain for now whether Economy will ever be harmed by the statute, making it likely that the court would dismiss the action as unripe.

(A) is wrong because the case is not ripe for decision (see the discussion of Choice (C)), so the court will never reach the constitutional merits. (Also, its highly doubtful that a relatively brief moratorium on rate increases would violate the due process rights of a utility.)

(B) is wrong for the same reason as (A): the case is not ripe for decision (see the discussion of Choice (C)), so the court will never reach the constitutional merits.

(D) is wrong, because the federal judicial power extends to any case raising an issue under the federal Constitution or a federal statute, and the fact that the controversy involves state-regulated utility rates does not prevent that controversy from raising a federal issue. For example, if a state utility commission were to prevent a utility from ever raising its rates again, this would raise a serious taking-without-just-compensation constitutional issue.

VI. THE ELEVENTH AMENDMENT AND SUITS AGAINST THE STATES

A. The Eleventh Amendment generally:

4. No bar against injunctions:

Question: In response to the need for additional toxic waste landfills in a state, the state's legislature enacted a law authorizing a state agency to establish five new state-owned and state-operated toxic waste landfills. The law provided that the agency would decide the locations and sizes of the landfills after an investigation of all potential sites and a determination that the particular sites chosen would not endanger public health and would be consistent with the public welfare.

A community in the state was scheduled for inspection by the agency as a potential toxic waste landfill site. Because the community's residents obtained most of their drinking water from an aquifer that ran under the entire community, a citizens' group, made up of residents of that community, sued the appropriate officials of the agency in federal court. The group sought a declaratory judgment that the selection of the community as the site of a toxic waste landfill would be unconstitutional and an injunction preventing the agency from selecting the community as a site for such a landfill. The agency officials moved to dismiss.

Which of the following is the most appropriate basis for the court to dismiss this suit?

(A) The case presents a nonjusticiable political question.

(B) The interest of the state in obtaining suitable sites for toxic waste landfills is sufficiently compelling to justify the selection of the community as a location for such a facility.

(C) The Eleventh Amendment bars suits of this kind in the federal courts.

(D) The case is not ripe for a decision on the merits.

[QA079]

Answer: Choice **(C)** is **incorrect**, because the Eleventh Amendment does not bar this type of suit. The Eleventh Amendment bars federal-court suits for *money damages* against a state, and it also bars federal-court attempts to have a *state itself enjoined* from acting in a particular way. But the amendment does *not* bar suits against state *officials* for an injunction, even if the injunction would, if granted, have the effect of barring implementation of an official state policy. Cf. *Ex parte Young* (1908); Chemerinsky, *Constitutional Law* (2d Ed., Aspen, 2005), p. 223. Since the question carefully specifies that the citizens' group sued "the appropriate officials of the agency" (not the state itself), the Eleventh Amendment does not apply. (The correct answer is **(D)**; see *supra*, p. 322.)

6. **Congress can't override:**

   b. **Exception for remedial powers:**

   Question: A federal statute enacted pursuant to the power of Congress to enforce the Fourteenth Amendment prohibits any state from requiring any of its employees to retire from state employment solely because of their age. The statute expressly authorizes employees required by a state to retire from state employment solely because of their age to sue the state government in federal district court for any damages resulting from that state action. On the basis of this federal statute, a retiree who had worked for State X sues the state in federal district court. State X moves to dismiss the suit on the ground that Congress lacks authority to authorize such suits against a state.

   Which of the following is the strongest argument that the retiree can offer in opposition to the state's motion to dismiss this suit?

   (A) When Congress exercises power vested in it by the Fourteenth Amendment, Congress may enact appropriate remedial legislation expressly subjecting the states to private suits for damages in federal court.

   (B) When Congress exercises power vested in it by any provision of the Constitution, Congress has unlimited authority to authorize private actions for damages against a state.

   (C) While the Eleventh Amendment restrains the federal judiciary, that amendment does not limit the power of Congress to modify the sovereign immunity of the states.

   (D) While the Eleventh Amendment applies to suits in federal court by citizens of one state against another state, it does not apply to such suits by citizens against their own states.

   [Q1027]

   Answer: Choice **(A)** is correct. The Eleventh Amendment generally forbids the federal courts from entertaining damage suits against states, and Congress cannot override this ban even when it is acting pursuant to some enumerated power (e.g., the Commerce Clause). But there is one exception: when Congress is using its special powers to enforce the post-Civil War amendments (the Thirteenth, Fourteenth and Fifteenth), it may authorize damage suits against the states that would otherwise be barred by the Eleventh Amendment. That is what's happening here.

   (B) is wrong because it is overbroad. As a general rule Congress, even where it is acting pursuant to some power given to it by a specific provision in the Constitution, may not override the state immunity from federal-court damage suits conferred by the Eleventh Amendment; enforcement of the post-Civil War amendments represents the only exception to this rule.

   (C) is wrong for essentially the same reason: the Eleventh Amendment *does* generally limit the power of Congress (not just the power of the federal judiciary) to modify the sovereign-immunity of the states, but the Supreme Court has held that in the special case in which Congress is enforcing the post-Civil War amendments this general limitation on Congress's power does not apply. *Fitzpatrick v. Bitzer* (1976).

   (D) is wrong because it is a flat misstatement of law: the Supreme Court has held that the Eleventh Amendment protects a state from federal-court damage suits even where the suit is brought by a citizen of a different state. *Hans v. Louisiana* (1890).

VII. POLITICAL QUESTIONS

B. "Commitment to other branches" strand:

Question: In response to the need for additional toxic waste landfills in a state, the state's legislature enacted a law authorizing a state agency to establish five new state-owned and state-operated toxic waste landfills. The law provided that the agency would decide the locations and sizes of the landfills after an investigation of all potential sites and a determination that the particular sites chosen would not endanger public health and would be consistent with the public welfare.

A community in the state was scheduled for inspection by the agency as a potential toxic waste landfill site. Because the community's residents obtained most of their drinking water from an aquifer that ran under the entire community, a citizens' group, made up of residents of that community, sued the appropriate officials of the agency in federal court. The group sought a declaratory judgment that the selection of the community as the site of a toxic waste landfill would be unconstitutional and an injunction preventing the agency from selecting the community as a site for such a landfill. The agency officials moved to dismiss.

Which of the following is the most appropriate basis for the court to dismiss this suit?

(A) The case presents a nonjusticiable political question.

(B) The interest of the state in obtaining suitable sites for toxic waste landfills is sufficiently compelling to justify the selection of the community as a location for such a facility.

(C) The Eleventh Amendment bars suits of this kind in the federal courts.

(D) The case is not ripe for a decision on the merits.

[QA079]

Answer: Choice **(A)** is **incorrect,** because the political question doctrine doesn't apply. The political question doctrine insulates from federal judicial review certain constitutional questions that the Constitution has committed either to the legislative branch or to the executive branch of the federal government. No such question is presented on these facts, which concern actions by a state government. (The correct answer is Choice (D); see *supra*, p. 322.)

2. Ratification of amendments:

Question: Which of the following acts by the United States Senate would be constitutionally IMPROPER?

(A) The Senate decides, with the House of Representatives, that a disputed state ratification of a proposed constitutional amendment is valid.

(B) The Senate determines the eligibility of a person to serve as a senator.

(C) The Senate appoints a commission to adjudicate finally a boundary dispute between two states.

(D) The Senate passes a resolution calling on the President to pursue a certain foreign policy.

[Q1087]

Answer: Choice **(A)** is **incorrect**, because, under *Coleman v. Miller*, the House and Senate together *do* have the right (indeed, the exclusive right) to determine whether a disputed state ratification of an amendment is valid. (The correct answer is Choice (C); see *supra*, p. 226.)